SEVENTH EDITION

EFFECTIVE SELLING

Charles A. Kirkpatrick, DCS

Professor Emeritus of Marketing
Graduate School of Business Administration
University of North Carolina

Frederick A. Russ, PhD

Professor of Business Administration
Graduate School of Business Administration
University of North Carolina

Published by

S56 **SOUTH-WESTERN PUBLISHING CO.**

CINCINNATI   WEST CHICAGO, ILL.   DALLAS   PELHAM MANOR, N.Y.   PALO ALTO, CALIF.

ISBN: 0-538-19560-6

Library of Congress Catalog
Card Number: 80-52061

2345678D876543
Printed in the United States of America

preface

Competence in selling is needed by everyone; we must all "sell" ourselves and our ideas. We recognize the salesperson as a communicator, an advisor, a problem solver, and a behavioral scientist.

This book is primarily a text for students who look forward to selling careers. It presents the principles and practices of professional selling. Emphasis is on information, skills, and attitudes.

We have tried to make this seventh edition an even better teaching and learning tool than the sixth edition. The two chapters in Part I introduce students to such basics as the role and the job of personal selling. Part II presents the background for selling. It includes the topics of behavior, communication, marketing, and promotion. Part III explains how salespeople prospect for buyers and plan their sales presentations. The focus of Part IV is the selling process, beginning with securing and opening the sales interview and ending with closing the sale. Part V helps the salesperson do a better job with customers and a better job of self-management. Chapter 16 is new. It comments on the legal, ethical, and social responsibilities of salespeople. Part VI examines special features of selling to organizational buyers and ultimate consumers. Finally, Part VII is a two-chapter unit on sales management.

Because this book is a combination of principles and techniques, it recognizes *why* as well as *what, how,* and *when.* The principles that receive emphasis are basic and lasting; they are the principles that students will apply in business. Techniques include practices to adopt and practices to avoid. There is no set of directions which can be followed by salespeople as a builder follows blueprints and instructions in building a house, but this is a practical book, comprehensive and thorough, based on what the better salespeople do.

The fundamental conviction that a salesperson is an adviser to buyers continues to be stressed in this edition. The salesperson is viewed as a counselor whose role is to help buyers make better buying decisions. This edition continues to emphasize creative selling which will lead to continuing, mutually profitable relationships between salespeople and their customers. Professional salespeople are not interested in making one-time sales; neither are they mere order-takers, unimaginative and devoid of resourcefulness.

As is always true, the authors are indebted to many. In particular, our thanks and appreciation go to companies which contributed, instructors who have used the book, students who have studied it, salespeople, and our colleagues.

C. A. Kirkpatrick
Frederick A. Russ

iii

contents

Part VI
SPECIAL TYPES OF SELLING

Part VII
SALES MANAGEMENT

PERSONAL SELLING BASICS
part 1

The Role of Personal Selling 1

After studying this chapter you should be able to:

- Summarize the positive and the negative attitudes toward selling
- Show how selling benefits our economy and our society
- Describe the three roles salespeople play
- Tell why selling offers an attractive career
- Argue that a person can learn how to sell

What do you really think about personal selling at this point? The first section in this first chapter reviews certain attitudes toward selling—some favorable, some unfavorable. The second section describes the roles personal selling plays and its effects on our economy and in our society. Next comes a section that shows how the salesperson provides a link between the salesperson's firm and its customers by persuading them, serving them, and informing them. The fourth section presents what a career in selling offers. The final section deals with how one learns to sell.

ATTITUDES TOWARD SELLING

When selling is understood fully, false ideas disappear, and in their place appears an appreciation of what selling means to us. Selling is not made up of jokes and drinks, backslapping and smiles, high pressure and high living, gifts, shady deals, and expense accounts. Salespeople are not away from home all the time. Their families need not suffer any more than other families. Salespeople do not have to resign themselves to a life less full, less satisfying, or less happy than other individuals enjoy.

Positive Attitudes

Many salespeople find much satisfaction and challenge in selling. They thrive on excelling in their field and take pride in their work and in satisfying the needs of their customers.

Selling Is Essential. It is a serious mistake to consider personal selling an optional activity as far as our economy is concerned. The products of our manufacturing and agriculture will not sell themselves, no matter how good or how big they are. The same holds true for intangibles. The advice that all one needs to do to succeed is to begin building the mousetrap better is as treacherous as it is untrue. Selling—aggressive, face-to-face selling—is necessary to move much of the volume of goods that comes from our factories and farms. As for intangibles, how many people buy insurance without any nudging from a salesperson?

Selling is essential for high employment. One study has shown that the typical salesperson of a manufacturer is responsible for the steady employment of 31 factory workers. Their dependents, plus the salesperson's, add up to 109 consumers. Furthermore, the salesperson contributes to the continued operation of other enterprises. Transportation firms get business because manufacturers' salespeople, as well as their own, sell. Wholesalers, retailers, storage companies, banks, advertising agencies, and advertising media stay in business because salespeople are out making sales.

A point sometimes overlooked is that new products are not alone in requiring personal selling. Established products, too, must be sold year after year. The changes forever going on will not allow otherwise. As examples, a manufacturer decides to enter a new market, or new competitors appear, or established competitors take some dealers away. All sellers see the buyer group changing every day, some disappearing and needing to be replaced. Advertising alone will almost never keep a product on the market; the manufacturer must make use of salespeople indefinitely. What would happen if personal selling were abandoned? Sales would drop, production would have to be cut back, workers would be laid off, inventories would rise, and eventually, the manufacturer would face bankruptcy.

Selling Is Productive. It is a misconception to think that selling adds no value to the goods and services it markets, or that it is a parasitic form of promotion. Selling is productive in that, to be successful, it must benefit the buyer as well as the seller. Practically all sellers must receive repeat orders and purchases from their customers if they are to survive profitably. Most sellers must hold a customer's patronage through many successive purchases and over many years. Clearly, no sensible buyer makes repeated purchases from a seller if those purchases are of no benefit.

Selling Is a Proud Activity. Every sincere, competent salesperson is entitled to a feeling of pride from a career in selling. As has been indicated, these activities assure jobs for many other individuals. Buyers are guided to better products and services; this is certainly a satisfying experience. Buyers, be they consumers, middlemen, members of a profession, or purchasing agents, benefit from good selling.

The salesperson is a key person in the economic well-being of our country. Salespeople, in part, make possible the massive production that contributes greatly to our national independence and security.

Negative Attitudes

There are some negative aspects of selling, and these may result in a negative attitude for some persons. Some selling jobs demand much travel and time away from home and family. The selling pattern can be one of irregularity with respect to hours, sleep, meals, and travel. The salesperson must see buyers where and when they can be seen. Those who sell insurance can testify to sales made in strange settings and at odd hours.

One difficult phase of the salesperson's job is buyers' hostility. Many buyers raise obstacles and defenses the moment a salesperson appears. Buyers tell themselves that they are being imposed on, and they worry lest the salesperson take advantage of them. Many buyers have no confidence in their own abilities to analyze products, prices, and proposals. They fear that their decision may not be sound and that their selections may be unhappy ones. They convert this fear into fear of the salesperson. Selling to buyers who are insecure and, as a result, distrust the salesperson is not easy work.

Personal selling lacks the glamor, prestige, and social status of such professions as medicine and law. Some students even think that a career in selling would be a waste of a college education.

In addition, there is disappointment when a sales presentation fails. Salespeople are under pressure to exceed last month's and last year's volume.

Some students think that salespeople to succeed, must stoop to deception, false promises, trickery, and misrepresentation; these students should not become salespeople. Unethical salespeople talk buyers into buying what they should not.

SELLING BENEFITS OUR ECONOMY AND OUR SOCIETY

Selling benefits more than just salespeople and the companies they represent. Personal selling plays a vital role in our free enterprise system and thus has an influence on our entire society.

Product Innovation

The competition among sellers in their selling activities exerts strong, even irresistible, pressure on those sellers to compete by producing better products. Manufacturers must constantly ask if they should bring out any new products, if there are product improvements that can and should be made, or if there are any new uses for their present products. In every proposal for product change, there is one basic and all-important question: Can the new product, or the improved product, or the new use of a product be sold profitably? Unless the answer is affirmative, the proposal has no practical value.

No new product or service can be placed on the market and kept there unless it can be sold successfully. Inventions and improvements mean nothing to the inventor, the worker, the business person, the consumer, or our national wealth until they are accepted, and that means they must be bought. In the case of new products, both the product and its market must be created from scratch. New and better products do not of themselves create buyer desire or buyer demand.

Salespeople encourage and often demand the improvement of current products and the invention of new ones. Their plea is for products which will give them an advantage over the salespeople and products against which they compete. In effect, they ask the inventor to create and improve products; they urge the engineers and production managers to manufacture the items; they encourage the advertising manager to go into action. These actions can be approved because the salespeople themselves are going to take the actual products and show and sell them to buyers.

The number of products on the market is increasing. These products must be sold. Many new products are being designed and tested. They will appear on the market as soon as it is thought that they can be sold in a volume that promises profit. There is a natural tendency on the part of buyers to be cautious about purchasing new types of merchandise. Consumers get new and better products only if salespeople can sell them.

High Standard of Living

The activities of salespeople help raise our standard of living. Salespeople influence our way of life by changing our consumption patterns. They start by making consumers dissatisfied with their present habits, decisions, and products. In this particular undertaking, the salesperson functions as both an informer and a reformer.

The public's reception of new products is characterized more by caution, hesitation, skepticism, and postponement than by impatience to own the new item today. The public is reluctant to accept change, preferring the old and familiar. Consumers resist new ideas and new products because these will disrupt their routines. Consumers know the old; they are not quite sure of the new; they delay change. That delay is ended usually by some salesperson who convinces them they should spend some of their money for new and better ways of living. Price cuts, merchandising, advertising, and other promotion will not prove to homemakers that they need air conditioning, trash compactors, microwave ovens, or food processors. Telephones, automobiles, vacuum cleaners, TV sets, and clothes dryers all had to be sold.

The United States consumer is the best-fed, best-housed, best-clothed, best-transported, and best-entertained consumer in the world. There are more comforts of life available to more people in our economy than anywhere else. Our high standard of living relies on selling. No product or service can affect a consumer's living level and increase that consumer's satisfaction until the consumer buys and tries that product or service.

Business Activity

Our economic well-being at any given moment is greatly influenced if not completely determined by three factors: *consumption, production,* and *employment.* It is obvious that these three are related; not one of the three can be at a high and healthy level unless the other two are healthy. When all three are at high levels, then we approach a balanced economy because production is matched by consumption, and unemployment is practically nonexistent. Full consumption and full production insure full employment.

Our consumption is the envy of the world. Two facts help explain this. First, competition among sellers is sharpened by the nature of the selling process, with a resultant break for the consumer. Second, lower prices are possible because of mass production, and mass production depends on the marketing of large quantities. Salespeople play a role in the marketing of such quantities.

If maximum production is to be had, large quantities of products and services must be sold. Mass production demands mass marketing, and this demands intensive and extensive selling. The production department looks to salespeople to locate prospects for what is manufactured and then to convert those prospects into buyers. It must be remembered that unless a product can be sold profitably, its manufacture must stop. The result is either unemployment or the use of the facilities to manufacture a more profitable product.

If maximum employment is to be had, then, as in the case of maximum production, large quantities of products and services must be sold. Selling increases consumer spending and thereby acts as a pressure to increase the efforts and activities of consumers to earn. Because of selling, we can have highly specialized labor with its efficient machines and its assembly lines.

The highly specialized worker is indeed at the mercy of selling. A high degree of specialization demands a large volume of production, and this demands large markets. Selling contributes in a substantial measure to employment throughout all industry and commerce, as these expand in direct proportion to the volume of goods and services sold. In summary, selling raises consumption, which encourages production and increases employment.

Economic Growth

The second half of this century deserves to be called the "Age of Marketing" as much as the first half of the century deserves to be known as the "Age of Production." Distribution is the major element in our economy today. Our production has in many cases outrun our marketing. Despite certain scarcities, our ability to supply normally exceeds our demand.

Economic growth assumes continued investment because investment causes the production of additional products. This means more jobs, and jobs mean greater consumer buying power. Growth feeds on buying power. The cycle is something like this: sales cause capital investment; capital investment causes jobs; jobs cause income; and income causes purchases and sales. Investors invest because salespeople assure a market for the product in question, thus reducing the investors' risks to a tolerable point. New companies and new products would never be financed unless salespeople could find or create markets for the products.

Personal selling and advertising are our two basic promotional forces. Advertising is both desirable and necessary, and only the unenlightened salesperson is hostile to it. But advertising cannot do the entire marketing job for the products of our manufacturing, mining, and agriculture. Indeed, the greater portion of this job must be assigned to personal selling. It is the salesperson who must shoulder the greater share of the responsibility for the satisfactory operation of our distribution facilities.

Economic Recession

Our discussion of the socioeconomic benefits of selling assumes a growth-oriented economy, able to meet its raw material needs at reasonable costs. But we must also address the question of the role of personal selling in troubled economic times.

It is tempting to say that the role of salespeople diminishes when there are fewer products (scarcity) or fewer buyers (recession), but such is not the case. A study conducted in the mid-1970s—when recession and scarcity were both problems—indicated that four times as many large companies intended to increase the size of their sales force as planned to decrease their selling emphasis. There were at least five reasons for this increased emphasis:

1. When there are fewer buyers, competition is even more intense. The firm that survives hard times (even just barely) will be in an excellent position once good times return.
2. Scarcities of raw materials and reluctance to increase capital expenditures (on new plants or machinery) mean that most of the competition will come not from new products but from new and better ways of selling.
3. Neither the buyer nor the seller can afford any slack. Both must become lean and hard. The seller cannot afford to produce something that will not sell. The buyer needs to know what will be available. The salesperson is a major source of information both for the buyer and seller.
4. The salesperson can help the buyer make intelligent purchases and decisions by informing the buyer about: (a) other products that can substitute for products in short supply, (b) ways to use the products more efficiently, and (c) sources of financing.

5. By showing buyers how to solve their problems, salespeople can play a major role in helping the country overcome recession. They can serve as catalysts in the process that turns pessimism into optimism.

SELLING LINKS THE COMPANY TO ITS CUSTOMERS

The salesperson is on the boundary between the firm and its customers, providing a personal link between the company and its customers (and often the rest of the outside world). The behavior and skills of the salesperson reflect well or badly on the image of the company and do much to determine its success.

More specifically, the salesperson plays three roles in the link between the company and its customers: a persuasion role, a service role, and an information role.

A Persuasion Role

As the name implies, salespeople sell. That is, they persuade buyers to meet their needs with the products or the company that the salesperson represents. How well salespeople play this role will depend on their understanding of the art of selling—the major focus of this text.

A Service Role

It is not enough for the salesperson simply to persuade buyers to buy products. Unless buyers get satisfaction from the products, the salesperson and the company represented will lose any chance of *repeat* business, the cornerstone of success for all but the shadiest fly-by-night operators. This means that the salesperson must provide service after the sale: showing the customer how to make effective and efficient use of the product, providing assistance if the product fails to perform well, and showing how the product can be used in new and better ways. This benefit to the customer results in increased sales and loyal customers for the seller.

An Information Role

Salespeople are important sources of information about new products for the customer. Salespeople for drug manufacturers tell doctors about new drugs or new methods of using them. Grocery products sales agents tell chain store buyers about new products that will increase their gross margin per square foot of selling space. Sales associates for office equipment companies tell office managers about new word processing systems that will promote greater secretarial efficiency. Sales representatives for book publishers tell professors about new books that will help the learning process.

Salespeople are also important sources of information for the seller. They help the company plan new products by identifying and reporting customers' needs that aren't being adequately filled. And they help the company adjust its current operations by providing feedback about what the customer likes or dislikes about the way the company is doing business.

SELLING OFFERS AN ATTRACTIVE CAREER

The aspects of selling that will probably be most important to a person who is contemplating a career in this field are: the opportunity for advancement, expected earnings, personal satisfaction from the job, security, respect, independence, variety, and interesting work.

Opportunity for Advancement

Few types of activity offer the bright future for an individual that personal selling offers. Broad trends are partially responsible for this. Our population has been growing and continues to grow. The increase in our capacity to manufacture also continues; the volume of goods and services that our productive facilities are able to pour out to our markets is staggering. More and more new products appear, needing salespeople, and consumers continue to want more and better products. The increase in the amount of leisure time each consumer enjoys is opening up new markets. And most important of all, the rise in national income has placed in consumers' hands buying power with which to pay for more and better goods.

Salespeople who deserve promotion are more apt to get promoted than are many individuals in other phases of business. From the moment they begin to succeed and to achieve, regardless of their age they must be considered for advancement. Hard work and resourcefulness will move them up faster and farther than they will move people in many other types of work. Good salespeople do not have to wait long for management to recognize their worth. They can stand on their records of successful performance, not on successful politicking; they can substitute a base that cannot be challenged—sales—for unsound bases, such as seniority.

Where does promotion lead? The successful individual can chart a course for the top in selling, or can move toward a position in management. These two are available, of course, within the salesperson's own company or in other organizations. Advancement in industrial selling is largely through territories or accounts. Advancement in management might be through such jobs as sales supervisor, branch manager, district or zone manager, regional manager, divisional manager, assistant sales manager, sales manager, vice-president of sales, and even president. Advancement in retailing might be to head of stock, assistant buyer, buyer, or selling supervisor. Then there are certain allied activities in marketing into which one might move—advertising, sales promotion, and market research.

Business used to get its senior management from the fields of production, law, and finance. Now, however, many top managers are coming from the field of selling. Management and leadership everywhere depend on the ability to get along with others and to influence them. Salespeople come in contact with all types of people. They learn to sell not only products but also their company and themselves. For individuals planning to enter business for themselves, the future is brighter if they have learned to sell.

Earnings

Good salespeople are paid well. Studies of college and university classes usually show that four or five years after graduation, the salespeople have risen more in earnings than almost any other group. Some of the highest income figures in business are found in selling. In addition, selling ranks highest among many fields in average earnings.

Practically all salespeople are paid a salary or commission, or some combination of the two. Many people flatly refuse to enter selling strictly on a commission basis, demanding the salary type of compensation. They group together such factors as steady salary, fringe benefits, size of company, and prestige of company; they consider these more desirable than incentive, opportunity to rise quickly, or even amount of pay.

The significant point is that salespeople set their own compensation, whether they be on salary or on commission. Their pay is determined by how much, how hard, and how well they work. Their income is in direct proportion to the time, energy, and thought they choose to spend. Proof of their control over their pay is the fact that to earn more, all they need to do is to sell more. There is no ceiling on the size of their income. In being paid on the basis of individual production, the salesperson differs from others in business. For example, no company can measure precisely what any one of its accountants contributes to the profitable operation of the business. The field of personnel is another in which the determination of personal output or worth of an individual can be done in only a rough, subjective manner. Not so for salespeople. They can reap what they sow because their sales volume, the gross margin thereon, and their cost to the company can be measured in dollars.

Personal Satisfaction

Dollar income is not the only kind of income a person must have in order to be and feel successful. Everyone needs psychic income, too. Unless a person's activities provide all the necessary amounts and types of incomes, then that person will be dissatisfied.

Selling offers the satisfaction of personal growth and development. Because salespeople must think of the needs, problems, hopes, and welfare of others, they cannot afford to be narrow or self-centered. They must learn to get along satisfactorily with all types of people and to deal with them pleasantly. They must work toward permanent, mutually profitable relationships with their buyers.

Selling lets the salesperson feel needed, and that feeling gives satisfaction. To know that buyers need help in finding better solutions to problems, to know that they count on you to help find those better solutions, and then to join buyers in a successful search for them—that is a most rewarding experience and gives the salesperson a feeling of personal worth.

Selling gives salespeople the thrill of accomplishment, a major form of satisfaction. Salespeople start by hunting buyers who will benefit from buying their products. They analyze the problems of those buyers in order to be able to make specific proposals. Then they persuade the buyers to become customers and to begin enjoying the advantages of using their products. Making each sale provides the salesperson with the feeling of accomplishment because not only the salesperson but also the company and new customer know of this performance. A second gratification is experienced by the salesperson who sees clearly that these efforts have benefited buyers.

Selling gives salespeople the personal satisfaction of knowing that they have been of service to others. Salespeople can feel that they have contributed to society. They make life safer, more pleasant, more convenient, or easier for their customers. Salespeople help business people increase sales volume and reduce costs. They sell satisfaction and, in return, find their own satisfaction.

Security

Almost everyone wants a good measure of security. That desire is both understandable and commendable. Some students consider selling as a career to be too risky and uncertain. They contend that they can take a long-shot chance and enter selling, or they can choose security. Even within the field of selling, some graduates insist that the only items to sell are large, complex, physical products. They want little to do with low-priced, small items, and absolutely nothing to do with intangibles.

One does not need extensive or exhaustive research to discover that companies can continue operating only if their salespeople make sales. When a recession develops, does a company fire its salespeople? As times get tougher, does the need for productive salespeople decline? Sales executives say that for a salesperson who likes to sell and can sell, there is no job more secure. They say that there have never been enough good salespeople and that, consequently, the ability to sell at a profit is the most effective type of security. Indeed, it is during depressions that demand for competent salespeople is greatest. When times are bad, inefficient salespeople may be fired along with production and office personnel, but the sound salesperson usually suffers no more than a drop in earnings.

Selling is security in other ways. The ability to influence human behavior, to persuade, is essential everywhere and at all times. Employers will pay for that ability. A person can be—or even become—a good salesperson at age 40, or

50, or 60. When the management of a company changes, many replacements may be made; but few will be replacements of salespeople, for salespeople are responsible for sales volume and for the sales income budget—the most basic of all budgets. Finally, no machine is going to replace or make obsolete the salesperson whose judgment is sound, whose tact and discretion are outstanding, whose thinking is keen.

Respect

Unless a person's economic activities are respectable, chances of being happy are slim. There are two phases to this matter of respect—self-respect and community respect. In the discussion of personal satisfaction, it was stated that salespeople can adopt a high purpose in life because they know that selling is as worthwhile as it is essential. They can be individuals of integrity. Their calling can be one of pride and dignity.

Some shy away from selling for fear that they might not be held in esteem by those close to them. The prestige of the professions is a dominant element in this desire for community respect. Social status is determined not only by the number of dollars one earns but also by one's personality, character, conduct, personal and civic accomplishments, and contributions to the community. And certainly members of no one occupation or profession have a corner on any of these elements of success. If salespeople accept as their sales philosophy the one of "helping prospects buy," they will include in their personal and social philosophy the concept of helpfulness and service.

Independence

Selling is an independent way of life. Salespeople have much control over their time and activities. They have so much freedom of choice that often they are virtually in business for themselves. Each works in a single territory, handling products, prospects, and customers as thought best. There is some supervision, of course, but salespeople, in a sense, are pretty free to draft a program or schedule of work and plan their routing in the light of the customer's needs and location.

More and more companies are coming to realize how dependent they are on their salespeople. They have developed sound procedures for selecting, training, and supervising new salespeople. Instruction for selling is extensive and intensive. Whatever guidance is necessary or desired is available on a continuing basis. In selecting a selling job, an individual can get just about the preferred mixture of independence and guidance.

Variety

The very nature of selling insures considerable variety for the salesperson. Some jobs in selling demand travel, others do not. There is the day-to-day type of travel, and then there is the infrequent move or transfer which perhaps can be classified as another type of travel. Normally, the amount and type of traveling the salesperson must do depend on the size of the territory. There are two or three advantages to travel. One is seeing new places; a second is seeing different people; a possible third is the additional compensation received in some jobs because of the travel required.

Because of loss of customers to death, retirement, or competitors, each salesperson must ever be on the trail of new prospects, some of whom must be converted into new customers. This means a stream of new contacts and new acquaintances. Each day is different from other days, each city or market differs from others, and, in a literal sense, no two interviews are identical. Always the circumstances vary. Because no two buyers are alike and no two calls the same, a salesperson finds each buyer a new challenge, each call a new test.

Stimulating variety can be found in broader areas. Prices, for example, vary from market to market, from time to time, and even from buyer to buyer. Products do not remain unchanged too long, or they may become dated or obsolete. Promotional strategy and tactics are always being revised and improved so that their effectiveness is increased. New types of middlemen appear and may be added to a manufacturer's distribution channels. Sales expectations and the potentials of individual markets can change overnight. One can certainly say that selling is not monotonous.

Interesting Work

The most challenging phase of the salesperson's job is the competitive nature of selling. Salespeople must be successful competitors. The salesperson, in one sense, competes with the buyer as to which will influence the other. Competition is the essence of another relationship, that between a salesperson and the salespeople of competing companies. Each salesperson tries to hold on to customers, to keep them from going to competitors. At the same time, each salesperson is trying to take customers away from those competitors. Finally, salespeople must compete with themselves, against their past performances. They want each year to be better than the last, and every order from each customer to be larger than previous orders. A salesperson's greatest challenge may be to exceed his or her past achievements.

While it is true that selling is hard, competitive work, it is the most interesting work in the world for those who like it. The salesperson is dealing with human beings and their motivation, working with personal values and personal satisfaction, and experimenting with various stimuli and analyzing buyers' reactions to each. For the individual who delights in coming to grips with buyers and selling to them, the basic enjoyment, excitement, and satisfaction found in selling can be matched nowhere else.

Some people take the position that one cannot learn how to sell. This contention is supported by their concepts of, first, the nature of selling, and, second, the nature of individuals. On the first point, the argument is that selling is an art and not a science and that, because it is not a science, it cannot be taught and learned. On the second point, it is believed that some individuals are born salespeople, while others just are not endowed with the ability to sell and there is little or nothing they can do about it.

It would seem more in line with facts to recognize that there are certain sound principles of selling that are so long-established and susceptible to proof that they cannot be challenged successfully. These principles can be examined and understood in a classroom and can then be proved by pragmatic testing on the outside.

Two conclusions must be drawn from the concept of the nature of individuals. First, it is true that some people are not attracted to selling as a profession. If they did enter the field, they would be miserable failures; whereas if they undertook some more suitable vocation, they could be happy and successful. Other people are better qualified to enter selling and to become outstanding in that field because of their likes and dislikes, their talents, and their basic natures.

The second and more significant observation is that each group, even the group without "natural" sales ability, can improve the quality and increase the quantity of its sales ability. Outstandingly successful people are not born ready-made that way, whether they are farmers, doctors, merchants, manufacturers, or salespeople. Much of their success must be attributed to hard work, practice, and a fierce determination to improve. Even the innate qualities and characteristics of those with an aptitude for selling need cultivating and developing. Companies would not conduct elaborate and expensive sales training programs if the principles of personal selling could not be taught and learned.

Advantages of College Courses

Some salespeople lose their jobs because of their lack of adequate training. It certainly seems reasonable to assume that a person who enters the field of selling with no sales training is handicapped. There are both major and minor ways in which college courses in selling can be helpful to you.

One major benefit is that you will learn of the need for training in selling. You will see that selling is a demanding, specialized activity for which preparation is necessary. Quickly discarded is the idea that a salesperson will automatically succeed because of personal charm, because of a well-known name, or because of "connections."

The second major benefit is that the college course serves as an introduction to selling. You learn something of what to expect and will be confronted later by fewer situations that are completely unexpected.

READING LIST

1. *The Lacy Techniques of Salesmanship*—Micali
2. *Sell Yourself Rich*—Hipple
3. *Enthusiasm Makes the Difference*—Peale
4. *The Art of Listening*—Morris
5. *Get Control of Your Time and Your Life*—Lakein
6. *Selling is Simple*—Herman
7. *Speak Your Way to Success*—Sazor
8. *Psychocybernetics*—Maltz
9. *Dress for Success*—Malloy
10. *Promotion: An Introductory Analysis*—Kernan
11. *Corporate Lives*—DeMear
12. *Psychological Aspects of Selling*—McCarthy
13. *Drucker: The Man Who Invented the Corporate Society*—Tarrant
14. *The Great Executive Dream*—Heller
15. *Passages*—Sheehy
16. *The Managerial Woman*—Jardin and Hennig

Source: *Gillette Sales Training Guide*, p. 249.

ILLUSTRATION 1-1. Salespeople should never stop learning. Gillette recommends the above reading list to its sales representatives.

Third, a college course in selling can help you as a future salesperson to work more intelligently and satisfactorily with your supervisor and with the sales training personnel of your company because you will know what they are trying to do.

Last of the major benefits is that you can acquire in a short time much of the fundamental selling knowledge that has been accumulated by others through years of experience in every field of selling.

As for lesser advantages, the course can help uncertain individuals decide whether selling is the proper field to enter. It may help all students to become better buyers. And it is a valuable adjunct to other business courses.

Limitations of College Courses

Despite the need for and the value of college courses in selling, this type of instruction has limitations, as would a classroom study of swimming, for example. Schools cannot turn out salespeople in the same way that schools turn out typists, mechanics, or accountants.

Because a sales situation involves human beings and because there are always some differences between any two interviews, prospects, or conditions, the salesperson is called on to exercise and demonstrate originality, mental agility, and ingenuity. If this were not true, the job of a salesperson would be as simple as that of a robot. Experience is needed as a supplement to give meaning to the principles learned in the classroom. Proficiency in selling can be acquired in no other way. For maximum progress, it is best to combine study and instruction with experimentation and practice.

Need for Continuous Study

There is no specific time period within which selling can be learned, whether it is a quarter, two semesters, a year, or a decade. The obvious inference is that salespeople can never afford to stop learning. The minute they become complacent, they begin to stagnate and slip. Instead of feeling that they have mastered the process of selling and are entitled to coast for a while, salespeople must search for new and more effective techniques if they want to insure success. They must always study people carefully. They must check books and trade papers for whatever material may be of value to them. The company and its personnel must be used as sources of selling aids. Observation and practice must not be neglected. Constructive suggestions about changes that will be beneficial should always be welcome. Only by adopting an inquiring, experimental attitude and maintaining it can the salesperson avoid drifting into mental ruts.

SUMMARY

Selling is necessary to move the goods and services our work force provides. Both new products and established goods must be sold year after year.

Selling is a productive function, benefiting both buyers and sellers. And selling to consumers and many others in the economy can be a proud activity. However, there are some negative aspects to a career in sales. Travel, odd hours, buyer hostility, lack of prestige, and pressure to excel past performance are a few drawbacks.

Competition among sellers places strong pressure on them to produce new and better products. Salespeople encourage and even demand these goods because without them, they will not be successful. They urge inventors and engineers to be more productive, and in the past few years, more products than ever are on the market.

Salespeople help raise our standard of living. They educate consumers about innovations and better products. Consumers are cautious and skeptical, and they require pushing to make purchases of new items, even when these goods will raise their standard of living.

Consumption, employment, and production are three factors that determine our economic well-being. Selling raises consumption, which encourages production. And high production results in increased employment. Therefore, selling is an important aspect of the well-being of our economy. Prosperity encourages economic growth. And growth generates demand, production, and employment. This cycle cannot continue without the influence of salespeople.

Salespeople are also very important when the economy is doing poorly. When recessions occur, firms may increase their sales staffs.

The salesperson is the link between a company and its customers. Salespeople persuade buyers to meet their needs with the product or company the salesperson represents. Salespeople also provide service to buyers, helping them to utilize the product for maximum advantage. And salespeople are information providers to customers and the seller.

Selling can be a very attractive career. Salespeople who deserve promotion are likely to be promoted; they can rely on their record of successful performance rather than in-house politicking. Advancement can either be in the form of new territories and accounts, or the salesperson can go into management.

Good salespeople are paid well, above the average in many other fields. Salespeople are paid a salary or commission, or a combination of the two. However, salespeople really set their own compensation, based on how much, how hard, and how well they work.

Selling offers great personal satisfaction. Growth and development, feeling needed, the thrill of accomplishment, and the knowledge that they are helping others and the economy all lead to a sense of accomplishment.

While some people believe that a sales career is risky, that really isn't so. Sales executives say that for a salesperson who likes to sell and can sell, no job is more secure. Companies always need good salespeople, especially during recessions.

Salespeople can gain respect from the community by participating in community life. Salespeople also can use the attitudes learned and used in selling to gain respect and friends.

Selling is an independent career, and salespeople have much control over their time and activities. At the same time, companies provide guidance to the sales staffs to help them be more effective. This combination of independence with guidance is an attraction of a selling career.

Sales careers have considerable variety. Travel, new customers, ever-changing market conditions, and new products and techniques provide a variety of challenges for the salesperson.

Selling is challenging work. An aspect of selling is its competitiveness. Salespeople compete against other salespeople and their own past performance. Selling is a tremendously interesting and exciting career.

Some people believe that selling is an art that cannot be learned. They contend that the nature of individuals is set and that you are either born a natural salesperson or you will never be able to sell. This view is not totally accurate. Certain principles of selling can be taught in a classroom. And, everyone can learn to become a better salesperson with hard work, practice, and determination.

College courses can be very helpful. Such courses show the need for specialized training. They serve as an introduction to selling and will help you as a future salesperson to work better with your supervisors. In a very short time, you will acquire knowledge that has taken years for others to accumulate. College courses are limited in scope, however. They can teach principles but not mental agility and ingenuity, qualities that are invaluable in selling. Experience and experimentation are necessary to round out an individual in selling. Continuous study and practice throughout a career are important for helping salespeople maintain high performance levels.

REVIEW QUESTIONS

1. Why is personal selling an essential activity?
2. Why is selling difficult work?
3. What are some negative beliefs people have about selling?
4. Why do salespeople push for new and better products?
5. How do salespeople raise our standard of living?
6. Where does selling fit into the cycle of economic growth?
7. What information do salespeople provide their employers?
8. What are the two primary compensation methods for salespeople?
9. How can your college courses help you become a better salesperson?
10. What are the limitations of college courses?

DISCUSSION QUESTIONS

1. What are your strengths and weaknesses as they relate to a career in sales? What traits do you have that will make you a good salesperson? What is the trait that will cause you the most problems in selling? How will you try to overcome this shortcoming?
2. What aspects of a career in sales are most attractive to you?
3. How do you think the role of salespeople will be changing between now and the year 2000?
4. Discuss the promotional opportunities of salespeople contrasted to those of other employees.
5. Discuss the variety aspects of selling.

CASE STUDY 1

Dr. Glenn Frank, former president of the University of Wisconsin, is quoted* as follows:

---

*Quoted by Dr. George W. Crane, "Salesmen Are the Sparkplugs of Civilization," *Sales and Marketing Management* (February 4, 1980), pp. 37–40.

Nothing of permanent value has come down to us from the past, save by the grace of good salesmanship on the part of somebody. . . . A time comes when peddler and President stand on the same footing: both must be good salesmen.

1. Do you agree? If so, why? If you don't agree, give examples of "things of permanent value" whose acceptance hasn't involved good salesmanship.
2. Using what you've learned in this chapter, write a brief essay describing the selling roles played by the President of the United States.

The Job of Personal Selling: 2
Traits and Tasks

After studying this chapter you should be able to:

• Define a professional salesperson

• List eight psychological characteristics that are commonly mentioned as essential to successful selling

• Point out social characteristics that help salespeople

• Comment on the physical characteristics of salespeople

• Name and explain the obligations of salespeople

• Distinguish among different types of selling jobs

To be successful at personal selling it is helpful for the salesperson to have certain personality traits and attitudes. Neither technical skill, nor experience, nor basic talent, nor size of income is the deciding factor. Instead, the salesperson's attitude is the main criterion.

THE PROFESSIONAL SALESPERSON

A professional point of view is the feature that identifies the professional salesperson. When the chief principle of selling is, "What can I do *for* my prospects and customers?" the salesperson is a professional. If the question is "What can my prospects and customers do for *me?*" or, even worse, "What can I do *to* them?" the attitude is less than professional.

True salesmanship is neither a game nor a racket. In calling attention to a product and asking the prospect to buy, the salesperson is doing a favor and not asking one, for the purchase is not recommended unless there is a deep conviction that it will benefit the prospect to buy. The successful salesperson is one who guides a customer's purchasing in order to benefit that customer. In performing this buyer-seller function, the salesperson sells ideas, not products or services, because the buyer buys satisfaction, not merchandise. A buyer appears to be buying a tire, but actually is buying safe, low-cost transportation. The buyer does not buy lamps, but lighting. The insurance policy is, in reality, protection.

Professional salespeople are dedicated to serving the needs and problems of buyers. Because they know their calling to be a proud one, they are jealous of their own reputations. Their basic honesty reflects high personal principles as well as the integrity of their companies. Their initial interest in buyers develops into loyalty to them. They tactfully advise them about their circumstances and about what should be done in the light of those circumstances. They instruct buyers about product features and product uses. True professionals are not content until customers are happy with what they bought. The professional knows that the buyer, too, must benefit from purchase-and-sales transactions. Only when professional salespeople see these results can they enjoy the long-term associations with customers that are customary in many industries.

A study of the professional salesperson reveals the following characteristics:

1. Possesses a satisfactory amount of basic ability to sell.
2. Consciously chose the selling field and is proud of it.
3. Is loyal to high ethical standards.
4. Is a skilled worker.
5. Has thorough knowledge of product.
6. Is true to obligations.
7. Has had actual selling experience.
8. Stays up-to-date because of continuous learning.
9. Has integrity above reproach.
10. Knows there is no substitute for hard work.
11. Maintains self-respect and independence.
12. Knows that to sell is to serve.

CHARACTERISTICS OF SUCCESSFUL SALESPEOPLE

A dynamic personality is one of the basic needs of all salespeople. Complete product knowledge is eminently desirable, as are such other features as strict obedience to company instructions, long hours of work, determination to keep up-to-date and accurate records on all prospects, and a mastery of selling fundamentals and techniques. It is quite true that these are examples of things the salesperson should try to achieve, but they and other similar accomplishments are not enough. An individual must also have a superior sales personality.

Psychological Characteristics

A pleasing personality by itself is not enough. Popularity and an engaging personality alone will not enable a salesperson to sell anything to anybody. The salesperson who relies solely on personality is at a disadvantage when competing with an all-around salesperson.

Personality is a broad concept that cannot easily be defined. A sales personality may be thought of as the impression that the prospect gets of the salesperson. It is how the salesperson appears to prospects. The sales personality is what the prospect likes or dislikes about the salesperson as a human being.

No salesperson can afford to be indifferent to or negligent about the cultivation of a superior sales personality because personality influences prospects. Every impression the salesperson makes helps or hurts chances of making the sale. If the reaction elicited is unfavorable, or even neutral, the sale will be more difficult.

In implementing a program of personality development, the salesperson starts with a self-analysis. Then it is necessary to work largely through control and change of habits because methods of operation, selling techniques, and even attitudes are matters of habit. It is the habit pattern that has good or bad effects on prospects and customers, the company, and oneself. Superior sales personality is largely the result of certain habits and ways of thinking, certain practices and policies that fortunately can be acquired by experimentation and effort.

It is not easy to develop a more pleasing personality. Most individuals are reluctant to admit even to themselves that something about them is wrong and needs changing. Because such an admission deflates the ego, it tends to be avoided or postponed. People with whom the salesperson comes in contact are hesitant to point out habits that need correction. Then too, new habits of a detrimental type have a way of insinuating themselves so quietly and gradually that the salesperson is usually unaware that they have been adopted until they are assimilated. Once established, a habit is difficult to break.

Eight psychological characteristics are commonly mentioned as essential to successful selling. They are optimism, enthusiasm, confidence, sincerity, determination, dependability, initiative, and imagination.

Optimism. Optimism is a characteristic of a success-minded salesperson—one who, within reasonable limits, does not admit to himself the possibility of failing to reach the objective. The first thing salespeople are optimistic about is themselves, for they are confident that they are going to better themselves as time passes. Second, they are optimistic about the products they sell. They feel that each one is an excellent value in its own price class and that each will give satisfaction to the proper user. A third source of optimism is the company being represented, its service to customers and the quality of its products.

Enthusiasm. Enthusiasm is a combination of interest and belief, of energy and activity. Salespeople need a broad curiosity about the products being sold, the prospects, themselves, and even matters unrelated to selling. Enthusiasm leads a salesperson to become acquainted with the work from all possible angles. Enthusiasm plays a dominant role in the sales interview in helping secure the interest and confidence of the prospect. It is a requisite for eloquence and, when translated into animated and persuasive delivery, it prevents the sales story from being a dull recital. If the salesperson is to inspire the prospect's enthusiasm over the proposition, the only safe course to follow is to carry infectious enthusiasm into the interview.

Confidence. Confidence is the result of knowledge plus experience, and for this reason it can be developed and is more easily acquired than optimism and enthusiasm. To a salesperson, confidence is a belief in oneself, a healthy respect for one's own capabilities and powers. It is the motivation that causes the salesperson to be not merely willing but eager to encounter hard-to-sell prospects. To a prospect, the confident salesperson inspires confidence.

Sincerity. Still another requisite of a successful salesperson is sincerity. Nothing is so vital to the continued trust and confidence of prospects as a sincere interest in their problems and well-being. Salespeople who are known to be high-powered individuals determined to sell at all costs, who have concern for their own interests above the interests of their prospects and customers, who make claims that will not be lived up to, who resort to half-truths and false information to influence customers, cannot expect to hold customers long. Prospects usually have little trouble in detecting an insincere presentation. Salespeople cannot hope to make other people believe that which they themselves know to be untrue.

Determination. Determination is the will to succeed. Successful salespeople are those who are determined to get ahead. Their urging, driving ambition makes them industrious individuals who are willing to work long hours under discouraging circumstances. This same ambition is responsible for their aggressive, competitive spirit and for their pride in wanting to be the best people on the sales force.

Patience and perseverance—parts of determination—do not allow salespeople to give up easily but instead make them stick to their jobs. The persevering salesperson makes calls on a desirable prospect repeatedly and regularly, knowing that the first order will come eventually.

Dependability. Buyers are always in search of elements of certainty in an area which is largely one of perpetual change. One such welcome element is a dependable salesperson. They know too many salespeople who have proved to be unworthy of confidence. Consequently, the salesperson who can be relied upon is received enthusiastically by buyers.

Initiative. A salesperson with initiative is a self-starter who, instead of being hesitant about undertakings, is both willing and desirous to get action under way. This is essentially a person with ambition implemented with a healthy amount of industry, thinking, acting, and continuously busy even when not under close supervision. Skill and intelligence give customers confidence.

Salespeople with initiative learn to rely on themselves, to make their own plans, and then to follow those plans. In their constant search for methods of increasing value to their company, they are a fertile source of new ideas, suggestions, and challenging questions.

Imagination. The salesperson finds imagination a tremendous help; unless the sales talk is shot through with imagination, it becomes boring. Because ideas are the real stock in trade—regardless of what the physical product may be—the

WHY SALESPEOPLE FAIL

Cause of Failure	Percent
Lack of initiative	55
Poor planning and organization	39
Inadequate product knowledge	37
Lack of enthusiasm	31
Salesperson not customer-oriented	30
Lack of proper training	23
Inability to get along with buyers	21
Lack of personal goals	20
Inadequate knowledge of market	19
Lack of knowledge of company	16
Lack of job satisfaction	15
Unsuited for selling career	14
Lack of adequate background	13
Insufficient self-discipline	12
Salesperson not company-oriented	12
No interest in self-development	11
Failure to follow instructions	11
Lack of self-confidence	11
Improper supervision	9
Inability to improvise	8
Lack of imagination	7
Personal problems	6
Difficulties in communicating	6
Dishonesty	5
Unfortunate appearance	5
Improper attitude	5
Failure to ask buyers to buy	3
Lack of tact and courtesy	2
Gambling and drinking	2

ILLUSTRATION 2-1. In a survey conducted by the authors, sales managers of 500 of this country's largest companies were asked what, in their experience, were the causes of salespeople's failure on the job. Here is their composite answer, with the percent mentioning each cause.

salesperson makes greatest use of imagination when painting word pictures. Consider, for example, an annuity. It is not presented merely as a legal document nor even as a certain number of dollars each month. Instead, the imaginative salesperson paints a picture of the retirement period of life, of trips and touring, of hobbies and longings to be gratified, of the feeling of security. Using imagination, the salesperson is able to translate the product into those exact things the prospect wants.

Social Characteristics

A salesperson's chances of long-term success are slight if a pronounced social inclination and a basic liking for people are lacking. One must be eager to meet and know new individuals and be friendly by nature.

Friendly Nature. The salesperson encounters all types of prospects in all types of situations. Prospects vary in point of view, age, pattern of living, background, ideals, knowledge, and in many other respects, yet the salesperson must be a friend to and of each. This demands extreme social adaptability. The only lasting basis for friendship between salesperson and prospect is the salesperson's genuine interest in the prospect and an accompanying desire to help with any problems. To be liked, the salesperson must like, and to know the prospect is to take a long step toward liking and becoming friends.

Social Grace. The mannerly salesperson tries to make each call a pleasant, enjoyable visit, marred by no violation of social custom. Tact and diplomacy should be used in arranging and opening the interview and in handling objections, interruptions, and other obstacles to purchasing. Courtesy must be evidenced from the moment of entering the prospect's office until it is time to go. Prospects should not be the only ones granted this social grace. Salespeople should also be courteous to clerks, receptionists, secretaries, assistant buyers, and all other personnel contacted in the prospect's place of business.

Conversational Ability. To be a good conversationalist, the salesperson should be concerned about four matters. First, the salesperson must assume the "you" point of view and talk from that position all of the time. Prospects are basically interested in only one subject, themselves, and in what the salesperson's products can do for them. The "you" point of view requires a sympathetic understanding of the prospect's buying problems, together with a spirit of tolerance. It also demands that the salesperson be attentive to what the prospect says.

The salesperson's second concern is to make the prospect feel important, and this calls for deferring to and complimenting the prospect. So the salesperson will find something to congratulate the prospect about; will ask for the prospect's advice and opinions; will be impressed by what the prospect has accomplished; will hold the prospect's judgment and experience in high regard.

The third concern is to control the conversation with finesse. By exercising subtle control over the subject matter and direction of the conversation, the salesperson prevents arguments, interruptions, undesirable domination by the prospect, and discussion of unnecessary topics.

A fourth concern is to guard against overusing certain words or expressions. This practice restricts the salesperson's ability to express a precise meaning. In addition, excess repetition becomes monotonous and annoying. The salesperson with an inadequate vocabulary cannot express thoughts intelligently.

Poise. Poise is the characteristic or power that permits people to be in effective command of themselves—physically, mentally, and emotionally. Nothing is more essential to a salesperson's personality than self-confidence, and that confidence permits poise. Poised salespeople are recognized immediately. Their bearing gives proof of selling maturity as well as of emotional stability. At least on the surface, the poised salesperson takes criticism or praise, disappointment or success with the same even manner.

How can one become a poised salesperson? Junior salespeople acquire poise in several ways. The first step involves thorough preparation for a selling career; this is then followed by painstaking preparation for each major sales interview. If salespeople know themselves, their products, their company, and their buyers, and if they know how to sell, they have every reason in the world to feel calm and collected. A helpful device is the rehearsal, in which the salesperson runs through a presentation before actually making it to a buyer. Over the long run, the salesperson will recognize that experience will provide in large measure the competence and confidence that result in poise.

Traits to Be Avoided. Thus far in looking at the image of a salesperson, the characteristics have all been good. There are also certain traits that salespeople should avoid. Obviously, almost every favorable feature has its unfavorable opposite. So, the list below contains just some examples of traits or behavior to be avoided:

Lying or cheating	Over-familiarity or -aggressiveness
Sarcasm or criticism	Self-importance or pompousness
Begging or complaining	Discourtesy or bad manners
Prejudice or intolerance	Indifference or complacency

Physical Characteristics

The physical image of the salesperson is the first factor to register on the prospect. Appearance is a big factor in personality, and thus it is a big factor in selling. The salesperson must appear to be both trustworthy and able, and must advise with authority. To do this, personal appearance must help instill confidence and respect in the prospect. The salesperson pays dearly for any indifference or inattention to appearance, for such neglect will cost sales. To be a success, the salesperson must look like one. A personal appearance that is beyond reproach goes hand in hand with success in selling.

Grooming, Clothing, and Bearing. Ability to sell is not limited to any one physical type. Tall or short, fat or slim, fair or dark, bald or bushy—each group has its share of outstanding salespeople. It is good that such physical differences are unimportant, for one is limited in what can be done about such matters as build, features, or vision. One is not limited, however, in what can be done about such controllable factors as grooming, clothing, and bearing.

The first controllable factors include the cut and grooming of hair, the condition of hands and nails, and the appearance of the teeth. Even the new salesperson knows from experience what is pleasing about these and should need no instruction. Clothes constitute the second group of controllable factors. The main requirement is neatness. Clean and neat clothes bear silent but powerful witness to the attention and care they receive. Personality is expressed in the choice of clothes. Extremes should be avoided. Clothes plus grooming do for a salesperson what a product's package does for the product.

Posture and bearing are also subject to control. They should be positive and confident. Sitting or standing, the salesperson should display both respect and assurance. The physical manner should be of such vigor and power that it bespeaks authority and gets attention. Because posture and bearing are revealing, the salesperson should see that they are a positive force rather than a negative one. The salesperson's walk is also important. It should be energetic and businesslike, with head erect and shoulders back. It should connote authority and purpose.

Mannerisms. Many salespeople acquire habits of which they are not conscious. Tugging at earlobes, fidgeting with glasses, scratching the head, constantly adjusting clothing, or rubbing a hand over the face repeatedly should be avoided. Tapping with a pencil, cracking the knuckles, chewing gum, or even talking with food in the mouth are other undesirable mannerisms. The trouble with such mannerisms is that they make concentration harder for the prospect and, in more extreme cases, create an impression that is definitely unfavorable. This, of course, hinders the salesperson in making the sale.

The salesperson must constantly be alert to detect such mannerisms and eliminate them so that there is complete, conscious control over the physical self. If feasible, the salesperson should encourage some associate, the sales manager, or even some long-established customer to observe a sales presentation and to suggest desirable changes.

Good Health. The sales job is exacting and exhausting. The daily grind of selling makes heavy demands on a salesperson, causing the expenditure of much physical effort and the depletion of energy reserves. Yet at all times the salesperson is expected to be the personification of vitality. Because appearance depends in large measure on physical condition, health should be guarded.

Nonvisual Physical Factors. The prospect's sense of hearing ranks second to the sense of sight in registering an impression of the salesperson. For the prospect to enjoy favorable reception, the salesperson's voice should be pleasing —clear and well-modulated, easy and warm. Its tone should be both courteous and respectful. Because the salesperson's job is that of persuading, a voice that is convincing, emphatic, firm, and purposeful is needed.

Since effective expression is the goal, the salesperson is obligated to eliminate vocal defects and then to continue improvement until vocal versatility has been acquired. A monotone is lifeless and boring and will not persuade a prospect to buy. Practice is required until voice, enunciation, and expression are all acceptable.

Distracting and irritating oral mannerisms can no more be permitted than can the visual. An odd-sounding laugh, a nervous cough, an objectionable clearing of the throat, a resort to "ahs" or "uhs" as prefaces to remarks, or a habit of humming or whistling should be eradicated, for some prospects and customers will certainly find these habits offensive.

ALL SALESPEOPLE HAVE SIMILAR OBLIGATIONS

We begin by examining the basic duties that apply to every person in the selling field.

Job Duties

A salesperson's basic job duties fall into three major areas: selling duties, auxiliary selling duties, and nonselling duties.

Selling. The salesperson's basic responsibility is to make sales against competitors' selling efforts to meet a sales quota. Salespeople must show ultimate consumers how to enhance their self-concepts and business buyers how to increase their sales or reduce their costs. They must add to the number of customers, and must sell more to present customers. Both customer and salesperson must benefit from sales transactions; this usually involves a period of time and a number of transactions. To make sales, an individual must have the need and the will to succeed at selling, and must be a successful communicator.

Auxiliary Selling Duties. To succeed in selling, most salespeople must do certain auxiliary or indirect selling duties. Finding prospects is such a job. Practically all salespeople perform some services to buyers, perhaps before the first sale, sometimes after getting an order. For example, manufacturers' salespeople help their retailer customers by building and maintaining displays and by checking inventories. Some calls by salespeople are literally service calls. By following up first sales, by counseling buyers on their problems, and by working with their customers wherever possible, salespeople try to make loyal customers, not just sales. Salespeople handle most complaints and make some adjustments. Salespeople should always work to improve their company's image.

Nonselling, Personal Tasks. All salespeople must manage and develop themselves. This demands sound planning and controlling; it often demands that the salesperson cooperate with company sales trainers and supervisors. Many salespeople must attend sales meetings and conventions.

Communication takes time: salespeople in the field should read communications sent out by their firms, and their reports to their sales managers should be correct and prompt. The credit manager may expect the salesperson to collect financial information about buyers—even to collect past-due accounts. The sales manager wants information about what competitors are doing, so other market research jobs may be assigned. Finally, some salespeople are expected to be active in public relations—at trade shows, for example, or in the community. The goal is to increase goodwill.

The Salesperson's Obligations to the Employer

A salesperson owes something in two directions; to the employer, and to the prospects and customers. This section and the next consider these obligations.

Selling at a Profit. From the company's point of view, the salesperson's major long-range duty is to sell at a profit. The company wants to continue in business, and this will not be possible unless its operation is profitable. The salesperson best serves personal interests as well as those of the employer by being of maximum benefit and assistance to the customers.

Selling at a profit demands that the salesperson explore the assigned territory and analyze it in order to find out just how much opportunity is present. Having determined what the area is capable of producing, the salesperson proceeds to draft a specific, detailed program for its development—the objective being to build sales and profit up to their full potentials. If a virgin territory is being opened, prospects must first be identified and then converted into customers; in an established territory, the program calls for the salesperson's holding present customers, making them larger customers, and adding new customers.

The beginning salesperson should learn that the real salesperson is the one who maintains prices at a level that returns a profit to the company. By making money for their companies, salespeople make money for themselves, too. It may be helpful for the junior salesperson to think of the territory as a personal business, in which case one cannot fail to relate selling expense to gross margin and to strive for a satisfactory relationship.

Although the selling of merchandise at a profit is the primary obligation to the employer, it may sometimes have to be postponed in favor of promotion of goodwill or building up a customer's desire for the product. Likewise, in an extreme seller's market when merchandise is being rationed or is unavailable to all, the salesperson's chief concern is that of keeping on good terms with those to be served in the future.

Working Industriously. In hiring a salesperson, the company assumes the risks involved with any new employee; the salesperson should justify this risk. In training the salesperson, the company spends both time and money; the salesperson should justify this expenditure. In making the salesperson responsible for a part of the company's activities, the company acknowledges belief in a certain capacity or potential; the salesperson should justify this faith.

Salespeople go about discharging these obligations by expending the effort necessary to do a successful job. They must be efficient managers—always in control, purposeful, active—and they must conduct themselves so as to get the greatest possible return from their efforts. Their time and energy are budgeted wisely, and there is no wasted motion.

When working at peak efficiency, when keeping fit and busy, the salesperson can safely trust the law of averages. This is possible because few relationships are more basically sound than those between calls and interviews, and interviews and sales. If the salesperson makes enough calls on properly selected prospects, there will be a satisfactory number of interviews and a satisfactory volume of sales.

Cooperating with Others. Immediately upon joining the company, the salesperson should try to fit into the spirit of its organization, learning as much about the company as possible—not operating details at first, but attitudes and policies. The salesperson should be eager to get acquainted with the personality of the firm, to appreciate its aims and ideals, and to understand its methods of doing business and the principles that shape its policies.

As soon as the new salesperson has the "feel" of the company and is considered a part of it, it is necessary to work in harmony with the rest of the organization so that a healthy spirit of cooperation may prevail. Because the new salesperson is in need of instruction, advice, information, and aid, there is every reason for cooperating with everyone. The credit manager and the opening of new accounts, the sales promotion manager and the influencing of dealers to use display material, the advertising manager and the letters of inquiry from prospects, the production manager and the scheduling of a rush order—these situations point up the need for the salesperson to cooperate with other units of the company.

When salespeople are considered as constituting one group and all other company personnel are considered another, it becomes clear that the two groups are responsible for the welfare of each other. Each depends on the other in a very literal sense, and if one suffers, so does the other. When each group keeps this fact in mind, cooperation is almost certain to result.

The Salesperson's Obligations to Customers

The salesperson has the primary obligations of providing fair treatment to customers and assisting them in finding answers to their buying problems.

Giving Fair Treatment to Buyers. No one, of course, questions the obligation of a salesperson to deal honorably with buyers. The relationship between salesperson and buyer must be characterized by mutual loyalty, trust, and dependence. The salesperson must respect the buyer's position, policies, and time; in return, the salesperson hopes for the buyer's confidence and goodwill. The buyer must certainly be able to count on the salesperson to keep secrets and promises. Unethical treatment and undependable behavior will destroy this trust.

To treat buyers fairly, the salesperson will not sell to anyone without truly believing the buyer will benefit adequately from the purchase. Here's a good test: if the salesperson can sit in the buyer's chair, assume the role of buyer, and buy what the salesperson is offering from across the desk, the purchase can be recommended. Because the typical salesperson is an optimist, there is a bias which must be discounted somewhat. There are, however, pragmatic as well as ethical reasons for being frank and fair. Hard, aggressive selling is sometimes necessary because some products and some buyers require it, but it is unwise to carry this type of selling so far that the result is a disgruntled or disappointed buyer.

Hard, aggressive selling is not to be confused with high-pressure selling, a type of selling which violates the principle of fair treatment. High-pressure selling operates when a salesperson offends by becoming too aggressive or offensive, or by stooping to tactics that are unethical, deceitful, or dishonest. High-pressure selling is flagrant when a salesperson uses extravagant means to sell something to a buyer which the buyer should not buy.

Sometimes fair treatment to the customer competes with fair treatment to the salesperson's company, as in the case of a complaint or a request for an adjustment. Clearly, the salesperson is in the middle of a conflict of interests, owing something to the customers and something to the company. There is no rule universally applicable. Whatever action is taken, the salesperson must be honest and fair to both, doing nothing to damage personal independence and self-respect.

Giving Assistance to Buyers. Because individuals have an assortment of desires with only limited purchasing power, they need assistance that will enable them more nearly to realize their desires and to provide for their needs. In general, buyers-for-consumption want increased satisfaction, whereas business buyers want to make or save more money. These facts make the salesperson a missionary charged with the responsibility of guiding prospects to a better mode

OUTLINE FOR A JOB DESCRIPTION HAVING GENERAL APPLICATION

Sales:
Make regular calls.
Sell the line, demonstrate.
Handle questions and objections.
Check stock—discover possible
product uses.
Interpret sales points of the line to
the customer.
Estimate customers' potential
needs.
Emphasize quality.
Explain company policies on price,
delivery, and credit.
Get the order.

Services:
Install product or display.
Report product weaknesses, com-
plaints.
Handle adjustments, returns, and
allowances.
Handle requests for credit.
Handle special orders for cus-
tomers.
Establish priorities, if any.
Analyze local conditions for cus-
tomers.

Territory management:
Arrange route for best coverage.
Balance effort with customer
against potential.
Maintain sales portfolio, samples,
kits.

Sales promotion:
Develop new prospects and new
accounts.

Distribute home office literature,
catalogs, desk pieces.
Make calls with customers' salespeople.
Train jobbers' personnel.
Present survey reports, layouts,
and proposals.

Executive:
Each night make a daily work plan
for the next day.
Organize field activity for minimum
travel and maximum calls.
Prepare and submit special reports
on trends, competition.
Prepare and submit daily reports to
home office.
Collect and submit statistical data
requested by home office.
Investigate lost sales and the rea-
son for loss.
Prepare reports on developments,
trends, new objections, and new
ideas on meeting objections.
Attend sales meetings.
Build a prospect list.
Collect overdue accounts; report
faulty accounts.
Collect credit information.

Goodwill:
Counsel customers on their problems.
Maintain loyalty and respect for
firm represented.
Attend local sales meetings held
by customers.

ILLUSTRATION 2-2. This outline—taken from *Sales Training for the Smaller Manufacturer,* a Small Business Administration publication by Kenneth Lawyer— gives a good summary of a salesperson's duties and responsibilities.

of living or improving the prospect's circumstances so that satisfaction or profits are increased.

The salesperson must have a sincere desire to serve and to help prospects and customers. Being of aid is more than permissible or desirable—it is mandatory. Since salespeople are going to serve, they must be qualified to serve. If they plan to act as experts, they should be experts; if they want to function as advisers on purchasing, they should have enough information to perform that function adequately.

In fulfilling the obligation to help prospects and customers, the salesperson must render whatever assistance is available, regardless of whether the prospect buys or not. Prospects and customers have problems, and they need help in coping with them on nonbuying days as well as on days when purchases are made. Whether there is a large order or no order at all, the salesperson should be a friendly counselor.

BUT THEIR DUTIES/TASKS DIFFER

Even though all salespeople have similar obligations to their employers, including working industriously to make sales and giving assistance and fair treatment to their customers, there are many duties and tasks that vary, dependent upon the product being sold and the type of customer being visited.

Selling to Wholesalers and Retailers

In selling merchandise to middlemen for resale, three principal relationships are found. First, a manufacturer's salesperson can sell to wholesalers. Second, a manufacturer's salesperson can sell to retailers. And, third, a wholesaler's salesperson can sell to retailers. Often the same individual will sell to more than one type of buyer. Thus, a manufacturer's salesperson may sell to both wholesalers and retailers, to wholesalers and institutions, or to wholesalers and chain store warehouses. A wholesaler's salesperson may sell to retailers, to business and industrial buyers, and may even sell to other wholesalers.

Middlemen display a wide range of buying skill, but in one respect they are identical: they buy mainly in response to rational, not emotional, motivation. Their principal concern is to make a profit, and they know that the only ways to increase profits are to increase sales volume and to reduce costs. Wholesalers and retailers think in terms of inventory requirements, turnover, unit and dollar sales volume, markdowns, and margins. The manufacturer, the wholesaler, and the retailer all know that merchandise is completely and satisfactorily sold only when the ultimate consumer buys, consumes, and returns to buy more. Thus, middlemen are serving ultimate consumers as well as themselves when they buy with rational motivation.

Selling to dealers for resale often consists more of service selling than of creative selling. *Service selling* is little more than order taking. It refers to transacting sales with buyers who want to buy and know what they want.

In *creative selling,* the salesperson discovers a buyer-need of which the buyer was unaware and sells a product as the answer to that need. Or, the salesperson entices a buyer away from a competing seller.

Regular Dealer-Selling Salespeople. A regular *dealer-selling salesperson* may work for a manufacturer and call on wholesalers and retailers, or may work for a wholesaler and call on retailers. The products sold to these two types of middlemen are items for resale, not for use by the wholesaler or the retailer in the operation of the business. For example, this type of salesperson sells toothpaste to a drugstore, not a cash register, or sells canned food to a grocery store, not tires for the grocer's delivery trucks.

Features of the Job. The regular dealer-selling salesperson travels over a planned route in a sequence. In the pattern of call intervals, there is a regularity which permits each buyer to know when next to expect the salesperson. This salesperson may make numerous calls each day. Much income may be in the form of a straight salary. The job provides the individual with a considerable amount of security and with a regular pattern of life.

The job of the regular salesperson who sells to dealers demands only a modest amount of creative selling. There is a certain amount of prospecting and identification of persons who are prospects, and their conversion into customers is considered to be a creative activity. In handling regular customers, the salesperson will occasionally discover a buyer-need that was not recognized before and then sell the product that will best fill that need. This, too, is creative selling. Finally, any success the salesperson has in getting promotional support from a wholesaler or retailer will be the result of creative selling.

For the most part, however, this salesperson will be doing service selling. The main activity will be that of writing up for established customers reorders of products that buyers need to replenish. In one sense, this service selling makes the salesperson's call more of a friendly visit than a product-promoting conference. Friendship between buyer and seller is a major factor in this type of selling.

Creative Selling Duties. As was just indicated, the typical salesperson who calls on wholesalers and retailers does not do much creative selling. Prospecting, discovering unfilled needs, and getting dealer support were mentioned as challenges to the salesperson's creativity and resourcefulness.

There is, however, one area of selling to middlemen for resale in which creative selling ability is most essential. This is the new-product area. Products can be new in regard to name of product or nature of product. When the name of the product is new to buyers, the salesperson must do creative selling to enter a group of brands already known and established. An example would be introducing to the Pacific Coast market a product formerly marketed only east of the Rockies. Another example would be a manufacturer's addition of an electric razor to its line of cigarette lighters.

When the nature of the product is new to buyers, the demand for creative selling is even stronger. Both electric razors and cigarette lighters, when first offered to retailers, were so different in nature as to be revolutionary. Middlemen stock new types of products with reluctance; they may fear that the item is ahead of its time, overpriced, a short-lived fad, or not yet rid of all its defects. To place a different type of product on the market is a real pioneering job. Only hard and able creative selling can open new markets.

Service Selling Duties. The big job expected of regular dealer-selling salespeople is that of service selling. Usually the seller and the buyer have been doing business with each other for some time. The products the salesperson is handling are generally well-known to the dealer and, more important, to the dealer's customers. Often the products are well advertised. In these circumstances, the salesperson's job is largely one of contact and service in a regular routine. The customers are steady customers. The salesperson's task is to keep them steady, to hold on to them. This is done by keeping them stocked at all times with an adequate supply of merchandise. Much of the time is occupied with writing up reorders after checking the dealer's stock and after looking at the dealer's want book, if one is kept. (A *want book* is a notebook or set of forms in which the retailer lists the items that will soon need to be replenished.) Thus, while it is true that the service salesperson hopes to expand present accounts, the main concern is for continued patronage.

Nonselling Duties. Great variety is found in the number and in the nature of nonselling duties performed by dealer-selling salespeople. Many do about 5 percent creative selling and 95 percent service selling, and nothing else. Others will undertake certain nonselling duties, either because they think they should or because their companies require them to. Collecting past-due accounts is such a duty. Handling complaints is another. Counseling is a broader nonselling duty that may have to do with any of the buyer's problems. Another even more general duty of the salesperson would be striving for goodwill, for both company and self.

Selling to Retailers for Wholesalers. The salesperson who works for a wholesale house may call on three types of buyers: retailers, business and industrial buyers, and other wholesalers. Our interest at this point is in selling merchandise to the retailers for resale. When salespeople sell to industrial and business buyers, they are in effect selling to purchasing agents, and that area of selling will be discussed later. When they sell to other wholesalers, nothing involved is so different as to demand our attention now.

Wholesalers stock thousands and thousands of items. In the grocery field, the number is often about 10,000; in drugs, 50,000 is not uncommon; in hardware, a figure of 60,000 is not unusual. This means, of course, that the wholesaler's salespeople must know something about a wide range of products.

Furthermore, they cannot push any specific product to a great degree, for they do not have the time.

In the drug field, one survey showed that four out of five retail druggists want advice and assistance from wholesalers on various problems concerned with retail store operation. The retailers desiring help wanted assistance in moving merchandise to the consumer. This included mainly sales promotion assistance and help in training retail store clerks—two major services wanted by about half the druggists. Two out of five wanted information about successful promotions of other druggists. About two out of five wanted wholesalers' salespeople to advise them on what to display and how to display it. Three out of eight wanted to know how and where to obtain special display materials.

The primary duty of the wholesaler's salesperson is to keep reorders coming in. Because products and prices are nearly identical to those of competing wholesalers, the salesperson must hunt for some unique selling points to stress.

Requirements. For any creative selling, the salesperson who sells to dealers will need to be confident and even aggressive. These salespeople must have initiative, and they will find enthusiasm and resourcefulness to be desirable. Obviously, they must know how to use the principles and techniques of effective selling.

Service selling calls for a different set of requirements. Here the demand is for a friendly, helpful type of person. The salesperson must have energy and stamina for a long and hard day. Because of the repetitive nature of the calling, sincerity and dependability are necessary for success. Persistence is more necessary than aggressiveness.

Missionary Salespeople. *Missionary salespeople* work for manufacturers and are relatively prominent in the marketing of drug, tobacco, food, and hardware products. The primary duty of the missionary salesperson is not selling goods directly to buyers; that assignment is given to other of the manufacturer's salespeople. The goal of the manufacturer's missionary salespeople is to move their products faster and in larger volume through the use of techniques that are more indirect than direct. These salespeople work to promote their customers' sales, thus increasing their own sales.

Features of the Job. The most common situation finds a manufacturer's missionary salesperson calling on wholesalers to develop greater interest in and support for the manufacturer's line of goods. Arrangements may be made for the missionary salesperson to talk to the wholesaler's salespeople. The follow-up might well be for the missionary salesperson to travel for a short time with each of the wholesaler's salespeople, making calls on the wholesaler's prospects and customers.

Another situation finds the missionary salesperson calling alone on retailers who might or do stock the manufacturer's merchandise. Still another possibility is found in industrial selling. A manufacturer who supplies fabricating materials or parts to other manufacturers might employ missionary salespeople to keep in close touch with those manufacturers.

Creative Selling Duties. The overall objective of the missionary salesperson is to stimulate the wholesaler's business by writing up a larger order than the retailer would have bought had the wholesaler's salesperson been calling alone. In other words, the objective is to improve, at least for awhile, a circumstance common to many manufacturers—the failure of wholesalers to push the manufacturer's products.

To achieve these goals, the missionary salesperson in most instances must persuade the retailer to stock a larger quantity of the manufacturer's goods. This can be quite a challenge when the manufacturer is launching new products on the market. In this case, the missionary salesperson wants to obtain the best location in the store for the line and to be given excellent shelf position in that location. Finally, the missionary salesperson wants as much retail support as can be obtained. This includes displaying the merchandise, advertising the merchandise, and putting stronger personal selling behind it. Clearly, the missionary salesperson must be competent in creative selling.

Service Selling Duties. Service selling is obviously neither an adequate nor an appropriate assignment for a missionary salesperson. Of course, the missionary salesperson can write up an order for a retailer's needs in the line while the wholesaler's salesperson is busy with other matters, but then the missionary salesperson must move immediately into creative selling or into performing services for the retailer.

Nonselling Duties. Missionary salespeople must be merchandising salespeople and, to some degree, management salespeople. If they build store traffic and sales volume for retailers, if they are able to improve their management techniques, then these salespeople almost automatically build goodwill, confidence, and profits for their employer.

One of the most effective techniques for the missionary salesperson is the service approach. (This is not to be confused with service selling, which is nothing more than filling the retailers' requests.) In calling on retailers, the missionary salesperson has an excellent opportunity to make effective use of the service approach. For example, point-of-purchase material can be offered to a retailer, even going so far as to change a retailer's window display or to build a floor display of the products. The salesperson can help retailers with their advertising and can teach the retailer and the retailer's sales staff about the merchandise, especially how to sell more of it more profitably. As an advisor on management problems, the missionary salesperson may analyze some of the retailer's problems and make recommendations. Such problems might involve store equipment, store layout, organization, credit, records, special promotion events, or customer services.

Requirements. For two reasons, missionary salespeople must be broadly informed and highly competent salespeople. First, their assignments are varied and challenging. They must be experts in their product line; they must know more than a little about the buyer's business; and they must be successful salespeople. Second, the buyers seen by a missionary salesperson present a special type of challenge. Retailers, upon seeing that a wholesaler's salesperson is not calling alone, may immediately become wary and feel that they are due for a matching of wits with a high-powered specialist. As for calling on wholesalers, getting them to show even a bit more interest in a manufacturer's products is not easy.

Selling to Purchasing Agents

Purchasing agents are professional buyers who are responsible for the procurement function in their organization. Authority and activities of the purchasing agent will vary from organization to organization depending on what the management thinks the purchasing staff should do. A salesperson must see and sell to the person who makes the organization's purchases, the purchasing agent.

Features of Selling to Purchasing Agents. In selling to purchasing agents, there are three important areas that the salesperson will want to consider: the market, the nature of purchasing agents' buying, and the general nature of selling to purchasing agents.

The Market. Many of the industries for which purchasing agents buy are actually very limited markets. The automotive industry, the aluminum industry, and the cigarette industry are examples of markets consisting of a relatively small number of buyers. Because buyers are few, geographic concentration is common; the result may well be that 85 to 90 percent of an industry is found in just a few locations. Where this concentration exists, salespeople have little trouble locating their buyers.

The individual buyers making up the industrial market are experts in buying; the contrast between their purchasing skill and that of the typical consumer is impressive. Purchasing agents are trained thoroughly for their roles. In addition, most of them are experienced buyers. They are hard, cost-conscious buyers. They are spending a company's money and not their own, and this means that their accountability for purchases is more serious and strict than that of a consumer.

Purchasing agents must be rational buyers. Whereas consumers can gratify some or many of their emotional desires, purchasing agents generally cannot. Because they make purchases that will be considered good or bad depending on whether profits go up or down, purchasing agents must try to act only on rational motivation. To do otherwise would jeopardize the buyer's standing within the company. Because advertising and sales promotion are usually more effective in appealing to a person's emotions than to reason, they are of limited use to sellers who sell to the industrial market. Purchasing agents are less influenced by these two marketing forces than are consumers or even middlemen buying for resale.

Nature of Purchasing Agents' Buying. Purchasing agents buy from manufacturers, from industrial distributors, from mill supply firms, and sometimes from wholesalers. There is much more buying direct from the manufacturer and less buying from middlemen than is found in the marketing of consumer goods. Several vendors are usually considered before a purchase is made.

The nature of the buying done by purchasing agents is interesting. To begin with, their demand is a derived demand—the result of actual or anticipated buying by consumers. If the sales force of the buyer's company is not moving merchandise, then no salesperson on earth can persuade the purchasing agent of that company to buy on a larger scale. In the case of capital items, the purchasing agent may not buy anything new for years; this makes infrequent purchase a feature for certain types of products. For many industrial goods, the business cycle is a significant factor. The natural longevity of some items, such as railroad cars or turbines, can be extended even further by a relatively small increase in maintenance costs. Replacement of such items can be postponed when times are bad.

The fact that certain purchases are made by a group of company officials suggests a few other features of purchasing agents' buying. For example, the decision on need can originate in one or more of various offices. When a salesperson does not know which individuals can request a particular type of product and does not know the relative influence of the members of the buying group, the question is whom to see. Suppose the salesperson is selling industrial lubricants. How much voice does the production manager have in such a purchase? What about the chief engineer, the plant engineer, and the plant superintendent?

A common feature of buying groups is their diversity of interests. For example, the sales manager may want to buy from firms who are also customers or potential customers. This factor of reciprocity may mean nothing to the production manager, whose main concern is to keep production costs low.

General Nature of Selling to Purchasing Agents. In selling to purchasing agents, selling efforts are understandably influenced by the buyers themselves and by the character of their buying. In many lines, the salesperson will make few sales, but each will be a large one. Often the salesperson can predict quite accurately when a certain buyer will be buying and can even make a shrewd guess as to when this buyer will begin thinking seriously about buying. Because buyers can postpone certain purchases for years, the negotiation phase can extend over a long period of time.

There can be great fluctuations in a salesperson's sales volume. It could happen that a salesperson might make infrequent sales in a year—if, for instance, the line was turbines and the year was one of recession. Prices must often be quoted or negotiated when a product is to be built to the specifications of a single buyer. If the salesperson's customer is also a manufacturer, that customer can be the salesperson's most dangerous competition in the sale of products such as parts. The customer has the choice of producing certain parts or of buying them.

Often the salesperson is active with the account both before and after the actual sale. The first big job in many situations is to sell need to the buyer. As has been noted, many industrial products can be made to last for one more year. Where appropriate, the salesperson may ask for permission to make a survey of the buyer's circumstances. If it is found that need exists, the salesperson may ask permission to demonstrate the product, hoping thereby to convince the buyer. After the sale, the salesperson may install or help to install the product and may take care of the product's maintenance. If the buyer's employees must be trained to use the product, that training may be conducted by the salesperson. Finally, the salesperson must help the buyer solve problems involving the product.

Requirements for Selling to Purchasing Agents. For most selling to purchasing agents, the salesperson will need a dual background consisting of a technical specialty plus marketing training. Engineering, accounting, chemistry, or electronics might be the specialty to which must be added knowledge of the selling function. In some lines, a person with a marketing background can be taught by the employer as much of the specialized field as it will be necessary to know. In other lines, specialists or technicians can be hired and given the necessary training in selling. In any event, there must be much study and learning, much knowledge of the laboratory and factory of the company, and maybe even a lengthy apprenticeship before a salesperson is given a territory.

In selling to purchasing agents, salespeople need a thorough understanding of what their technical products or intangibles can do for buyers. They need the ingenuity necessary to see how their present products can be adapted to provide better solutions to buyers' problems. And the salesperson must be keen enough to spot waste, inefficiency, and unnecessary expense of which the buyer is unaware. This demands an analytical mind and a knowledge of the production, equipment, and operating problems of plants.

Selling to Professionals

Members of certain professions exert great influence over certain purchases made by their clients or their patients. For example, when architects are designing homes for their clients, they are often asked which plumbing fixtures or which brand of floor tile is the best to use. Probably few days pass without someone in a dentist's chair asking about toothpaste. Engineers are asked about brands of petroleum products. Clearly, certain professional people are in positions of significance to certain manufacturers because of their practice of specifying or recommending products.

One type of selling, then, is that done by a manufacturer's salesperson who works to get the goodwill and favorable influence of professional men and women. In the drug field such salespeople are called *detailers.* Their activities will be considered as being typical of this type of selling and will be examined briefly.

Detailers constitute the major link between drug manufacturers and physicians. Their importance in the manufacturer's promotion mix and their role as a channel of communication to the doctor is suggested by the following estimate of the typical promotion program:

Type of Promotion	*Percent of Promotion Budget*
Detailers	75 percent
Ads in medical journals	15 percent
Direct mail	10 percent

A detailer is (1) a salesperson and (2) a reporter of information about new products, calling on medical doctors, dentists, hospitals (if a hospital is huge it may be the detailer's entire territory), nursing facilities, and drugstores. The detailer must be able to meet professional medical people and impress them favorably; must talk intelligently about the problems and needs of the world of medicine; and must literally speak the language of medicine. When leaving a doctor to call on a druggist, the detailer must switch from a professional vocabulary to a commercial one. In drug stores, the detailer bids for good public relations, and works for more promotional support from the prescription department. In selling nonprescription drug products, the detailer tries to persuade the retailer to give this brand more and better shelf space, more mentions in ads, and stronger promotion by retail salespeople.

A typical detailer might try to see five doctors and four retailers a day, and two dentists a week. A typical doctor averages seeing eight detailers a week. The detailer does paperwork in the reception room while waiting to be seen. In brief presentations, the detailer promotes three items, then leaves promotional material and samples. Publishers' sales representatives calling on professors are, in reality, detailers.

Selling to Ultimate Consumers

Salespeople who sell to ultimate consumers may perform their selling activities either in retail stores or in the consumer's home or office.

Selling in Retail Stores. It is quite probable that, of all types of selling, the least complex type is found inside retail stores. It is true, of course, that some retailers employ outside salespeople to sell certain high-priced products, such as draperies, and that with these salespeople, effective selling is a prerequisite to success. Within the store these same kinds of products also require capable salespeople. But the bulk of the transactions over the counter are *purchases* rather than *sales*.

Typically customers seek out the retail store in which they expect to find what they want and may even seek out a favorite salesperson. The customer typically enters the store wanting something or at least favorably inclined toward the possibility of buying. A customer comes in, selects two ties, tells a salesclerk that he wants them, pays for them, gets the ties and a "thank you" from the salesclerk, and the purchase is completed. This is service selling. If the retail salesclerk just mentioned had sold a better quality tie to the customer, had sold three ties instead of two, or had sold three shirts to the customer in addition to the ties, that would have been creative selling.

There is much service selling and little creative selling in which the salesperson uses both imagination and persuasion. Self-service has simplified the retail selling job, making attendants out of many salespeople.

Duties of Retail Salespeople. The selling duties of a retail salesperson can be stated simply. First, the salesperson must greet and size up the customer, determining the customer's needs and wants. Next, merchandise is selected that is thought most suitable in the light of the customer's circumstances. Third, the customer is told and shown how and why that particular merchandise will best fill the requirements. Fourth, the sale is completed. Then, if it seems desirable, an attempt may be made at suggestion selling—recommending some product the customer had not asked about. Finally, the salesperson makes a bid for the customer's goodwill so that the customer will be inclined to return for future purchases.

Certain nonselling duties are usually assigned to retail salespeople. Integral phases of the sale are such activities as making change, operating the cash register, writing up a salescheck, and bagging the merchandise. In addition, salespeople must know the location of stock throughout the store, must see that their own department's stock is always adequate, and must keep their stock in place and their selling area neat. Many salespeople are asked to participate in taking inventory. It is also not uncommon for some to be asked to do some of the store's displays.

Features of the Job. On the plus side, selling in retail stores does not make extreme demands on an individual. This area of selling can be entered and mastered adequately by almost anyone who is attracted to it. Average amounts of courtesy, tact, patience, and endurance will enable one to get along satisfactorily. The activity offers a measure of security because a store must have employees to serve its customers. There are internal promotion possibilities to such positions as buyer or assistant manager. Retail selling is good preparation for other types of selling and for marketing jobs other than selling. It is almost a prerequisite for people who plan to open their own stores.

Selling in Consumers' Homes. A salesperson can call on an ultimate consumer at home, a place of business, a farm, or even in a restaurant over lunch. Because customers do not always visit sellers' places of business often enough to buy or be sold, some salespeople take the initiative by locating and going to see buyers. Such salespeople can be working entirely for themselves, for a retailer, or for a manufacturer. They may sell intangibles such as insurance, securities, or travel tours. Or they may sell physical products such as appliances, shoes, books, brushes, or cosmetics. Calling may be as mechanical and unscientific as going from house to house, or it may be highly selective and done only by appointment.

Consumers can look upon house-to-house salespeople with either favor or disfavor, depending on the product and the person selling that product. The family can make a group purchase with a minimum of inconvenience if the salesperson will call at their home at an appointed hour. The homemaker can experiment with and operate certain products under the same conditions as they will be used. Instruction is typically available from the salesperson. The homemaker may well feel under less pressure at home than in a retail store. Of course, most people have knowledge of or have had experience with dishonest and otherwise objectionable house-to-house salespeople. Many have been subjected to the rude behavior or the almost insulting aggressiveness of high-pressure salespeople selling everything from brushes to encyclopedias.

Certain aspects of selling to consumers on their own ground deserve special mention. One of these is that locating prospective buyers is often a considerable job. Then there is the problem of getting in to see the buyer. Homemakers needn't open the door when a stranger rings the bell, and requests for appointments can be refused. Obviously, these two aspects mean that there is a high percentage of failure when calling is nonselective. Another factor is that in house-to-house or office-to-office selling, the salesperson has little specific information about the person being interviewed. If a salesperson can persuade a prospect to hold a "house party" to which other prospects are invited, send out direct mail to a large list and offer an incentive to prospects, or request appointments with individuals whose names were acquired from satisfied customers, the number of unproductive calls and the amount of wasted time are reduced.

In this type of selling, the hours worked and the income received vary from salesperson to salesperson and from month to month. Many calls must be made every day. Finally, the salesperson must often sell the need to the buyer before the product can be sold to fill that need. Want or desire must be established where the prospect feels none.

Selling to the consumer at home demands that the salesperson meet certain requirements. The salesperson must be rugged; this type of selling affords no place for thin skins and easily discouraged personalities. The salesperson must work hard and long hours each day; this demands control and self-discipline. The salesperson must be able to find and then stay in the middle ground between too much and too little aggressiveness. The salesperson must be able to meet strangers easily, to make a favorable impression on them quickly, and to capture the buyer's attention almost instantly and convert it without delay into interest in the product. A smooth and persuasive selling style must be developed.

SUMMARY

A professional point of view identifies the professional salesperson. A professional salesperson is dedicated to serving the needs and problems of buyers in a tactful, honest way.

Successful salespeople are dynamic. Technical expertise and the willingness to work long and hard are important, but to be really effective, the salesperson must also have a superior sales personality.

A sales personality can be thought of as the impression that a buyer gets of the salesperson. Individuals can improve and refine their sales personalities, starting with self-analysis and moving to the control and change of habits.

Optimism, enthusiasm, confidence, sincerity, determination, dependability, initiative, and imagination are eight psychological traits commonly thought essential to successful selling. There are also a number of social characteristics that are valuable assets of a good salesperson. These include a friendly nature, social grace, conversational ability, and poise. Lying, sarcasm, and discourtesy must be avoided.

The salesperson's physical image is important because it is the first factor to register on the prospect. The salesperson must appear competent and worthy of confidence and respect. Ability to sell is not limited to any one physical type. But, one should be conscious of good grooming, clothing, and bearing. Cleanliness, neatness, and proper posture are under the salesperson's control and are vital to a good appearance. Nervous habits and mannerisms are undesirable and should be eliminated. Good health is important because the salesperson's appearance depends much on physical condition. Nonvisual physical factors such as the salesperson's voice and oral mannerisms are important.

A salesperson's job responsibilities fall into three areas. First, the salesperson must sell products to existing customers. Increased sales are to be encouraged. Prospects must be converted into customers. Next, the salesperson has auxilliary duties, such as checking inventories and maintaining displays. Third, salespeople have nonselling, personal tasks. Attending sales meetings and being active in public relations are examples.

A salesperson owes something to the employer and to prospects and customers. To the employer, the salesperson's major responsibility is to sell at a profit. To maximize long-run profits, the salesperson must analyze the territory and create a plan. Gross margin on sales is the most important dollar amount the salesperson must worry about. Salespeople also owe to the employer the obligation of working industriously, operating at peak efficiency. Finally, the salesperson should try to fit into the organization, working in harmony with managers and other salespeople.

Salespeople have to give fair treatment to buyers. The relationship between the two must be characterized by mutual trust, loyalty, and dependence. Hard, aggressive selling is commendable; high-pressure selling is not. Salespeople should also give assistance to buyers, supplying information, helping with problems, and advising them when appropriate.

Salespeople can sell to wholesalers, retailers, purchasing agents, professionals, and ultimate consumers. The responsibilities, tools and techniques, and duties are different for each, although certain elements do overlap.

Wholesalers and retailers are middlemen—they come between producers and ultimate consumers in the distribution chain. They buy mainly in response to rational motivation.

Service selling is order taking and is common in selling to dealers for resale. Creative selling is more difficult, requiring the salesperson to discover a buyer-need.

Regular dealer-selling salespeople work for a manufacturer and call on wholesalers, or for a wholesaler and call on retailers. They usually travel over planned routes at regular intervals. Dealer-selling salespeople do both service selling and creative selling, with 95 percent of their time spent on the former. Creative selling usually requires more aggressiveness and confidence than service selling because the salesperson is taking the initiative.

Missionary salespeople work for manufacturers and are used in the drug, tobacco, food, and hardware industries. Their goal is to move their products faster and in larger volume using indirect selling techniques. They generate goodwill, instruct and work with wholesalers' salespeople, and do much creative selling. Theirs is a service function since they do little order taking.

A purchasing agent is a professional buyer who is responsible for the procurement function in an organization. Purchasing agents must be experts. They do much direct buying based on demand. Salespeople to purchasing agents usually must be experts in their field in order to spot buyer needs that the purchasing agent may not recognize.

Professionals often exert great influence over purchases made by their clients or patients. As opinion leaders, their preferences are important to salespeople in these fields. Detailers sell to professionals in the drug industry.

Salespeople who sell to ultimate consumers either sell in retail stores or in the consumer's home. In-store selling is the least complex type of selling because it usually involves just order taking. Selling in homes gives consumers the chance to try out products in the environment in which they will be used. In addition, consumers may feel less pressured in their homes than they do in retail stores. Selling in homes requires stamina and confidence. Over-aggressive door-to-door salespeople have given this type of selling a bad image, so the successful salesperson often has to overcome consumers' fear of being taken advantage of.

REVIEW QUESTIONS

1. What is required of a professional point of view?
2. List eight psychological characteristics essential to successful selling.
3. Why do some salespeople fail?
4. What factors are important for good conversational ability?
5. What traits must good salespeople avoid?
6. What physical traits can people improve?
7. What are some auxilliary selling duties?
8. What is service selling?
9. How is creative selling different from service selling?
10. Why must salespeople use creative selling for new products?
11. What is a missionary salesperson?
12. What are the special requirements for selling to purchasing agents?
13. What are the responsibilities of a drug detailer?
14. Why is selling in retail stores considered to be the least complex type of selling?
15. What advantages does the buyer have when a salesperson comes to his or her home?

DISCUSSION QUESTIONS

1. Gross margin and total profit from sales are the best measures of a salesperson's performance. Do most companies really measure this, or is total sales the variable that most firms use to evaluate performance?
2. Salespeople act as the link between sellers and buyers. One of the salesperson's responsibilities to the seller is to provide the seller with information. How in performing one's duties as a salesperson can that be accomplished? What information should be gathered?
3. What type of selling would you like to do? What are the attractions of that alternative?
4. Would your approach to a purchasing agent be different from your approach to a professional? If so, how?

CASE STUDY 2A

Jordan Reaves is a salesperson for Putt-Putt Golf Courses and is calling on Stephen Biggs at a Putt-Putt Golf Course in Jacksonville, Florida. Mr. Biggs has four other courses in Florida, three in Texas, and two in California. He has been buying supplies from the Putt-Putt wholesale establishment, Southern Golf, Inc., for the past two years. On his last visit four months ago, Reaves sold Biggs

3,000 golf balls, 100 tee mats, and four rolls of carpet. It is now June, and the course has been open for three and a half months. This is Reaves' first trip to Florida for the year.

Salesperson:	Good afternoon, Mr. Biggs. It's good to see you again. I believe this is the first time I've seen your golf course this year. You certainly do have it in good shape.
Customer:	Thank you, Mr. Reaves. We've worked hard on it, and we're very pleased with the results.
Salesperson:	I visited your course in Miami about two weeks ago, and it was doing extremely well. Even with that big parking lot of yours, it was hard to find a space for my car.
Customer:	The Miami course is doing an excellent business. We might even set a new course record in receipts this season. Our manager down there is doing a terrific job.
Salesperson:	Mr. Biggs, I would like to show you something that your Miami manager was very interested in. It's our new putter, the "7–11," with a brand new feature called the Pride Grip.
Customer:	Mr. Reaves, you know we do most of our business with you because we like your products. But we are almost at the point of being overstocked with clubs right now. If you remember, I placed a large order with you at the beginning of the season.
Salesperson:	Yes, sir, I certainly do. And I appreciate your business. It makes us very proud to see excellent miniature golf courses like yours using our equipment. And I do realize your position, Mr. Biggs. I just want you to look at this club because it is our newest and best club. I know you're always thinking ahead, and you'll probably need clubs for some of your other courses before long.
Customer:	Well, I may need clubs later on, but I certainly don't need any now.
Salesperson:	Mr. Biggs, you will notice (handing him a putter) that this shaft and face are coated with chrome to give a lasting and clean appearance at all times. In the manufacturing process for this putter, the shaft and face are dipped into the chrome not just once, as most putters are, but three times. This will give it three times the life of regular putters and will prevent the chipping and scraping of chrome from becoming noticeable. This is why we call it the "triple-dipped shaft."
Customer:	You mean there are three separate coatings of chrome instead of one?
Salesperson:	Yes, sir.
Customer:	And you're absolutely positive that it will last three times longer than the regular putters now in use?

Salesperson:	Mr. Biggs, the 7–11 carries with it a two-year Putt-Putt guarantee, fully backed by us. We have never had a 7–11 putter turned in to us and have not heard a single complaint about its performance.
Customer:	Well, then, with this supposedly long life, I imagine the 7–11 costs more, doesn't it?
Salesperson:	Considering the advantages that this putter offers, Mr. Biggs, it is relatively cheaper. I've already mentioned the added life of the shaft. It also has features in the face and grip which give longer life and durability to the club.
Customer:	I believe you did mention something about a grip a while ago. What were you talking about?
Salesperson:	Here's the feature of our putter which makes it stand head and shoulders above everything else in its field. This is the "Pride Grip." No other putter has this, Mr. Biggs. This grip will come off the shaft when it becomes too dirty or too sticky for play, and it can be replaced with a similar grip.
Customer:	That's really nice. I've never seen that before. But how do I know some kids won't jerk it off by accident?
Salesperson:	Well, it's not exactly that easy to take off. You notice the tape at the bottom of the grip which holds the grip to the shaft. It has to be cut—like this. (Demonstrates.) Then it has to be worked loose like this. (Does so.) It is not easy for small kids to do, and it takes about half a minute to take one off completely. Besides, this feature isn't known outside of the golfing business, so I doubt if you would have any trouble with kids tampering with the grip.
Customer:	What is the purpose of this grip coming off? So I won't have to replace the whole club?
Salesperson:	Exactly. You know that the grip gets sticky and dirty long before the shaft and face of the club are damaged. This way—with the Pride Grip—only a part of the club is replaced, and you wind up with a seemingly brand-new club at a minimum price—only $1.50 per grip. This price is hard to beat.
Customer:	What about the price of the whole putter?
Salesperson:	They sell for $6.50 a piece. That includes everything.
Customer:	That's a little higher than the average club, isn't it?
Salesperson:	Yes, it is, Mr. Biggs; but considering the two-year guarantee and all of its features, especially the Pride Grip, it is a relatively inexpensive club, don't you think?
Customer:	Well, I guess so.
Salesperson:	The grip feature alone would save you the purchase of a new club in a year or so. This club at the present is in great demand.

	Do you happen to know of any other club that offers as many advantages as our 7–11 putter does?
Customer:	No, I don't believe I do.
Salesperson:	Well, here's what I'd like to do, Mr. Biggs. I know your inventory of clubs is full at the moment, but you will be needing some next season. Let me put you down for 500 clubs now; we can send 50 clubs to any course you desire, and you can use them now. It would be on sort of an experimental basis. Look at the response that you receive from your customers, and if you aren't satisfied, we can cancel the order before next season. But I'm sure that you'll be more than pleased with the performance of this club.
Customer:	You mean if I don't like the club, I don't have to take the order?
Salesperson:	That's exactly right. If you aren't satisfied, the 450 won't be charged to you at all.
Customer:	But the 50 will.
Salesperson:	You may even return those.
Customer:	That sounds all right to me. But will the 450 clubs have to be sent to the same course as the 50 experimental clubs? If so, I can't take them.
Salesperson:	No, sir. If you wish, we can ship the clubs to different courses. It's all up to you.
Customer:	All right. I'll take 500. When do I get my bill? Now?
Salesperson:	No, sir. You may, if you prefer, but otherwise you won't be billed until after you receive all of your clubs.
Customer:	Fine! When can I get my 50 clubs?
Salesperson:	Where do you want them shipped, sir?
Customer:	I would prefer 25 shipped to Miami and 25 sent to Dallas if possible.
Salesperson:	Well, we can have the clubs in Miami in four days and the clubs in Dallas within seven to nine days. Will that be satisfactory?
Customer:	Fine. It's a pleasure to do business with you, Mr. Reaves.
Salesperson:	Thank you, Mr. Biggs. It's our pleasure.

1. Did Reaves make a sound presentation?
2. Does the sale strike you as being "too easy" for the salesperson?

CASE STUDY 2B

Women are playing an increasingly prominent role in nonretail selling. Personnel managers are actively recruiting women for sales positions, and they often find that women have advantages over men in certain selling situations. Nevertheless, there are obstacles to be overcome.

I. When Ann Baker began selling business machines, her (male) sales manager was convinced she would never succeed, so he assigned her the least desirable sales territory, one that no one else seemed to want.
II. Carol Denson found that all of the sales representatives for the competing companies were male. They couldn't stand the idea of competing with a woman, so they used whatever tactics they could to keep her from being successful, even if it meant handing the sale to another (male) competitor.
III. Eleanor Friedman found that despite her three years experience, few of the purchasing managers with whom she dealt would believe that she had the necessary technical knowledge. To test her, they gave her really tough problems, problems so tough that her sales manager said that he'd never encountered them before.
IV. Gloria Holly discovered that entertaining clients could lead to sticky situations. Some of her prospects considered their meetings with her social rather than business.

What, if anything, would you do to handle each of these situations?

BACKGROUND FOR SELLING
part II

Chapter 3

Buying Behavior

After studying this chapter you should be able to:

- Explain the influences culture, social classes, reference groups, and family have on behavior

- Discuss self-concept, perception, learning, motivation, and attitudes as they relate to behavior

- Trace the steps in consumer buying behavior

A salesperson needs to understand how and why buyers behave the way they do. To explain the why of buying behavior, many marketers and sellers draw upon the principles of three behavioral sciences: psychology, sociology, and anthropology. Behavioral sciences, as the name implies, are those sciences concerned with the study of human actions. Psychology concentrates upon individuals and their mental processes and behavior. Sociology is the study of the development, structure, and function of human groups in a society. Anthropology is concerned with the study of total cultures comprised of individuals and groups of individuals.

One who considers the broad dimensions of consumer buying behavior is concerned with the nature of such *social institutions* as culture, social class, reference groups, and family. Each of these factors has considerable influence on why and what a consumer buys.

Unless they understand a *culture,* sellers cannot appeal to the goals and respect the values of buyers constituting that culture. The *social class* of a buyer is something that most salespeople should know about because social class membership influences what consumers buy and from whom. Salespeople need to identify the *reference groups* (especially the smaller, more intimate groups) of which a consumer is a member. *Family,* the most influential reference group, greatly affects the buying actions of its members, both individually and as a unit.

There are *individual aspects* of a consumer's buying behavior that are of great interest to salespeople. These include self-concept, perception, learning, motivation, and attitudes.

Consumers do not make voluntary purchases unless they believe that the product or service bought will do good things for their *self-concept.* What a buyer does about and with a stimulus involves *perception;* a salesperson's presentation is an example of a stimulus. *Learning* is reflected in subsequent behavior; a buyer senses a need, buys, then learns whether or not the purchase filled the need. Those needs that initiate behavior or action represent *motivation;* each consumer has an innumerable assortment of needs. *Attitudes* are the opinions, views, beliefs, or convictions a person holds about some object. Most attitudes influence whether the person takes favorable or unfavorable action toward the object.

SOCIAL INFLUENCES ON BUYING BEHAVIOR

Some of the social influences which affect our buying behavior are our culture, our social class, the reference groups to which we belong, and our families.

Culture

A culture includes a broad grouping of people and the geographic area the group occupies. Material items and nonmaterial concepts are elements of a culture. Examples of the material are cars, TV, books, and water beds; these are parts of a pattern of daily living. Examples of the nonmaterial are ideas, attitudes, values, and beliefs; these influence human behavior. Each culture reflects the customs and standards of most of its members. So, a culture is a manner of behaving, a way of living for a group of people.

Prominent in a culture are the symbolism, artifacts, and behavior patterns that an older generation passes on to an upcoming generation, using language and systems of abstract thought, within a society over time. The receiving generation learns about the culture. Each individual in it can accept all that is transmitted, reject all, or accept some elements and reject others. In short, the individual can conform, deviate, or do some of each. In addition to learning how to behave from others, an individual can also learn by evaluating the results of personal behavior.

Although all cultures are different, each of them has its set of beliefs and attitudes concerning social structure and organization, sex, age groupings, kinship, marriage, social stratification and status, economic relations, rituals, political relations, and social control.

Subcultures. Within many societies there are subsocieties or subcultures. As the total population of a society or a culture grows in number and as it expands and inhabits a larger geographical area, homogeneity declines, and subcultures appear. This occurs because each individual feels the need for closer, more personal, and more specific identification than is possible with the total population. Increase in the size of this total population denies the individual satisfactory contact with the whole. A *subculture* may be defined as a grouping of people who exhibit patterns of behavior sufficient to distinguish them from the embracing culture or society.

There are a number of bases on which subcultures may develop. Geographical region is one; urban-rural breakdown is another. Many subcultures are based on ethnic factors resulting from race, religion, or national origin. In New York City, for example, there are four major subcultures based on ethnic considerations: Italian, Jewish, Black, and Puerto Rican. Language, color of skin, age, and social classes can also be bases for the development of subcultures.

Norms of Behavior. *Norms* are customary, approved modes of behavior which develop over time as a result of personal interaction within a culture. Every culture, subculture, social class, and group has its norms of behavior. Norms probably play their greatest role as influences on behavior within reference groups.

Individuals tend to learn, accept, and respect the norms of their culture. They seldom question them, and rarely do they abandon or replace them. Because they reflect behavior which is allowed or approved, norms supply standards which can be used as behavior guides. One who has learned what is proper and then does it knows the pleasant feeling of identification through conformity. Norms operate to make decision making easier by reducing the number of options considered. Some norms tell members of the culture what to do and some tell members what not to do.

There are three general types of norm: folkways, mores, and laws. *Folkways* are those behavior patterns we call customs; having turkey for Thanksgiving is an example of a folkway. *Mores* are behavior patterns concerning moral conduct. An example would be the disapproval of cheating. *Laws* are those norms which are written down and enforced by sanctions levied by recognized authority. All norms bring sanctions with them—punishment of some kind for those who violate the norms, and rewards for those who obey them.

Social Class

Whether we admit it or like it, we do have social inequality in our culture. Our society consists of several layers that form a structure of social classes, each above or below, inferior or superior, to other classes. A social class is a relatively homogeneous and permanent segment of society to which individuals and families belong. Members have only limited social contact with social classes other than their own.

Social stratification reflects the ranking of persons by other members of the culture or society into high, middle, or low social positions. The result is a hierarchy of prominence and prestige, respect and admiration, responsibilities and privileges.

Each social class has its own norms of behavior, its own consumption patterns, its own tastes. Social class norms influence individual behavior in two ways. First, the typical person feels pressure to conform to the norms of his or her own class. Second, the socially ambitious person feels pressure to conform to the norms of the social class just above the present class, the class to which the person aspires. The person whose ambition is quite strong may even flout some of the norms of the peer group.

Within any social class, the members tend to have the same hopes, attitudes, and preferences; feel the same needs; share the same values, tastes, and emotions; consume the same goods and services; and buy from the same sellers. Members want the approval of their social class so that they can feel good about themselves.

Social Classes in Our Society. Most sociologists stratify this country's population into five or six classes. These classes are not, of course, separated by sharp lines; there is considerable overlapping, especially concerning the criterion of income. A common classification with a few features of each class follows:

1. *Upper.* Quality of breeding is high. Respectful of family reputation and values. Much civic responsibility. Gracious living. Some nouveaux riches, some top executives, some doctors and lawyers.
2. *Upper middle.* Owners of medium-size firms. Managers. Successful but not top professionals. Want to appear successful. Ambitious for their children. Expensive status symbols such as large houses. College graduates. The upper and upper middle classes constitute the *class market.*
3. *Lower middle.* Ambitious; college for their children. Owners of small firms; highly-paid blue-collar workers; salaried white collar workers. Small homes or multi-family dwellings. Strong on respectability.
4. *Upper lower.* "Ordinary" working class. Semi-skilled workers. Comfortable living. Don't save much. Spend less on clothing and services than do upper middle and lower middle classes. Lower middle and upper lower classes are the *mass market.*
5. *Lower lower.* Sporadic employment. Unskilled workers. Low pay. Battle for life's necessities. Slums.

Bases for Social Stratification. Perhaps the three most common criteria for assigning individuals to certain social classes are the factors of income, occupation, and education. Other bases used include type of residence, neighborhood, kinship, ethnic factors, political position or power, associates, public service, and property ownership. The bases for grouping individuals in social classes change over time, as do the weights given to each.

Social mobility is the movement of an individual from one social position to another, either upward or downward. The term is most commonly used in connection with upward movement. In theory, our society offers complete mobility, but in practice there is relatively little mobility. There is no agreement on the degree of mobility in our social class structure, but rarely does an individual rise more than one rank. Mobility is more restricted at the top and bottom of the social class structure.

Reference Groups

A reference group consists of two or more individuals who have something in common; members of the more influential reference groups communicate and interact in group activities on a continuing basis. Because the member refers (and defers) to the group for guidance and direction, we call them *reference* groups. The "something in common" usually includes experiences, problems, interests, and goals. Its members form and change attitudes as a group. The group serves its members as a model, a standard of comparison, and a source of approval. It influences its members' tastes, beliefs, and behavior.

There are reference groups everywhere because groups are essential. For example, there are *work groups* (job associates) and there are *play groups* (non-work groups). Much of your behavior is as a member of groups. Indeed, your behavior cannot be understood or explained without reference to the groups of which you are a member. Those groups have much influence on your decisions involving your behavior.

Choice of Reference Groups. The range of reference groups is wide. Reference groups to which an individual may belong include family, friends, neighbors, professional and work associates, relatives, political groups, fraternities and sororities, civic clubs, church groups, PTA, athletic groups, country clubs, student body, classmates, and service organizations. Reference groups can be either membership groups (family), aspirational groups (country club), formal membership groups (labor union), informal groups (coffee break associates), or groups consisting of categories (based on age or vocation). Some reference groups exert a positive influence, some a negative influence, and some even evoke both types of reactions from different people. Some reference groups are primarily concerned with the continuation or survival of the group—bridge or garden clubs, for example. Other groups are primarily concerned with the successful accomplishment of some project—a research and development unit or a district sales force, for example. Certain features of social class are also features of reference groups, but it must be remembered that some reference groups cut across social class lines.

Affiliation with some groups is more automatic and unavoidable than is true of others, but there is considerable freedom to exercise personal membership preferences. Many persons use one, two, or three groups as the main points of reference, identifying closely with and depending heavily on those particular ones even though they are also members of other groups.

Use of Reference Groups by an Individual. Individuals use reference groups to provide *identification.* Almost everyone feels a need to belong, to be accepted and approved by other people. Reference groups provide support, comfort, and well-being. They enhance one's sense of personal worth and provide stability and a reduction of risk. One contributes to the group and also draws from the group. A pleasant feeling of superiority may be experienced when one finally becomes a member of some aspirational group which is considered prestigious.

Individuals use reference groups as a *source of information.* Members assume that other members have information they will pass on to the group.

Individuals also use reference groups as their major *source of norms.* By respecting the norms and by holding the attitudes that are common in a reference group, each member's conformity contributes to the group's uniformity.

Individuals use reference groups to satisfy their social needs and permit social fulfillment. Reference groups provide association and fellowship. For all members who conform, esteem and warmth will be forthcoming from companions and friends.

The typical reference group establishes its qualifications for membership and its standards of proper behavior so as to be able to screen prospects for membership and then to control its members. The group rewards those who observe its norms and punishes those who flout them. Punishment can actually start with the group's refusing membership to someone who violates its norms. Punishment of members may involve neglect, shame, ridicule, penalties, sanctions, or as a last resort, expulsion. Rewards may take the form of support, security, protection, encouragement, honors, awards, praise, or election to high office. The more highly a member esteems the group, the more the member values his or her membership and the more likely is that member to respect and obey the group's norms. Sometimes group preferences will even prevail over personal preferences. Much of an individual's behavior cannot be understood apart from the behavior of some reference group.

Position and Role. *Position* concerns where an individual stands in the structure of a reference group. Position determines status within the group; it influences who says what and to whom. Each position has its own rank and measure of prestige. Each position has its own rights—the demands its occupant can make on others—and its own responsibilities—the obligations its occupant owes to others. Position implies some specialization and ability. The more ability demanded and the larger the number of persons the occupant supervises, the higher the status of the position. A position requiring unusual talents should obviously be filled by an unusual occupant. The status of each member is always relative to the status of each of the other members. Many positions in many reference groups continue over time but are filled by different persons as time passes. For example, the captain of this year's football team is almost never the person who was captain last year.

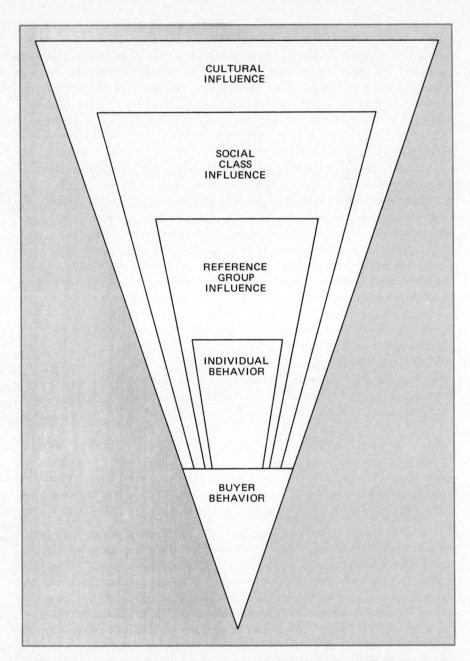

ILLUSTRATION 3-1. Professional salespeople should try to understand why customers buy as well as how and what they buy. Gaining this understanding involves knowing about cultural influences, as well as about individual buying behavior. This chapter starts with the broad behavioral dimensions and narrows down to the behavior of buyers.

An individual may occupy positions in several reference groups at the same time; the football captain may also be president of the senior class, for example. Sometimes an individual qualifies for high-level positions in two reference groups, but more often people occupy low-level positions in several groups or have a high-level position in one reference group and a low-level position in another.

Role is based on position. Role is that behavior considered acceptable for and in a specific position. For each position, certain types of behavior are appropriate and other types are not. The group of norms (role) suitable for Robinson Crusoe did not fit his man Friday. Each occupant of a position is under pressure to see that his or her behavior is in harmony with the position and with what is expected of its occupant. Roles must be learned, sometimes from instruction, sometimes from trial and error. Each person plays many roles because each individual is many different persons in different groups and in different situations. A person plays one role in a golf foursome, another role in interviewing for a job, still another role when serving as a student counselor. The individual tries to play each role satisfactorily. Most role playing is done in situations of personal interaction, and the individual stays alert for indications of how his or her performance is being received and evaluated by the other members of the reference group.

Opinion Leaders. Most reference groups consist of opinion leaders and opinion followers. Opinion leaders are tastemakers because their tastes tend to be adopted by the other members of the group. By definition, followers look to leaders for leadership. Opinion followers ask their opinion leader for information and advice, for recommendations, and even for instruction in the leader's area of specialization. If the leader is inclined to "sell" personal attitudes, this influence can be quite powerful. The direction of this influence is largely horizontal because individuals wanting guidance usually look for it inside their own reference groups. Only the socially ambitious are inclined to follow leaders in a higher social class or in an aspirational reference group.

There are opinion leaders in every social stratum, income level, and reference group. In business firms, opinion leaders may be found in any department and wearing any title. For example, picture four homemakers who are close friends and neighbors. One has taken many steamship cruises, the others none. Another is a wizard at bridge. One's cooking and baking skills are the envy of the other three. The fourth knits sweaters that are a joy to behold and receive. In each specialty, one communicates, informs, recommends, persuades, and may even exert a bit of social pressure. An opinion leader in one field is seldom an opinion leader in another field. Indeed, the typical opinion leader is quite similar to followers in almost every context except a specialty.

There is no simple, satisfactory technique by which outsiders can identify opinion leaders inside a reference group. Position, of course, sometimes helps because certain positions imply a type of leadership by requiring particular competence in the specialty. The very fact that a certain person is the golf pro (position) at a country club automatically makes that person an authority (opinion leader) on golf.

In reference groups of the social type, opinion leaders are usually gregarious, easy to reach, and easy to communicate with. In many types of reference groups, an opinion leader will have contacts and sources of information outside the group. Opinion leaders are generally more exposed to mass media than are opinion followers. Who they are, what they own, what their great interest is, what they have done, what they can do, what they know, and whom they know may all be clues to the identity of opinion leaders.

The identification of opinion leaders has great implication for sellers. Communication is often made more effective if, instead of trying to communicate directly with the total audience, a seller tries to communicate with opinion leaders in the hope that they will pass both the seller's message and their influence on to their followers.

Family

For most individuals, the family unit is the most influential reference group. It is so powerful that we treat it separately.

Technically *family* is two or more people who live together and are related by marriage, blood, or adoption. By way of contrast, a *household* is a person who lives alone, or two or more people who are unrelated but live together. We usually think of a family as consisting of a father, a mother, and their children. Almost everyone starts life as a child in his or her parents' family. In later life, many persons marry, become parents, and head their own families.

From birth, children have needs. As they grow older, they have more to say about what is bought to fill their needs, and, later, family needs. Teenagers are consumers. They make certain individual buying decisions and influence certain family buying decisions. The family as a group may decide where to go on vacation, or which house to buy.

The family is a major influence on the behavior of its members. The family has great influence on its members' attitudes, motivations, values, norms, and habits. The family has a strong influence on the decisions of its members. Year after year, children find their values, consumption patterns, and habits shaped by those of the family unit. In the family, if one member is treated to some expensive item, the other members expect to receive their turns later.

Most ultimate consumers are strongly influenced by two families, the one into which they were born, and the one each individual helps form. Each member is influenced by and influences the other members. What you experience, absorb, adopt, and learn as a child is not easily abandoned when you become an adult.

As for buying behavior, our predominant interest, the role of each family member is somewhat traditional. Many women dominate decision-making in the areas of food, household supplies, and clothing (including the clothing of their husbands). Recently, the growth of seven-day-a-week and 24-hour-a-day retailing has enabled men to play a larger role in those areas. Many men dominate in buying decisions involving high-priced, "big-ticket" items, such as automobiles, insurance, and investments.

To the concept of the family as a consuming unit must be added two relatively recent developments. They are working wives and singles. Many families have two incomes because the wife works and earns; so, those families can increase their purchases of products and services. Just as more husbands are shopping with their wives in retail stores, working wives are joining their husbands in making buying decisions involving such items as automobiles, TV sets, and insurance.

About one fourth of our 75 million households consist of single persons. A single's buying behavior is featured by heavy spending for such services as entertainment, travel, and domestic help. Singles are also buying houses or condominiums.

INDIVIDUAL ASPECTS OF BUYING BEHAVIOR

The individual aspects of buying behavior include self-concept, perception, learning, motivation, and attitudes.

Self-Concept

As an individual, your voluntary behavior is controlled by your concept of self and by the concept of self you are eager to achieve. Your actions reflect how you view yourself.

The most obvious dimensions of self-concept are physical. Are you skinny or heavy? Tall or short? Coordinated or clumsy? Then, there are moral dimensions. Do you tell only the truth? Do you "cut corners"? There are social dimensions. What social class are you in? Are you married? Are you a leader? Finally, there are mental dimensions. What is your IQ? Your grade-point average? Your views of yourself are truly complex and powerful. Your self-concept is a valued possession, for it influences your feelings of worth, your motivation, and your initiative.

The Impact of Self-Concept. The formation of self-concept starts very early in life. Family, friends, circumstances, and experiences can all be determinants of it. Many facets of self-concept remain virtually unchanged over long periods of time, often throughout life. Self-concept is a significant feature of a person because it is the key to behavior. The individual is anxious to avoid any behavior that downgrades self-concept, and is alert for opportunities to improve self-concept.

Each person tries to live according to a concept of self, and tries to project certain personality traits. If a person succeeds in these two endeavors, behavior is in harmony with self-concept. If you sense at some point that others do not attribute to you the same image as you attribute to yourself, this discrepancy may force you to revise your behavior.

Environment. To think of an individual apart from everyone and everything else is unrealistic. Environment must be included when behavior is examined because at any given time, the individual is behaving in the environment of that moment. There is continuous interaction between a person and environment because they are mutually dependent variables, each capable of changing the other and being changed by the other. Actions are taken within the context of the situation or environment. An individual's behavior reflects how the total environment of the moment is seen. Obviously, the way one person evaluates a situation may be quite different from the way someone else evaluates it. In all instances, an individual tries to integrate self-concept with concept of environment.

Other persons are often present in an individual's environment. They can be very influential because interpersonal relations have a powerful effect on behavior. For example, you have shopped many times alone and many times with another person. You know that there were differences in your behavior in each situation. And consider the difference between your topics of conversation when with your peers and topics of conversation when with your parents. Whom you are with has much to do with how you behave.

There are other environmental elements besides people. Some are animate —dogs and cats, for example—and others are inanimate—tables, books, clothes. Some are even less obvious but are still influential: hour of the day, temperature, season, and geographic location, for example.

The attention or awareness a person gives to environment is highly selective. How many items in a supermarket attract your attention? How much of the bulk of a Sunday newspaper do you notice? In most situations, a person can be conscious of only a small portion of the elements or potential stimuli in environment. Usually you could take account of many more than you do. You may note some objects or people in passing, then pay no further attention; such items may never gain your genuine awareness. Occasionally, however, a person seeks out some environmental elements. A generalization is that individuals pay attention to a potential stimulus only if that stimulus is thought to affect self-concept. What one does take account of in one's environment is usually evaluated in ways acceptable to the self-concept.

Perception

The perception process is based in large part on stimulus-response relationships. An *external stimulus* is something in a person's physical environment which excites a sense organ enough to cause a response. The stimulus can be a physical element, an act, a situation, a change, or an event. Each of these stimulates the senses because of some attribute such as size, intensity, color, movement, position, contrast, or isolation. An *internal stimulus* originates inside the individual;

it is a condition calling for attention. Pain, fear, discomfort, hunger, and thirst are examples of internal stimuli. A *response* is a person's reaction to a stimulus. Complex stimuli are sometimes called *situations,* and the responses to situations are sometimes called *behavior.*

Steps in the Perception Process. There are several kinds of perception, each of which leads to the formation of concepts. A *concept* is a thought, an opinion, or an idea which grows out of a stimulus-response pattern. A concept can be an image or an inner representation of an act, an object, a person, an event, a condition, or a relationship. In the most common type of perception, the individual takes in some stimulus through one or more of the five senses. There may be a simple stimulus (a police officer raises his arm to halt a line of automobiles), which leads to perception (in this case, by sight), which leads to the formation of a concept (my line of traffic is to stop).

Another kind of perception may be called unconscious perception. For example, picture a student starting to write a theme but facing the basic problem of how to organize it. Then, perhaps during some other activity, the sections fall into place in a logical sequence. There were stimuli which eventually resulted in the concept of how to organize the theme, but they were not consciously defined.

Perception does not stop with the awareness of some outside stimulus. It shades into and includes the interpretation as well as the selection of stimuli for attention. It includes fitting perceptions and their resulting concepts into the individual's personal world in a coherent way. Perception is the major determinant of how you adapt to your world.

Perceptual Field. Each individual has his or her own perceptual field—everything that a person sees or knows about the world. The dimensions of the perceptual field depend upon an individual's past experiences, needs and wants, emotional makeup, mental set (readiness to react almost automatically to a stimulus), membership in a particular social class and in various reference groups, and the physical environment.

There are two elements of a perceptual field—figure and ground. *Figure* is the portion of a perceptual field that is in focus at any given time. Once a concept is in focus, it is said to be differentiated. This simply means that it is recognized as being distinct from other concepts. The more intense the differentiation, the longer forgetting is postponed and the longer recall back into focus is possible. *Ground* is all the rest of a perceptual field that is not in focus. Every concept, after being in focus, becomes part of the ground. Old concepts can be recalled into focus, and new concepts can be developed by combining or relating old concepts to form a new concept. Ground expands as more and more experiences are perceived and as more and more concepts accumulate.

Your self-concept controls entry to the figure of your perceptual field. It can pre-set the figure to reject or to accept certain stimuli instantly and automatically. For example, your figure may be set to pick up any announcement of an upcoming quiz, or telephone rings. Most figures are set to hunt and accept stimuli which can affect self-concept. Your figure does not function on the basis of chance—nor on the basis of random selection.

No two perceptual fields are alike because no two people are alike. Individuals' perceptual fields reflect everywhere that they have ever been; everything that they have seen, heard, tasted, smelled, and touched; everything that they have experienced, thought, and learned. Differences between individuals' perceptual fields affect what and how they perceive. These differences pose a great problem to sellers. For example, imagine how the different perceptual fields of the following people would cause them to perceive a television commercial: marketing student, English instructor, advertising instructor, Better Business Bureau investigator, copywriter, advertiser's lawyer, media representative, artist, and prospective buyer.

Learning

Although learning is a complicated process and one which is not yet fully understood, we must acquire some basic facts about it because of its influence on behavior. The stimulus-response relationship is the essence of learning. To learn is to accumulate associations or relationships between certain behavior patterns (including the purchase and consumption of specific products or services), and the satisfaction or dissatisfaction which results from that behavior. When the probability increases that a certain act will be repeated, or when the probability decreases that some other act will be repeated, there has been learning.

Simplified Learning Process. Learning is reflected in behavioral changes which often are more or less permanent. The subsequent behavioral change can be brought about by practice, training, observation, repetition, or experimentation. Experimentation generates experience, permitting one to compare previous behavior patterns in similar situations.

Here is an example of a simplified learning sequence:

1. Awareness of need (pain of a headache).
2. Examination of alternatives (take two aspirins, go to bed, do nothing).
3. Selection of which response to make to the stimulus (take two aspirin).
4. Response (actually take two aspirin).
5. Evaluation of the outcome of Steps 1, 2, and 3. (What did Step 4 do for Step 1? Was Step 3 the correct choice?).

Over time, by trying various selections in Step 2, one learns which response best answers the need in Step 1. After identifying the most satisfactory choice of response, the individual can store it in the ground of the perceptual field for future reference, and can recall it later to the point of focus.

Reinforcement. Reinforcement is necessary if learning is to take place. When a person experiences gratification because of a particular response to a stimulus, there has been positive reinforcement. The greater the satisfaction, the stronger is the stimulus-response relationship and the incentive to repeat it. Continuing positive reinforcement encourages automatic reaction to the stimulus involved and recommends that the selection of response be based more and more on habit.

Reinforcement also leads to the assigning of ratings to concepts. Ratings may range from very positive to very negative. Those valued "very positive" are approved and sought. Those valued "very negative" are unpleasant and are avoided. Ratings can be assigned to concepts concerning such things as persons, institutions, activities, and products.

Habit-Based and Problem-Solving Behavior. Positive reinforcement and high concept values lead to repetition, and over time repetition becomes habit. The relationship between a stimulus and its most satisfactory response becomes largely fixed, usually operating below the conscious level. In habitual behavior, little or no consideration is given to other possible responses.

More of a person's behavior is of the habitual type than of the problem-solving, or decision-making, type. In problem-solving behavior, the individual makes a conscious choice from among several options. The more serious or infrequent the situation, the more likely problem-solving behavior is to be used. Sometimes habitual behavior is not possible. If a store is out of your regular product brand, for example, you are forced into problem-solving behavior.

Motivation

Psychologists do not agree on just how motivation operates. Over time, we must learn more about needs, the most basic factor in all voluntary behavior. We do know that each individual has needs. As soon as one need is satisfied, another appears.

A *motive* is an impetus for an individual to act; it results from a felt need or want. An individual's overall motivation is to maintain a certain self-concept by behaving in accordance with it. When a situation demands the protection of self-concept or when it offers an opportunity to enhance self-concept, the individual experiences a feeling of need. This prompts the individual to initiate and direct behavior in a particular direction, a direction determined by the perception of self and the environment.

Motives. Current literature on motivation reveals disagreement about its nature and about the manner in which motives can be classified. Our purposes in this book are best served by recognizing a two-way classification of motives: physiological motives versus nonphysiological motives.

Physiological motives result from the biological needs for survival plus the strong preferences of the human organism. Absolute needs for survival include food, clothing, shelter, and sleep. Typical of the strong preferences of human beings are the desires for comfort and freedom from pain. Physiological needs are powerful and repetitive motivators.

There are many different kinds of nonphysiological motive. Four important kinds are:

1. *Pyschological,* the needs for consistency within oneself, praise, pleasure, banishment of fear, prestige, and unity within one's world of reality.
2. *Social,* including the needs for affection, acceptance, and happiness of others.
3. *Learned,* including the desires for efficiency, economy, cleanliness, dependability, convenience, beauty, and profit.
4. *Self-fulfillment,* including the desires to learn, to work for a cause, to work for self-improvement and growth, and to achieve a higher standard of living.

There is really no foolproof method of identifying the needs of any one person. Thus, those who try to influence behavior must base their efforts on less than they would like to know about the presence of certain needs in an individual and about the urgency of each need to that individual.

Variations in Buying Motives. Motivation is an intensely personal matter. No two persons have exactly the same needs or buying motives because no two persons are identical. Each individual establishes goals and decides, subject to personal limitations, what he or she is willing to pay to achieve those goals. Consumers decide which benefits and advantages they want to enjoy, then buy those products and services which promise the chosen benefits.

A seller very quickly discovers that buying motives vary in strength and that this variation can be from person-to-person and time-to-time. Person-to-person variations in buying motivation reflect the fact that no two individuals are alike. Hereditary background is one factor which helps explain why one person's buying motives are different from another's. Other important factors are personality, capabilities, training, education, experience, environment, social status, occupation, and income.

Time-to-time variations in buying motivation reflect the fact that each individual buyer experiences changes in the pattern of motivation. Age is obviously a variable that affects desires and abilities. Season of the year, phase of the business cycle, mood, and immediate circumstances can also cause variations in an individual's buying motivation.

Life Styles. Life style is total behavior. The life style of an individual can be determined with great accuracy if one learns how that individual spends money, particularly for status symbols, and how he or she spends time. Sometimes a life style is adopted by a group, a family, or some other reference group. A group's life style may be unusual—even bizarre; however, more consumers conform to common life styles than deviate. Whatever your life style, it expresses you or you would change it.

Goals and Goal-Objects. *Goals* are the conditions, objects, experiences, or activities which motivate behavior. All voluntary behavior is goal-directed behavior. A goal reflects the concept of a desired state of affairs; a *goal-object* is a specific item which will help to produce that state. Consumption or use of a goal-object allows one to achieve a goal. For example, if one feels thirsty, the goal is alleviation of that thirst; the goal-object is some type of beverage.

The typical goal-object is an assortment of features, some of which are positive and some of which are negative. For example, a product of high quality (positive) usually has a high price (negative). Most products, when they function as goal-objects, consist of physical features plus various attributes such as credit terms, store location, manufacturer's image, buying assistance, design, and status. The best goal-object is the one best assortment of features for the need in question.

Motivation cannot be correctly deduced from a person's behavior or from the goal-objects used to satisfy needs. Goal conflict compounds this difficulty. In *plus versus plus conflicts,* two goal-objects are attractive, but each blocks the other. Here are some examples:

1. Buying a sports car versus buying a sailboat.
2. Buying 100 shares of stock versus buying bonds.
3. Taking a mountain vacation versus taking a beach vacation.
4. Maintaining a large bank balance versus taking a trip to Europe.

In *plus versus minus conflicts,* the individual is caught between gaining a plus goal-object versus avoiding a minus goal-object. Examples are:

1. Buying a premium-quality tire versus paying a higher price.
2. Eating a fudge sundae versus adding calories.
3. Playing golf versus mowing the yard.
4. Sleeping versus missing an 8 o'clock class.

In *minus versus minus conflicts,* the individual must choose between two unattractive alternatives. Some examples are:

1. Stealing food versus going hungry.
2. Taking an extra job versus doing without something one wants.
3. Cheating on a final exam versus getting an F in the course.
4. Staying in a boat which is on fire versus diving into shark-infested waters.

Rationalization. In studying motivation, the concept of rationalization is an important one to consider. *Rationalization* is the individual's attempt to justify behavior on logical and proper bases. The outcome of some behavior is embarrassing because it is disappointing. Also, the motivation for some behavior is base, unethical, or illegal. The self-concept cannot live with behavior that fails in its undertaking or with motivation that incriminates. Both are repulsive to the self-concept and to other individuals. Thus, an individual may resort to the practice of assigning respectable explanations to the behavior in question so as to disguise the truth.

Suppose that a retailer enters a manufacturer's window display contest but does not win a prize. Instead of admitting that the display did not deserve to win, the retailer rationalizes by saying that the manufacturer awarded the prizes to friends. Or suppose that because of the faulty buying of a purchasing agent, a small hand tool used by certain production employees turns out to be unsatisfactory. Instead of admitting that the buying proposition was not carefully evaluated, the purchasing agent claims to have been misled by the tools salesperson. A cruise taken for fun could be claimed to be for the traveler's health. An executive whose expensive wardrobe is bought for pride may say business demands it. Rationalization helps reduce mental anguish by helping to protect one's self-concept.

Attitudes

Attitudes are the views or convictions a person holds about or toward something. Every person brings to every situation an assortment of predispositions—needs, interests, goals, motives, opinions, values, beliefs, and preferences. They are the expectations which reflect the person's anticipation of events or experiences. They are the evaluation, feeling, and inclination to take favorable or unfavorable action toward an object. Attitudes are similar to what we call tastes. Here is a list of objects of particular interest to salespeople:

Product type	Brand or make
Retailer	Manufacturer
Salesperson	Advertising
Sellers' policies	Ideas

Attitudes vary in basic ways. They can be positive (favorable), neutral, or negative (hostile). They can be easy or difficult to change; most strongly held attitudes cannot be changed quickly. An attitude can be powerful or weak as a determinant of behavior.

How Attitudes Develop. An individual acquires attitudes from experience. Social interaction, experimentation and trial, and interpersonal communication are powerful determinants of one's attitudes. The odds are that many of your attitudes were learned while you grew up as a member of a family.

Attitudes are being formed whenever you examine or try a new type of product, brand, or retail store. When a friend, neighbor, or opinion leader reports on purchase and consumption of a product or service, your attitudes are likely to be affected. The promotional communication of sellers affects your attitudes.

Attitudes and Behavior. Attitudes influence total behavior. They incline a person to look with favor or disfavor on elements in the perceptual field. They influence an individual to be ready to respond in a predetermined way to certain experiences. Attitudes influence reaction to all communication—exposure (attention), learning (decoding), perception (grasp), and remembering (retention). Generally, changes in attitudes cause behavioral changes.

Buying behavior is greatly influenced by a buyer's current attitude toward types of products, brands, salespeople, manufacturers, retailers, prices, etc. We interpret and respond to sellers' promotion favorably or unfavorably mainly according to our experience, values, and expectations. Sometimes, a change in attitude can trigger a change in buying behavior. For example, an impressive advertisement or a persuasive presentation by a salesperson can induce a buyer to try a product or a brand for the first time. Sometimes such a change in buying behavior can change an attitude. If a skeptical buyer tries a new product or brand and likes it, skepticism may change to favorable enthusiasm.

A seller may try to change unfavorable attitudes or may try to strengthen favorable attitudes. It is possible to revise the product offering more easily than it is to change an unfavorable attitude. The revised product offering may increase the number of favorable attitudes.

MODEL OF CONSUMER BUYING BEHAVIOR

Our glance at motivation leads naturally into an attempt to build a model of what actually takes place when an ultimate consumer buys a product. Salespeople must influence buyers to buy. Purchase-sale transactions are the core of all business because each business firm must sell at a profit if it is to survive. Only if salespeople have adequate understanding of the steps or phases of the buying process can they persuade individuals to become buyers. Does this model fit many of your purchases?

Step 1—Need

A sense of need appears when an individual perceives either a threat to self-concept or an opportunity to enhance self-concept. Either of these causes tension or disequilibrium and puts pressure on the individual to take corrective action. Either makes the individual aware of a difference between actual condition and a better condition which is possible to obtain.

Step 2—Definition of Goal

You recall that achieving a goal is something which makes a need disappear; the goal involves the satisfaction that the buyer wants. Imagine a husband, Bill, at work. He has experienced a vague concern several times during the day. Then late in the afternoon, he suddenly realizes that today is the birthday of his wife, Ann. Need is clear. Bill's goal then becomes the satisfaction of bringing happiness to someone he loves by doing something nice for her.

Step 3—Selection of Goal-Object

In this step, Bill consciously or subconsciously checks on whether habit-based behavior ("Each birthday, add to her strand of Oriental pearls") or problem-solving behavior is indicated. If he chooses the latter, he moves toward his definition of goal-object by narrowing his selection down to buying a gift or taking his wife out to dinner. If he decides on a gift, he might consider perfume, a robe, or candy. The moment he settles on candy, he has defined his goal-object. If he had wanted to, he could have sought information and advice before selecting candy as the goal-object. He could, for example, have searched through his perceptual field for any guidelines which might be there. Or he could have gone to external sources, such as checking advertisements in the day's newspaper. He could even have delayed selecting a goal-object until he had examined various items in stores.

Step 4—Selective Elements in Choosing the Goal-Object

In this step, Bill lists the brands of candy from which he will make a final choice. Whereas Step 3 dealt with primary demand, this step deals with selective demand. Brands are put on Bill's list only if he feels that they qualify as being acceptable. They will be considered only: (1) if the brand's name has occupied the buyer's point of focus and was then favorably differentiated, and (2) if the buyer has the ability to recall the brand name from ground back into his point of focus.

Step 5—Evaluation and Choice of Goal-Object

Suppose that in Step 4, Bill listed three brands of candy from which to choose: Blum, Barton, and Godiva. Now he weighs all the positive and negative values of each brand. He is much concerned with how the goal-object expresses his affection to Ann. Bill decides to give Ann a box of Godiva candy because of what it will mean in terms of brand image and taste. In this step, there can be possible frustration; if a box of Godiva candy cannot be obtained, Bill must decide whether Blum or Barton will do. If not, then he goes further back and looks again at the possibility of giving Ann either a robe or perfume. If these alternative goal-objects do not look promising, he may go even further back and decide to take her out to dinner.

Step 6—Purchase

Bill buys a two-pound box of Godiva candy. At the moment of purchase, that item is in closer harmony with his expectations than is any other.

Step 7—Consumption

Bill gives the candy to Ann. Now is the time for reinforcement to operate. If Ann's sweet tooth has been demanding some exceptional candy and if the gift pleases her, there is positive reinforcement. Bill is encouraged to repeat the procedure because the goal-object lived up to his expectations, too. Sometimes, of course, reinforcement is negative. If Ann had gone on a rigid diet the day before her birthday without telling Bill, reinforcement could have been negative.

Step 8—Possible Post-Purchase Dissonance

Everyone knows the experience of buying and then questioning the wisdom of the purchase. Every purchase has the potential to cause such anxiety; the probability of its development is in direct proportion to a product's price or importance in use. Every item bought promises satisfaction, but it also demands the expenditure of money, time, and shopping effort. Practically every product finally chosen has some negative features, and practically every other product on the list for consideration has its share of positive features. The result is that the compromise reflected in every purchase can cause post-purchase dissonance.

One technique that buyers use to combat post-purchase dissonance is to initiate interpersonal communication soon after buying. A consumer may stimulate communication with a member of the family or a friend. The substance of ads promoting the item bought may be thoroughly read. Reassurance and support are needed, and information consonant with the buying decision is welcome.

Sometimes a consumer obtains information which, if it had been received sooner and if the decision had been made on that basis alone, would have caused different buying behavior. After the purchase, the consumer may learn of better products, lower prices, negative case histories, or hostile attitudes and norms. If post-purchase dissonance is strong, an order may be cancelled, payment on the check stopped, or the good may be returned.

When a discrepancy develops between a buyer's expectations and a subsequent experience, when a state of disharmony is detected among actions and attitudes, when it is sensed that the purchase was inconsistent with one of his or her reference group's norms, then there is the psychological discomfort called post-purchase dissonance. The individual tries to avoid any experience which will cause post-purchase dissonance and welcomes experiences which will cause post-purchase consonance.

SUMMARY

A culture a is broad grouping of people and the geographic area the group occupies. Material items and nonmaterial concepts are elements of a culture. Each culture reflects the customs and standards of most of its members.

Subcultures are smaller groups within the embracing culture. They have different behavior patterns. Norms are customary modes of behavior within a culture. Folkways, mores, and laws are three types of norm.

A social class is a relatively homogeneous and permanent segment of society to which individuals and families belong. Each class has its own norms. This country's population is often broken into five classes: upper, upper middle, lower middle, upper lower, and lower. Class members are distinguished by income, occupation, and education.

Reference groups consist of individuals who have something in common, such as experiences, goals, and attitudes. Reference groups act as models for their members. Individuals use groups as a means for identification, a source of information, and to satisfy social needs. Position is where a person stands within the reference group. Role is acceptable behavior for that position. Opinion leaders provide guidance to opinion followers.

The family unit is the most influential reference group. Families shape almost everyone's attitudes, values, norms, and buying habits. The increase of seven-day-a-week and 24-hour-a-day retailing and of working wives has in many cases altered traditional roles.

Your voluntary behavior is controlled by your self-concept, your view of yourself. You want that opinion of yourself to remain high. Individuals avoid behavior that downgrades that concept. One's environment must be included when behavior is examined because every action is taken within the context of the situation or environment. The attention a person gives to environment is highly selective.

Perception is based in large part on stimulus-response relationships. Stimuli can be external or internal. Situations are complex stimuli, and the responses to situations are called behavior. A concept is a thought which grows out of a stimulus-response pattern. Perception can be conscious or unconscious.

Perceptual field is everything that a person sees or knows about the world. The two elements of perceptual field are figure and ground. Self-concept controls entry to the figure of the perceptual field.

Learning is a complicated process. The stimulus-response relationship is the essence of learning. Learning is reflected in behavioral changes. Awareness, examination of alternatives, selection of response, and evaluation are the steps in learning. When a person experiences gratification because of a particular response to a stimulus, there has been positive reinforcement. Positive reinforcement leads to habit-based behavior.

A motive is an impetus for someone to act. Needs create motives. Motives can be separated into two groups: physiological and nonphysiological. Physiological motives result from biological needs and strong preferences of the human organism. Nonphysiological motives include psychological, social, learned, and self-fulfillment motives. No two individuals have exactly the same buying motives because everyone has different goals and needs. Personality, occupation, and age variations affect buying motives.

Life style is total behavior. It can be determined by watching how one spends time and money.

Goals are the conditions, objects, experiences, or activities which motivate behavior. A goal-object is a specific item which will help to produce a desired state or goal. Rationalization is a person's attempt to justify behavior on logical and proper bases.

Attitudes are the views a person holds about something. They are the sum of needs, interests, goals, motives, opinions, values, beliefs, and preferences. Attitudes can be positive, neutral, or negative. They can be easy or difficult to change. Attitudes are acquired from experience. They are formed whenever one tries a new product or when another person expresses a fact or opinion about that product. Attitudes influence total behavior. Buying behavior is greatly influenced by a buyer's current attitude. Sellers try to change unfavorable attitudes or to strengthen favorable ones.

Models have been built to explain buyer behavior. One popular model has eight steps:

1. Need—an individual perceives a threat to self-concept or a chance to enhance it.
2. Definition of goal—the individual establishes a goal for meeting the need.
3. Selection of goal-object—the individual chooses the type of goal-object that will help achieve the goal.
4. Selective elements in choosing the goal-object—the choice of goal-objects is narrowed.
5. Evaluation and choice of goal-object—the individual analyzes and chooses the specific goal-object to purchase.
6. Purchase—the individual buys the goal-object.
7. Consumption—the individual uses the goal object.
8. Possible post-purchase dissonance—the individual may question the choice of the goal-object.

REVIEW QUESTIONS

1. What is a subculture?
2. What are the three general types of norm?
3. List the five different social classes.
4. How are social classes determined?
5. How do individuals use reference groups?
6. How is a person's position in a reference group determined?
7. Who are opinion leaders?
8. How does self-concept affect behavior?
9. What is the difference between external and internal stimuli?
10. What is a perceptual field?
11. Describe four types of nonphysiological motive.

12. How can a salesperson determine a prospect's life style?
13. Why do people rationalize?
14. How is buying behavior influenced by attitudes?
15. How can buyers reduce post-purchase dissonance?

DISCUSSION QUESTIONS

1. In what fields are you an opinion leader? In what fields are you an opinion follower?
2. Give examples of folkways, mores, and laws that can affect a buyer-seller relationship.
3. In reference to a well-known television commercial in your area, discuss the differences in perception that you, your parents, and your professor might have.
4. How does your life style reflect your self-concept?
5. Discuss your attitude toward the last salesperson you dealt with face-to-face. Did you buy anything from that salesperson? Why or why not?

CASE STUDY 3A

Alan James came home from work and picked up the newspaper to read the sports news and the automobile ads. His next-door neighbor had just bought a new car—air conditioning, power steering and power brakes, vinyl top, large engine. In short, the car was really loaded and James was already feeling a bit jealous. The more he thought about his neighbor's car and the more he read the car ads, the older and shabbier his car seemed. James had just been promoted to day-shift supervisor at the factory where he worked, so he was especially busy; he didn't have much time to think about cars until the weekend. But on Saturday afternoon, James, his wife, and their two children went over to the local car dealer. They told the salesperson they were just looking, but he followed them around offering useful information as they looked at the new cars.

James was particularly interested in the large cars like his neighbor had just purchased. He felt a large car would provide more comfort for his family and would be safer if they were ever in an accident. His wife kept pointing out such features as air conditioning, plush upholstery, and power windows. The children seemed to be most interested in a bright red sporty car. After spending about an hour looking, James decided not to buy a car for a while; so they all went home.

On Sunday, James saw his neighbor washing his new car and went out to talk with him. When he asked his neighbor how he liked his new car, the neighbor replied that it was the best buy he had ever made. Then he asked James how long he was going to keep driving his old car now that he had been promoted.

On Monday, James drove over to the car dealer during his lunch hour and traded his car in for a new intermediate car—a fully loaded model. That afternoon after work he drove it home and surprised his wife and children.

1. What decisions did James make?
2. How might culture have played a role in his decisions?
3. How might social class have played a role in his decisions?
4. How might reference groups have played a role in his decisions?

CASE STUDY 3B

Ross Thompson is a salesperson for Downtown Chevrolet. He recently sold two identical, fully equipped Impalas to two completely different types of customer. He assembled the following information about the two customers and is examining what seems to be inconsistent buying behavior.

Earl Meyer is the owner of a very successful drugstore in Westwood, a nearby suburb, but does not live in that area. His family founded the store many years ago and has always enjoyed a high standard of living. Meyer's annual salary is now about $45,000, and he could easily afford a higher priced automobile. Meyer has a great deal of personal contact with both his customers and his suppliers. He does not wish to create an image of wealth, for he fears his customers might think he is becoming wealthy at their expense through high prices at his store. Thompson recalled that Meyer thought his purchase was one of economy.

Al Williams works for an accounting firm and hopes someday to become a partner. He often entertains clients and must use his own car. Williams and his family have difficulty living as they wish on his $18,000 annual salary, but he decided to purchase his Impala in the hope that it would favorably impress his clients and his superiors at the office.

1. What was the primary motive which prompted Meyer and Williams, two very unlike persons, to make like purchases?
2. What variations in buying motives might account for seemingly inconsistent buying behavior?
3. Both men chose the same goal-object in this case. Do you think their goals are the same? Why or why not? Is there a goal conflict for either man?
4. Thompson's study revealed several principles of individual buying behavior. How can his findings be of most benefit to him in his selling efforts?

The Communication System

Chapter 4

After studying this chapter you should be able to:

- Identify the elements in a communication system
- Discuss sources of communication and receivers of communication
- Understand the encoding process and the transmitting process
- Demonstrate familiarity with the receiving and decoding of messages
- Present a clear picture of responses to messages
- Relate promotional communication to the adoption process

The simplest communication system consists of a sender, a message, a medium, and a receiver. A communication sign, signal, or stimulus is whatever our five senses detect. Communication transmits information and ideas or other stimuli by the use of symbols. Each symbol must have a common meaning to communicator and receiver. When two people communicate back and forth, each is a complete communication system; each transmits and receives.

The basic function of our marketing system is to communicate. The communication system consists of a salesperson, a sales story, a way of communicating that story, and a potential buyer. A seller's basic job is to relate products and services to buyers' consumption framework. Anything that reduces effective communication must be eliminated or at least held to a minimum by salespeople.

Our most common version of communication is face-to-face, person-to-person *oral* exchange. *A*'s communications are stimuli to *B,* and *B*'s communications are stimuli to *A.* Most oral communication is fast moving, characterized by little preparation and editing, instantaneous feedback, and instant disappearance. Much *written* communication is deliberated, planned, lasting, organized, outlined, and rewritten more than once.

SOURCES OF COMMUNICATION

Sources of communication are almost limitless. Individuals, groups of people, business enterprises, and other institutions try to communicate with you on practically a daily basis. One learns to communicate by interacting with others.

On first calls, the salesperson is usually viewed by buyers as an agent who delivers the company's sales message; the company is considered the source of the message. After mutually satisfactory dealings, the salesperson tends to become a source. Buyers judge messages according to their sources, and each salesperson needs to be considered by buyers as a trustworthy source.

Objectives of Sources

In selling, the all-inclusive objective of sources is to influence the attitudes and behavior of buyers and people who influence buying. Some experts see the seller as trying to achieve awareness, change attitudes, and stimulate favorable action. To others, the seller tries to move the potential buyer through the definite stages of attention, interest, desire, conviction, and action. To still others, the seller tries to obtain affirmative answers to the five buying decisions, concerning need, product, source, price, and time. Some picture the seller as communicating to establish a brand image and corporate image. Others see the seller as trying to effect changes in the buyer, in the buyer's environment, or in both. A seller has also been described as communicating for the purposes of converting nonusers of a product into users, of wooing customers away from competitors, and of increasing the volume of purchases by present users. Finally, some state that the seller communicates to inform, persuade, and remind.

Among these ideas, there is agreement that the seller tries to influence perceptions, concepts, and attitudes—either by changing them or perhaps more often by reinforcing them. Whatever their specific objectives, successful persuasive communications from a source cause an internal response in the receiver which predisposes a prospect to buy and a customer to continue buying.

The objective of every salesperson (essentially a communicator) is to present to each buyer a promise that will appeal so strongly that the buyer will take the action the salesperson desires. Why is that the case? The heart of every sales presentation is a promise. One can say, indeed, with confidence and correctness that every sales presentation (and every ad) should be built on and actually be just that—a promise. What is promised? Satisfaction. What is satisfaction? The disappearance of a feeling of need, the solution to a problem, the gratification of a desire. Unless the communicator promises the receivers something desirable, the promotional communication fails.

Source Credibility

The more credible the source, the more likely the receiver is to accept the message. The greater the respect for the source, the more likely it is that the receiver will be persuaded to take the action the source desires. If a source is perceived to be credible, the receiver is less wary of being manipulated and is more inclined to accept immediately the source's ideas and recommendations.

Two basic determinants of source credibility are trustworthiness and expertness in a given area. Firms seek to establish source credibility by building favorable corporate images both through their advertising activities and through their salespeople. The credibility standing of a salesperson determines the confidence that a buyer puts in that salesperson.

Some communication research suggests that a *sleeper effect* may operate where source credibility is concerned. This means that a message which was quite ineffective when transmitted, due to low source credibility, may become increasingly effective over time while another, initially more effective message from a highly credible source may become less effective over time. In one experiment, the same message was transmitted from two sources to two similar groups of people. Source 1 ranked high in credibility and its message immediately produced considerable attitude change in Group 1. Source 2 ranked low in credibility, and its message was largely discounted by Group 2. Some weeks later, without intervening messages, the attitudes of both groups were again checked. Each group then registered about the same number of changed attitudes. In Group 1, some persons had gone back to the attitudes they held before transmittal of the message. But in Group 2, many more attitudes were changed than had been indicated at the time of the first survey. Apparently some group members remembered and accepted much of the message but had forgotten the low credibility of the source. Message impact seemed to have lasted longer than source impact.

There is another interesting phenomenon regarding source credibility. Messages from a credible source may actually be misinterpreted by the receiver as being closer to the receiver's own attitudes than will messages from a less credible source which in actuality are closer to those attitudes.

Both source and message are influential. Changing only the message can change the prestige of the source; changing only the source can change the meaning of the message. Sometimes, in fact, a communication can be thought of as a two-part stimulus—a source-message stimulus.

Betty Crocker, the well known trade character of General Mills, is a good example of the influence of source on message reception. Betty was introduced in 1936. Homemakers perceived the artist's conception of Betty as young, reserved, and not very experienced domestically. That reduced Betty Crocker's potential influence on and acceptance by homemakers. So, in 1955, Betty was given more warmth and maturity; more recently, a smile was added. Betty was modernized again in 1969. The result? Better acceptance by homemakers.

RECEIVERS OF COMMUNICATION

Actually, receivers, and not senders, determine whether communication takes place, and, if so, what is communicated. The sender must, therefore, be aware of the audience for a message. What communicators call audiences, the marketing manager calls markets. Just as a communicator needs a profile of the potential audience, a marketer needs a profile of the potential market. A market consists of those buyers who share certain characteristics of interest to a source in selling. The source sends persuasive messages to those persons for the purpose of accomplishing some marketing objective. Salespeople typically talk to an audience of one buyer, and advertisements are carried by mass media to mass audiences.

Those who communicate through mass communication find the techniques of market or audience segmentation particularly helpful. Communication efforts are more effective if the total audience can be broken down into a number of smaller segments. This process consists of three basic steps. First, the total audience is defined as specifically as possible. Second, the total audience is divided into smaller, reasonably homogeneous segments. Each segment consists of persons who have some similar characteristics, especially concerning circumstances, motivation, and decision making. Ideally, the source wants a minimum of differences within a segment and a maximum of differences between segments. In the third step of this process, the source tailors a different message to fit each segment of the audience.

A basic audience segmentation in selling separates the industrial audience from the ultimate-consumer audience. Other divisions may be the domestic market and the foreign market, or the government market and the private market. Many sellers must segment the ultimate-consumer audience, and the techniques of doing so are complex. Factors which may be considered in segmenting the ultimate-consumer audience for purposes of effective communication are income, education, occupation, geography, age, sex, marital status, composition of the household, social class and group membership, type of residence, and political affiliation.

No segmentation structure lasts indefinitely. Because the number of segments and the characteristics of each are always changing, continual audience research is essential.

ENCODING THE MESSAGE

A source must know exactly the behavior he or she wants to bring about before building the message which is to cause that behavior. If the communicator is to influence and persuade and if the receiver is to respond favorably, the communicator must transmit information which reaches the receiver through one or more of the senses. The receiver must then take in those data and find them meaningful.

When a source undertakes to put an idea into a form that a receiver is capable of understanding, the source is *encoding* a message. Encoding is mainly concerned with meaning—the definitions and effects of words—and communication is faulty unless the meaning of a given message is virtually the same to both source and receiver. The fundamental element of every encoded message is a promise of satisfaction to the receiver if the receiver buys and uses the seller's product. This satisfaction may be in the form of the disappearance of a feeling of need, the solution to a problem, or the gratification of a desire. Unless the source promises the receivers something significant and desirable, the selling communication is likely to fail.

Communication Symbols

Communication symbols are substitutes for real objects, concepts, actions, or sensations. Words are communication symbols. The object, concept, action, or sensation for which a given word is used as a symbol is called the *referent*.

The most common kind of communication is face-to-face oral exchange, and words are the most basic communication symbols. The source uses words to convey impressions of the world. These word-symbols are stimuli to another person, and that person's word-symbols are stimuli to the source. Other commonly used communication symbols are illustrations, numbers, and sounds.

Each symbol used must have a common meaning to source and receiver, or the message will not be interpreted as the source desires. In actuality, each receiver will interpret symbols somewhat differently because the meaning of each verbal and nonverbal symbol is determined largely by the dimensions of each receiver's perceptual field. It is impossible for any source to be certain that the message will be decoded exactly as it is intended. However, it is possible to control the decoding process in some measure by understanding the norms and frames of reference of the intended receiver and by encoding the message accordingly.

Communication symbols must be suitable for the source, the medium, the intended message, and receivers. The symbols selected should be ones which the intended audience knows and uses.

Words and Sentences

Communicators must choose words carefully. Specific words (apple pie) are better than general words (dessert). Words which refer to objects (shoes) are safer than words which refer to intangible concepts (security). Short words are usually superior to long ones (do vs. accomplish); the same is true of phrases (because vs. for the simple reason that). Every word should be correct; "infer" is often used when the communicator means "imply," "since" is often used for "because." The words in parentheses are unnecessary: consensus (of opinion), (final) outcome, (as a matter of fact).

Even though there are 500,000 to 600,000 words in the English language, the average conversational vocabulary consists of only 2,000. One half of the typical consumer's conversation makes use of only 44 words. Some communication experts recommend that about 75 percent of the communicator's words be of one syllable. Of the 66 words in the Lord's Prayer, 48 (72 percent) are of one syllable. In Lincoln's 268-word Gettysburg Address, 196 (73 percent) are words of one syllable.

A short, direct sentence is easier to understand than a longer, more complex sentence. Familiar nouns, pronouns, and action verbs strengthen sentences and contribute interest.

Wordless Communication in Selling

Salespeople send wordless (nonverbal) communication to buyers and buyers do the same to salespeople; signals flow back and forth continuously. The salesperson must be an expert in both verbal and nonverbal communication. Because most buyers "read" the salesperson's signals, all of these signals should be positive. The salesperson must be sensitive to the buyer's signals, "read" them, and then use them as guides as to what to do and not to do. For a salesperson to ignore or miss a buyer's signals can be fatal to a sale.

These are four examples of buyer-to-salesperson wordless communication:

1. A buyer remains standing at the desk and does not invite the salesperson to sit.
2. A buyer treats the product with care and respect when examining it.
3. A buyer gazes out the window as the salesperson moves into the presentation.
4. A buyer's voice becomes harsh and the facial expression hostile when the name of the salesperson's firm is heard.

Here are four examples of salesperson-to-buyer wordless communications:

1. A door-to-door salesperson takes two steps back as the door is opened.
2. A salesperson makes a totally silent product demonstration.
3. A salesperson's breath, grooming, and dress are not what they should be.
4. A salesperson extends (offers) something for the buyer to take (accept).

The salesperson's wordless communication can be less specific than the examples given. The salesperson's mood or frame of mind is usually sensed by the buyer; it can help or hurt. Interest in and respect for the buyer (or the lack of either) are not easily concealed; the same is true of the desire to help the buyer. General demeanor is an asset or a liability. Above all, the salesperson's attitudes communicate with powerful impact and have much to do with the salesperson's performance.

Five Construction Questions

There are five basic questions which a source (sender) will want to consider in constructing or encoding the selling message. First, the source must decide where the most important idea should be placed. Should the message begin with it? If the idea is placed first, the source is observing the principle of *primacy*. If it is placed last, the source is observing the rule of *recency*. There is no agreement as to which procedure is better. Communication experts do know that the concepts at beginning and end are more likely to be remembered than are those concepts placed in the middle of the message. The more powerful the beginning, the more likely it is that receivers' attention will be gained. The more powerful the ending, the more likely receivers are to recall the message later.

The second question concerns which should be featured, need or answer to need. Unless receivers identify with the need that is being referred to, they will pay little attention to the message; gaining attention is requisite to gaining acceptance and recall of the message. If the communication is to succeed, the receiver must admit to the presence of need and then perceive the source's recommended answer to that need. As far as position within the message is concerned, the statement of need or problem should precede the solution to that need or problem.

What about appeals to fear? Such appeals can be effective in gaining attention, but they can produce an emotion that may cause the receiver to reject either the message or the source. There is some indication that strong appeals to fear are not as successful as less extreme appeals. If an appeal to fear is used, an escape route should be provided for the receiver. This escape route, of course, is the seller's product or service. The effectiveness of the communication will be directly related to how easy the escape route is to implement.

Should the source present just one side of an issue (the source's side), or should both sides be included? Few messages transmitted through nonpersonal channels present both sides of an issue. In personal selling, many salespeople are forced at least to admit their products' limitations, because buyers generally hear the competitor's side, anyway. Some sources present one side only if the audience is friendly and no counterargument is expected, but present both pro's and con's if the audience is hostile. The more capable and informed the audience, the safer is the inclusion of both sides of an issue.

Should selling communications include the conclusions the sender hopes the receiver will draw? Because every promotional communication is intended to produce some response favorable to the source and receivers will sometimes miss some of the source's selling points, the inclination is to include some conclusions. This practice is recommended particularly when the substance of the message is complicated or personal, and when receivers' potential interest is likely to be low.

TRANSMITTING THE MESSAGE

Messages can be transmitted from source to audience through several channels. The salesperson engages in face-to-face conversation with buyers. The advertiser places ads in newspapers, magazines, television, radio, outdoor signs, and transit media. Many sellers also use direct-mail promotion and point-of-purchase promotion. Informal contacts and word-of-mouth exchanges are other forms of communication. No one channel of communication is best universally. Most large sellers use a combination because of the many differences in audiences, objectives, messages, and situations.

Generally speaking, personal channels are most effective when the product involved must be tailored to a customer's needs, when it must be demonstrated, when a trade-in is involved, when the product is costly or infrequently bought, when the seller is small and cannot afford mass advertising, or when the market segment is small. Nonpersonal channels are effective when the product is well known but the customer must be periodically reminded of its availability, the differences between competing brands are slight, the product is inexpensive, a special price concession is being offered, or the statement of a single point of differentiation may influence customers' buying decisions.

RECEIVING AND DECODING THE MESSAGE

Raw data are inputs into the receiver's physiological and psychological systems. The receiver takes note of these data and converts them into concepts, and communication takes place. The receiving and decoding of a message involve three basic questions for the source:

1. Did the intended receiver pay attention to the message?
2. Did the receiver perceive in the communication the same meaning the source built into it?
3. Did the receiver accept and believe the communication?

Selectivity of Attention

There is potential reception of a message when an individual is physically able to receive it through one or more of the five senses. Potential reception becomes actual reception when the message makes contact with one or more of those senses. In an individual's typical sensory environment, various stimuli are always present and bidding for attention. Add a communicator's message, and there is one more competitor to be recognized. At any given moment, one can attend to only a fraction of the stimuli in his or her environment. Thus, the individual exercises power to select those stimuli which will be allowed to reach the senses.

Attention may be either voluntary or involuntary. When one cannot help but notice a gaudy electric spectacular advertising some product, one is giving involuntary attention. Most attention related to selling communication is voluntary, and a person is inclined to attend to messages about matters of interest. A person is also inclined to pay attention to messages consistent with the role of the moment. A couple who are planning their vacation are more likely to be interested in a message about vacation cruises than a message about garden equipment. The best way to gain a receiver's attention is to appeal to needs and wants of the moment.

Perception and Meaning

How the receiver will decode the meaning of a message is a real problem for communicators because communication is not precise. Perceptual fields differ, and perceptual fields determine the meaning of communication symbols.

Symbols have no inherent meaning except that given to them by communicators and their audiences, and concepts often differ from person to person. Adding to the imprecision is the fact that many words have several accepted meanings and slightly different meanings to different persons.

In determining how a receiver decoded a message, three questions must be asked:

1. Did the receiver interpret the symbols in the same way the source did? (Interpretation.)
2. Is the message as reconstructed by the receiver the same as the message constructed by the sender? (Reconstruction.)
3. Is the receiver's understanding of the message content the same as the sender's? (Understanding.)

Unless the answers are affirmative, communication has been faulty.

One barrier to effective communication is a receiver's mental set which, as you have learned, predisposes almost automatic reaction to a certain stimulus. Individuals tend to perceive what they want to perceive and what they expect to perceive. Indeed, of the various determinants of perception, expectancy may well be the most important as far as communication is concerned. Sources cannot determine each individual's mental set; but by understanding the buying behavior of their receivers, they can learn what mental set receivers are likely to have in a given communication situation and can encode their messages accordingly.

Another problem in communicating effectively is the different meaning of symbols, particularly words, to receivers. Every word has its literal or *denotative* meaning and its *connotative* meaning—the emotional meaning that a receiver attaches to a word. In encoding their messages, sources should consider what connotative meanings their word symbols are likely to have and then avoid those words which are likely to have unpleasant connotative meanings. Sources run a risk when they use vague, general words which are open to many interpretations. The broader the classification to which the general word applies, the wider the range of interpretation. The more precise the words used, the more likely the communication is to be decoded as the source intended.

Noise is a real problem in determining whether a message will be received and decoded as the source intended. Anything that interferes with the communication process, that obstructs either sending or receiving, or that distorts the message, is a form of noise. At any given moment, every receiver has many personal concerns demanding attention. The current emotional state of receivers can be a powerful factor; it can encourage them not to question what they want to hear and not to hear what they do not want to hear. In addition to this internal competition, there are competing stimuli of an external nature—the ring of a telephone, appearance of a third party, or malfunctioning, such as static —in the channel of communication. Any competing stimulus which distracts the receiver from the message constitutes noise.

Acceptance and Belief

Exposure and attention to a message are essential to communicating effectively, but they alone are not enough. Perception and meaning are essential, but they are not enough. Also essential are the receiver's acceptance and belief of the message. When the communication effort is successful, the receiver infers that the message is correct and then absorbs the substance of the message so that it becomes an integral part of his or her perceptual field.

How does a person conclude that one communication should be accepted and believed but that another communication should not? First, one must recognize that each person is the product of both heredity and experience. A person tends to believe what is in agreement with this heredity and experience. Belief tends to be founded not so much on reason as on emotion. Also, an individual acts and reacts in the environment in harmony with the mood of the moment. To be accepted and believed, the meaning of the message must be within the receiver's experience and capabilities, and it must be compatible with the receiver's attitudes, circumstances, and self-concept.

Just as individuals tend to see and hear what they want to see and hear, so also do they tend to believe what they want to believe. They will not accept what is true if they believe it to be untrue. This has been demonstrated in advertising; ad illustrations which were true-to-life and realistic were not accepted because consumers thought them too extreme to be possible. On the other hand, let someone offer those same consumers a "free" set of encyclopedias, an "inside" stock market tip, or "irresistible" sex appeal. Those claims are often accepted because most of us want to get something for nothing, to get rich quickly, or to overwhelm the opposite sex.

RESPONSE TO THE MESSAGE

The responses, either overt or covert, that a source hopes to achieve with a message may be a new or increased desire to buy the product or service with which the message is concerned, increased brand preference or brand insistence, or a favorable association of the advertised product with a concept which has selling value. A source wants a receiver to learn from the communication, to be favorably influenced by it, and to recall it for future use. The ultimate response desired is, of course, buying action. Just as attention, perception, and belief are selective, retention is also selective. The individual can keep a concept in the ground of the perceptual field so that it can be recalled, or the concept can be discarded. Obviously, every seller wants the messages to be stored and recalled for later use.

If there is to be a favorable response to a seller's message, the communication must produce tension in the buyer. This tension results because the buyer senses either a threat to self-concept or an opportunity to enhance self-concept.

Buyers feel involved because they identify with a problem or an opportunity. Response of the receiver must be related to and evaluated against the communicator's objectives.

Feedback

In one-way communication, the sender transmits but does not receive, and the audience receives but does no transmitting. A salesperson in a radio or TV commercial is a one-way communicator. In two-way communication, the sender and the receiver exchange ideas. There is action and reaction or transmitting and feedback. Feedback, thus, is communication that flows from the original receiver back to the original communicator. Some feedback is volunteered by the original receiver. Some is initiated unintentionally, such as a facial expression, but can still be interpreted as feedback by the original source. Some feedback is promoted and brought about by the original source. Feedback can be either verbal ("I missed that last point. Will you please repeat it?") or nonverbal (nodding, smiling).

Senders of messages rely on feedback to determine whether they are securing attention, understanding, and acceptance. A salesperson, for example, can use feedback as a continuing indicator of success or failure. The salesperson can present a buyer-benefit, obtain feedback, revise the presentation, obtain feedback to the revision, take further corrective action, and so on. In personal selling, feedback can be instantaneous. The salesperson and buyer are each a sender and a receiver of communication; each generates and uses feedback. In advertising, feedback is delayed and is both difficult to obtain and to interpret.

Response to Hostile Communication

Hostile messages produce internal disharmony and pose a threat to self-concept. Various ways in which an individual may respond to hostile communication are to avoid it, to reject it and the source, or to distort it so that it is interpreted in a way that the communicator did not intend.

An individual can seek to avoid all communications that are transmitted through certain disapproved media, are originated by certain disapproved sources, or are incompatible with self-concept. In theory at least, avoidance can be lasting and complete.

An individual can also reject the medium or the message. Instant rejection is closely akin to avoidance. Prompt rejection may result in the individual's receiving only part of the message or quickly removing the message from the point of focus and replacing it with a more pleasing concept. Or, the individual may absorb the entire message and then reject it.

Another reaction is to find something wrong with the message or deny respectability to the source or medium. A person may claim that the communication was a prank, done with tongue-in-cheek; that the reporter erred and misquoted the source; that the communication does not represent the communicator's true position; that the source or the medium just did not know any better; that receivers were expected to make automatic adjustment for exceptions or overstatements; or that the source was irrational when composing the communication, or at least biased.

In distortion, the receiver recasts the meaning of the message in order to perceive it in a manner consistent with predispositions toward the subject of the message. The receiver who adds interpretations or meanings that were not in the source's message is said to be "sharpening" the message. This is sometimes called *mirage distortion.* The receiver who overlooks or ignores the disagreeable parts of the message is said to be "leveling" the message. This is known as *fog distortion.*

THE COMMUNICATION PROCESS

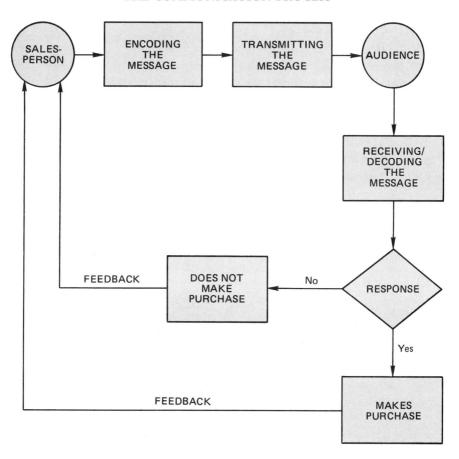

ILLUSTRATION 4-1. Selling is a form of communication.

PROMOTIONAL COMMUNICATION AND THE ADOPTION PROCESS

The *adoption process* is closely related to promotional communication. Sellers' communication, obviously, does not succeed unless buyers adopt (buy) the products and services of those sellers.

Sellers need to know as much as possible about what goes on in buyers' minds. Only by so doing can sellers tailor their communication to the buyers whose patronage they want, thereby maximizing the effectiveness of that communication.

The adoption process as it concerns products is considered to consist of five steps:

1. *Awareness.* The individual becomes informed about a product, but feels no urge to obtain more facts.
2. *Interest.* The individual in the marketplace who now relates need, product, and price, often seeks more information.
3. *Evaluation.* There is speculation about the matter, and the individual wonders if the object involved will really fill the need.
4. *Trial.* The individual decides to try the product, if possible, on a limited scale.
5. *Total adoption or rejection.*

There are five general classes of adopters: innovators, early adopters, early majority adopters, late majority adopters, and late adopters or laggards. Here are some characteristics of each class:

1. *Innovators.* Venturesome and urbane. Have money to risk. Grasp new information quickly. Attracted to change and new experiences. Little influenced by peers and have little influence on group members because they are not in positions of leadership. Some are eccentric. Not over 5 percent of population.
2. *Early adopters.* Many are opinion leaders in various fields. Are among the first to buy when a product becomes available locally. Younger, and have more purchasing power than the next three classes. A bit more cautious about accepting the new and different than are Class 1 members. More education than the next three classes. Their approval is a "must." Not over 15 percent.
3. *Early majority adopters.* Older, with fewer dollars to spend than Class 2 members. Are not opinion leaders. Identify closely with friends and seek their approval. Not over 30 percent.
4. *Late majority adopters.* Cautious, read less, are less inclined to change, older, and have less education. Greater conformers to group norms. Not over 35 percent.

5. *Late adopters or laggards.* Oldest, most skeptical, and least educated. Hold to traditional values and to the past and are suspicious of change and those who favor it. Not over 15 percent.

Now, let's look at the standard product life cycle and see how it fits the adoption process and the classes of adopters. In the first stage, *introduction,* the product's sponsor launches a revolutionary product. There is no awareness at the start, but limited awareness comes somewhat later. The problem is one of generating primary demand. Consumers examine the new product closely concerning basic utility. Because product models or versions are few, consumers' choices are narrow. Advertising and various inducements may be used to promote the item. Competition, sales, and profits are low. Promotion costs may actually exceed sales revenue.

Stage 2 is that of *growth.* Production expands, heavy advertising typically continues, and sales volume increases rapidly. Wholesale and retail distribution grow, and competitors appear. Buyer resistance is still noted, but opinion leaders influence followers.

Stage 3 is *maturity.* Sales continue to increase, but at a slower rate. Brand differentiation begins. Price reductions appear. Profit margin declines because of price cuts. Manufacturers strive to improve their respective products, search for new product uses, and intensify competition. Some attrition of firms appears as marginal sellers drop from competition.

Stage 4 reveals a state of *saturation.* Sales volume reaches a plateau, prices are reduced even more, and the rate of profit drops even more. Manufacturers try to further differentiate their brands, perhaps in the area of packaging.

Stage 5 is that of *decline.* The product that was revolutionary in Stage 1 loses out to better products or to substitute products. Decline may end in abandonment.

SUMMARY

A communication system consists of a sender, a message, a medium, and a receiver. A communication sign, signal, or stimulus is whatever our five senses detect.

The major job of our marketing system is to communicate. Anything that reduces effective communication must be minimized or eliminated. Initially, the buyer views the salesperson as an agent delivering the company's sales message. Over time, the salesperson becomes a source.

Sources of communication are almost limitless. In selling, the objective of sources is to influence attitudes and buying behavior. A promise should be made that buyers' needs will be satisfied. The more credible the source, the more likely the receiver is to believe the message. Trustworthiness and expertness are basic determinants of credibility. Both source and message are influential. Communication can be thought of as a two-part stimulus—a source-message stimulus.

In selling, the audience is the market. The sender should understand the market before sending the message, so the message composed will be optimally effective. Communication efforts are more effective if the total audience is broken down into a number of segments. These market segments are homogeneous within themselves, but different from all other segments. Income, education, age, sex, and social class are a few of the bases used for segmentation.

Encoding is the process by which senders put ideas into a form which they expect the receiver to understand. Communication symbols include words, illustrations, numbers, and sounds. Each symbol must have a commonly understood meaning. Communication symbols must be suitable for the source, the medium, the intended message, and receivers. Words and sentences should be short.

Wordless communication plays an important role in transmitting a sales message. Both buyers and sellers communicate wordlessly, and the salesperson must be expert in this type of communication to be successful.

There are five basic issues a source should consider in constructing a message. These are the placement of the most important idea, the relative importance of need and answer to need, the use of appeals to fear, presenting one or both sides of an issue, and the use of conclusions.

Messages can be transmitted through many media. The salesperson can engage in face-to-face conversation. Advertisers can place ads in newspapers, magazines, television, radio, outdoor signs, and transit media. Direct-mail, point-of-purchase promotion, and word-of-mouth can be effective channels.

Raw data is an input into the receiver's physiological and psychological systems. The receiver notices the data and converts them into understandable concepts. The receiver is selective and may perceive only part of the message. And the receiver may decode the message in a way other than the sender intended. A barrier to effective communication is the receiver's mental set. Individuals tend to perceive what they want and expect to perceive. They also tend to believe what they want to believe.

The source wants the receiver to be favorably influenced by the communication. The ultimate response desired is buying action. Response of the receiver must be evaluated against the communicator's objectives.

Feedback is the process by which the receiver transmits to the sender an indication of acceptance or rejection of the original message. Senders rely on feedback to determine whether they are securing attention, understanding, and acceptance. They can revise a message to improve communication.

Hostile messages produce internal disharmony and pose a threat to the buyer's self-concept. Receivers may avoid or reject a hostile message, or may distort the message, making it more acceptable.

The adoption process has five steps: awareness, interest, evaluation, trial, and total adoption or rejection. There are five classes of adopters: innovators, early adopters, early majority adopters, late majority adopters, and late adopters.

The product life cycle stages are introduction, growth, maturity, saturation, and decline.

REVIEW QUESTIONS

1. List the parts of the simplest communication system.
2. What is a seller's basic job?
3. What are the two determinants of source credibility?
4. What is the sleeper effect where source credibility is concerned?
5. How are market segments determined?
6. What factors make written and oral communication effective?
7. What role does wordless communication play in a sales presentation?
8. What are the five questions to consider in encoding a selling message?
9. What media are most popular for advertising?
10. Why is a receiver's mental set sometimes a barrier to communication?
11. Why is connotative meaning important?
12. What factors are important for acceptance and belief of a message?
13. How do salespeople use feedback to improve their presentations?
14. What are the steps in the adoption process?
15. What are the stages of the life cycle of a typical product?

DISCUSSION QUESTIONS

1. Generally speaking, what kind of adopter are you? Are you an innovator or early adopter with some products and a laggard with others?
2. Relate the classes of adopters and the product life cycle. Which adopters will buy the product at the various stages of the life cycle?
3. Why does the sleeper effect operate when source credibility is concerned?
4. Choose a popular product. What are the factors that are most important in dividing this market?
5. What steps can a message sender take to insure that the receiver is receiving and decoding the same message the sender is transmitting?

CASE STUDY 4A

Barbara McGowan, sales representative for DeLancy Business Forms, Inc., has been assigned a sales territory that includes Washington, Oregon, Idaho, and western Montana. DeLancy is a newcomer in the business forms field, and McGowan is its newest sales representative. DeLancy does very little advertising and relies heavily upon its salespeople to inform prospective customers about its products. The company hopes that its salespeople can sell complete systems rather than just individual forms. The company has no formal training program for its sales personnel. Instead it expects its salespeople to familiarize themselves with the product features and company services.

McGowan's first selling effort is to a large manufacturer of automobile parts. This company, Marshall-Vollman, Inc., is involved in revamping its accounting and bookkeeping system. Unfortunately, McGowan is unaware of this. In fact, she has taken very little time to acquaint herself with Marshall-Vollman's operations or the automotive parts industry as a whole.

McGowan enters the office of Marshall-Vollman and asks to see the chief accountant. Although he usually sees salespeople only by appointment, Hal Maples consents to see her. They meet briefly, and Maples calls Rick Findlay, systems analyst, and asks him to join the meeting.

McGowan emphasizes the low price of her products, their convenient size, their practicality, the color coding used to help the accountant, the ease of ordering, prompt delivery service, and easy credit terms. The meeting is interrupted by several telephone calls for Maples and Findlay and by a visitor looking for Findlay. McGowan tries to point out the merits of each form but fails to present them as a totally integrated system. Maples and Findlay ask several questions, but McGowan senses that their interest is artificial. When she is ready to leave, she offers some sample forms for Maple and Findlay to examine and use. They decline the offer and tell McGowan they will call her after they have better determined their needs.

1. What basic tenet of communication theory did McGowan violate which, had she observed it, might have saved the situation for her?
2. Identify some of the barriers to effective communication in this case, and suggest ways in which they might have been eliminated or reduced.

CASE STUDY 4B

Don Rankin is the newly appointed director of marketing for a new professional soccer team located in a major southern city. The city is a center for financial institutions (banking, insurance), has relatively little heavy industry, and because of its moderate climate and its many good restaurants is a favorite spot for conventions. The inhabitants of the city and its suburbs are relatively diverse. Unemployment is traditionally low and the work force is well paid despite the absence of many unions. There are two major ethnic minorities in the city, one of which has a long history of interest in soccer. Soccer interest has also been growing as a result of the introduction of soccer into the physical education programs of the area schools. One of the local colleges is frequently nationally ranked.

Rankin's job is to build attendance up to 15,000 per game. This means that he is responsible for season-ticket sales, local advertising, promotional events at games, and community and school relations.

1. With what audiences might Rankin try to communicate?
2. What messages should he use to try to reach these audiences?
3. What communication problems is he likely to face?

Chapter 5

Product, Price, and Distribution

After studying this chapter you should be able to:

- Tell what salespeople need to know about their industry and their company

- List what a salesperson should know about terms of sale

- Indicate what product attributes are of great interest to salespeople

- Agree or disagree with the claim that salespeople can know too much about their products

- Answer questions about what information salespeople should have about the distribution system.

One area in which information is essential involves the company for which the salesperson works. Acquiring company facts should include the industry of which the company is a part. Information about the salesperson's company can play an important role and be a basic tool in the selling process. For example, if a prospect has a problem that the salesperson's firm confronted and solved earlier, then the salesperson may be of specific help. A suggestion in such a situation may be instrumental in making a sale.

A second area involves the product behind which the salesperson puts selling effort. Product information is used mainly to show prospects how they will gain by buying. Essential facts here include product research, the terms of sale (prices, discounts, and credit procedures), the physical product (its physical features, brand name, and packaging), the product guarantee, and the service the company supplies to buyers. Salespeople need to know about products other than those they sell, such as other products put out by the company, and, certainly, competing products.

A third area involves distribution systems. The makers of Xerox copiers, Dial soap, Zenith TVs, and the orange growers of Florida all have a common problem—how to get their products to the ultimate consumer. Solving this problem consists of two steps: (1) the producer selects a distribution channel of middlemen through which title to the products moves to ultimate buyers, and

(2) the producer plans a physical distribution system to perform storage and transportation functions.

Salespeople operate on the boundary between buyer and seller. They may also perform some functions that a wholesaler or retailer may be expected to perform.

A knowledge of company policies and procedures, the company's products, and the distribution strategies for those products helps the salesperson. It speeds personal progress; increases confidence, enthusiasm, and professional selling skills; and raises income. This knowledge also has benefits for the company, encouraging higher sales performance, greater loyalty to the company, increased cooperation, and better customer relations.

COMPANY BACKGROUND

A salesperson's advancement will be based largely on ability to produce at a profit, and this ability reflects knowledge and understanding of the company's objectives and methods. The salesperson should also be aware of the company's relationship with the industry as a whole.

The Industry

The salesperson should study the industry of which the company is a unit. The logical starting point would be the beginning of the industry and its evolution. Then the salesperson might branch out into the industry's relationship to and dependence on other industries. Knowledge of current developments, particularly those that are being referred to in various news media, and also the activities of the industry's trade association, will most certainly be in demand by customers. If the nature of the industry is such as to be affected by current legislative proposals or the activities of some outstanding personality, the salesperson can count on being asked for the detailed story.

Many individuals will ask the salesperson about the future of the industry, simply taking for granted that a salesperson connected with the industry is an expert source of information. The salesperson will be expected and encouraged to talk knowledgeably about trends within the industry, and about problems and their solutions.

In certain cases, the size and nature of the industry will be interesting to customers. For instance, the national significance of an industry might be impressive. The number of persons it employs and the volume of its output, both in units and dollars, will interest customers. Likewise, the number of companies making up the industry and the relative rank of the leaders will be essential information. The salesperson will automatically learn who the chief competitors are. The salesperson should also know where his or her company fits into the industry picture (what rank it holds), what rank it has held in the past, and the explanation for its competitive position. Even more important are the reasons why buyers should patronize a company so located within its industry.

Company Features

Three features of the company with which the salesperson should be familiar are: the physical aspects, the financial aspects, and its reputation.

Physical Aspects. Nothing is more basic or necessary than for the salesperson to be informed about the physical makeup of the company. The salesperson must know the various parts that combine to make the complete physical plant and should know what each part looks like. In addition, the salesperson should understand why each of the component parts is needed and how it fits into the broad picture. It may help to know where certain machinery was bought, what it cost, and its principal features. Acquaintance with other facilities and holdings, such as mines, office buildings, ships, trucks, and metropolitan offices, is desirable.

These facts about the physical company are of little value unless they are properly presented to prospects. For instance, size is a most impressive feature about many companies. Size can be expressed in terms of daily consumption of raw materials, amount of floor space, daily output, annual output, number of employees, size of payroll, and extent of dealer representation. Statistics on such matters should be presented in graphic, understandable style.

Financial Aspects. Fiscal topics frequently enter the conversation between salesperson and prospect, and the prospect is only exercising ordinary caution when requesting information about the financial condition of a possible supplier. Because this is a common salesperson-buyer topic, the salesperson must be prepared to answer questions concerning it. There is also a second angle. Potent reasons for the prospect's buying may be found among the financial aspects of the salesperson's firm.

Reputation. A manufacturer's good reputation with wholesalers and retailers may be indicated in various ways. Prominent dealers may be included among the middlemen handling the manufacturer's line. The relationship between the manufacturer and its better customers may have been established quite a long time. If the manufacturer belongs to a trade association that is well recognized and respected in its field, this might be a favorable point. If the company is having no difficulty in adding new dealers to its list of customers, that can speak well for its trade reputation.

The company's standing with ultimate consumers is of greater significance than its trade standing because the public helps influence—and may almost determine—what the trade reaction will be. If the public has passed through the earlier stages of brand recognition and brand acceptance and has moved on into one of the later stages, brand preference or brand insistence, then the manufacturer has solved the most serious problem of reputation. Evidence of continued patronage by the consuming public or proof of increased buying may be emphasized by the salesperson as indicating an excellent standing with the consuming public.

PRODUCT KNOWLEDGE

The salesperson should be familiar with the history of the product being sold, such as significant improvements that have been made in the product. Each type of product knowledge should be sales-oriented, if possible.

Product Research

The two types of product research that are of interest and value to salespeople are manufacturing research and market research. Favorable research results are useful because they can offer evidence that a product is just what the prospect needs and that it is the best quality for the price. When the company uses tested methods and builds up a store of facts over years of research, the salesperson is better able to meet the exact needs and wants of prospects and customers.

Manufacturing Research. The salesperson needs to know the nature of manufacturing research, where it is carried on, under whose supervision, with the use of what facilities, and, above all, with what purposes and results. For example, the company might be experimenting with a new type of machine, a change in manufacturing sequence, other methods of storing raw materials, more complete utilization of fuel, or the use of substitute raw materials. All this information could be of value to a prospect.

Product quality can be improved as a result of a continuous manufacturing research program. Reductions in price can also result. Information on manufacturing research assures prospects that a never-ending study of all manufacturing phases is being made and that operating methods and practices are continually being reviewed.

Market Research. Market research can also make the salesperson's job easier. Examples of market research with product significance include the determination of consumer attitudes toward a product, acceptance of the package, selection of a brand name, and the identification and evaluation of the market for a new product. The salesperson needs information about what research projects the company undertakes, why they are undertaken, and whether the projects are handled by the company or turned over to a commercial research organization. The salesperson should learn as much as possible about the studies that are made, and certainly should learn about the findings.

Statistics are needed on the trend of public thinking and on the thinking of the trade in regard to the product. The salesperson who sells to wholesalers should know what retailers and consumers think; and the salesperson who sells to consumers should know how various types of consumers react.

Market research influences both buyers who use the product and those who resell. Both groups are pleased to know that the manufacturer is making a popular product year after year and that it keeps a sensitive finger on the consumer's pulse.

Terms of Sale

When terms of sale are discussed, each salesperson should be familiar with product prices, allowable discounts, and the credit and collection policies of the company.

Product Prices. Prices are of vital interest to buyers and consequently to salespeople. A salesperson's ideas about prices are significant to the company in making pricing decisions, although salespeople do not establish prices.

The salesperson must justify prices to buyers. If the firm's prices are above the market, the salesperson points to top quality and reminds the prospect that the lowest-priced item is rarely the most economical, that quality is remembered long after price has been forgotten. The salesperson may say that the company, knowing that the quality trade includes the most satisfactory customers, will never sacrifice quality in order to be competitive. If the firm's prices are at the market, the salesperson may point out aspects of the product that are superior to the competitors' product. If the firm's prices are below the market, the salesperson emphasizes economy, volume, and competitive position. The price structure may give the merchant a generous markup that will increase the profits, and the inducement to take advantage of a cash discount may be made irresistible to the buyer.

List Price. List *prices* are published, basic prices. They are found in price lists, advertisements, and sellers' catalogs. List price can be thought of as the highest price on a product because it is often subject to discounts.

List price is of less interest to buyers than is the net cost, delivered, of the salesperson's product and of competing products. The salesperson must recognize that if prices are soundly set, they should be matched by product utility or satisfaction and that the buyer has no grounds to ask for an extra discount. These "extra" discounts reduce profits and incur the wrath of sales managers.

Net Price. When one reduces list price by the discounts applicable, one arrives at the *net price.*

Zone Price. Sometimes a seller divides the total market into a number of geographic areas, such as Southwest and Pacific Coast, and quotes the same price to all buyers within any one area. These are *zone prices.* Because like buyers in a given zone pay the same freight rate, each gets the product at the same delivered cost as every other buyer in that zone.

FOB Price. Much merchandise is sold *FOB (free on board)* shipping point. This means that the buyer pays transportation charges on the goods from a specified shipping point. Goods may also be shipped *FOB destination* (seller pays all charges until goods reach the buyer), *FOB factory* (buyer pays all charges from the seller's place of business), *FOB destination, charges reversed* (buyer pays all charges), or *FOB factory, freight prepaid* (seller pays all charges). It is obvious that FOB terms cause different buyers to have different cost-of-goods figures.

Guaranteed Price. A *guaranteed price* can be a powerful selling point in getting big orders, early orders, or long-term buying contracts. The guarantee is against certain reductions or increases in the seller's prices. A manufacturer might agree to protect a customer on price cuts or increases made after the customer places an order but before the customer takes title to the goods, receives them, uses them, or resells them.

Discounts. Some of the common discounts granted to buyers are quantity discounts, trade discounts, and cash discounts.

Quantity Discounts. *Quantity discounts* are offered to buyers in return for buying in large volume. They encourage buyers to place large orders and discourage hand-to-mouth, small-scale purchasing. Discounts usually are for single orders but may be cumulative, which means that they are applicable to a buyer's purchases for a month or even for a year. Quantity discounts permit a seller to share savings in administrative, production, and marketing costs from volume operation with the customers who make that large-scale operation possible.

Trade Discounts. When a manufacturer sells to different types of middlemen, *trade* or *functional discounts* may be offered. A manufacturer groups buyers according to their position in the distribution channel, according to the jobs or functions they perform. Status of buyer is the key issue, not quantity bought. For example, retailers might be allowed a 33 1/3 percent discount on purchases from the wholesaler, and wholesalers might be allowed a larger discount because they perform an extra distributive function for the manufacturer and must be able to give a discount to the retailer. Discounts for each group are intended to cover the typical buyer's operating costs plus an amount for profit.

Cash Discounts. *Cash discounts* are incentives that the seller offers for prompt payment for merchandise bought. A common base is the invoice date. A common set of terms is 2/10, net 30, meaning that the buyer gets a 2 percent discount on payments made within 10 days from the invoice date and that the net is due in no more than 30 days from the invoice date. Suppose the order totals $100, and the invoice date is August 1. If the buyer pays by August 11, the seller will accept $98 (reflecting a 2 percent discount) as payment in full. Otherwise, the buyer is obligated to pay the full $100 not later than August 31.

Credit and Collection. Every salesperson should understand the fundamentals that underlie sound credit management. Salespeople should comprehend fully the role of the four *C*s—character, capacity, capital, and conditions—and should be familiar with financial statements and credit reports. They should keep informed on how their company feels and what their company does about these matters. The young salesperson should learn the firm's credit and collection policy, and then follow it, and should never override a company decision. In most cases, the company has been operating for years and has no doubt experimented with a variety of credit regulations. The new salesperson is in no position to challenge this background of experience.

A credit policy cannot be sound if it is either too conservative or too liberal. The policy that is too strict may keep bad-debt losses down to a very low figure, but it does so at too great a cost in the form of low sales volume. Conversely, the overly lax policy encourages a large sales volume but at the same time encourages heavy costs. A firm, middle-of-the-road policy maximizes sales and minimizes expenses most satisfactorily.

The salesperson must know credit procedure in its entirety, and it is related closely enough to credit policy to be taken up at this point. The salesperson must know what the credit manager requires prior to the opening of a new account. The salesperson responsible for any part of this first step should understand every detail. In addition, the salesperson should know the credit limit of each customer. It is also necessary to remember just what the company policy is on credit limits for new customers.

As for collection policy, the salesperson first must become acquainted with the collection techniques adopted by the company. The salesperson needs to be able to explain and defend them to customers who, as a result of an unhappy credit experience with the company, hesitate to reopen their accounts. New customers should be informed of collection policy. Detailed instructions should be given to the salesperson if any collecting is to be handled for the home office.

Each salesperson should be impressed with the individual responsibility for helping the company avoid bad-debt losses. The salesperson should help keep the total cost of handling credit at a low figure. It is easy for this expense to grow and take away from net profit.

Product Attributes

The salesperson must be familiar with the physical features of the product being sold as well as brand names, trademarks, and packaging. Then the features of the product must be translated into fulfillment of the buyer's need.

The Physical Product. The salesperson must be able to describe his or her merchandise clearly and adequately. Then the salesperson must translate these features into product benefits. For example, the person selling electric blankets may point out that four new and improved precision resistance elements are used to insure absolute control. The features of an electric blender may be translated into the user-benefits of safety, simplicity of operation, convenience, and dependability of performance.

PRODUCT INFORMATION SHEET

CRICKET - INTRODUCED 1972

#3402

PRODUCT KNOWLEDGE

1. Preferred feminine round shape.

2. Nylon pressure vessel with visible fuel supply.

3. Black, red, and blue male color plus marbleized fashion colors to appeal to all tastes.

4. Easily adjustable for variety of lighting uses.

5. Comfortable actuation.

6. $1.49 suggested retail price.

PRODUCT PERFORMANCE AND ADVANTAGES

1. Gives thousands of sure fire lights.

2. Eliminates need for refilling (flint, fluid, etc.).

3. Easily displayed in any location with self-service package.

4. Last for months.

Source: *Gillette Sales Training Guide*, p. 75.

ILLUSTRATION 5-1. The salesperson must be familiar with the physical product being sold as well as brand names, trademarks, and packaging.

Two final aspects of the physical product concern *type* and *selection*. The salesperson needs to know how each product in the line will perform. The type of product available can be matched to the needs of the customer. This calls for a knowledge of such things as dimensions, capacity, design, and adaptability. Selection refers to choices available to buyers. It involves models, grades, sizes, colors, styles, quantity per package, minimum orders, and dealer assortments.

Brand Names and Trademarks. *Brand names* lend familiarity to the product. They are serious, significant, and costly to establish in the marketplace. Brand names can be comprised of personal names, company names, foreign words, numbers, letters, or coined names. Good brand names are usually short, appropriate to the product, and distinctive. They are easy to pronounce, spell, and remember. They are suitable for all types of promotion and for a family of products. They should not be commonplace or negative in connotation and must not infringe or misrepresent.

The term *trademark* is the official legal designation for brand names as well as for certain symbols and devices used with a product. A trademark can be a word, name, symbol, device, or a combination of these. Coke, Ivory, Ford, and Jello are both brand names and trademarks.

BRAND NAMES

THE ORIGIN OF THE NAME "KODAK"

The origin of the name "Kodak" has run the gamut of human curiosity. Romance, mystery, superstition, legend—all have been in the minds of thousands of persons who have tried to guess the source of the name.

As a matter of fact, there is nothing obscure about it. The word came straight from the mind of George Eastman, who coined it.

In 1888 George Eastman designed the Kodak. The photographic inventor also devised the name for his new instrument—devised it by experimenting with the letters of the alphabet in much the same way in which he was accustomed to trying out the various elements of a camera.

The mental processes that went into the name "Kodak" are quite simple. Mr. Eastman wanted a word which was easily spelled and readily pronounced in English or in a foreign tongue. To that end, he toyed with the letters of the alphabet until he had arranged the since famous combination of consonants that remain constant and vowels that have no greater vagaries of accent than are found between Kent and Kansas.

ILLUSTRATION 5-2. The origin or construction of the brand name may be good for a bit of dialogue between salesperson and prospect. The Eastman Kodak Company says its product was named in this fashion.

Packaging. A salesperson's interest in how the product is packaged is understandable because the package is a competitive and a promotional matter as well as a production matter. The package can have a significant influence on the decision to buy.

The package has three basic functions. It must protect, identify, and promote. All the while, it must not add too much to the selling price. Consumers know what they like and dislike in packages, and the same holds true for retailers.

Company Support of the Product

When, where, and how a company stands behind its products constitutes essential product information. There will be reasonable and unreasonable requests as well as honest and dishonest claims made by buyers who regret something about their purchases.

Product guarantees are one type of company support. Information on guarantees should include the precise terms of the guarantee, the mechanics of handling, and, for the salesperson's own personal knowledge, the strictness with which the company observes the letter of the agreement.

Product service is another type of support. The necessary facts here include the amount, kind, and availability of company service; the details about charges for it; and the time limit for the services.

The handling of defective merchandise is another phase of this subject. Time limits, repairs, credit memorandums, refunds, replacements, proof, and transportation charges are typical of the matters involved.

The salesperson's first duty in these matters is to know what the company's policy is and to make sure that every buyer understands this policy clearly so that friction will not be caused by misinterpretation. The salesperson must also know exactly what areas are covered by personal authority and responsibility. Finally, he or she should transform the company's product support policies into reasons for buying.

Can Salespeople Know Too Much About Products?

Sometimes an informal discussion develops around the question of whether or not a salesperson can know too much about the merchandise. Two pitfalls in this matter must be considered. The first to be avoided is the mistake of overburdening customers with technical data. The second is stressing product features at the expense of user-benefits. Because they are apt to be attracted to and impressed by product features, inexperienced salespeople often spend much time describing them to prospects. Nothing could be more unproductive than unduly stressing product features because nothing is more certain to cause a "so what?" reaction from the prospect. Instead of selling product features, salespeople should sell the product benefits that result from buying. They should not sell insulation, they should sell economy. They should not sell dancing lessons, they should sell social popularity.

The conclusions seem to be that the salesperson cannot know too much about his or her product, and that it is not necessary to memorize every possible product fact. The greatest danger is overburdening the sales talk with so many technical data that the customer is either confused or indifferent.

The salesperson must be familiar with related products produced by the company and competitive products. Knowing the strong and weak points of the competitor's product enables the salesperson to stress the advantages of the product being sold.

Composition of the Product Line. The salesperson should also be familiar with the composition of the product line. If the salesperson happens to work for a manufacturer who makes only spark plugs and markets them only under a single brand name, the line is that one brand of plugs. If the company manufacturers a family of products, the salesperson may benefit from knowing which was the original item, the sequence of additions, and how, when, and why each related item was added to the line.

Related Products. In learning everything possible about what the product will do for its buyers and just how it can be best applied to users' needs, a salesperson frequently must acquire information about complementary or auxiliary products. One who sells vacuum cleaners must know rug construction and types of dirt found in rugs. The salesperson of furniture needs to have a better than casual acquaintance with accessories of various types. Windows should be sold only by an individual who knows something about both architecture and construction.

Competitive Products. Salespeople must know their competitors' products almost as well as they know their own. They must identify and study the outstanding features of competing brands—and their weak points. They must also know about their competitors' market coverage, the customer service they provide, and the prices they charge.

Market Coverage. Every salesperson should know, for his or her territory, the market coverage of each competitive seller. The concept of market coverage includes both geography and buyers. The geographical aspect often involves sales organization (districts, territories) and selling effort (areas getting stronger or weaker sales power). The buyer aspect includes knowing who are the large volume customers of each competitor, the types of buyers given special attention, and the buyers who are neglected. The salesperson needs at least a rough estimate of how the firm and its competitors share the market, how those shares have changed over the last five years, and forecasts of how each major competitor may do over the next five years.

Customer Service. Sellers compete in providing services to their customers. Examples of services include the following:

1. Outstanding knowledge about products and their uses
2. Speedy and satisfactory handling of complaints
3. Quick order handling and delivery by the dates promised
4. Answering buyers' questions fully, accurately, and promptly.

Prices. Competitors' prices are a major concern—sometimes the most perplexing problem—of our salesperson because, in most situations, some competitor is quoting to buyers lower prices than our salesperson's prices. Some competitor mistakenly assumes that quoting the lowest price will result in dominating the market and getting rich almost overnight. Or, a competitive salesperson has authority to quote special discounts or laxer credit terms which put these prices below our salesperson's prices.

THE DISTRIBUTION SYSTEM

Many distribution channels for industrial products and a few distribution channels for consumer products are *direct* channels. The producer deals directly with the industrial purchaser or ultimate consumer. Such direct channels involve no middlemen; the producer and the customer perform all the activities necessary to get the products distributed. These direct channels are possible or necessary in the following situations:

1. When the product for sale is very technical (and the customer requires much assistance in understanding, using, and servicing the product)
2. When the product is expensive to store, handle, or transport (due to bulk, weight, or perishability)
3. When the product and company are exceptionally strong (in items of high brand loyalty, much marketing expertise, etc.)
4. When the selling company wishes to exercise much control over the circumstances in which the product is sold.

When channels are indirect, middlemen are involved. In the traditional distribution channel for consumer goods, a producer sells to a wholesaler who sells to a retailer who sells to the ultimate consumer. Growing more popular with the growth of larger retailers (Sears, Ward, Safeway, Federated Department Stores) are channels that bypass the wholesaler: producers sell direct to retailers who then sell to the ultimate consumer. And there are some channels for consumer goods, particularly those for agricultural products, in which, in addition to a retailer, two or more wholesalers are involved.

A salesperson's task will depend to a great extent on the length of the distribution channel. In a direct channel the salesperson must call upon the ultimate consumer or the industrial purchaser. In longer channels the salesperson may call on retailers or wholesalers.

Let us now look in more detail at the middlemen with whom a salesperson must interact if the channel of distribution is to be an efficient, effective one.

Wholesalers

Wholesaling is selling to buyers for resale (wholesalers, retailers), to producers (manufacturers, farmers, and such), or to institutional users (governments, universities, and such). The U. S. government identifies the major categories of wholesalers. We discuss three major types here: merchant wholesalers, merchandise agents and brokers, and manufacturers' sales branches and offices.

Merchant Wholesalers. Merchant wholesalers take title to the goods they sell. Almost 70 percent of all wholesaling firms are merchant wholesalers. An average merchant wholesaler has sales in excess of a million dollars per year.

There is a class of about 7,000 merchant wholesalers called limited function wholesalers because they do not provide all the services which producers and customers expect of regular merchant wholesalers. For example, drop shippers buy and sell bulky items like coal and construction materials, but they never handle these products physically. Instead, they store the products they've purchased at the producer's plant or warehouse and have them shipped directly to the buyer when one is found. Truck distributors or wagon jobbers deliver small, perishable items (potato chips, bread, beverages, and tobacco products) to supermarkets and grocery stores on a very frequent basis. Truck distributors carry only the amount of inventory that will fit on their trucks and rarely extend credit to their customers.

Merchandise Agents and Brokers. Merchandise agents and brokers are different from merchant wholesalers because they do not take title to the goods they sell. Average sales of an agent or broker are more than double the average sales of a merchant wholesaler. The income of an agent or broker is derived from commissions on sales rather than the difference between selling prices and buying costs. Agents and brokers typically emphasize selling—in fact, they often supplement or substitute for a manufacturer's sales force. But they typically perform very few of the other services that merchant wholesalers provide. Two kinds of merchandise agents perform tasks that a producer's salespeople would normally perform: manufacturers' agents and selling agents.

Manufacturers' Agents or Representatives act as independent salespeople for one or more noncompeting manufacturers in a specified, exclusive territory. Because they usually sell the related products of several manufacturers, they can write orders large enough to allow them to handle many customers to whom a single manufacturer could not afford to sell direct. Although a wide variety of products (groceries, furniture, books, chemicals, steel) is handled by manufacturers' representatives, they are most often used when a company is new and small and cannot afford to hire and train its own sales force, or when a company is selling a new product or in a new market with which it has little previous experience. When manufacturers subsequently decide to hire their own sales force in these situations, manufacturers' agents are often prime candidates for the sales jobs.

Selling Agents. When manufacturers find themselves insufficiently skilled or financed to conduct an effective marketing program, they hire a selling agent to handle the entire marketing program for all their products. Selling agents have such broad responsibilities that they often actually manage the company for which they are supposedly working.

Manufacturers' Sales Branches and Sales Offices.

Manufacturers sometimes establish their own wholesaling operations, especially when suitable middlemen cannot be found or when the potential volume of sales appears likely to lead to large profits. Sales branches carry inventory but sales offices do not.

These manufacturers' outlets are becoming more and more popular because (1) they can sell a manufacturer's products more aggressively than can a wholesaler carrying the products of several manufacturers; (2) they can reduce the time to fill a customer's order; and (3) they can provide better technical service than the wholesaler.

Retailers

Retailers sell to ultimate consumers for personal or household use. The retailers of products in the U. S. range in size from giants such as Sears, Safeway, and Macy's down to retailers with sales of less than $100,000. Although the number of retail establishments has remained fairly constant for many years, many retail stores fail each year and many new ones are established that take their place. This creates a special problem, for the salesperson must be worrying continually about bad debts from defunct retailers and be searching for potential customers among the new firms that spring up.

We will now take a look at several types of retailers and retailer organizations: department stores, supermarkets, discount stores, corporate chains, and contractual chains.

Department Stores.

The Department of Commerce has defined department stores as retail establishments employing 25 or more people and engaged in selling merchandise in each of the following lines: (1) furniture, home furnishings, appliances, radios, and TV sets; (2) a general line of family apparel; (3) household linens and dry goods. About 10,000 establishments fit this definition. Although they number less than 1 percent of the total retail establishments, these stores generate 10 percent of all retail sales volume.

Supermarkets.

A supermarket is basically a large store specializing in groceries and carrying convenience items. Annual sales of $1 million are usually considered the minimum volume for a store to be considered a supermarket.

The 25,000 or so stores which meet this criterion account for almost two-thirds of all grocery sales, about 15 percent of all retail sales.

Supermarkets typically operate on a self-service basis (except, perhaps, in the meat or produce sections) and rarely offer credit or delivery. Because of the large volumes of business they do and the absence of much service, supermarkets take a very small profit margin—often only 1 percent or 2 percent per sales dollar—and sell at low prices.

Discount Stores. A discount store offers merchandise at a lower than normal price. Examples are discount shoe stores, discount furniture outlets, discount department stores, and discount supermarkets. Although there have probably always been stores which sold for less, discount stores did not gain prominence until the 1950s. Now there are national and regional chains of discount stores (Best Products, Gibsons, K Mart, and Woolco), some of which have been started or acquired by traditional retailers.

The growth in discount retailing has had enormous impact on traditional retailing and on manufacturers' marketing policies. Retailers have lowered their profit margins (hardly anyone sells at the suggested list price these days), reduced or eliminated many services, and adopted other tactics of discount retailers. Manufacturers who were initially reluctant to sell through discount stores have had to reevaluate their channels of distribution. Most have discovered that they must sell through discount retailers if they desire widespread distribution for their products. This, of course, has resulted in a new type of customer on whom the manufacturers' salesperson must call.

Corporate Chains. A corporate chain is a group of stores under one ownership. U.S. Bureau of the Census figures suggest that about one-eighth of all retail stores belong to corporate chains operating eleven or more stores. These stores transact about 30 percent of all retail business. They transact a particularly important portion of business in drug stores (one-third of all sales), grocery stores (more than one-half) and general merchandise stores such as department and variety stores (more than three-fourths).

In addition to centralized ownership, corporate chains typically have standardized operating policies in all stores, centralized advertising developed at corporate headquarters, centralized buying for all stores, and centralized management. Most corporate chains bypass the wholesaler and buy direct from the manufacturer. The large size of most corporate chains gives them tremendous buying power and leads to intense competition among sellers who hope to persuade the corporate chain to carry their products.

The importance of corporate chains to the distribution system of many manufacturers has created two distinct types of selling jobs. The first, and therefore most important, task of salespeople for Company B is to convince buyers for a corporate chain to recommend or require that each store carry Company B's brands. The second task is to help each store in the chain to sell as much of Company B's brands as possible. Some firms have one group of salespeople who specialize in the first task—another group who specialize in the second task. For example, Armstrong Cork has a Corporate Market Sales Department whose salespeople call at the headquarters of major department store chains, large building contractors, and so on. Then there are other salespeople, specialists in the types of products they sell (floor and wall coverings, residential ceilings, carpet) who act as consultants to the individual stores in each chain. These salespeople help set up displays, provide advice about advertising, and offer assistance in many other areas of the business.

Contractual Chains. The advantages of corporate chains have resulted in attempts to organize independent retailers into chains that are linked by contract rather than common ownership.

Voluntary Chains. Wholesalers have reacted to the possible loss of business that occurs when corporate chains purchase direct from the manufacturer by persuading independent retailers to join together in voluntary chains. Members of voluntary chains guarantee to buy certain volumes of certain products through the wholesaler forming the chain. In return, they receive lower prices on the merchandise they buy, and operating and marketing help from the wholesaler. The voluntary chain provides the wholesaler with guaranteed customers and, therefore, with significant buying power. IGA Supermarkets, Western Auto Stores, and Walgreen Pharmacies are good examples of large voluntary chains.

Selling to voluntary chains is similar to selling to corporate chains: the salesperson must convince chain headquarters to adopt the product or there is little chance of getting individual stores to carry it.

Retailer Cooperative Chains. Sometimes independent retailers initiate action to improve their buying power. They band together and establish a jointly owned warehousing/wholesaling facility which gives them opportunities for mass purchasing. Over time, the distinction between a voluntary chain and a retailer cooperative often becomes blurred. Usually, however, individual retailers in a retailer cooperative chain maintain their own store names and operating procedures.

Franchise Systems. A franchise is a legal agreement in which a franchisor (usually a manufacturer or service supplier) grants to a franchisee (usually a retailer) the right to sell the franchisor's brand of product or service in a particular location or market area. The franchisor typically promises to supply managerial assistance, a national or regional advertising program, and some portion of the equipment, products, and supplies necessary for doing business. In return, the franchisee agrees (a) to produce or market the product according to procedures established by the franchisor and (b) to pay a franchising fee and, possibly, royalties on the basis of sales or profits.

Franchises of many types have become household words: McDonald's, Kentucky Fried Chicken, Holiday Inn, Hertz, Midas Mufflers, and so on. Most automobile dealerships are franchises; so are soft drink bottlers.

Salespeople and the Distribution System

Physical distribution, or logistics, is the physical flow of goods. Physical distribution management has two goals: (1) to maximize the service provided to customers and (2) to minimize the costs of providing the service. Unfortunately, the better the service the more costly it is likely to be. This often puts the salesperson, who wants to provide rapid, accurate delivery to customers, in conflict with the traffic manager or warehouse manager, who want to use slower, cheaper methods of transportation and materials handling. Thus, it is very important that the salesperson understand the distribution system so that customers can be given the best service possible, and conflicts with physical distribution management can be reduced or eliminated. Furthermore, good service is an excellent talking point for salespeople.

Basic to understanding the distribution system is awareness of what affects the length of the order cycle and a knowledge of storage and transportation, the two basic decision areas which determine physical distribution costs and service.

The Order Cycle. The order cycle is the time that elapses between placement of the order by the buyer and the receipt of the products ordered. If a manufacturer's order cycle is rapid and consistent, customers are happy because they can get the products they need when they need them (and don't have to order long in advance of a possible need). Salespeople and middlemen are happy because it gives them an important edge over their competitors. Finally, rapid and consistent order cycles typically reduce the amount of inventory which must be stored throughout the system.

Three major components of the order cycle are order placement, order processing, and order shipment. Each of these activities takes time, but customers see only the end result. They care very little whether a slowdown or speedup occurs because of one activity or another.

Order Placement. The salesperson influences the order cycle most during the order placement stage because he or she is usually responsible for it. Customers sometimes place their orders directly with the main office, but they ordinarily deal with the salesperson. Therefore, the salesperson's accessibility is very important: the frequency of calls on customers and the ability of customers to reach the salesperson between calls can mean the difference between rapid order placement and a delay. Another important facet of order placement time is how the salesperson handles an order. Orders may be transmitted to the main office or warehouse immediately, or the salesperson may wait until there are enough orders on hand to make a telegram, a telephone call, or a letter worthwhile.

Order Processing. Order processing involves paperwork and the physical assembly and packaging of the order. The main office may need to run credit checks and make credit granting decisions; it must transmit a work order to the warehouse or plant indicating what should be assembled or produced; and it must prepare an accurate invoice so that the customer is properly billed. The salesperson can speed up order processing by making sure that the order form is filled out accurately and completely.

Order Shipment. Order shipment is the transportation of the product from seller to buyer. If a company chooses to use its own transportation system, it must decide what and how many vehicles (trucks, railroad cars, barges) to own and how to schedule their use. If neither the seller nor the buyer provides transportation, a third party enters the picture: a transportation firm (Southern Railway, Flying Tiger Airlines). The customer often specifies the type of transportation preferred and even the company to provide it. The salesperson has an opportunity to help the customer avoid costly and frustrating errors when making that decision.

Distribution Decision Areas. Two important decision areas of physical distribution management are storage and transportation. These areas cannot be managed separately: storage decisions and transportation decisions affect each other. For example, choosing to store a large quantity of a product at a single, centralized warehouse can reduce warehousing and inventory costs, but it can also force a company to use speedier and more expensive modes of transportation to reach far-flung customers quickly. In making decisions in each area, the distribution manager needs to consider their impact on costs and customer service and on other decisions.

Storage. Product storage is needed when demand or supply is uncertain and when demand or supply is seasonal. For example, Macy's does not know how many television sets, shirts, or electric mixers it will sell on a given day; so it buys a quantity large enough to meet expected demand for several weeks or a whole season and stores those products until they are all sold. Heavy equipment manufacturers are dependent on the supply of steel available to them; they stockpile steel when shortages are threatened due to possible strikes in the steel industry.

Three major decisions must be made about product storage:

1. What quantity should be stored? (inventory management)
2. Where should it be stored? (location)
3. Should public or private warehouses be used? (facility)

Inventory Management. Holding large inventories of products helps to provide better customer service, but it also creates costs. Storing inventory ties up capital that might be used elsewhere, requires costly warehousing space, and involves the risk that the inventory will lose some of its value—due to theft, spoilage, or loss of fashion appeal.

The jobs of inventory management are to keep accurate records of the inventory available and to adjust inventories to the point where expected demand can be met satisfactorily at the lowest possible cost. This involves a consideration of inventory carrying costs (warehouse rent, spoilage), setup or ordering costs, the costs of losing sales and customers due to product scarcity, and the speed and consistency of order cycle times.

Location. Warehouse location strategies may be production-oriented or market-oriented. A production-oriented warehouse acts as a collection point for products manufactured at a number of plants. A production-oriented warehouse is used when there are many factories and relatively few (or widely scattered) customers desiring an assortment of goods from the factories. This usually reduces the costs and time taken to fill the customer's order when compared to separate shipments for each type of product.

A market-oriented strategy is used when there are many customers located close together and few supply points. Food wholesalers and supermarket chain store warehouses are usually located close to concentrations of supermarkets so that local store inventories can be quickly replenished.

Public vs. Private Warehouses. Manufacturers, wholesalers, or retailers can decide to build or purchase their own warehouses. Such a decision requires a commitment of money and labor and may be justified if it allows the firm to provide better services or lower costs. Public warehouses offer their services to anyone for a fee based on the volume of goods stored and the length of time for which they are stored. Many companies use private warehouses for normal storage needs and public warehouses for seasonal or unusual storage needs.

Transportation. Transportation decisions initially involve the choice of transportation mode: railroads, trucks, waterways, pipelines, and airplanes. The salesperson should understand the cost and service characteristics of each in order to make realistic delivery promises to customers or advise customers when they specify the transportation mode to be used.

Choosing the lowest-cost or best-service transportation mode depends on the products being shipped and the distances and locations involved. A salesperson should be able to help customers make a wise decision. The salesperson should have some idea of the shipping costs and times from the company's warehouse to each major customer, and know when increased weight and bulk or special handling characteristics makes shifting from one mode to another desirable. It may even be appropriate to use intermodal methods of transportation. Railroads load truck trailers on flat cars (piggyback service) and transport them by rail as far as possible before shifting them to a truck tractor to be delivered to the customer's door. Ships, combined with trucks, offer a similar "fishyback" service.

At various stages in this chapter we have examined how the salesperson's tasks and the firm's distribution strategies affect each other. These relationships can be described in terms of two roles: a boundary role and a substitute role.

The Boundary Role. Salespeople operate on the boundary between buyer and seller. They must meet certain expectations of the seller in order to keep their jobs. They must live up to buyers' expectations in order to keep their customers.

When a producer decides to establish or expand its distribution system, the salesperson has primary responsibility for establishing, maintaining, and improving relationships between the manufacturer and middlemen. The depth of the relationship will depend on the number of accounts the salesperson must service. This, in turn, depends on the type of distribution strategy employed by the manufacturer.

If the manufacturer chooses to use *intensive* distribution to market products (typically convenience goods), it will want to sell through every available, suitable outlet. The salesperson's job becomes one of "getting distribution," that is, seeking out suitable outlets and persuading them to stock the product. The salesperson may have too many accounts to develop a close relationship with any of them, and may call only infrequently—for the purpose of checking quantities in stock and writing new orders.

On the other hand, if the manufacturer uses *exclusive,* or *fairly selective,* distribution—selling through only one or a few outlets in a given market—the salesperson may call on only a few accounts but spend much time with each of them. The salesperson may advise them on local advertising and sales promotional techniques, help in training the retailer or distributor salesperson, or offer aid in operating the business in a profitable manner.

In this boundary role, the salesperson is also responsible for introducing new products. Employers look to salespeople to get adequate distribution for a new product. Middlemen customers look to salespeople for information about new products that can help them improve the profitability of their product lines.

The salesperson's boundary role involves communication about more than new products. As we noted earlier, the salesperson controls the speed and accuracy of the order placement portion of the order cycle. He or she also encourages, gathers, and transmits feedback to the manufacturer about customers' attitudes and practices. This feedback enables the manufacturer to adjust policies and products to meet the challenge of the changing competitive environment, and to cement profitable relationships and dissolve unprofitable ones.

The Substitute Role. A manufacturer's salesperson may perform some functions that a wholesaler or a retailer may be expected to perform. For example, salespeople for manufacturers of tobacco products often call on retailers along with or in lieu of a wholesaler's salesperson. Salespeople for detergent manufacturers deliver, install, and maintain displays and other sales promotional devices in the supermarkets on which they call. This service may even extend to marking prices.

Certain types of selling jobs are direct substitutes for wholesalers or retailers. Manufacturers who distribute their products through door-to-door or in-home selling (Avon, Electrolux, Tupperware) use salespeople in place of retail outlets. A manufacturer's sales office may assume the role of a drop shipper by taking orders from customers and having them shipped direct to customers from a warehouse at some other location. A manufacturer's sales branch may perform practically all the functions of a merchant wholesaler. And we noted earlier that manufacturers often substitute company salespeople for manufacturer's representatives (who are, you remember, independent middlemen) once the manufacturer has successful experience with selling the product in the territory.

SUMMARY

Industry origins, current developments, and future prospects all must be understood if the salesperson is to live up to the title of expert. The salesperson should look at his or her firm and the company's place in the industry. The size of the company, including the facilities and number of employees, is an important physical aspect. Financial condition and the company's reputation must also be considered when studying the business.

Product research includes manufacturing research and market research. Manufacturing research deals with the production process, storage methods, materials used, and product quality. Market research measures consumers' attitudes, product acceptance, and new product possibilities. Salespeople must know what the manufacturer, wholesalers, retailers, and ultimate consumers are thinking so that they can interact effectively with each group.

Prices are extremely important to buyers and salespeople. Although salespeople have little control over pricing, they must deal with the prices established for them by management. Depending upon the price, the salesperson has to emphasize quality or economy.

There are a number of different prices for a product. List prices are published, basic prices. Net price is list price minus discounts. Zone prices are prices established by a seller for a given geographic area. FOB price indicates who pays shipping costs. A guaranteed price protects a customer against price cuts or increases made after the customer places an order but before the customer receives the goods.

Quantity discounts are offered to buyers in return for buying in large volume. Trade discounts are given to middlemen according to their position. Cash discounts are used as an incentive for buyers to pay promptly.

Character, capacity, capital, and conditions are the four *C*s of credit management. Credit policies should be neither too liberal nor too conservative. Salespeople must be concerned with credit management because they are responsible for helping their company limit bad-debt losses.

Salespeople must be very familiar with their products' physical attributes, brand names and trademarks, and packaging. The salesperson must know the product's features, the types and selection offered, and the needs each satisfies.

Brand names lend familiarity to a product. Good brand names are short and catchy. Trademark is the offical legal designation for brand names as well as for certain symbols and devices used with a product.

Packages protect, identify, and promote products. Salespeople must know how the product is packaged because the package plays an important role in selling the product.

The company's support of its products is vital product information. Guarantees, product service, and the handling of defective merchandise are elements of company support of a product. The salesperson must know all the details and make sure that the buyer is familiar with the company policy.

Salespeople cannot know too much about the products they sell. But they must be careful not to overburden customers with technical data. Also, the salesperson must not stress product features at the expense of user-benefits.

Product line composition and related product information are important areas of study for salespeople. The salesperson must know how his or her products relate to each other and to other products. Salespeople must also be familiar with their competitors' products, identifying the strengths and weaknesses of those products in order to give a sales presentation that will show off their own product in the best possible light. Market coverage, customer service, and prices are three important areas of concern here.

Product distribution channels can be either direct or indirect. Direct channels occur when the producer deals directly with the industrial purchaser or ultimate consumer. Indirect channels occur when middlemen are involved. Wholesalers and retailers are middlemen.

Wholesaling is selling to buyers for resale, to producers, or to institutional users. Merchant wholesalers, the largest class of wholesalers, take title to the goods they sell. Their sales average over a million dollars per year. Merchandise agents and brokers never take title to the goods they sell. Instead they earn commissions on their sales. Manufacturers' agents act as independent salespeople for manufacturers in a specified area. They are used by new and small companies that cannot afford to hire and train their own sales forces. Selling agents conduct an entire marketing program for manufacturers who for some reason cannot conduct an effective marketing program for themselves. Manufacturers' sales branches and offices are wholesale operations set up by manufacturers.

Retailers sell to ultimate consumers. They range in size from giants like Sears to small businesses selling less than $100,000 annually. Department stores sell furniture, apparel, and household dry goods. They are usually very large.

Supermarkets are large stores specializing in groceries and carrying convenience items. They usually operate on a self-service basis. Discount stores offer merchandise at low prices. In recent years, their growth has been great, and this has had an impact on traditional retailers.

Corporate chains are groups of stores under one ownership. They are important in drug stores, grocery stores, and general merchandise stores. Corporate chain stores have standardized operating policies. They often bypass the wholesaler and buy direct from the manufacturer. Contractual chains are the result of independent retailers joining together to gain the advantages of chain ownership. Voluntary chains guarantee to buy certain volumes of certain products, and in return they pay lower prices to the wholesaler forming the chain. Retailer cooperative chains are independent retailers banding together to improve their buying power. Franchises are legal agreements in which a franchisor grants to a retailer the right to sell the franchisor's brand in a particular area.

Physical distribution is the actual flow of goods. Maximized customer service and minimized costs are the goals of physical distribution management.

The order cycle is the time that elapses between placement of the order by the buyer and receipt of the products ordered. Order placement, the first step, is influenced directly by the salesperson. The salesperson is the one usually responsible for gaining that order and transmitting it to the main office or warehouse. Order processing involves paperwork and the assembly and packaging of the order. Order shipment is the transportation of the product from seller to buyer.

Storage and transportation are of concern to physical distribution managers. The quantity of items stored, storage location, and type of facility used are the three major storage decisions. Transportation decisions involve the choice of the mode of transportation.

Salespeople operate on the boundary between buyer and seller. They are responsible for establishing, maintaining, and improving relationships between the two. The manufacturer's decision to use intensive versus exclusive distribution affects the salesperson's ability to spend enough time with customers to establish a close working relationship. Intensive distribution is used when the manufacturer sells through every available, suitable outlet. Exclusive distribution occurs when only one or a few outlets are sought in each area.

Manufacturers' salespeople may perform some functions that wholesalers or retailers usually perform. They may maintain displays and mark prices. Manufacturers who distribute their products through door-to-door selling use salespeople in place of retail outlets.

REVIEW QUESTIONS

1. What industry characteristics should be understood by salespeople?
2. Which is more important: reputation with consumers, or trade reputation? Why?
3. What is the difference between list price and net price?

4. What does FOB mean? Why is it important?
5. Why are quantity discounts given?
6. What is the purpose of a cash discount?
7. Why must salespeople be attuned to credit and collection issues?
8. What is a trademark?
9. How do merchant wholesalers and merchandise agents differ?
10. Why have manufacturers set up sales branches and offices?
11. How has the growth in popularity of discount stores influenced other retailers?
12. Why are voluntary and retailer cooperative chains organized?
13. What is a franchise?
14. How do salespeople influence the order cycle?
15. List the three major product storage decisions.
16. What are the different responsibilities of salespeople under intensive versus exclusive distribution?
17. How do salespeople act as substitutes for wholesalers and retailers?

DISCUSSION QUESTIONS

1. Why do people care about the seller's financial condition?
2. How can a thorough understanding of the manufacturer's reputation be used to advantage by a salesperson?
3. Why are brand names and trademarks carefully protected by their owners?
4. Give three examples of department stores, discount stores, corporate chains, and franchises.
5. Why do some manufacturers use intensive distribution while others use exclusive distribution? List three products distributed with each method.

CASE STUDY 5A

Sam Rubley was the owner and chief production official of a small plant. Rubley tinkered in his spare time, often coming up with innovations of genuine utility. He was an avid sports fan who hated to sit on bleachers when viewing sports events. Rubley did not care for splinters, dirt, stains, dampness, and the discomfort of sitting for long periods of time with his back unsupported. Deciding to do something about this, Rubley went to work designing a portable stadium seat. He and some of his friends experimented, tested, and improved this seat until it seemed ready to be marketed.

Rubley decided that he himself should make the first sales call because the product had been his brainchild from the start; consequently, he knew more about it than anyone else. He selected his state university as his first prospect and decided that the man who managed the football stadium concessions was the individual to see. The university had a well-known football team and a stadium which seated 65,000. Rubley made an appointment for August 2nd.

Rubley entered the office at the appointed time.

Salesperson:	Good morning, Mr. Cruz. I'm Sam Rubley of Rubley Company. You were good enough to clear a little time for me.
Prospect:	I'm glad to meet you. What's on your mind?
Salesperson:	I have an item you should have in your concession stands here at the stadium.
Prospect:	As crowded as we get, I don't know where we'd put it. What is it?
Salesperson:	(Hands a seat to Cruz.) It's a portable stadium seat. Just the thing in a stadium where the bleachers don't have backs. We call it The Seat.
Prospect:	That gadget doesn't look substantial to me.
Salesperson:	Mr. Cruz, let me tell you about this stadium seat. I know it's good because I happen to have invented it. The Seat has a back and a bottom of high-quality plastic. There are no sides, but when the user sits down, his weight causes the seat to mold to his back. Unique slits along the edges allow the seat to give and fit. Feel how light it is. See how small and compact it is. That special clasp keeps it closed and those finger holes make it easy to carry. The thin layer of foam rubber on the bottom makes sitting more comfortable. Special glue holds the layers together. Two strips of plastic prevent the seat from opening beyond 90 degrees. These strips have been tested and found to withstand 500 pounds pressure. A total of 15 patents cover The Seat, so you will not be seeing it duplicated. Each shipping case contains 50 seats and opens into an attractive display case. I'm sure you want to know about prices. The spectator pays $6 for The Seat. Your cost is $142.50 for a case of 50, plus transportation and handling charges of $7.50 per case; so, you gross $300 minus $150, which is $150. You can give vendors 15% ($45 on $300) and net $105.00 per case. If you like, we can print your school insignia on the back at a low cost. Well, Mr. Cruz, that's about it. Your first home game, I believe, is on September 30th. How many cases do you want here by then?
Prospect:	Not so fast, Rubley. I don't think that flimsy thing will sell well enough for us to stock it.
Salesperson:	If you sold 10 cases on September 30th, you'd net $1,050. At $6 each, The Seat will sell like hotcakes. Spectators are in a frame of mind to make impulse purchases at football games. They will be eager for something that will prevent tired backs and dirty clothes. Why don't I put you down for 10 cases on this first order?
Prospect:	What do you want me to do with my rental seats?
Salesperson:	Rental seats? What rental seats?

Prospect:	I've got a lot of money invested in the fabric-and-metal rod seats I rent to spectators. I get $3.00 an afternoon for each one rented.
Salesperson:	I'll bet they are rusty, weather-beaten, and dirty. They can't be as attractive as The Seat, and they certainly can't be as well designed. I ought to know—I designed The Seat.
Prospect:	If you can figure out something about my rental seats, give me a call. I'm due downstairs at once.
Salesperson:	I see. Thanks for your time.

Why did Rubley fail to make the sale?

CASE STUDY 5B

Jeff Andrews is a sales engineer for Baxter Metal Products Company, manufacturer of stock and custom metal parts for industry. Baxter has been in business for more than 100 years. Its founder was a blacksmith who diversified his business by making replacement parts for the new machines that were being manufactured then for the first time (the steam engine, the reaper).

Andrews has just discovered that he has lost a major customer—a customer whose orders have averaged over $50,000 annually for the three years that Andrews has serviced the account.

When Andrews calls the purchasing agent to find out why the customer has stopped buying from Baxter, the purchasing agent doesn't hesitate: "I'll be quite frank. Jackson Metal parts quoted me a lower price and I couldn't afford to pass it up. After all, your products and theirs are just about the same quality."

As Andrews thought about ways to regain a competitive advantage, he recognized that improvements in Baxter's distribution customer service (delivery time, etc.) might help to counteract the effects of Jackson's lower price.

1. What changes could Baxter make that might improve distribution customer service?
2. What changes in distribution methods could be made that would allow Andrews to quote lower prices (because of lower costs)?

Chapter

The Promotion Program

6

After studying this chapter you should be able to:

- Tell what advertising is and identify the groups engaged in advertising

- Give some ideas of what ad managers do

- Suggest how salespeople can benefit from the advertising their firms do

- Contrast sales promotion for dealers with sales promotion for ultimate consumers

- Describe the elements in a promotion program

There are three *direct promotional forces* available to sellers. The first, *personal selling,* is the subject of this book. Personal selling is a "push" technique, pushing a manufacturer's products down through the distribution channel.

The second direct promotional force is *advertising.* Manufacturers may direct some of their advertising to their wholesalers and retailers. They may direct some to certain professional groups (architects, dentists) whose members influence certain purchases. Most advertising, however, is addressed to ultimate consumers. Advertising is a "pull" technique, urging consumers to ask for and buy advertised brands, pulling those brands down through their channels of distribution.

The third direct promotional force consists of a group of auxiliary activities labeled *sales promotion.* This includes the coordination of personal selling and advertising. Sales promotion can influence retailers and stimulate the purchase of the manufacturer's products by ultimate consumers.

Publicity is an *indirect promotional force.* There are two types of publicity: (1) information about a firm or product considered news by communication media and reported by them to the public at no charge, and (2) two or more persons conversing about a seller or the seller's product.

Personal selling, advertising, sales promotion, and publicity are the only forces of which promotional programs or mixes can be built. Each seller faces the challenging problem of combining them in what will be the most profitable promotion program. Most medium and large sellers of consumer products include all four promotional forces. They talk individually with certain buyers through their salespeople, communicate impersonally with large groups of buyers through their ads, use the amounts and types of sales promotion they deem desirable, and build publicity schedules to appear in media.

Promotion programs must be planned. Management sets up goals or objectives, the major ones involving sales, share of market, and profit. Management next develops strategies of attaining its goals. Time, effort, dollars, and personnel are budgeted. The result is the promotion mix of the firm.

ADVERTISING BASICS

Advertising is the mass communication of a promise of satisfaction. Advertising is both informative and persuasive. The content of advertisements should give buyers the facts about buyer-benefits which will help them make better buying decisions.

Advertising is a form of communication which can tell a seller's story to millions of consumers quickly. Because advertising is mass communication, the low cost-per-buyer-impression makes it quite economical. Advertising is uniform communication, being under the rigid control of the advertiser and not subject to revision without the advertiser's consent. Because advertising is impersonal communication, it is much more easily ignored than is a salesperson.

The characteristics of advertising make its most logical assignment that of preselling. When a manufacturer's advertising presells middlemen on products, salespeople actually have an easier job in selling to those middlemen. When the manufacturer's advertising presells consumers, the selling done by retailers is made easier. In preselling, advertising introduces products and their manufacturers to buyers. In subsequent contacts, buyers recognize the products, their names, and the names of their manufacturers. If this recognition is favorable, buyers will often buy one of the items when that purchase is recommended by a retail salesperson, suggested by a friend, or when the product is seen in another advertisement.

Because of its limitations, advertising is seldom asked to complete sales to buyers. Advertising suffers from the absence of personal contact and the impact of a salesperson's personality.

Groups Involved in Advertising

There are four major segments involved in the advertising process: advertisers, buyers, media, and advertising agencies.

Advertisers. This chapter will emphasize the manufacturer as an advertiser. Of course, many of the principles and techniques of creating effective advertising apply equally to retailers. For manufacturers of such consumer items as soap, cereals, beverages, and automobiles, the typical promotion mix is one that directs advertising to ultimate consumers and sends salespeople to wholesalers and retailers. Manufacturers of industrial products and sellers of industrial services usually direct advertising and personal selling efforts to the same buyers.

Buyers. Within the ultimate consumer group of buyers, the advertiser recognizes three types of consumer. One consists of persons who do not consume the advertiser's kind of product. A thin person would not use a weight loss product. A second type is composed of people who use the advertiser's kind of product but who buy competitors' brands. Included in the third type are those who buy the advertiser's brand but do not buy as much as the advertiser might wish. Advertisements are constructed and transmitted with these three types in mind.

Media. Advertising media are the third segment involved in the advertising process. Four of these media sell space and use print promotion through newspapers, magazines, outdoor billboards, and the public transit system, such as space in buses and subways. The other two media sell time. Radio broadcasts verbal promotion and television combines verbal and visual promotion.

Advertising agencies. Advertising agencies are the fourth segment involved in the advertising process. These specialized firms have two principal functions: (1) to build effective advertisements for their clients, the most typical of whom are manufacturers of consumer goods, and (2) to contract with advertising media to transmit these ads.

Types of Advertising

Three common classifications of advertising are primary advertising versus selective advertising, brand advertising versus institutional advertising, and direct-action advertising versus indirect-action advertising.

Primary and Selective Advertising. Primary demand is the demand for a type or class of product or service, such as wine, leather, insurance, or investment counseling. Primary advertising promotes a generic product or service, not any one brand. Seldom does a salesperson's company engage, by itself, in primary advertising. Instead, the typical sponsor of primary advertising is an industry trade association—a group of competitors who unite in the hope of achieving something beneficial to the entire industry. For example, the Institute of Life Insurance can advertise life insurance in general and thereby aid the promotional efforts of individual companies such as Prudential, Metropolitan, and New York Life. Such a primary advertising campaign is sometimes called a horizontal cooperative campaign.

The individual seller is concerned mainly with the stimulation of selective demand. The seller wants consumers to buy a particular brand within a broad class of products. Whereas primary demand determines total market, selective demand determines each competing seller's share of the market. To each seller, the selective demand for a particular brand is a segment of the primary demand. Most salespeople are more concerned with selective demand and selective advertising than they are with primary demand and primary advertising.

Brand and Institutional Advertising. Product-promoting or brand advertising seeks to promote the sales of a specific brand; thus, it is essentially the same as selective advertising. Brand advertising tries to differentiate a particular brand from other similar brands and to endow that brand with a favorable image. A brand image is the consumer's impression and evaluation of a certain branded product.

Institutional advertising does for the company what promotional advertising does for the brand. It attempts to endow the firm with a favorable corporate image. Corporate image is the buyer's picture of the character and personality of that corporation. There are three types of institutional advertising: that of a patronage nature, that of a public relations nature, and that of a public service nature. Institutional advertising of a patronage nature hopes to establish the company as the preferred source of the types of products or services it sells. Institutional advertising of a public relations nature is used by a company to improve or maintain relationships between the company and prospects, customers, competitors, suppliers, middlemen, employees, suppliers of capital, and government. Institutional advertising of a public service nature promotes the public welfare. Companies use it to publicize health, savings, safety, conservation, security, education, and so on.

Direct-Action Advertising and Indirect-Action Advertising. Some advertising tries to stimulate immediate response on the part of the buyer. An advertisement containing an inquiry coupon is an example of direct-action advertisement. Few manufacturers who maintain capable sales forces use direct-action advertising, but much retail advertising is of this type. Advertisements try to persuade consumers to visit the store promptly to look for or buy some specific merchandise.

Most salespeople work for firms whose advertising is mainly of the indirect-action type. This advertising has long-range goals; it wants to influence buyer attitudes rather than stimulate immediate action. Most television and magazine advertisements are indirect in nature. They encourage the development of respect for and confidence in a certain product. Of course, the advertiser hopes eventually for buying action brought about because of the influences attitudes have on action.

ADVERTISING MANAGEMENT

Advertising management includes working with the advertising organization in advertising campaigns, scheduling, budgeting, and evaluating advertising.

Advertising Organization

A company's advertising may be managed by the firm's own advertising department, by an outside advertising agency, or by a combination of the two.

Advertising Departments. Many advertising departments engage in marketing research, particularly in advertising research. All departments must do certain recordkeeping. All should check the appearance of scheduled ads. All need to learn what can be learned through contacts with outside advertising firms.

What do ad managers do? That depends on whether they are actually part of top management or mere figureheads. They should formulate advertising policy; translate ad strategy into an ad budget and program; evaluate ad performance; help select, then work with ad agencies; keep management informed about advertising matters; and build and administer a sound advertising department.

Advertising Agencies. An advertising agency is a group of advertising specialists plus marketing, merchandising, public relations, communication, behavioral, and allied specialists. Its business is advertising. Advertisers (usually called *clients* or *accounts*) patronize agencies.

Very briefly, agencies study their clients' advertising needs, draft and recommend ad programs, build the ads, schedule the ads, and contract with the advertising media to transmit those ads. Of the dozen or so departments in the typical agency, the *copy, art,* and *media* departments are clearly the basic creative ones.

The Campaign Concept

The salesperson of a manufacturer who advertises needs to be acquainted with the firm's advertising campaigns because they can be presented to buyers to advantage, and because buyers will ask about them. A campaign is a planned, orderly, unified series of ads. It has its own theme and objective. The ads look or sound similar through intent. They start on a certain date and end on a certain date. Campaigns vary in length. Salespeople need acquaintance with two types.

Brand campaigns encourage the purchase of specific brands. The substance of these campaigns is the satisfaction, the buyer benefit, which the advertiser promises. A second type of campaign is the *corporate* campaign, also known as an institutional campaign. This campaign promotes the advertiser, not the brand. Either type of campaign can be directed toward trade customers (wholesalers, retailers) or users (ultimate consumers, industrial customers).

Scheduling

Reach is coverage. Reach is the number of buyers "reached" by ads during a certain period of time. The advertiser obviously wants to reach 100% of the audience it hopes to persuade and influence.

Frequency is the number of ads run during a certain period of time. Radio is probably the medium offering the highest potential frequency. Just as advertisers want complete coverage, most if not all feel that high frequency is desirable. There is an inevitable trade-off between the two.

Budgeting

Many times the manufacturer's salespeople are asked how much their firm is spending on advertising. Some of their customers chide them about how small that figure is—others about how large it is. How do advertisers determine how much to spend for advertising next year?

There are two basic approaches. In the *percent-of-sales* approach, the advertiser estimates next year's net sales, picks a multiplier (perhaps 3%), multiplies one by the other, and has the amount of the ad budget. The other basic approach is the *task* approach. Here again the advertiser estimates next year's net sales. Next, the advertiser estimates the task of advertising in the attainment of that forecast. In the third step, the advertiser estimates the cost of an advertising program that will perform that task. Ad budgets must be broken down by sales territory, product, ad medium, and time period.

Evaluation

Checklists are a type of *pretest* evaluation. A list is built of the values an ad should have—attention value, conviction value, memory value, and such. Proposed ads are checked against the list and scored. If an ad is weak on attention value, then back it goes for revision. *Consumer juries* pretest ads. A sample of representative buyers looks at proposed ads and says what's good and bad about them.

Concurrent evaluation is best known in the broadcast field. Telephone calls are made to a sample, say, between 8 p.m. and 8:30 p.m. to learn if the TV is on and, if so, to what station. Commercial firms do this research.

Readership studies are a *posttest*. The number of inquiries received, samples requested, contest entries received, or incoming telephone calls are posttests. Without any question, the greatest handicap in all advertising is the absence of a measure which will tell what an advertiser's ads do to sales.

ADVERTISING AND PERSONAL SELLING

Advertising and personal selling can each contribute significantly to the more effective functioning of the other. As was mentioned earlier, advertising can presell merchandise and stimulate demand for the products the salesperson sells. Advertising that invites inquiries from interested buyers can also locate prospects for salespeople. Advertising helps to keep sales in balance, whether the problem of balance is among products, types of buyers, markets, or seasons of the year.

Good advertising, then, does a superb job of increasing a salesperson's sales power. Because advertising can build buyer's confidence in the salesperson and can endow a product with prestige, the results are more sales interviews, shorter interviews, and more successful interviews. Advertising makes for stronger sales presentations because salespeople get both facts and ideas from their company's advertisements. The presentations sound stronger to the buyer because points which were seen are now heard from the salesperson. A final way in which advertising increases sales power is to help keep customers sold between the salesperson's calls. The advertising that buyers see during these intervals reduces the chance of the salesperson's being forgotten.

In return, advertising efforts can be aided by the sales manager and staff. First of all, the sales force helps stock wholesalers and retailers before an advertising campaign breaks. The sales staff can also provide feedback information that keeps the company's advertising slanted in the proper direction. Salespeople are often in a position to supply some of the raw materials from which advertisements are fashioned—case histories, experiences, testimonials, and product information not previously known by the company.

"Selling" Advertising Policy to Middlemen

A salesperson has an obligation to understand the company's advertising policy and to be able to make a creditable case for it. Obviously, the salesperson's company can adopt one of two general policies: it can do no advertising, or it can incorporate that activity into its promotion program. Salespeople for manufacturers who do not advertise usually contrast their products with advertised products of higher price and comparable quality. These salespeople will stress that their lower prices permit wholesalers and retailers to sell the unadvertised lines at lower prices than they can sell the advertised lines, and that dealers will have greater freedom in pricing the merchandise and avoiding price wars.

If the company *does* advertise, the salesperson will stress that advertising builds consumer demand for the product. Concerning dealer sales, the salesperson will stress high turnover and ease of selling because the manufacturer has presold the merchandise through advertising. The salesperson will point out that markdowns, dealer advertising expenses, and inventory can be reduced as a result of the manufacturer's advertising. These reduced expenses can mean greater profits for the middleman.

Cashing in on the Firm's Advertising

There are many ways for a salesperson to cash in on the advertising the company does. Here are some examples:

1. Read the ads so as to know what the firm is saying.
2. Make the same points and promises to buyers.
3. Help retailers buy and promote more profitably.

Salespeople using reprints may do one or more of the following:

1. Write a buyer's name at the top of the reprint; continue with a request for an appointment; staple a business card and a small photo at the bottom; and mail the reprint.
2. Use the reprint instead of a business card, or attach a reprint to a business card when calling.
3. Show the reprint as well as tell about the ad. Many buyers accept the written word as authoritative.
4. Use reprints as visual aids in presentation. Select the best ad to dramatize and prove each sales point.
5. Attach a reprint to a thank you note.
6. Use reprints as reminders. Leave reprints with buyers after the call, or mail reprints to buyers between calls.

ILLUSTRATION 6-1. Reprints of ads may be used in many ways. A few of those ways are listed in this illustration.

4. Show each retailer the ad schedule for the coming season and copies of the ads to appear. Tell each retailer which ads will run in its market.
5. Use the ad program to create and reinforce brand image; the program has prestige value.
6. Use responses to coupon ads as a source of potential prospects. A salesperson can clip prospect P's coupon to his or her business card when calling on P.
7. When calling on the most desirable prospective buyers, take (and then leave) a copy of the magazines containing the ad.
8. Use reprints of ads. See the examples in Illustration 6–1.

SALES PROMOTION BASICS

Any element of a promotion program other than personal selling, advertising, or publicity is properly considered to be *sales promotion.* Some forms of sales promotion try to stimulate ultimate consumers; some try to persuade retailers to buy and sell a manufacturer's products in greater volume. One estimate is that about 40 billion dollars are spent each year for sales promotion activities.

Sales promotion should not be viewed as replacing or substituting for either advertising or personal selling. Instead, it supplements them and makes them more effective. Most manufacturers promote their products with salespeople and advertisements year after year, but many sales promotion activities are short-lived. Examples include a World Fair or State Fair exhibit, distribution of samples of a new product, one-cent sales, and sweepstakes. Sellers who use sales promotions almost always rely heavily on personal selling, or advertising, or both.

The Uses of Sales Promotion

The sales promotion area is much less simple and unified than is personal selling or advertising. Actually, the term is defined by different sellers in different ways. That fact is clear when one reads the description of sales promotion of the American Marketing Association, "those marketing activities, other than personal selling, advertising, and publicity, that stimulate consumer purchasing and dealer effectiveness, such as display, shows and exhibitions, demonstrations, and various nonrecurrent selling efforts not in the ordinary routine."

Sales promotion is part of a seller's overall promotion program. It is persuasive communication intended to influence buyers. Sales promotion offers prospects an additional reason for buying the product the seller is promoting. It suggests to middlemen, especially to retailers, that they buy and promote the manufacturer's product. It suggests to ultimate consumers (sometimes to purchasing agents) that they examine and try the manufacturer's brand. If successful, a sales promotion can get some habitual users of other brands to test, now, a different brand.

Sales promotion can be used in an aggressive manner when a new product is put in the marketplace. It can be used to respond when competitors are promoting their brands vigorously, and the seller feels the need to do something about their promotion. The increase of self-service in retail stores has encouraged manufacturers to resort to more sales promotion.

Some buyers may be encouraged to buy a new type of product (an electric toothbrush, for example) and, of course, the promoter's brand. If the trial is a happy one, repeat purchases are probable. Buyers may buy more of a satisfactory brand than they did in the past. This can be true if the seller shows that the item can be used in various ways. Sales promotions can back up and strengthen what the seller's salespeople and ads claim.

Sales promotion techniques can influence retailers to begin carrying and selling a manufacturer's brand. They can do what's known as *loading*, urging wholesalers and retailers to buy and stock more than they have in the past. Some promotions aim to increase the number of ultimate consumers in stores and their purchases. Some may get for a manufacturer more or better display in a retailer's store.

Sales Promotion for Dealers

One area of sales promotion consists of certain relationships between a manufacturer and the middlemen, especially retailers. In selling, there are problems, questions, and activities for which neither the sales manager nor the advertising manager should be responsible. Good working relationships with middlemen contribute so much to the company's overall promotion program that they must be given serious attention by someone, and this function falls to sales promotion personnel.

A manufacturer's promotion program for dealers must be merchandised; salespeople must "sell" dealers on the sales promotion techniques the manufacturer uses. Well before the start of the next year, the manufacturer explains the upcoming promotion program to the salespeople. The sales promotion manager takes pains to see that the salespeople know how advertising and sales promotion activities contribute to the total sales effort and that they know what techniques to use in "selling" the firm's promotional program to dealers. The sales meeting is the vehicle commonly used for this project.

Direct-Mail Promotion. Direct-mail promotion consists of sales letters, cards, folders, circulars, booklets, broadsides, and catalogs sent by the manufacturer directly to buyers. The bulk of a manufacturer's direct-mail promotion is aimed at middlemen, so it makes sense to assign this type of promotion to the department in charge of dealer relations. Some of the possible achievements of direct-mail promotion are:

1. It can locate prospects.
2. It can send precall information to buyers or request it of them.
3. It can be used to make appointments.
4. It is useful in following up a salesperson's call and in maintaining contact with buyers between calls.
5. It helps keep the goodwill of customers and helps keep them sold on the manufacturer's product.
6. It can be used in sampling and in answering inquiries.

Direct mail is a flexible type of promotion because it offers wide choices in the cost of each mailing, the frequency of follow-up, the composition of each mailing, timing, volume, and the geographic area to be covered. Direct mail is the only advertising medium of a confidential nature. Furthermore, it can often reach buyers whom salespeople find difficult to see.

Point-of-Purchase Promotion. Those advertising materials that retailers display near the point of sale to stimulate customers to buy are called *point-of-purchase advertising.* Such materials include window displays, counter displays, floor displays, and items for wall, ceiling, and exterior displays—ad reprints, banners and streamers, decals, and posters. Some point-of-purchase materials are really considered part of fixtures and equipment; these items include racks, stands, clocks, store signs, thermometers, and cabinets.

Point-of-purchase advertising backs up a manufacturer's other advertising at the most crucial point: the point of sale. Point-of-purchase advertising gives a manufacturer a last chance to communicate with the customer before that customer makes a purchase; it stimulates impulse buying and reminder buying.

Point-of-purchase advertising is important because many of the persons reached are close to the act of buying.

Some manufacturers ship their point-of-purchase items direct to the retailer, either packed with the merchandise or sent separately. Often such direct shipment is made only upon the retailer's request, but the manufacturer may have invited the request by sending the retailer an inquiry advertisement through direct mail or trade papers. Occasionally a manufacturer makes use of an installation crew, especially with costly items. In most cases the crew is from a commercial firm specializing in this type of work. The most common method of distributing point-of-purchase materials makes salespeople responsible for this task.

The salesperson plays a key role in the company's effective use of point-of-purchase advertising. Retailers can use a manufacturer's display or they can throw it away. First, the salesperson must see that the retailers are stocked with enough merchandise to justify their use of the company's materials. Then there is a continuing job of selling retailers on the company's point-of-purchase program. By persuading more retailers to use more of the items for greater lengths of time, the salesperson helps the company reduce waste. The salesperson tries to encourage retailers to synchronize their point-of-purchase activities with the promotion schedule of the company. The salesperson is always trying to obtain the most desirable locations for the materials, and reports to the company on the use of the various items. To the sales promotion manager, the salesperson comments on the company's point-of-purchase program, the programs of competitors, and the thinking of the customers.

Cooperative Advertising. In their promotion programs, manufacturers may encourage retailers to advertise their products locally by offering to defray part of the advertising cost. This is commonly done by a manufacturer whose distribution is restricted to one retailer in a market or whose distribution is highly selective. The manufacturer drafts the advertising program, adopts rules and controls, builds the ads, and makes them available to retailers. The most common arrangement for sharing costs of cooperative advertising is for manufacturer and retailer to split the costs equally. Sometimes the manufacturer will limit the amount that will be paid to a certain percent of the retailer's yearly purchases. For example, if the limit is an amount equal to 5 percent of the retailer's yearly purchases and the retailer's purchases amount to $100,000, the manufacturer will match the retailer dollar for dollar up to $2,500, one-half of the limit of $5000.

Other Dealer Services. Counsel on managerial matters is another aid which the sales promotion staff should make available to middlemen. Retailers should be able to obtain recommendations about store location, layout, equipment, and organization. Guidance should also be available in such operations as buying, pricing, credit, and control. Certainly retailers should be able to obtain from the sales promotion department all the aid they need in the areas of personal selling, advertising, and display.

Manufacturers can produce external house organs aimed at their retailers. These publications can encourage greater understanding between the manufacturer and retailers. Such a publication might include tips on how to increase sales, counsel on management problems, product information, and case histories of successful retailers.

Manufacturers design contests for their retailers, promote them to those retailers (the manufacturer's salespeople do some of this promotion), administer the contests, and award prizes to the winners of the contests.

Manufacturers' ads in trade publications *(Progressive Grocer, Hardware Retailer)* are to stimulate sales to manufacturers' middlemen. These ads stress sales and profit potentials. Typical trade ads urge retailers to stock and push the line, announce new products or policies, or promote the manufacturer's consumer promotion program.

Deals are special concessions manufacturers offer to retailers. The deal can usually be earned by the retailer's placing a large order. Sometimes the retailer gets free goods, reduced prices, a promotional allowance, or some exceptional point-of-purchase display. Sometimes the deal involves more liberal credit—dating, billing, or terms. Sometimes the manufacturer includes retailers' names and addresses in ads, particularly in regional magazine ads.

Manufacturers can give *executive gifts* to deserving retailers, gifts for the individual merchant. These are given in appreciation of past business and in anticipation of future business. Popular for short-run consumption are steaks, tickets, and fruit. Popular for long-run use are cameras, glassware, and luggage. Some gifts are delivered by salespeople.

A final activity of the sales promotion department in its handling of dealer relations is one of stimulating retail salespeople. A promotion program may include sales manuals, sales training courses, films on selling, and sales instruction given by the manufacturer's salespeople. Retail salespeople may be offered *PM's* (push money) to encourage their support of the manufacturer's merchandise. Gifts, discounts, and contests are other possible elements of a sales promotion program used by the manufacturer to stimulate a retailer's sales force.

Sales Promotion for Ultimate Consumers

The various elements which make up another area of sales promotion mesh with the other phases of the manufacturer's promotion. Prominent in this area is the creation of stimulants to consumer buying. A by-product of favorable consumer buying action is, of course, the demand that prompts middlemen to buy. If great numbers of consumers can be presold on a manufacturer's brand of merchandise, strong pressure is felt by retailers to stock or feature that brand. It is not uncommon for the manufacturer to include retailers in the promotion, as, for instance, when a contest is staged and the entry blanks are made available in retail stores. Consumer services consist of a manufacturer's activities intended to make better buyers and happier users of individuals who purchase the products.

Contests. One technique to provoke consumer reaction is the consumer contest. Some goals of contests are to build greater retail distribution, build store traffic, persuade consumers to try a product for the first time, increase the units of purchase, and stimulate new uses for old products.

The sales promotion manager is responsible for the design of a contest. He or she may schedule simultaneous contests for the company's middlemen and its salespeople. There are many patterns along which a contest can be constructed. Some call for word-building, some for slogan-writing. Some ask the contestants to add the last line to a poem or limerick, some are based on puzzles, and many ask for a written statement or letter. The execution of contests poses many problems, such as the type which will be most successful, the period for which the contest should run, the number, nature, and size of prizes, the contest rules, legal aspects, the judging, and obtaining retailers' cooperation.

Sampling. A second type of sales promotion for ultimate consumers is the sample, which may be given away free or may bear a small charge. Its virtue lies in the claim that nothing promotes the consumption of a good product so effectively as a trial of that product. Like contests, sampling presents problems for the manufacturer. Is the product one that can be sampled satisfactorily? What is the optimum size of the sample? Should the offer be a free one? If not, what charge should be made? What method or methods of distribution should be adopted? Should retailers be given a role in the project? Retail cooperation is usually most desirable, and seeing that retailers are well stocked is usually the first step in a sampling operation.

Premiums. For the many consumers who at any given time are close to buying and trying a manufacturer's product, only a small inducement is needed to bring about such a purchase and trial. The inducement needed is often a premium—something of value given to the consumer at no cost or at a very low price. Premiums can take many forms. They may be items of merchandise packed inside the containers which hold the manufacturer's products. They may be products offered free or at a small price with a combination purchase or a certain amount of purchase from the seller.

A good premium should be attractive and, if practicable, not available in the consumer's local shopping area. A quality brand name also helps make the premium seem desirable. If the consumer must pay for the premium, the premium should be worth at least twice the amount charged. The premium should be useful, dependable, not instantly consumed, up-to-date, and in good taste.

Trading Stamps. In some areas, consumers can save trading stamps to exchange for premiums. Food stores distribute most stamps. Shopping goods

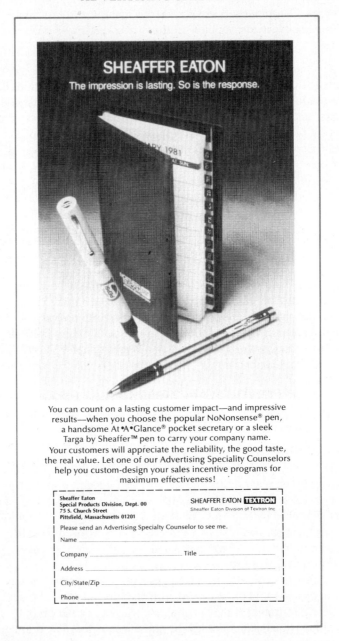

Source: Sheaffer Eaton Division of Textron Inc.

ILLUSTRATION 6-2. The advertisement above shows several gifts that salespeople can give to customers or prospects. These gifts help to remind the customer of the salesperson's company. The coupon in the advertisement is used to generate sales leads for Sheaffer Eaton's sales force.

dominate the premiums offered. The consumer can often get a nice premium with the stamps saved over a six-month period.

Most retailers offering stamps buy them from a stamp company. The retailers then give one stamp for each ten-cent purchase. The consumer pastes them into a book, and exchanges the number of books stipulated for a premium. The retailer hopes the stamps increase regular patronage.

Trade Characters. The growth of TV encouraged manufacturers to explore the creation and promotional use of trade characters. The Green Giant and Betty Crocker are two well-known trade characters.

Some trade characters are masculine, some feminine. Some are popular cartoon characters. Each is a unique personality, able to move, act, and talk. Some are named, some are not. Many deliver advertising messages for their sponsors.

Advertising Specialties. Promotional novelties dominate the advertising specialty group. Their main goal is to build goodwill. Of the many wall, desk, and pocket calendars given away, three fourths are used. Other examples of novelties are thermometers, pens, rulers, and ashtrays. Novelties are distributed by mail, by retailers, through advertising offers, and by salespeople.

Consumer Deals. There are four types of consumer deal. Cents-off coupons are one of the types. Consumers commonly receive these coupons through the mail, in a newspaper or magazine ad, or in the package of a product. When the shoppers buy the promoted brand, they present the coupon and are given a price reduction.

Cents-off packages are a second kind of consumer deal. Here the manufacturer features the price cut on the package of the product. A jar of instant tea, for example, might bear a "25 cents off regular price" label.

The cash refund is a consumer deal which retailers like. The consumer buys an item at its regular price, then sends proof of purchase to the manufacturer, and is sent a cash refund for the purchase price.

Finally, there is the one-cent sale, in which the consumer buys two items for the price of one plus one cent.

Consumer Services. The last element of the consumer program for sales promotion is sometimes referred to as consumer education, but it seems that consumer services is a broader and more accurate term. The idea behind a consumer service program is that the better the manufacturer serves ultimate consumers, the better customers they will be. Information and advice given before the purchase teach the consumer to buy more expertly. Unless the consumer selects and buys wisely, experience with the manufacturer's product cannot be satisfactory. The buyer must use the product correctly and care for it properly to get the most out of it. Teaching consumers how to use and care for their merchandise is part of a manufacturer's program of service.

SALES PROMOTION MANAGEMENT

Selecting promotional activities and evaluating promotion results are aspects of sales promotion management.

Selecting

Sometimes a manufacturer identifies a need that some sales promotion be sponsored. Sometimes a manufacturer concludes that there is a chance to achieve a sales or profit coup because time or circumstance is favorable.

Before choosing a sales promotion technique, the manufacturer must set a goal. Then it is necessary to decide how much to spend for the sales promotion. It is also necessary to analyze the competitive situation and to review previous sales promotions.

Some activities may be directed to retailers. For example, executive gifts may be given to retailers who have done outstanding jobs. A cooperative advertising program may get retailers to advertise the manufacturer's brands over retailers' names. Or, direct mailings may be sent to follow up salespeople's calls and to maintain contact with retailers between calls.

Some activities may be directed to ultimate consumers. A contest may be run to get consumers to use the manufacturer's product in new and different ways. A premium may be offered to increase the number of consumers who buy and try the manufacturer's brand. Cents-off coupons may be distributed to reduce the price to consumers.

Evaluating

Pre-evaluation may be attempted. The manufacturer may poll salespeople and retailers. The support of each group is essential. In addition, the manufacturer may poll a group of consumers who are prospective buyers. Limited test marketing may be done using samples or comparing cents-off coupons and low introductory prices.

Post-evaluation is not easy or certain. The manufacturer must try to establish quantitative goals and measure actual performance against them. To isolate and measure what a sales promotion accomplished is very difficult.

SALES PROMOTION, PERSONAL SELLING, AND ADVERTISING

The sales promotion department may be responsible for training salespeople and may provide materials and incentives for them. In addition, it frequently supplements some of the work of the advertising department.

Sales Promotion and Personal Selling

Many companies have found that the training of their salespeople is best assigned to the sales promotion department. Sales promotion personnel first teach the salespeople about their company, their products, their buyers, and then about how to sell to those buyers. The sales promotion department may also be asked to be responsible for the continuous education of and incentives for salespeople. For example, the sales promotion manager is often in charge of sales meetings and conventions, and it is not uncommon for intracompany sales contests to be designed and executed by sales promotion personnel. In companies whose missionary salespeople are under the line control of the sales promotion manager, the education of and creation of incentives for those salespeople obviously should be duties of the same executive.

The sales promotion staff should also teach the company's salespeople about advertising activities. This project breaks down into three phases, the first of which is a general explanation of what advertising is and why sellers use it. This overview provides a basis for the next two phases. The second phase involves the company's advertising policies and plans. Here salespeople are told of the role advertising plays in the company promotion program, and the various advertising activities are described. A major aim of sales promotion in this second phase is to "sell" the advertising program to salespeople. The third phase involves the salesperson's advertising relationships with middlemen. Salespeople will be expected to "sell" the advertising program to wholesalers and retailers in largely the same manner in which it was sold to them. Then, as part of this third phase of learning about advertising, salespeople examine the advertising problems of their middlemen and equip themselves to advise middlemen on those problems. The advertising portfolio, one of the salesperson's most impressive selling aids when talking to a retailer, is put together by the sales promotion department. Salespeople are taught how to use this tool most effectively in their selling.

Incentives for Manufacturers' Salespeople

Many manufacturers believe that their salespeople can be advantageously stimulated through the proper use of incentives. Salespeople who qualify for some special incentive feel that their efforts have been recognized, that they were rewarded for their achievements. Incentives can be offered for performing jobs management wants done (new customers, product demonstrations made). And, they provide a change of pace for salespeople.

Merchandise is an effective incentive because the salespeople can win it for their families or their homes. It does not slip away as money so often does. Travel is offered as an incentive as, of course, is cash. There are commercial firms which specialize in designing and executing sales incentive programs.

Sales Promotion and Advertising

The sales promotion department coordinates some of its work with that of the advertising department. As has been mentioned briefly, sales promotion personnel put together the advertising portfolios given to salespeople. These contain two types of material. First, copies of future advertisements are included, along with information about media and dates the ads are to be run. The second type of material consists of items to be used by middlemen, particularly retailers. Examples of these items are mats of newspaper advertisements, commercials for broadcast media, point-of-purchase materials, and direct-mail pieces that the company provides for retailers' use.

If the manufacturer makes a cooperative advertising program available to retailers, its management is a responsibility of the sales promotion department. The handling of the manufacturer's direct advertising to the trade also sometimes falls within the province of sales promotion responsibilities. Responses to company advertisements are usually sent to the sales promotion department for processing. Those which come from prospects are forwarded at once to the appropriate salesperson for follow-up.

Persons in the advertising department are not commonly in contact with wholesalers and retailers. In most cases, the only personal contact with them is through the company's salespeople, so the sales promotion department usually handles advertising matters through the salespeople or directly with the customer. The sales promotion department tries to solve the advertising problems of middlemen, often transmitting the solutions through the salespeople. The department constantly strives to encourage retailers to tie their promotions in with the manufacturer's promotion, an arrangement that makes the efforts of both retailer and manufacturer more productive. A successful joint promotion plan may often be attributed to the work of a salesperson.

PUBLICITY

Sellers do not want a single month to pass in which they receive no publicity. They want good publicity, not bad publicity. A television newscast that reports and shows the wreckage of a large plane of a major airline is an example of bad publicity. Editors of newspapers, magazines, television, and radio decide which firms get publicity, so publicity directors are eager to have a good relationship with editors. This is best achieved by supplying the editors with material that is truly newsworthy. News releases, press conferences, and feature stories are common.

Another form of publicity, word of mouth publicity, can help or hurt a firm. Its influence is particularly powerful. Sellers hope that opinion leaders like them, their personnel, and their brands, and they hope that the opinion leaders will pass these attitudes on to opinion followers.

SUMMARY

There are three direct promotional forces available to sellers: personal selling, advertising, and sales promotion. Publicity is an indirect promotional force. Promotion programs must be planned to create an effective promotion mix.

Advertising is the mass communication of a promise of satisfaction. It is informative and persuasive. The role of advertising is that of preselling, making salespeople's jobs easier. Because of its limitations, advertising is seldom used to complete sales to buyers.

Primary advertising promotes a generic product, while selective advertising promotes a specific brand. Brand advertising promotes a product, and institutional advertising is used to endow the firm with a good image. Direct-action advertising tries to stimulate an immediate buyer response. Indirect-action advertising has long-range goals, such as influencing buyer attitudes.

Advertising may be managed by a firm's own advertising department, by an outside agency, or a combination of the two. Salespeople need to be familiar with the firm's advertising campaigns because they can be presented to buyers to advantage. A campaign is a series of planned, similar ads. Campaigns can be either brand oriented or corporate-image oriented.

Scheduling is composed of two factors. Reach is the number of buyers reached by ads during a certain period of time. Frequency is the number of ads run during a certain time period.

Manufacturers set advertising budgets using either the percent-of-sales approach or the task approach. Ad budgets are broken down by sales territory, product, ad medium, and time period.

Checklists are a type of pretest evaluation. A list of desirable ad characteristics is built, and proposed ads are then checked against the list and scored. Concurrent evaluation is used in the broadcast field. Readership studies are posttests, measuring the number of inquiries received, for example.

A salesperson has an obligation to understand the company's advertising policy and be able to make a creditable case for it. Whether the company advertises or not, the salesperson must show why that policy is the most advantageous to the buyer. There are many ways for a salesperson to use the firm's advertising to increase sales.

Sales promotion is any element of a promotion program other than personal selling, advertising, or publicity. It can be used to encourage buyers to try a new product and retailers to begin carrying a manufacturer's brand. A manufacturer's promotion program for dealers must be merchandised. Salespeople must sell dealers on the sales promotion techniques the manufacturer uses.

Direct-mail promotion includes sales letters, circulars, and booklets sent directly to buyers. Direct-mail promotion can locate prospects, transmit precall information, and increase customer goodwill. It is a flexible type of promotion, and it can reach buyers whom salespeople find difficult to see.

Point-of-purchase advertising is the material that retailers display near the point of sale. It backs up the manufacturer's other advertising. Salespeople are usually responsible for getting retailers to use the displays.

Manufacturers may encourage retailers to advertise their products locally by offering to pay part of the advertising cost. This is commonly done when distribution is exclusive. The manufacturer creates the advertising program and makes ads available to retailers.

The sales promotion staff should also help middlemen with store location, layout, and equipment problems. Guidance should be available in operations like buying, pricing, credit, and control. Manufacturers design contests for retailers, place ads in trade publications, give special concessions, and offer executive gifts to deserving retailers.

Another area of sales promotion activity is stimulating purchase by ultimate consumers. Contests, samples, premiums, trading stamps, trade characters, advertising specialties, consumer deals, and consumer services and education are all possible elements of consumer-oriented sales promotion.

Sales promotion management includes selecting promotional activities and evaluating promotion results. Pre-evaluation is carried out to help managers make the correct choice. Post-evaluation is not easy or certain. Measuring what a sales promotion accomplished is very difficult.

In many companies, the sales promotion department trains salespeople and provides sales incentives for them. Merchandise and travel are two incentives offered by manufacturers to salespeople.

The advertising department is not commonly in contact with wholesalers and retailers. In most cases, the only personal contact with them is through the company's salespeople, so the sales promotion department usually handles advertising matters through the salespeople or directly with the customer.

REVIEW QUESTIONS

1. Why is advertising a "pull" technique?
2. List some limitations of advertising.
3. What is the difference between direct-action advertising and indirect-action advertising?
4. What is an advertising campaign?
5. How does advertising increase sales power?
6. List four ways that a salesperson can take advantage of the firm's advertising.
7. What is the purpose of sales promotion?
8. What are the advantages of direct-mail promotion?
9. When is cooperative advertising used?
10. What problems are involved in product sampling?
11. List four examples of consumer deals.
12. Name several methods of pre-evaluation of a sales promotion.
13. Describe the training given to salespeople by promotion departments.
14. List several sales incentives for manufacturers' salespeople.
15. What two types of material are contained in the portfolios put together by sales promotion personnel and given to salespeople?

DISCUSSION QUESTIONS

1. Describe an ad campaign that you are familiar with that was successful. Why was it successful?
2. Some television advertisers use commercials that are irritating. Why do they use such ads when they know the ads will upset viewers?
3. Give an example of each of the following: a primary, selective, brand, institutional, direct-action, and indirect-action ad. Can an ad be of more than one type?
4. Some advertisers use well-known people, such as actors and sports stars, to promote their products. Is this more effective than using unknown people? Does it enhance the image of the product?

CASE STUDY 6A

A television network found itself on October 1 under contract to broadcast a postseason football bowl game early in January but having no sponsor for the game. Network executives got in touch with a toiletries and cosmetics manufacturing firm and its advertising agency and proposed sponsorship of the game. Special inducements were offered.

The toiletries and cosmetics firm was large but relatively young. In its few years of operation, it had achieved respectable retail distribution and sales volume in 60 markets. It sold to a number of wholesalers, chains, department stores, and drugstores. The firm was a heavy advertiser, including cooperative advertising with its retailers, and it supplied many promotional display materials to its retailers.

The company president's first reaction to the advertising proposal was that not enough time remained between October 1 and the scheduled game time to get the most out of the television advertising. The game was to be broadcast in 75 major markets, including the 60 in which the firm had its own salespeople. On October 15, after discussion with key retailers, the company's salespeople, and the managers of the company's production, sales, advertising, marketing research, and legal departments, the president decided to accept the proposal.

Was this a wise advertising decision? Why?

CASE STUDY 6B

Marsha Feinman is a salesperson for one of the nation's largest insurance firms. The company offers a complete range of business and personal insurance policies and advertises them heavily in business publications, in consumer publications, and on television (including the sponsorship of shows on public television). It even sponsors and has its name associated with a major professional golf tournament.

Feinman graduated from college last year and is still learning the ropes from the experienced salesperson who was assigned to conduct her on-the-job training. Feinman is receiving a salary right now, but when she completes her training program all her income will come from commissions on the policies she writes. She's a bit concerned because she thinks that the commissions are a little low. She wonders out loud one day when eating lunch with the senior salesperson why the company can't spend much less on advertising and use the money saved to pay higher commissions. She concludes by saying, "I don't see how advertising can help at all. Salespeople are the only ones who can persuade the prospect to buy: so why shouldn't we get all that money that's being wasted on advertising?"

If you were the senior salesperson, how would you answer this question?

PRESELLING ACTIVITIES

part III

Prospecting for Customers

Successful salespeople must continually prospect for new customers to replace those who die, go out of business, retire, move away, switch to a competitor's product, cease to qualify financially, or go into another line of business. In addition to finding prospects, the salesperson needs to find out about them. Actually, these two activities overlap because a salesperson cannot separate prospects from those unlikely to buy without obtaining certain information about them. Outstanding salespeople spend their time selling to the most promising prospects, whereas weak salespeople try to sell to anybody.

TECHNIQUES FOR PROSPECTING

The first thing for the salesperson to do in prospecting for customers is to make an exhaustive study of the product line. When the salesperson has learned what the products do, it is possible to determine what kinds of customer the products can help. For instance, a study of electric water heaters reveals that businesses as well as homeowners would be prospects. A manufacturer of glass containers may find that the product can be sold to beverage, dairy, food, pharmaceutical, cosmetic, and chemical companies. The next step is to isolate individual prospects within these broad categories.

Endless Chain

The *endless chain technique* can be quite successful in yielding names of prospects. In using this technique, the salesperson asks satisfied customers or former customers to suggest individuals who logically could use the product

SALESPEOPLE'S OPINIONS ON THE MOST EFFECTIVE WAY OF
ACQUIRING NEW ACCOUNTS

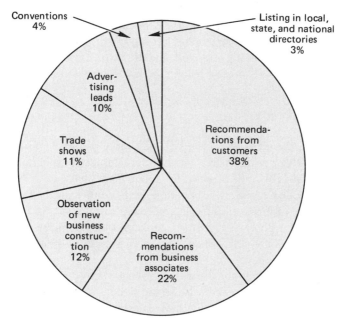

Source: "Two Views of Those Vital 30 Seconds," *Sales and Marketing Management*
(October 30, 1972), p. 29.

ILLUSTRATION 7-1. Successful salespeople must continually prospect for new
customers.

being sold. Customers are inclined to be cooperative with the salesperson who
works hard to serve them.

Referrals

The *referral technique* goes beyond the endless chain. In the endless chain,
customers only supply names of prospects to salespeople, but in the referral
technique customers do more. They may give the salesperson a personal card
or note of introduction for the suggested prospect. They might recommend the
salesperson to a prospect through a telephone call to that prospect, perhaps
trying to set up an appointment for the salesperson. Or they might arrange to
introduce the salesperson personally to the prospect.

To get referrals, the salesperson has only to ask for them. Requests for
referrals can be made upon completion of the first sale, on the next call, or after
allowing a reasonable length of time for the customer to become accustomed
with the purchase. Most customers will cooperate with the salesperson. Some

want their friends to know of the wise purchases they have made, and most feel that their decisions and actions carry weight with their friends.

There are several advantages to the referral technique. Prospecting time and approach time are minimized, permitting more face-to-face selling time. Appointments are more easily arranged, and they are generally made with likely prospects because the customer's recommendation serves as a screening procedure.

Centers of Influence

Centers of influence can also be used as a source of prospect names. These centers are friends or perhaps customers of the salesperson who have influence over other individuals and information about them that can be used by the salesperson. An office manager, for example, can identify for the salesperson of home study courses those employees who have promise enough to be good prospects. Lawyers, doctors, ministers, bankers, public officials, and business executives serve as centers of influence for their friends, employees, neighbors, associates, and relatives.

Centers of influence do the job of referral and then some. They may supply all the prospect information the salesperson needs. They may make appointments and then go on to recommend the salesperson and the proposal to the prospect. Sometimes they are even present at the selling interview. Why do people use their influence in this manner? Sometimes the explanation is personal —perhaps just friendship for the salesperson, or perhaps the salesperson returns the favor by helping the center of influence in some way. Or perhaps the center of influence owes a debt of some sort to the salesperson and is making a bid for goodwill and patronage for the company.

Centers of influence are more likely to function for the salesperson's benefit if the salesperson keeps them fully informed about how matters develop and expresses appreciation for their aid.

Junior Salespeople

Junior salespeople, sometimes referred to as spotters or bird dogs, do specialized prospecting for some salespeople. Automobiles, major appliances, tires, and lines of housewares are suitable products for prospecting by junior salespeople. Homemakers who give house parties, police officers, waiters, barbers, beauty shop operators, meter readers, and milk and laundry delivery drivers make good junior salespeople who can give names of likely prospects to the salesperson.

Other Sellers

Other sellers can be used as sources of prospects. Contractors and architects can give clues to the sellers of plumbing and heating equipment. A seller of oil furnaces can persuade an oil dealer to supply a prospect list. In similar fashion, service station operators can pass valuable tips on to automobile salespeople. Even competitors sometimes help the salesperson, usually unintentionally, when they disclose something of their own activities.

Cold Canvassing

Some salespeople use the cold canvass technique in their search for buyers. This technique is also called cold prospecting. The salesperson locates prospects by contacting people who may or may not be prospects and about whom little or nothing is known. Those who are not prospects are then eliminated. Usually the salesperson starts by knowing the type of individual to whom sales can be made. Next it is necessary to find how and where that type of person can be located. Then the salesperson talks briefly to many people to identify those who are real prospects.

House-to-house selling is a prime example of cold canvassing. Another is working an office building from top to bottom in selling. Often the salesperson can do nothing to pave the way for a call on a person whose name is not known; the sales work must be done after meeting a prospect.

FINDING THE PROSPECT

You should organize your work and build a list of prospects from:

The neighborhood bank.
Present users.
Architects, contractors, builders.
Telephone and business directories.
New car registrations of owners of higher priced automobiles.
Main street businessmen's association (or similar organization).
Friends and acquaintances.
Building permits, construction reports.
Members of various clubs, such as Rotary, Kiwanis, Lions, chamber of commerce, and country clubs.
A local lettershop's list of larger income taxpayers. (See "Mailing Lists" in the classified telephone directory.)
Various supply houses which deal with air conditioning markets.
The "cold canvass" method.
The utility companies.
Old files of prospects and propositions.
Other sources used in the past.

ILLUSTRATION 7-2. This excerpt from the training materials of Carrier Corporation tells that firm's salespeople how to go about finding prospects.

Prepared Prospect Lists

Some companies supply their salespeople with prospect lists. These lists may have been compiled by the company itself. A list may represent individuals who have made inquiries of the company. Sometimes the lists come from *list brokers,* who compile lists in return for payment. Advertising media may also compile prospect lists for the localities which they serve. Organization membership lists, professional lists, and various directories may provide the salesperson with a virtually ready-made prospect list. However, even a prepared prospect list does not relieve the salesperson of the duty of using ingenuity in looking for prospects.

Publications

Various publications can also give the salesperson names of prospects. Trade papers with their information about new companies, new functions, or personnel changes justify the salesperson's examination. Even a medium as general as the newspaper can frequently be scanned and yield profitable results. Some salespeople can consult public records, such as tax lists, and published building permits in their search for prospects.

Direct Mail and Technical Surveys

Sometimes direct-mail pieces containing inquiry coupons for the customer to fill out and return are sent out for the purpose of identifying prospects. Returned coupons, which may ask that additional information on the product be mailed to the individual or may ask that a salesperson call, yield prospects' names and addresses. Such mailings are commonly executed by the salesperson's company.

In some product lines, the salesperson finds it profitable to make technical surveys to locate prospects. The salesperson of lighting equipment, for example, may make a study of an industrial plant or office to see if lighting is adequate. Insurance, air conditioning, and heating equipment are other products for which surveys have been effectively used in identifying prospects.

Telephone

The telephone makes possible many more contacts with buyers than the salesperson can make in person. And some prospects will talk on the phone but would not see the salesperson who called in person. The phone call can identify prospects, then gain their interest, then make appointments that permit economical routing. Much travel, waiting time, and expense are thus saved, and the salesperson's face-to-face selling time with buyers is increased. The call is a speedy way to determine if certain buyers are prospects, and most of those buyers have telephones. Telephone prospecting eliminates the distance limitation; a buyer 100 miles away can be reached by phone as easily as one only 100 yards away. Salespeople for home improvements do much prospecting by telephone.

The Salesperson's Personal Contacts and Observations

Friends and acquaintances of the salesperson can supply prospect leads, either in casual conversation or in conversation directed specifically toward uncovering prospects. If the salesperson's friend is also a friend of the prospect, so much the better. A salesperson's own powers of observation can also help in the search for prospects. For example, an insurance salesperson who sees ground being broken for a house needs no better clue to a likely prospect.

Company Records

Information present in the firm's files and records can be used in prospecting. Included is correspondence with buyers. Records in the service department may point to owners who are prospects for the replacement of old models with current models. Records in the credit department can identify inactive accounts which may be excellent prospects. Sales department records may identify active accounts which buy only part of the selling firm's product assortment but could buy more.

BUYING INFLUENCES

A salesperson must not assume that the person who actually places orders is the only person whose goodwill is significant. Picture the sale of small hand tools to a manufacturer. The purchasing agent may place the order, but may be influenced by supervisors and workers who will use the tools. The firm's director of public relations may have a voice in delivery drivers' uniforms, and what is painted on the trucks they drive. Department heads and high-priced production executives are often hidden influences on buying decisions. In some cases, the purchasing agent can make only small purchases; larger purchases are made by the treasurer. Because a buying influence can be favorable or hostile toward the salesperson's firm, the salesperson should identify such influences and determine appropriate selling points for each influential person. Such a project may require months.

NEED FOR AND USE OF PROSPECT INFORMATION

The salesperson who is to convert prospects into customers and then develop those customers to the greatest possible degree must have prospect information. The more complete and comprehensive the information, the better the salesperson can serve the people called upon and make these efforts produce.

A salesperson's four main uses of prospect information are in qualifying prospects, visualizing prospects' needs, increasing sales effectiveness, and respecting the prospect's wishes.

Qualifying Prospects

The first use the salesperson makes of prospect information is in selecting from a group certain individuals who warrant future attention. The larger group can be called the "suspect" group. Some people in this group will deserve the salesperson's time and sales effort; others will not. Suspects are those who do not qualify now for sales attention; some may in the future. The smaller group becomes the "prospect" group because the salesperson determines that each member needs the product, can finance the purchase, and has authority to buy.

In qualifying the prospect, the salesperson will check first those aspects which are key matters for the product. The major consideration may be location, credit rating, or freedom to buy on the part of the prospect. In other cases it may be a matter of age, vocation, home ownership, or marital status.

It should be mentioned here that many prospects are not aware of needs and wants until they have been shown a product that performs a task more efficiently. Most prospects are not ready to buy until some salesperson shows them the product. Furthermore, criteria change. This fact requires the salesperson to keep informed on new trends and developments; on the changing demands of various age, sex, or income groups; on the appearance of new markets; and on new uses for old products.

Regardless of time, place, product, or criteria, the process of qualifying the prospect provides the salesperson with answers to a single question: "Should I spend more time with this person?"

Visualizing Prospects' Needs

A second use of prospect information is in picturing the prospect's buying problems and requirements. The salesperson who is to help the prospect buy must have a grasp of the prospect's current situation in sufficient detail. The salesperson cannot fit the offerings to the prospect's needs until those needs are known. Prospect information identifies and describes those needs. It reveals why the prospect needs the product and how it will solve a problem. See Illustration 7–3 for problem areas in which salespeople can be helpful.

Increasing Sales Effectiveness

A third use of prospect information is in making sales efforts more productive. Because facts enable the salesperson to weed out those people who are not prospects, fewer wasted calls and fewer costly call-backs are made. Prospect facts help, too, in securing interviews with the right people. Less time during the first

The Ralston Purina Company lists the following problem areas in which their salespeople must be helpful:

1. *Products.* They must be thoroughly informed about the products which we make, and they must be able to give genuine help to their customers in their farm management.
2. *Profits.* They must be competent financial counselors to their dealers. Unless they can teach the firms that handle our Purina products how to be sound financially, they will never have successful outlets for the sale of our products.
3. *Plant.* They must be able to advise our dealers on how to arrange their buildings and warehouses conveniently, efficiently, and with good sales facilities.
4. *Promotion.* Then they must be able to teach their dealers how to advertise and market their products in the modern way.
5. *Personnel.* Finally, they must be competent in helping their dealers to hire the right kind of people, pay them a fair working wage, and make it worth their while to improve themselves.

ILLUSTRATION 7-3. These are some of the areas where salespeople can be helpful to customers.

calls need be given to the job of collecting prospect information, and more time is thus available for selling.

A prospect is favorably impressed when a salesperson can discuss specific problems on the first visit. When the salesperson shows that time and effort have been spent in getting to know the prospect's circumstances, the salesperson makes a strong bid for attention, interest, and confidence. The salesperson has a justification for taking up some of the prospect's time, and can invite the prospect to communicate facts which could not be determined prior to the call.

Prospect information also helps in the selection of the most promising approach and appeals. It makes the salesperson better able to anticipate objections and to overcome them skillfully before they are voiced. For example, if the prospect has a commitment to another vendor and the salesperson knows about it in advance, it will be easier to handle this situation satisfactorily.

The salesperson's presentation is stronger because of what is known about the prospect. Specifics rather than generalities can be discussed. By examining the prospect's problems from the very first contact and showing what the product will do, the salesperson makes the sales story easy to understand, believe, and act on. The more the salesperson knows about the prospect, the more expertly the product can be fitted into the picture and the more convincingly the benefits of the product can be shown.

The salesperson must often be a friend before being accepted as an advisor, and one of the salesperson's first objectives is to be accepted by the prospect as a friend. Because of having obtained prospect information in advance, a more friendly atmosphere can frequently be created in which the salesperson and prospect can become acquainted.

Respecting the Prospect's Wishes

A fourth use of prospect information is concerned with information of a general nature that applies to practically all prospects. This information answers the salesperson's question, "What does the prospect expect of me, and what must I avoid doing?" Knowledge that is deposited in this fund of facts guides the salesperson in trying to please the prospect and in trying to avoid annoying or irritating the prospect.

Any set of recommendations will probably need to be adjusted in the light of such matters as the stage of the business cycle, nature of the product, type of prospect, characteristics of the salesperson, and section of the country. Each salesperson will certainly want to compile a list of "do's" and "don'ts" that have been observed by experience.

TYPES OF PROSPECT INFORMATION

Most salespeople need two types of information about prospects—personal information and business information. The amount of each required for a satisfactory job varies, as do the specific items. A salesperson may find little or no use for business information in selling to homemakers. Another salesperson may be helpless in qualifying prospects unless it is known whether or not they are parents.

It is the salesperson's duty to build a list of facts which can be used to maximize the effectiveness of sales efforts. However, the salesperson should not spend a disproportionate amount of time in getting ready to sell. The salesperson does not get orders signed while digging up prospect facts.

Personal Information

Personal information refers, of course, to facts about the individual whom the salesperson interviews. The salesperson may be hoping to sell something to the individual for personal use, or the individual may be the purchasing agent or buying representative of a company. Obviously, the salesperson will need and make use of personal information when selling for personal use.

Objective personal information that the salesperson should obtain may include name, home address, telephone number, and purchasing power. Subjective

Personal information that the salesperson will want to obtain may include the following:

OBJECTIVE INFORMATION

1. Name (including initials, spelling, and proper pronunciation)
2. Age and birthday
3. Home address and telephone number
4. Ownership of specific items, such as houses or automobiles
5. Education and background
6. Purchasing power
7. Marital status
8. Family data (including names, schools, and interests of spouse and children)

9. Social circle
10. Reputation
11. Organization memberships (including fraternal, civic, political, and religious ties)
12. Job (including company name, job title, nature of work, responsibilities, approximate salary, training, experience, years with the company, and years on the present job)
13. Daily routine

SUBJECTIVE INFORMATION

1. Character
2. Beliefs
3. Mental type
4. Traits

5. Interests
6. Likes and dislikes
7. Buying problems
8. Aspirations

ILLUSTRATION 7-4. Salespeople need personal information when selling for personal use.

personal information may include character, interests, and buying problems. See Illustration 7–4 for a more complete list.

Business Information

Business information consists of facts about the company or institution with which the buyer is connected. The salesperson will need to make use of business information when selling for business use.

Business information that the salesperson will want to obtain may include the name of the company, the type and size of business, the location and most efficient route of reaching it, company organization, credit rating, and company policies. See Illustration 7–5 for a more complete list.

Business information that the salesperson will want to obtain may include the following:

1. Name of company
2. Type of business
3. Size of business
4. Location and most efficient route of reaching business
5. Product line
6. Markets served
7. Organization
8. Type of management
9. Credit rating
10. Prominent executives and other key personnel
11. Policies
12. Pertinent routines and procedures
13. Terminology
14. Major income and expense items
15. Competition
16. Previous experience with the salesperson's company
17. Problems
18. Future prospects
19. Where, how, when, why, and by whom the products will be used
20. Volume possibilities
21. Frequency of purchase
22. What the prospect now does about the salesperson's type of product

ILLUSTRATION 7-5. Salespeople need business information when selling for business use.

The salesperson will be particularly concerned with what the prospect now does about the salesperson's type of product. If the prospect does not currently buy the salesperson's product, the salesperson will want to know what competitive line is bought, why this line is bought, how long the prospect has been buying from the present supplier, prices paid, type and duration of present contract or commitment, attitude toward the salesperson's line and the line currently being used, and the dollar volume of purchases in this field. If the buyer already purchases from the salesperson's company and if the salesperson is new, information will be needed on which of the company's products the buyer currently uses.

SOURCES OF PROSPECT INFORMATION

Much prospect information can be obtained from the prospect or people close to the prospect. Mail, telephone, or personal contacts between a salesperson and prospect can supply information. The prospect's family, friends, and acquaintances are also good sources. People in the prospect's company, noncompetitive vendors from whom the prospect buys, customers who buy from the prospect, and the prospect's competitors are additional sources. If there have been previous contacts by the salesperson's company, this can also provide prospect information.

In addition, the salesperson can obtain prospect information from such general sources as chambers of commerce; directories and registers; trade associations; rating agencies; official records; list brokers; advertisements and stories in newspapers, magazines, and business and trade papers; and publicity releases of the prospect's company.

Personal observation is one of the most valuable sources of prospect information. Sometimes it is scheduled to be done prior to the sales interview. The salesperson may need to inspect and analyze the situation and to collect and classify the facts before making a recommendation. For example, the majority of furnaces are sold during the second half of the year, but this does not mean that the salesperson is idle during the spring. It is then that the salesperson qualifies prospects by making surveys.

In other cases, where surveys have not been made, the securing of an immediate order is not the salesperson's only objective. The salesperson makes use of the sales interview to explore in many directions. Use of personal powers of observation—operating every minute from the time the prospect's home or place of business comes into view—corrects and supplements advance information.

In choosing sources of prospect information, the salesperson should keep four things in mind. First, sources should be selected for their simplicity, adequacy, promptness, and economy. The telephone and the mail inquiry recommend themselves in many situations. Second, there should be no snooping. When people feel that they are being investigated, they tend to resent it. Third, when the prospect is a middleman, there is less need for an elaborate fund of facts. Fourth, the salesperson should always be looking for new methods of obtaining prospect data that will make all selling efforts more productive.

PROSPECT INFORMATION IN TERMS OF GROUPS

The individual prospect is the smallest and most basic unit in the salesperson's territory. In the final analysis, a territory is nothing more than a certain number of people, with a certain amount of purchasing power and a certain inclination to buy, who need the product. For each of these prospects, the salesperson will want to fill out a record card. This card will provide for the compilation of the specific prospect facts that the salesperson has found are needed if selling activities are to be successful. Continuous revision keeps these cards up-to-date.

While it is true that the salesperson properly thinks of the territory as a number of individual prospects, even a cursory examination of these prospect cards usually shows that these individuals naturally fall into groups, with each group having common characteristics. So, in addition to thinking about the territory as consisting of individual prospects, a salesperson frequently must recognize the need for prospect information in terms of groups of prospects. Classifying the total prospect group into a small number of markets and combining similar individual prospects into homogenous groups makes for selling efficiency.

The salesperson should group individual prospects into appropriate classifications, and worthwhile prospect data should be collected for each class. One classification might be made according to geography. Each state or city might constitute a separate group, or an urban-rural breakdown might be made. A second classification might be made according to type of retail outlet—separating, for example, drugstores from department stores, or chains from independents. Class of trade is a third possibility; examples include merchants or industrial buyers, banks or manufacturing establishments, and groups that use the product for different purposes. A fourth basis could be desirability of account. Customers could be rated on such factors as prominence, volume of purchase, size, and purchasing power.

PROSPECT INFORMATION IN TERMS OF THE ENTIRE TERRITORY

Just as the salesperson needs prospect information in terms of individuals and in terms of homogenous prospect groups, sometimes the sales area must be considered as a single prospective market, as a marketing entity in which both prospects and groups of prospects are united.

The salesperson must have certain market information in terms of that one unit. The salesperson must keep abreast of all territory-wide trends and developments such as population shifts, changes in total income, and other factors that affect sales potential. The salesperson must ask whether the territory contains any neglected markets and must stay informed about general conditions throughout the territory. The salesperson must study and understand the characteristics of the territory, its physical makeup, transportation facilities, attitudes, economic foundations, types of inhabitant, and other significant features.

SUMMARY

Successful salespeople must continually prospect for new customers to replace those they have lost for various reasons. The salesperson also needs to find out about prospects.

First, the salesperson studies the product line. When the salesperson has learned what the products do, it is possible to determine what kinds of customer the products can help. Then the salesperson isolates individual prospects.

Often salespeople will use other individuals as sources of prospects. The endless chain technique is sometimes used. Satisfied customers are asked to suggest individuals who logically could use the product being sold. The referral technique goes beyond the endless chain. Here, customers recommend the salesperson to other prospects. Centers of influence are friends or customers of the salesperson who have influence over other individuals and information about them that can be used by the salesperson. Lawyers, doctors, bankers, and such serve as centers of influence.

Junior salespeople do specialized prospecting for some salespeople. Other sellers can also be used as sources. In cold canvassing the salesperson calls on firms which may or may not be prospects and about which little or nothing is known. House-to-house selling is another example.

Some companies supply their salespeople with prospect lists. These lists are either prepared by the company or by list brokers. Publications and direct-mail pieces containing inquiry coupons are other sources.

The telephone makes possible many more contacts with buyers than the salesperson can make in person. Travel, waiting time, and expense are sharply reduced.

Friends are good sources of prospects also. Personal observation is another tool in locating buyers. Finally, company records can be used in prospecting.

Buying influences must be identified if the salesperson is to be successful. Rarely is just the purchasing agent's goodwill sufficient. Because a buying influence can be favorable or hostile toward the salesperson's firm, the salesperson should identify such influences and determine appropriate selling points for each.

Salespeople need prospect information if they are to turn prospects into customers. The information is first used for qualifying prospects. A "suspect" group is formed, and then it is narrowed into the prospect group. The most important question is "Should I spend more time with this person?" Next the salesperson visualizes the prospect's needs, fitting those requirements to attributes of various products in the salesperson's line. A third use of prospect information is in making sales efforts more productive. Inefficient use of travel, time, and money is reduced.

Prospects are favorably impressed when a salesperson can discuss specific problems on the first visit. Specifics rather than generalities can be covered. Finally, prospect information helps the salesperson respect the prospect's wishes and avoid annoying or irritating the prospect.

Salespeople need personal and business information about prospects. Mail, telephone, or personal contacts are useful. Information can be obtained from people close to the prospect. Noncompetitive vendors, directories and registers, newspapers, personal observation, and surveys are other good sources. Sources should be selected for their simplicity, adequacy, promptness, and economy. Snooping must be avoided.

Prospect record cards can be used to keep and update information. Salespeople should group individual prospects into appropriate classifications, based on geography, type of outlet, or other criteria.

The salesperson must also keep abreast of information affecting the entire territory, or all prospects. Population shifts, income changes, and other factors affecting sales potential as a whole should be monitored.

REVIEW QUESTIONS

1. Why should salespeople study their product line before prospecting for customers?
2. How does the referral technique improve on the endless chain technique?
3. How can centers of influence be sources of prospects?
4. Why is cold canvassing used?
5. What is a list broker?
6. What advantages are there to telephone canvassing?
7. Give two examples of buying influences.
8. Describe the process of qualifying prospects.
9. Why is it important for a salesperson to visualize the needs of prospects?
10. How does processing prospect information increase the effectiveness of salespeople?
11. What are the characteristics of good information sources?
12. Suggest a few possible bases for grouping prospects.

DISCUSSION QUESTIONS

1. In reference to collecting information, what dangers exist in selling to long-standing customers?
2. What are your personal feelings about having your name placed on lists that are sold to companies and salespeople by list brokers? Is this an invasion of your privacy for someone else's gain? How does your name get on these lists?
3. Assume you sell homes. Suggest three personal facts to know about a prospect. Why are these facts needed?
4. When is a salesperson likely to spend the greatest percentage of his or her time prospecting?

CASE STUDY 7A

The J. H. Reid Company is a wholesale firm whose salespeople call on hardware retailers and other retailers who handle hardware. A credit department and credit facilities are included as part of the Reid wholesaling operation. Up until the first of this year, salespeople of the Reid company had not been asked to assume any credit duties because the credit manager had been following a procedure which did not call for participation of the company's sales force. Early this year, however, the credit manager proposed an innovation—the salespeople would begin submitting a credit report when sending in initial orders from new customers.

The credit manager, Ms. Evans, felt strongly that the salespeople should represent the entire company, not just the sales department, and that they should be primarily concerned with net profit, not just sales volume. Ms. Evans was of the opinion that new orders could be approved or disapproved more quickly if accompanied by a credit report written by the salesperson. Moreover, she hated to see a salesperson spend time working on a prospective customer who would later be denied credit.

The Reid sales manager, Mr. Michaels, was skeptical but not hostile. He wondered how willing his salespeople would be to spend time in an activity which could irritate or even infuriate prospective customers. He wondered if a salesperson's makeup was as suitable for credit work as it was for selling. What changes would have to be made in the sales training program? Would the salespeople's reports be sound or slanted? Would the salespeople be reluctant to report unfavorable information about prospects? Would they refuse to assume credit duties? Would they be serious about or indifferent to their new assignment? Would the salespeople feel that their selling was handicapped and their earnings were jeopardized?

Ms. Evans reassured Mr. Michaels by promising him that the salespeople's credit reports would be of only slight inconvenience. Only a few factors would be included in the report because it would be just one of several sources of information about retailers. Furthermore, the facts would be limited to those easily checked by salespeople. Ms. Evans reminded Mr. Michaels that the salesperson was the only company representative to interview retailers face to face, the only personal contact with retailers, the only employee to observe personally a retailer's store, stock, and staff. She asked Mr. Michaels to agree to asking salespeople to be the eyes and ears of the credit department.

The final decision was to adopt the plan recommended by Ms. Evans. Immediately, the sales manager and the credit manager scheduled a conference to draft the credit report form.

What factors should be included in the credit report form?

CASE STUDY 7B

Jane White is a salesperson for Eastern Mills, Inc., a manufacturer of ladies' sleepwear. She is meeting a prospect—Andrew Hall—face-to-face for the first time. The presentation takes place in the office of Mr. Hall, who is owner and manager of Hall's Department Store in Monroe, Louisiana.

Salesperson:	Good morning, Mr. Hall, my name is Jane White and I am with Eastern Mills, manufacturer of Daisy sleepwear.
Prospect:	Good morning, Mrs. White, won't you have a seat?
Salesperson:	Mr. Hall, I was talking with Mr. Hobart Morris last week. He's a good customer of mine and a friend of yours, I believe. He told me that you had just retired from the Navy and opened a store here in Monroe.
Prospect:	Yes, we opened about a month ago.
Salesperson:	I understand that you have not stocked a full line of ladies' sleepwear.

Prospect:	That's right, we have just not had time to stock our store completely.
Salesperson:	Mr. Hall, you have built a very fine store, one which should handle goods which complement its physical appearance. I am very impressed with your window displays. Also by locating in Monroe you have a very good market for the young college set, and I know you want to carry goods that will please this group.
Prospect:	Yes, we think that we have chosen a very good location.
Salesperson:	This is the reason I'm here. I think that if you were to carry our line of ladies' sleepwear, we at Eastern Mills could help you obtain the patronage that you have set as your goal.
Prospect:	I know very little about your line. In fact, I have always felt that sleepwear was sleepwear. What makes your line any better for me to carry than any other line?
Salesperson:	The Daisy line of ladies' sleepwear is a nationally advertised, branded line of sleepwear. We offer prices beginning at $8 retail and ranging to $30, on which you are allowed a 45% average mark-up which is guaranteed. By this we mean that any goods left in your inventory at the end of a season can be marked down from one price level to the next at your discretion and you are still allowed your 45% mark-up; we at the factory take the loss. As some of our retail prices are in the most popular price level, they have a high turnover rate. Now wouldn't you like a 45% mark-up on fast moving items?
Prospect:	Well, yes, . . .
Salesperson:	Our goods are of excellent quality. They are made from cotton, nylon, rayon, tricot, and our latest is a perma-press dacron material. These are manufactured by the top textile mills. The craftsmanship of our goods is far superior to what you would expect on such a popular priced line. And to insure this craftsmanship we have a very modern system of quality control. Each garment is inspected six times before it is shipped. But, Mr. Hall, we are only human. If you receive any goods that are not up to your specifications, you may return them and receive full credit on that item plus transportation. I am sure you want to handle a line that would send you what you order.
Prospect:	Yes, I certainly would.
Salesperson:	Also, one of our factories is located in Mt. Gilead which is only 50 miles from here. This will enable you to get quick delivery on your orders and I might add, Mr. Hall, we at Eastern are known throughout the industry for our prompt delivery on both original orders and reorders.
Prospect:	What you have said sounds good, but I can't understand how you can help me build up the patronage that I desire.

Salesperson:	Mr. Hall, we manufacture garments which appeal to younger women. Our materials, colors, and styles are those which will please this group. As you can see in our catalog which I have here, we have a very wide line of garments. In fact we have over 500 styles from which our retailers can choose. So, as you can see, it would be impossible for me to show you here today our line of goods, but I would like to invite you to come to Mt. Gilead at our expense to look over the entire line. I will be glad to meet you there to assist you.
Prospect:	I would like to do that, but I won't be able to come until next week.
Salesperson:	I know you are busy. Why not come next Thursday around one, or better still, why don't you come a little earlier and have lunch with me?
Prospect:	That sounds fine with me. It has been a pleasure talking to you and I'm looking forward to seeing you on Thursday.
Salesperson:	Thank you for your time, Mr. Hall. I will leave this catalog with you so you can look over our line a little between now and next Thursday. It's been a pleasure for me also.

How has prospect information been valuable to Mrs. White?

Planning the Sales Presentation

After studying this chapter you should be able to:

- Explain the steps in selling
- Describe the preapproach salespeople should make
- Discuss the five buying decisions
- Show how salespeople should plan for the first "no"
- Discuss the advantages and the disadvantages of canned presentations
- Comment on what a story plan is and why it is needed

A salesperson needs a plan for each call to be made, just as motorists need road maps. In planning a sales presentation, the salesperson learns about each prospect's personality, experience, and motivation; the circumstances of the moment; attitudes toward the salesperson's product and competing products; and purchasing preferences and problems. In planning the presentation, the salesperson seeks the best approach to use in adapting the products or services to each individual customer. The salesperson plans to point out need, plans to show how the product's utility outweighs its price, identifies probable objections, drafts plans to overcome objections, and plans a presentation which is both believable and complete enough to close the sale.

Empathy, an important quality for all salespeople to have, is valuable in planning the sales presentation. Empathy in selling refers to the salesperson's understanding of the prospect's viewpoint and the ability to see and feel matters as the prospect sees and feels them. A salesperson who has empathy will be sympathetic to the preferences, perceptive about the attitudes, sensitive to the hopes and fears, receptive to the ideas, and appreciative of the objectives and values of the prospect.

AN OVERVIEW OF THE STEPS IN SELLING

The traditional view holds that a salesperson makes a sale by leading the prospect through five steps. The salesperson must get the prospect's attention, gain the prospect's interest, create the prospect's desire for the product, secure the prospect's conviction that a purchase should be made, and, finally, get action from the prospect in the form of a purchase. The presentation the salesperson plans should be constructed so as to have these five effects.

Attention

The salesperson must get and then hold the prospect's attention if a sale is to be made. This is not always easy because the prospect has problems and other interests, thoughts, and things to do. The prospect may have the attitude, "I'm not interested in you or what you are selling. I don't need your product." Often prospects will close their minds and not give their attention to the salesperson because they are afraid of being sold.

Interest

A prospect can be said to be interested in the salesperson and the salesperson's products when the prospect becomes willing to hear more of the salesperson's story. The best start the salesperson can make toward gaining the prospect's interest is to use effective attention getters because they help shift attention into interest. Also effective are the salesperson's expressions of interest in the prospect. Because prospects are interested in themselves, salespeople should plan to talk about prospects' interests—their hopes, problems, possessions, family, accomplishments, and such. The result of this approach is to encourage the prospect to link together thinking about *need,* the *product,* and its *price.* The prospect who does this is interested.

Desire

The way to sell is to present a sales story that will make the prospect want to buy the product. A product or service is desired only if it will do something the individual wants done. It is necessary to establish a need or want. This requires much tact if, in effect, it asks the prospect to admit carelessness, ignorance, or that decisions or purchases made earlier were mistakes. Then, of course, it is necessary to get the prospect to agree that the salesperson's product seems a desirable answer to a need or want.

Conviction

A salesperson has succeeded in this fourth stage when the prospect admits a desire to buy. The prospect now sees a problem or situation about which something must be done. The prospect agrees that the salesperson's product will do the job better than any other product. The prospect now sees the price of the product to be reasonable when related to the satisfaction resulting from the purchase. No longer bothered by doubt, the prospect agrees to buy.

Purchase

There can be only one act that will make a salesperson's undertaking a success. This, of course, is a purchase by the prospect.

In the light of the steps comprising the selling process, one seems entitled to claim that the first objective of the salesperson's story is to create prospect dissatisfaction with the present consumption pattern. This has been accomplished when the prospect agrees with the salesperson that (a) the prospect has a problem or need about which something must be done or (b) the prospect has a problem or need that is receiving attention but not the best attention. Next, the prospect must accept the salesperson's recommended solution to the problem. This is the salesperson's product. The prospect who recognizes a lack and sees that much of what is wanted can be found in the salesperson's product is ready to buy. The salesperson's presentation is the tool that sells the merchandise.

THE PREAPPROACH

The preapproach is the salesperson's preparation for the coming sales interview. To be more specific, the preapproach is the salesperson's finding the basic problem which the product will solve for the prospect, and then planning how best to concentrate on the problem and its solution when talking to the prospect. The preapproach gives the salesperson a clear and detailed picture of each prospect so that a personalized presentation can be built for each one. While the major emphasis is on the salesperson's getting ready emotionally, mentally, and physically for the call, there will be certain instances in which the preapproach includes some preparing of the prospect to hear the sales story. In every instance, the purpose of the preapproach is to insure for the salesperson the best possible odds for a sale.

A salesperson does most of the preapproach groundwork before ever seeing the prospect. The first step in the preapproach is to identify prospects, a step which was described in Chapter 7. The second step, and the most time-consuming, is the collection of information about the prospect and the planning of the sales presentation. The final phase of the preapproach takes place during the first few minutes of the salesperson's call on the prospect. During the introductory period, the salesperson can requalify the prospect, verify the information already collected, and expand the information already obtained.

Information Needed by Salespeople

The most important information to be obtained in the preapproach concerns the problems, needs, and wants of the prospect and any special circumstances that have bearing on the salesperson's presentation. Other information to be obtained concerns which product or products to recommend and the quantity to suggest. The buying philosophy and practices of each prospect should be determined as well as any personal preferences. If other people will have something to say about the purchase to be recommended, they should be identified.

Then there are matters pertaining to the actual sales interview. The salesperson must determine what seems to be the most persuasive sales presentation. The best way to contact the prospect must be determined. It is helpful to know which are the most compelling buying motives of the prospect, which buyer benefits to stress, and which satisfactions and goals are of greatest interest to the prospect. The salesperson will need to know what type of demonstration will be of greatest influence and through which of the prospect's senses to communicate. It will be particularly helpful to determine in advance the resistance to buying that will probably be encountered. Finally, the salesperson should try to predict which type of closing to make.

Benefits of Thorough Preapproaches

In a preapproach, it is essential that the salesperson consider a future sales presentation from the prospect's point of view. Certainly the salesperson must see, think, and feel as the prospect does before being successful in getting the prospect to see, think, and feel as the salesperson does about the salesperson's products. A thorough preapproach limits the number of facts a salesperson takes for granted; his or her selling strategy can be developed out of a firm background of knowledge.

Thorough preapproaches result in more interviews of higher quality with better prospects. Those interviews get off to good starts because the salesperson can justify the request for some of the prospect's time with meaningful, individualized reasons. The salesperson knows what each prospect wants and, consequently, can skillfully interpret the product in terms of those wants. The presentation the salesperson makes reveals the planning that went into it—the planning of appeals to emphasize, of product features to stress, and of demonstrations to perform. Thorough preparation increases the salesperson's confidence; it also helps convince the prospect of the salesperson's competence in making buying recommendations. Preapproach work results in sounder selling efforts and in shorter, more successful calls.

THE FIVE BUYING DECISIONS

No purchase is ever made, whether the product is a candy bar or a car, until the buyer has said "yes" to five questions. Because the five affirmative answers result in a purchase, the salesperson's basic job in any sales situation consists of identifying which of the five decisions are missing and then securing a favorable verdict on each. Once the five assents have been obtained by the salesperson, the prospect buys.

These are the five admissions a prospect must make before buying: that there is a definite *need* for certain advantages, benefits, or satisfactions that the prospect does not now enjoy; that a specific *product* is the best answer to that need; that a specific *source* is the best one to patronize; that the *price* is acceptable; and that the *time* to buy is now.

There is no standard sequence in which prospects make the five buying decisions. This means, for example, that *source* may be selected or *price* determined before *need* is admitted. Similarly, prospects observe no time schedule in making the decisions. Seconds or months may elapse between any two decisions. These two uncertainties make it possible for a prospect to have made one or more of the decisions before the salesperson comes into the picture and to make the other decisions in any order he or she chooses.

If you run a classified advertisement in a newspaper saying that you want a baby carriage, sellers start with Buying Decision No. 1, *need,* already made in their favor. If you have been wearing ABC brand shoes for years and have no intention of changing, then Buying Decision No. 2, *product,* is settled at least for the time being when any shoe salesperson starts talking to you. If you have been buying your clothes at the BCD store for years and plan no change, Buying Decision No. 3, *source,* is already made. If you have decided that X dollars is the right amount for you to spend for a suit, then that much of Buying Decision No. 4, *price,* is settled before you see the salesperson. Finally, if you walk up to a retail salesperson and say that you must have a birthday gift, Buying Decision No. 5, *time,* clearly has been made.

Salespeople cannot assume that each prospect really means what is said relative to the buying decisions. The prospect may say that there is not time available to spend listening to the salesperson when what is actually not available is money to spend. Much of the time, however, the prospect will make a comment or ask a question that throws light on the missing buying decision. No need is felt when the observation is made, "My car is only three years old; it's certainly good for two more years." There is an objection to the product in the exclamation, "Venetian blinds? I hate them!" The prospect's feeling about source must be changed if the reply is, "But I've bought all my insurance from *A.*" Price is the objection when the prospect asks, "What's it made of, gold?" And, finally, there is a refusal to make the time decision when the salesperson is dismissed with, "See me next week."

By ascertaining quickly which buying decisions are missing—and these are the ones that must be won before the sale can be closed—the salesperson avoids wasting time on any matter which the prospect has already decided in the salesperson's favor. The salesperson also avoids expounding on a topic that needs no expounding and thus reduces the risk of irritating or antagonizing the prospect. To determine how the prospect feels about the five buying decisions, the salesperson will rely heavily on two techniques. First, the prospect's voluntary comments are analyzed, particularly the objections. Second, the prospect is sounded out—indirectly, if possible—on each matter.

Buying Decision 1—Need

In Chapter 3 we recognized that all voluntary behavior of ultimate consumers—including their voluntary purchases—is intended either to protect or to enhance self-concept. So, individuals always have needs. Let's see how a salesperson for a realty firm secured an affirmative buying decision concerning need. The prospect was trying to sell his house himself before leaving to take a job in another community. Prior to calling on the prospect, the salesperson inspected the house from the outside and talked with the contractor who had built the house.

Salesperson:	Mr. Holmes, my name is David Morgan. I'm with Belmont Realty. I'd like to talk to you about your house.
Prospect:	Come in, Mr. Morgan. I'd like to sell it to you.
Salesperson:	Well, what I'd like to talk about are the advantages of your having us sell it for you.
Prospect:	I don't mind talking, but I don't want to waste your time. I don't need any help selling my house. Of course, I guess it would be convenient for you to handle it, but I don't need you badly enough to pay your commission.
Salesperson:	Are you having good luck showing it?
Prospect:	Things could be better, but I suppose it will come out all right.
Salesperson:	How many people have looked at the house?
Prospect:	Two people came by, but they weren't really too interested. And then there were three others who came by with their families.
Salesperson:	Were they all interested or just riding around?
Prospect:	They seemed interested enough at the time; but I haven't seen or heard from them since, and it's been almost a week now.
Salesperson:	There could be several reasons why they didn't come back. Maybe the house wasn't what they wanted; maybe the price was too high or maybe even too low.
Prospect:	Too low? I didn't think that ever happened. Even if it did, that would be just the buyer's good luck, wouldn't it?
Salesperson:	Maybe. But haven't you noticed that a low price can scare people off? People may think that they aren't getting quality.
Prospect:	You may have a point there.
Salesperson:	Have you thought of the risks you're taking if the price isn't right? If the price is wrong, you scare people away. If it's too high, you may have to lower the price and maybe take a loss.
Prospect:	Yes.
Salesperson:	When you list your house with Belmont Realty, you don't have to worry about your house being priced incorrectly. Because

we're experienced in this business, we know the neighborhoods, we sell houses like yours often, and we know what people are willing to pay for a house like this one. How much have you been asking for it?

Prospect: Well, I think I should get about $72,000 for it.

Salesperson: How did you arrive at that figure?

Prospect: I've got about $60,000 in the house, and I think I ought to make a 20 percent profit on it. Isn't that about as good a way to figure it as any?

Salesperson: That's one way to figure it, but what you have in the house doesn't always have that much to do with what you can sell it for, does it?

Prospect: What do you mean?

Salesperson: What you get for the house depends mostly on what someone is willing to pay for it.

Prospect: That's true, I guess. Well, if you were going to arrive at a price, how would you do it?

Salesperson: I've already come to a price, and this is how I did it. First, I did some thinking about the neighborhood. This is based on my years of experience—I've sold over 300 houses in the $50–100,000 price range. Then I talked to Jim Lyon, who built the house. He told me about how you insisted on such things as ceramic instead of plastic tile and the highest quality kitchen cabinets.

Prospect: He told you right. This is a quality house.

Salesperson: And a quality house should bring a good price, shouldn't it, Mr. Holmes?

Prospect: Of course, it should. What did you decide it should be priced at?

Salesperson: I would list it for you at $80,000.

Prospect: This is sort of a shock to me. Why is it $8,000 higher than I had priced it?

Salesperson: Because we keep up with the market so that we can price our clients' houses at market prices to sell them rapidly. How long have you been trying to sell the house?

Prospect: I put my sign out about two weeks ago.

Salesperson: Can you afford to have just five customers look at the house in a two-week period? How long before you'd planned to leave the community?

Prospect: Well, I have to be in Baltimore by the first of March. That's a little more than a month away.

Salesperson: What had you planned to do about selling the house when you're in Baltimore?

Prospect:	I was going to worry about that problem when I came to it. I suppose I'd have wound up letting a real estate firm sell it for me, even though I do hate to pay the commission.
Salesperson:	Had you considered that it's a lot easier to sell a house by showing it with a family living in it? A house doesn't look as attractive when there's no furniture or people in it, and customers can't picture themselves living there. Often the price has to be lowered to sell it.
Prospect:	Well, naturally I don't want to cut the price and then have to pay your commission, too.
Salesperson:	This happens all too often to people who try to sell their houses themselves and then find they can't. By listing your house with us, Mr. Holmes, you eliminate two big problems: possibly taking a loss, and also handling the legal red tape yourself. Another problem is that this house probably represents a big investment for you, doesn't it?
Prospect:	Yes, a lot of my net worth is tied up in this house.
Salesperson:	I doubt that you want to move into an apartment when you get to Baltimore and then have to wait until this house is sold to buy another house.
Prospect:	Not if I can help it.
Salesperson:	Let us list your house so that we can free your investment, and you can go to Baltimore and move into your own new home.
Prospect:	Well, I still think I can sell it myself before I leave.
Salesperson:	Clients who want a house are my main asset. Right now, I have the names of 10 people who are actually looking for a house in this size and price range. These are real prospects, not just people riding around. Also, we can show your house only by appointment. You don't have to worry about keeping everything bright and shiny all the time. We'll give you a call before coming out so that you can have the house ready to be seen.
Prospect:	You're probably right.
Salesperson:	Mr. Holmes, let me protect your interests by listing and selling this house for you before you have to leave for Baltimore. I can have customers here to look at the house day after tomorrow.
Prospect:	Maybe you're right. I guess I do need you to sell this house for me.

Buying Decision 2—Product

Once need has been established, the next step is to show how the salesperson's product fills that need. If the prospect is buying for personal use, the salesperson points out the many satisfactions—safety, comfort, economy, approval, affection, prestige, and so on—desired by the prospect and found in the product. If the prospect is buying for resale, the salesperson points out how and why the product will make more money for the prospect. Here is an example of how a salesperson obtained the second buying decision from the prospect, a woman who was shopping for a floor polisher.

Salesperson: Let me point out some of the outstanding features of this Apex floor polisher.

Prospect: Well, we certainly are in the market for a polisher but just can't decide which to buy. We are rather interested in the brand sold by the store across the street. It seems to be a good polisher and to have all the necessary equipment.

Salesperson: I'm sure it's a fine polisher, and, of course, doing the scrubbing and polishing by hand is a real chore. Do you know what equipment comes with our polisher? As regular equipment, you get one rug-scrubbing attachment, two scrubbing brushes, two polishing brushes, and two felt pads for buffing.

Prospect: That seems to be standard equipment on all polishers. What makes your brand so special? I want to compare brands so that I'll be sure I'm getting the best.

Salesperson: That's always the wisest thing to do, and I'm anxious to show you all the features of our polisher. Let's outline first some of the features you'd want in a polisher. Certainly you'd want one that is easy to operate, that will save you time, that will do a variety of jobs, that is durable, that is attractive, and that will be serviced quickly if necessary. Are there any other features you would want in a floor polisher?

Prospect: That seems to cover about everything.

Salesperson: Fine. Now let's take these one at a time and see how this Apex polisher meets these requirements. First, we said that a polisher should be easy to operate. This polisher weighs 14 pounds, which means that you get enough weight for scrubbing and waxing without having to apply pressure yourself. It also means that it's easy to lift and store the polisher.

Prospect: That seems to be a bit heavy. Most of your competitors' models weigh somewhat less.

Salesperson: That's true; I believe they run about 8 to 10 pounds. We feel that through experimentation we have hit upon the ideal compromise for efficient work and easy handling. The weight of this polisher gives controlled pressure for cleaner floors and better shines.

Prospect: I guess that much weight would do a better job, and 14 pounds isn't too much to lift when I have to.

Salesperson:	Also, this polisher has a built-in light which helps you see into corners and spot areas that you may have missed in the middle of the floor.
Prospect:	I see that your polisher has two brushes instead of one like some of the polishers I've looked at.
Salesperson:	These two brushes rotate in opposite directions and make the polisher more stable. You don't have to use force to guide it and hold it in position the way you do with a single-brush polisher. Just try it and see how easy it is to handle. Another feature which makes the polisher easy to operate is the way the brushes and pads are attached. The scrub brushes slip down on these shafts, the clamp is moved into place, and the polishing pads just snap on. You'll also be interested in these vinyl bumpers which keep it from scarring or denting furniture.
Prospect:	That looks good; it's impossible to keep from hitting furniture.
Salesperson:	Now let's move to the area of time-saving and see what features this polisher has which save time. First, the polisher has a two-speed action. Most other polishers have only one speed. Low speed is for scrubbing so that the polisher doesn't splash soap and water. The faster speed can be used for waxing and polishing to give a better, more durable shine. With these two speeds, you can get the job done in a hurry.
Prospect:	That may all be very true, but with the large single brush you can cover more area.
Salesperson:	Because this polisher has two 7-inch brushes, you get a full 14-inch path at every stroke. To equal this coverage with a single brush would mean getting a machine too large for household use. Also, at high speed, these brushes operate faster than do those of our closest competitor. Now, for perhaps the best feature of this polisher. What kind of floors do you have in your home?
Prospect:	Hardwood floors in four rooms, tile in two rooms, and carpeting in two rooms.
Salesperson:	This polisher will scrub and wax the tile floors and wax the hardwood floors with the same two brushes: you polish with these two polishing brushes. Then, without removing the brushes, just snap on the felt pads for buffing. I suppose you have your carpeting professionally cleaned, don't you?
Prospect:	Yes, that's right.
Salesperson:	Well, with this polisher, you don't have to do that any longer. Just attach this rug-scrubbing attachment, put some cleaning compound on the rug, and you can do a professional job yourself. It's just as easy as using the polisher for scrubbing or waxing.

Prospect:	That does sound good.
Salesperson:	And this polisher is as durable as it is versatile. Both the body and the brushes are made of high-impact plastic, with the handle made of a high grade of steel. Also, it comes in several attractive colors, as you can see. Another important thing to remember is that if you should ever need service on this polisher, you can get it quickly from our store.
Prospect:	Well, I just don't know. I still can't decide. It sounds good, but some of the other polishers have good points, too.
Salesperson:	Let's just review the facts we've gone over. First, this polisher has all the features which make it easy to operate. Second, it has timesaving features. It can do a variety of jobs, is very durable, and is quite attractive. Finally, if it ever needs service, we guarantee fast service from our store.
Prospect:	I've made up my mind. I believe your polisher is the one for me.

Buying Decision 3—Source

From the prospect's point of view, the source decision may involve one, two, or three types of source. The first type of source is the salesperson. The prospect must approve of the salesperson before the purchase is made. A second type of source is the middleman. Individual consumers give approval to retailers by patronizing them, and the customers of other middlemen, notably wholesalers, do the same. The third type of source is the manufacturer who must be accepted before purchases are made.

The product involved in our example of winning the source decision is a vaporizer which is used mainly to produce steam to relieve breathing difficulty but which can also be used to warm baby bottles. The prospect, an experienced drugstore proprietor, has stocked and sold a competing vaporizer in the past in another market.

Salesperson:	Good morning, Mr. Baugh. I'm Joan Temple, representing the Lion Electric Company. I'd like to talk to you for a few minutes about carrying the Lion Electric Vaporizer as a regular item in your stock.
Prospect:	Good morning, Ms. Temple. I'm glad to meet you.
Salesperson:	I understand that you were the manager of a large drugstore in the eastern part of the state and that as a result you decided to go into business for yourself.
Prospect:	That's correct.
Salesperson:	I also understand that you're not carrying any vaporizers in stock right now.
Prospect:	That's true. We've been open for only two months and haven't been able to stock the store completely with all the merchandise we need.

Salesperson:	Are you familiar with the Lion Electric Vaporizer?
Prospect:	Only to the extent of knowing it's on the market. I've never carried it in stock before. I was carrying the Val Vaporizer in the store I used to manage and was very pleased with its sales performance. In fact, I'd thought about stocking the same vaporizer in this store.
Salesperson:	Judging from your past sales and managerial performance, Mr. Baugh, I know that you're a well-qualified retailer and that you naturally want to carry only the best merchandise in your store. That's just the reason for my being here today. I'd like for you to consider stocking the Lion Electric Vaporizer in your store.
Prospect:	I haven't had any experience with your vaporizer and don't know what its sales performance would be. I have had experience with the Val and know that it's accepted by consumers as being a reputable product.
Salesperson:	I certainly understand your point of view, but I'd like to tell you a few things about my company. The Lion Electric Company is one of the nation's largest appliance manufacturers. We're proud that we have modern research facilities, highly qualified engineers, and plenty of technical expertise. With this combination, we can produce the best and most profitable in electrical appliances. We know what consumers want and supply this to them in our appliances. We have a reputation that can't be disputed, and we stand behind every single item we produce as being the tops in technological achievement. Don't you think that you might benefit by carrying a product associated with a company reputation such as ours?
Prospect:	Well, you have a good point there, and I'll agree; but I imagine that by dealing with such a large company, you would expect me to order several dozen vaporizers at one time. I don't have that much capital or storage space. As for Val, I know that I can order from them in much smaller quantities which better fit my needs.
Salesperson:	I'm glad you brought up that point, Mr. Baugh. Our company is just as aware of this inventory investment and storage problem. As a result, we've devised means by which a retailer would be able to carry our vaporizer in stock and yet not be compelled to battle this inventory and storage problem. My company has made arrangements with selected drug wholesalers throughout the country to stock and distribute our vaporizer to retailers along with their other drug merchandise.
Prospect:	Are you trying to say that a wholesale drug house is carrying an appliance that should be carried by appliance distributors?
Salesperson:	Our vaporizer is an item closely associated with drug products because of its nature. Greater economies can be achieved by

	distributing such an item through the same channels which distribute related products. Since you buy your drugs from drug wholesalers, why not buy your vaporizers from the same source?
Prospect:	Ms. Temple, I can imagine the type of service I'd get if I bought such an item through a wholesaler! They're the hardest people to deal with. I don't believe I'd be interested in carrying your vaporizer if I had to buy it through a drug wholesaler.
Salesperson:	Good service is just what you'd be getting, and much more than if you bought directly from the manufacturer. The reason for this is that the wholesaler is located close to you. In fact, you have a wholesaler within 15 miles of your front door! This means that the wholesaler can give you efficient, fast service and cut down the length of delivery and storage time in rendering service to you.
Prospect:	What do you mean, cutting down the length of time? Do you mean I'd get fewer deliveries by buying from this wholesaler you're talking about?
Salesperson:	Oh, no. I'm sorry if I wasn't clear. What I was trying to say is that the wholesaler will be able to give you more deliveries. In fact, you'd be able to get deliveries each day. The wholesaler's main office in Durham delivers to Chapel Hill on Monday, Wednesday, and Friday; and the branch office in Raleigh delivers on Tuesday, Thursday, and Saturday. This means that you can phone in an order whenever you need to replenish your stock, and within hours you'll have a new shipment of vaporizers in your store. This also means that you could maintain a minimum stock requirement of, say, about six vaporizers. As they sell, all you have to do is call the wholesaler for a new shipment, and within hours your stock will be replenished.
Prospect:	I'm still not sure I'd be interested in carrying your vaporizer. What kind of guarantee do I have that the wholesaler will take care of warranties and returns of defective vaporizers?
Salesperson:	My company has authorized the wholesaler to replace any defective vaporizers returned by its retailers, at no cost to the wholesaler. This feature is passed along to you, and you can likewise pass it on to your customers. Whenever a defective vaporizer is returned to you by a customer, you can replace it with a new one. You actually benefit from this in two ways. First, there's no cost to you in replacing the defective vaporizer. And second, you build customer goodwill because of prompt and satisfactory service.
Prospect:	Well, that certainly is an advantage I never received in buying direct from the Val Company. It took about two weeks to return defective vaporizers to the service center and then get them back

	to the customer; and, of course, during that time the customer was far from happy about the whole deal.
Salesperson:	Would you like to carry six vaporizers as your minimum stock requirement?
Prospect:	Hold on a minute here. I haven't said that I was going to carry your vaporizer. How do I know it will sell?
Salesperson:	Mr. Baugh, the sales performance of our vaporizer has been outstanding, and the demand for it is increasing steadily. My company has a promotional campaign that is very effective. Also, we've prepared some attractive and eye-catching point-of-purchase displays. I'm ready to set one up in your window right now at no cost to you. Now let me tell you about the Standard Drug Center over in Raleigh. They'd been carrying a competitive vaporizer for the past several years and were getting only average sales results. Six months ago I sold them on the advantages of carrying the Lion Electric Vaporizer and also set up a window display for them. Well, I was over there just last week; and Cynthia Waters, the manager, told me that her sales from our vaporizer had doubled the sales performance of the other vaporizer over the same period of time. Now isn't that proof that our vaporizer is a popular product with the consumer?
Prospect:	Yes, I suppose so.
Salesperson:	My company likes to deal with reputable wholesalers, so we've chosen the Durham Wholesale Drug Company to handle our vaporizer. I'll be happy to call them up right now and place your first order for delivery this afternoon.
Prospect:	Are you going to set up the window display this morning, too?
Salesperson:	I'll be happy to. How many vaporizers would you like for me to order for your stock requirement?
Prospect:	Let's see—I'll take six to start with.

Buying Decision 4—Price

The fourth buying decision is made by the prospect when it is agreed that the price of the salesperson's product is acceptable. This decision on price is closely related to those concerning need and product. Only after the prospect has decided on those two matters can the satisfaction that the product will give be related to its price, and that satisfaction be compared with the satisfaction which could be obtained in another product bought for the same amount of money. The greater the satisfaction and value the salesperson has built up, the more easily and promptly the prospect is able to approve of price.

In the following interview, a salesperson recommends an irrigation system to a tobacco farmer whose opposition to buying is based largely on the belief that the installation costs too much.

Salesperson:	I see you have a nice, large pond. Have you ever considered putting in an irrigation system?
Prospect:	Yes, I've thought about it, but those things cost too much money. I can't afford one.
Salesperson:	Well, there's no denying that an irrigation system does cost a lot to purchase. However, if I can show you how you can pay for one in about two years with a minimum of about eight additional years in which to realize further profits, the price would seem more reasonable, wouldn't it?
Prospect:	Yes, but I believe you're dressing that thing up a little. The fact that you said it will take about two years to pay for it shows that.
Salesperson:	I know it's hard to believe that you can recover the cost of a system like this in such a short time, but let me show you how it can be done. First, how many acres of tobacco do you grow each year?
Prospect:	Thirteen acres last year, but my allotment has been cut to nine for next season.
Salesperson:	Let's say that your irrigation system will cost $14,000. I can't determine the exact cost until we measure your property. We engineer the Rex Rain System to fit each customer's particular needs. We don't sell a system that is considered to be adequate for the average needs. If we did, it would be more than some people need and less than others need. When you buy a system from us, you can be sure it fits your requirements.
Prospect:	$14,000 is a lot of money.
Salesperson:	That's true, but let's consider some figures recently published by the Department of Agriculture. According to these figures, irrigating tobacco results in an average increase of $800 per acre in income. If you raise nine acres next year, the total increase in revenue would be $7,200. That's a substantial increase, isn't it?
Prospect:	It certainly is, but where did the Department of Agriculture get those figures?
Salesperson:	Here's a copy of the report. The department made a survey covering the last five years, and, as you can see, $800 was the average increase per acre.
Prospect:	That's surprising. I had no idea it would be that much.
Salesperson:	There's another matter to consider, also. How much fire insurance do you carry on your buildings.
Prospect:	Well, I have about $55,000 on the house, $36,000 on the barn, and $3,000 on the garage. That makes a total of $94,000.
Salesperson:	And how much are your total premiums a year?
Prospect:	About $582, I think.

Salesperson:	Well, by investing an extra $50, you can buy a fire hose which will fit on the pipe for your irrigation system. This means that you can save about 50 percent, or $296 a year, on your total premiums.
Prospect:	I see. The insurance company will figure I'm a better risk.
Salesperson:	Right. Now, if we add this savings on insurance to the increased income per acre you get from irrigating, it gives us a figure of $7,496. This will enable you to pay for the irrigation system in two years with money left over. Then for each additional year you use your system, you can realize an additional $7,496 a year. That'll certainly help you get the maximum profits from your crops, won't it?
Prospect:	I guess you're right. I'll tell you what—if we don't get enough rain this spring, I'll give you a call about getting an irrigation system.
Salesperson:	You can't afford to wait to buy one until it gets too dry. By the time you could get it delivered and installed, you could lose a large part of your crop.
Prospect:	I certainly don't see how I can afford to own one if we have enough rain. It would be just sitting around here, and I wouldn't get any use out of it. I hate to think of spending $14,000 for something I'm not even sure I'll need.
Salesperson:	I'm sure I don't need to tell you that even if we do get enough total rainfall next spring and summer, the quality of your crop is very likely to suffer if the rain doesn't come at proper intervals.
Prospect:	Yes, but the question in my mind is whether the quality will suffer enough to warrant my buying an expensive irrigation system.
Salesperson:	According to the figures I showed you from the Department of Agriculture, it has more than paid many other farmers to buy. As I stated before, this report covers the last five years. If you will recall, the rainfall for those five years was about average, but the use of irrigation still resulted in an average revenue increase of $800 per acre.
Prospect:	There's still one big problem. What am I going to do with all that equipment this winter?
Salesperson:	You could easily store it in your barn. The pipe comes in 20-foot sections and is lightweight because it's made of aluminum. The pumping unit could also be stored there. That would take care of your storage problem, wouldn't it.
Prospect:	I guess so.
Salesperson:	What will be the most convenient time for me to have someone come out to measure your fields?

Prospect:	I guess tomorrow morning will be all right.
Salesperson:	Fine. I'll figure up your requirements, then, and come out to see you next Monday morning. Will that be agreeable?
Prospect:	Yes, that'll be fine.
Salesperson:	I'll see you Monday, then. Thank you very much.

Buying Decision 5—Time

When the salesperson makes a bid for the time decision, it is an attempt to close the sale. When the decision is an affirmative one, the prospect buys. The prospect finds specific reasons for accepting the salesperson's recommendations in conflict with pressures and fears regarding buying. The prospect wants the salesperson's product because it will fulfill a desire, but knows that a choice must be made between this product and other items that are needed.

In the following interview, the prospect is in an office supply store where a salesperson has just demonstrated and described a portable typewriter. The prospect is a college senior and expects to go into graduate school next year. He is married, and his wife works as a secretary. The prospect has been thinking about purchasing a typewriter. He needs one, he can afford to buy, and he likes the one he has seen; but he does not want to buy now.

Prospect:	Well, I don't know. This looks like a good machine, but I just don't know about buying now.
Salesperson:	You told me that you need to type papers for some of your classes, didn't you?
Prospect:	Yes, that's right; but I don't have too many, and I can usually get them typed for me or rent a typewriter. Either way, the cost doesn't amount to much for the work I have to do.
Salesperson:	And when you're in graduate school, you'll have a lot of typing to do, especially for your thesis and for all those reports and book reviews.
Prospect:	That's right, I will, but I don't need to buy a typewriter until then.
Salesperson:	And before you get out of school you'll be writing companies for job interviews, and you'll always be writing other letters. What I'm trying to point out is that a typewriter is something you can and will use all your life—not just while you're in school.
Prospect:	I know there would be plenty of opportunities to use it after school, but I'm still not sure I want to buy. Let me think about it awhile and let you know in a few days.
Salesperson:	If you have more questions to ask, I can answer them now.
Prospect:	No, I don't have any more questions about the machine, but I think I ought to look around awhile before I decide so that I can make a few comparisons.

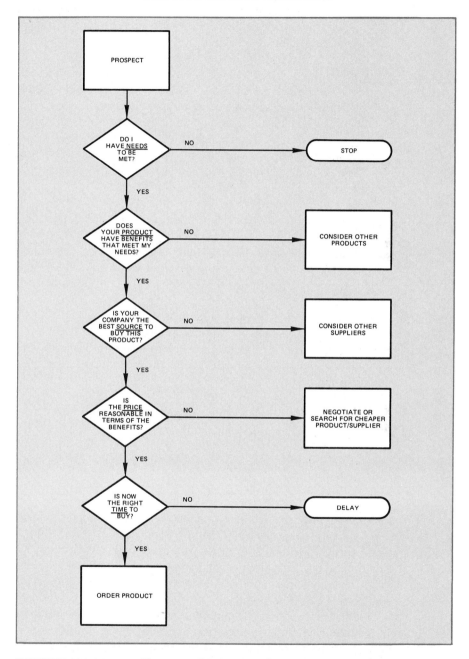

ILLUSTRATION 8-1. There are five hurdles that the salesperson must help the customer surmount. Planning for them will help avoid disappointment.

Salesperson:	It's smart to compare before you buy, but I can tell you truthfully that you won't find a better typewriter than this one. As I pointed out earlier, it has features that aren't found on other portables, such as the patented ribbon changer. Do you mind if I ask you why you don't want to buy now?
Prospect:	Well, for one thing, I want to talk it over with my wife. You see, she's worked as a secretary for the last three years, and she can tell me from her experience how typewriters rank.
Salesperson:	That's a good idea. If anyone would recognize a good typewriter, she would. The manufacturer of this typewriter has a very wide acceptance with its office models. Just last week, the Globe Company bought five new office models. I think that speaks well for the manufacturer, don't you?
Prospect:	Yes, I guess it does.
Salesperson:	If you brought this typewriter home with you today, I'm sure your wife would be surprised and pleased. She should be able to use it often, particularly for letters that she writes. A working wife can use all the time-saving devices she can find, and typing letters instead of writing them out by hand would save her a lot of time.
Prospect:	Well, that's true.
Salesperson:	And starting tomorrow, you wouldn't have to worry about renting a typewriter or finding someone to type for you. Both you and your wife could immediately begin enjoying the advantages of owning your own typewriter.
Prospect:	Well, I suppose you're right.
Salesperson:	Would you rather have this one or one that is still boxed?
Prospect:	Well . . . I guess one that is still in a box.

ADOPTING THE PROSPECT'S POINT OF VIEW

One of the most critical questions confronting a salesperson approaching the task of constructing a sales presentation is where the emphasis should be placed. Should the sales effort be centered on the prospect or on the product? The answer is clear: on the prospect. Letting the prospect be the focus of attention requires that the salesperson's own thoughts, words, and actions be fashioned accordingly. It means locating the prospect's buying problems, then finding solutions for them. This is sometimes called taking the "you" point of view. The salesperson gets in step with the prospect and stays there. Another phase of the "you" attitude consists of putting a strong service flavor into each presentation; instead of selling to the prospect, the salesperson helps the prospect make a sound purchasing decision. In the construction of a sales presentation, the salesperson must remember that the efficiency of a product, its inexpensiveness, or its style appeal mean little to a prospect until the effect of these features can be seen. As the salesperson gives the sales presentation, it is the satisfactions the product will or will not bring that enter the prospect's mind.

The salesperson's adoption of the prospect's point of view demands that the prospect be encouraged to do some of the talking during the sales interview. By intentionally arranging to do some listening, the salesperson insures the prospect a chance to take part in the interview and to express opinions. Prospect participation in the conversation helps the salesperson in several ways to understand and adopt the prospect's point of view. First, conversation helps the salesperson to recognize early in the interview the buying motives which seem dominant. Second, an unhampered exchange between prospect and salesperson can be had only if the prospect tells the salesperson what is needed. The prospect is encouraged to do this if the salesperson is tactful, receptive, and a respecter of confidences. Third, the salesperson who listens to the prospect's ideas and opinions is held in high regard by the prospect; the prospect feels that the salesperson understands and respects the prospect's opinions. Fourth, by talking and listening, the salesperson keeps a close check on the prospect's thinking. The salesperson can tell what the prospect takes exception to and what is accepted. Finally, the prospect's comments provide the salesperson with clues which enable the salesperson to adapt the sales story so as to personalize it best.

PLANNING FOR THE FIRST "NO"

There are many explanations of why qualified prospects say "no" to salespeople. Let's look at a few. (1) A prospect says "no" to a price to show toughness and superiority. (2) Or, the prospect may want to put off making a decision. (3) Perhaps the salesperson's presentation was not clear. (4) The prospect may be mistaken about his or her needs, or about a product's uses and benefits. (5) Maybe the prospect is trying to end the interview, or at least shorten it. Because real selling can start after the prospect's first "no," the salesperson should plan to cope with such "no's."

Here are a few suggestions to salespeople: (1) Do not be afraid of a prospect's first "no." (2) Try to learn to identify what each "no" really means. (3) Question the prospect tactfully. (4) Become an expert listener. (5) Try to estimate how strong and serious each "no" is; it can mean "maybe." (6) Get the prospect to express some favorable (even if minor) agreements early in the call. (7) Occasionally, offer a secondary recommendation for the prospect to shoot down, then switch to the primary, important recommendation. (8) Remember, there can be no single "best" technique.

Sometimes, the prospect's first "no" should be accepted to mean just that. Examples include (1) when a callback is clearly indicated, (2) when the prospect checks the time quite often, asks no questions, shuffles papers about, or refuses to examine the salesperson's samples, and (3) when a prompt and gracious exit will build goodwill and leave the door open.

ADVANTAGES AND DISADVANTAGES OF THE CANNED PRESENTATION

The question of whether a memorized sales talk—usually called a canned presentation—is superior to an extemporaneous one is controversial. The canned presentation, or story, is one that a salesperson memorizes word for word and delivers exactly as memorized. In its extreme form, a single presentation is memorized literally from beginning to ending. In a less extreme form, the salesperson memorizes elements or sections but uses some discretion in deciding which sections to include and which to omit from the presentation for a specific prospect.

There are some strong arguments in favor of canned presentations. One is based on the logical assumption that canned presentations have been well constructed. This should be the case because the builder of the presentation can test the component parts and identify and eliminate those that are weak. The phrasing of the canned presentation can be superior to the phrasing that the typical salesperson would use in making a sales presentation extemporaneously. Another argument is that the sound construction of the presentation gives salespeople confidence, particularly beginning salespeople. There should also be fewer objections to bother the salesperson because of the completeness of the presentation. All important points are included, and they are arranged in the most effective sequence. Carefully built canned presentations can avoid undesirable repetition or omission of important facts.

The canned presentation is open to criticism on several scores. For one thing, its use is impossible when a salesperson makes frequent calls on the same buyers, and it appears equally unusable for salespeople who handle a wide line of products. The inflexibility of the presentation makes it impractical in at least three respects: (1) it does not recognize that a prospect can be completely ignorant about the product, hostile toward it, or impatiently ready to buy; (2) it does not recognize the motivational differences which are present in different prospects; and (3) it does not recognize the differences among sales interviews —differences such as length, place, or atmosphere of interview. Its lack of originality can bore prospects, and its rigidity can cause irritation. Countless recitals of the same presentation are apt to lead to a delivery that sounds mechanical and listless.

THE STORY PLAN

The position of this text is that what a salesperson needs is not a memorized presentation but a story plan. This story plan is, in a sense, a program which appropriates all the good that it possibly can from the memorized presentation, yet tries to avoid the canned presentation's defects. The story plan is an outline, in considerable detail, of the complete presentation that the salesperson is competent to make. It is an agenda of the points the salesperson will make, unless, of course, a change is demanded. It is a framework and schedule of the main features of the salesperson's most effective presentation. The story plan has a single purpose: to enable the salesperson to make a sale.

The construction of a story plan calls for a salesperson to identify and then to memorize in four areas. First, the salesperson will identify and memorize the buying motives that can be stimulated.

Second, the salesperson will identify and memorize for each buying motive the ways in which the prospect will enjoy that particular benefit. For example, a product can be economical to buy, to operate, to service, or to replace.

Third, the salesperson will determine and then memorize the most potent sequence by which the buying motives can be appealed to. In some cases, this can be done best by making a memory scheme of the initials of the buying motives that the salesperson selects to compose the framework of the story. For example, the code word might be C-A-S-H-E-D, as:

Comfort   Approval   Safety   Health   Economy   Durability

Fourth and last, the salesperson will experiment to discover any key phrases and key sentences valuable in forestalling objections or in describing what the product will do. These phrases and sentences should be memorized.

The story plan, thus, is the raw material of which the salesperson's actual presentation is fashioned. In itself, it is a standard presentation, and as such it will fit the typical situation in the same way that a memorized presentation fits. The standard presentation embodied in the story plan will be made without change unless conditions demand some revision. When, however, circumstances put pressure on the salesperson to adapt and tailor the presentation a bit, then the story plan proves to be superior to the memorized presentation in that its elasticity provides for just such situations.

The more the presentation is personalized, the more convincing and persuasive it will be. If Prospect A places great importance on comfort, the salesperson will concentrate on that particular buying motive; if Prospect B ranks economy as the most desired feature, the salesperson translates the same product into economy for Prospect B and emphasizes economy instead of comfort. Personalizing the presentation, of course, demands of the salesperson the ability to diagnose accurately and to modify skillfully on short notice; otherwise, the salesperson had best stick to the standard presentation.

Why a Story Plan Is Needed

Regardless of how the salesperson feels about the memorized presentation, the duty of organizing the presentation cannot be avoided. If organization is lacking, there is a loss of cumulative strength. If the presentation is random, the prospect is confused. Because erratic selling is unsound selling, the presentation must be planned intelligently. No interview is adequately planned if conscious study has not been given to the organization of the presentation.

The resistance or objections that a salesperson encounters form a pattern that is almost statistically constant. Out of each group of 100 prospects successively interviewed, probably 40 will object to the product's price. Perhaps 20 will always want to "think it over." Because opposition from prospects shapes into a pattern, a patterned sales presentation must be prepared if that opposition is to be successfully forestalled.

A well-planned and organized presentation enables any salesperson to make a more favorable impression than would otherwise be possible. Instead of hoping the sales presentation will achieve the desired results, each salesperson must know how to make it do that. This requires planning.

The Story Plan in Operation

When put in use by the salesperson, a story plan has several advantages:

1. The basic presentation is a sound one. No strong selling points are omitted; there is no repeating or backtracking unless the salesperson intends to do so; and there is no overemphasizing or underemphasizing.
2. The presentation can be tailored to each prospect. This permits the product to be described in terms of the hopes and dreams of each individual prospect. Because the salesperson can construct a complete, specific presentation for each prospect seen, the presentation is more impressive and persuasive. The job of tailoring the presentation delineates an area wherein the salesperson's initiative, imagination, and resourcefulness can operate and grow.
3. The presentation is made in the salesperson's own words. As a result, the salesperson delivers a presentation that is natural and not one that is awkward or artificial.
4. With a story plan in mind, the salesperson can concentrate on prospect reaction and watch for indications of how the presentation is being received without any sacrifice of effectiveness.

A Minority Point of View

A few sales managers do not look with favor on a planned sales presentation. Because some students may go to work for companies which hold this view, this attitude is presented.

These sales managers do not think it advisable to outline a sales talk, offering as a basis for their feeling the fact that no two calls are alike. They do give each salesperson information about the product, prospects, and how the company operates, and they may even indicate points to be brought up in the interview, but they stop there.

If the salesperson is intelligent, fully familiar with the merchandise, posted on current market conditions, and strives for a close personal relationship with prospects, these, it is felt, are sufficient for the interview. Experience, they say, will enable the salesperson to handle interviews satisfactorily.

This text is in disagreement with the point of view just expressed. Instead, your authors believe that the new salesperson should write out several presentations, revise and improve them, and then memorize the best. Rehearsing in this manner results in a strong presentation until the day when, with experience, the salesperson can do better by improvising. Even if the memorized presentation is never delivered, it inevitably renews and increases belief in the product, and this conviction will be present in whatever presentation is made.

SUMMARY

A salesperson needs a plan for each sales call. The salesperson learns about each prospect's personality, experience, attitudes, and problems. Empathy is important in planning the presentation.

The traditional view holds that a salesperson makes a sale by leading the prospect through five steps: attention, interest, desire, conviction, and purchase. The sales presentation should be constructed with these five steps in mind.

The preapproach is the salesperson's preparation for the coming sales interview. It gives the salesperson a clear and detailed picture of each prospect so that a personalized presentation can be prepared. Three steps in the preapproach are (1) identifying prospects, (2) collecting information about each prospect and planning the sales presentation, and (3) requalifying the prospect, verifying the information already collected, and expanding the information already obtained. Step 3 takes place during the introductory period of the interview.

In the preapproach, the salesperson should obtain information concerning the problems, needs, and wants of the prospect and any special circumstances that have bearing on the salesperson's presentation. Product selection and quantity, the best sales presentation and which buyer-benefits to stress must also be determined.

Thorough preapproaches lead to more interviews of higher quality with better prospects. These interviews get off to better starts and result in more successful calls.

Five buying decisions must be made before any purchase is made. The prospect determines that there is a definite need, that a specific product is the best answer to that need, that a specific source is the best one to patronize, that the price is acceptable, and that the time to buy is now.

No specific sequence is required, nor is a definite time schedule necessary. Sometimes one or more of the decisions are made before the sales interview is conducted. It is the salesperson's responsibility to determine what decisions need to be made.

The sales presentation should be focused on the prospect rather than on the product. Instead of selling to the prospect, the salesperson helps the prospect make a sound purchasing decision. Prospect participation should be planned for and built into the presentation.

Qualified prospects say "no" to salespeople for many reasons. Salespeople must be prepared to cope with "no's." A few suggestions are (1) learn what each "no" really means, (2) tactfully question the buyer, and (3) become an expert listener.

A canned presentation is one that a salesperson memorizes word for word and delivers exactly as memorized. Advantages include (1) the presentation is well constructed, (2) increased salesperson confidence, especially when the salesperson is new, and (3) there will be fewer objections because all important points are covered. The canned presentation is criticized for several reasons. It cannot be used on repeat sales calls. And the canned presentation is inflexible.

The story plan is an outline of the sales presentation. It is a complete agenda of the points the salesperson will make. Four areas must be identified and memorized: (1) buying motives that can be stimulated, (2) the ways the prospect will enjoy product benefits, (3) the most potent sales presentation sequence, and (4) key phrases and sentences that have proved effective.

The story plan is a standard presentation with enough flexibility built in to tailor each presentation to the prospect. A well-planned, organized presentation enables the salesperson to make a more favorable impression than would otherwise be possible. A story plan has several advantages:

1. The basic presentation is a sound one.
2. The presentation can be tailored to each prospect.
3. The presentation is made in the salesperson's own words.
4. The salesperson can concentrate on prospect reaction.

A few sales managers do not like planned sales presentations, offering as a basis for their feeling the fact that no two calls are alike. They feel that if the salesperson is intelligent, fully familiar with the merchandise, and otherwise fully competent, that is sufficient for the interview.

REVIEW QUESTIONS

1. List the five steps that salespeople lead prospects through to make a sale.
2. How can salespeople gain the prospect's interest?
3. What is the purpose of the preapproach?
4. When is most of the work on the preapproach done?
5. What information must be obtained in the preapproach?
6. How do salespeople benefit from thorough preapproaches?
7. List the five buying decisions.
8. Is there a standard sequence of the five buying decisions?
9. Describe the "you" point of view.
10. Why should salespeople adopt the "you" point of view?

11. List four explanations for a prospect's "no."
12. What is a canned presentation?
13. Describe two advantages and two disadvantages of memorized sales presentations.
14. What is a story plan?
15. Why is a story plan needed?

DISCUSSION QUESTIONS

1. Describe the last canned presentation a salesperson gave you. Did you buy the product? Why or why not?
2. What preparation would you make for a sales presentation to a longstanding customer?
3. Identify the point in the sales presentation concerning need (pages 165–167) where the salesperson really makes the sale. What information generated in the preapproach was vital to closing the sale?
4. Before any sale is made, the customer must answer "yes" to five buying decisions. How would you explain impulse purchases then, when a purchase is made practically on a whim with no real conscious decision making?

CASE STUDY 8

Below is a sales presentation suggested in the *Gillette Sales Training Guide* for the Cricket disposable lighter. Read it carefully, and then answer the questions which follow it.

CRICKET PRESENTATION

Approach

Good morning, _____, I'm with the Gillette Company, Safety Razor Division; and today, I would like to talk to you about a profit opportunity that other stores, such as yours, have found to be very lucrative. That opportunity is Cricket Lighters; and for this reason, I would like to show you how to increase your sales and profits in the disposable lighter category without increasing your investment in inventory.

Reasons to Buy

1. Selling Cricket disposable lighters will increase your sales and profits because it is a number one selling item. Cricket and Super Cricket represent high profit, quick turn items as they allow you to retain a high profit margin on Super Cricket while promoting our Cricket Lighters. Both are available in a space saving "A" frame display for maximum impact, thus reducing the need for carrying many different lighters.

2. By reducing the number of different lighters you are carrying and devoting that display space to the faster moving Cricket line, you will be investing fewer dollars in inventory per dollar of sales than you are right now.
3. Our heavy advertising support generates consumer interest and awareness and thus pre-sells Cricket for you. All you have to do is keep them in stock and displayed properly.

Product Knowledge

See Product Knowledge section of the I.O.P.

Close

I am sure you will agree that Cricket and Super Cricket disposable lighters should be kept in stock and displayed. They are the highest volume and profit contributors in the lighter category. From whom [which wholesaler] should I send your displays of Cricket and Super Cricket?

1. Is this a canned presentation or a story plan?
2. What sales elements are included in this presentation?
3. What needs do each of the reasons to buy meet?

THE SELLING PROCESS

part IV

Securing and Opening the Sales Interview

Having planned the sales presentation, the salesperson's next concern is to deliver it to the buyer for whom it was prepared. Before the presentation can be made, the salesperson naturally must be with the buyer and must have permission from the buyer to make the presentation. The first portion of this chapter, then, will be concerned with securing the buyer's approval to meet and talk with the salesperson. Later parts of the chapter will discuss techniques of getting the interview off to a good start.

SECURING AN INTERVIEW

The chance of securing a sales interview is maximized if the salesperson (1) contacts the proper person in the organization, (2) selects the proper time to call for an interview, (3) considers the desirability of making appointments, and (4) knows some techniques for handling barriers to securing the interview.

Whom to See in a Business

In many kinds of selling, particularly in selling to ultimate consumers, the question of whom to see is readily answered. In some business selling, however, identifying the proper person to be contacted in a certain business can pose a real problem. For example, does the credit manager of a corporation order the typewriters used in the credit department or does someone else order them?

The salesperson naturally wants to deal with the person who is most influential in the purchase of the product. This individual will be the one most interested in the advantages to be gained from making the purchase, will be more likely to take the time to hear the salesperson's presentation, and is most able to grasp the benefits that will be gained from buying. The salesperson who has adequately qualified prospects should know the name of the proper person to contact for a sales interview. The well prepared salesperson should never walk into a firm and say something like, "Can you tell me who buys your typewriters?" This is almost sure to result in the salesperson's being turned down for a sales interview.

When to Call for an Interview

Very little help can be given in a textbook about the matter of timing or scheduling calls. About all that can be said is that the salesperson should try to tell the firm's story at the time that the prospect is most nearly receptive to buying. It does not take much time or ingenuity for the salesperson to learn what is the best time to call about a particular line of merchandise. A salesperson quickly learns, for example, that certified public accountants are extremely busy from January 15 to April 15, that retailers are less busy between one and three in the afternoon than at other hours, that professional people such as lawyers may often be best approached between 8:30 and 10 in the morning, and that ultimate consumers often should be seen at home soon after the evening meal. In determining the proper time to call for a sales interview, the salesperson must consider not only the time of day but also the time of week, month, and year.

Making Appointments for Interviews

In the entire field of selling, there are, at one extreme, some salespeople who find the selling-by-appointment technique impracticable if not impossible. For instance, appointment making is not easily adaptable to house-to-house selling and to much selling in retail stores. At the other extreme, there are salespeople who sell only to people with whom they have appointments. Certain salespeople in the insurance field, certain missionary salespeople, and certain salespeople selling to purchasing agents are examples. Between these two extremes is a large group of salespeople who can, if they wish, make some use of appointments to see specific buyers. Undoubtedly, more salespeople can make profitable use of the appointment technique than do. Generally speaking, appointments are easier to arrange with customers than with prospects and are easier to arrange for subsequent calls on buyers than for first calls.

Advantages and Disadvantages of Making Appointments. Making appointments saves the salesperson's time and energy. Appointments reduce

WHEN TO TELEPHONE

To save time and build prestige with a replier, it is usually best to arrange for an appointment by telephone. Because timing of the call can be as important as what you say, here, based on the experience of many salespeople, is a schedule of the best time to call various prospects:

Prospects	*Best Time To Call*
Chemists and engineers	Between 4 P.M. and 5 P.M.
Clergymen	Thursday or Friday
Contractors and builders	Before 9 A.M. or after 5 P.M.
Dentists	Before 9:30 A.M.
Druggists and grocers	Between 1 P.M. and 3 P.M.
Executives and business heads	After 10:30 A.M.
Homemakers	Between 10 A.M. and 11 A.M.
Lawyers	Between 11 A.M. and 2 P.M.
Merchants, store heads, and department heads	After 10:30 A.M.
Physicians and surgeons	Between 9 A.M. and 11 A.M.; after 4 P.M. Some between 7 P.M. and 9 P.M.
Professors and schoolteachers	At home, between 6 P.M. and 7 P.M.
Public accountants	Any time during the day, but avoid January 15 through April 15.
Publishers and printers	After 3 P.M.
Small-salaried people and government employees	Call at home.
Stockbrokers and bankers	Before 10 A.M. or after 3 P.M.
Prospects, at home	Monday nights between 7 P.M. and 9 P.M.

ILLUSTRATION 9-1. Mutual of New York gives its salespeople these suggestions on when to telephone various types of prospects.

wasted activity and make it possible to obtain more interviews which are productive. The most significant advantage of making appointments is that an appointment helps get the actual sales interview off on firm footing. The buyer recognizes that the salesperson understands the value of the buyer's time. With an appointment, the salesperson is expected by the buyer and is received on a higher level; the buyer is more inclined to give the sales presentation a better hearing. By agreeing to an appointment, the buyer has agreed to listen courteously if not sympathetically to the salesperson.

Making appointments also benefits buyers. First, this gives the buyer greater latitude in seeing salespeople because calls can be scheduled so that they will be most convenient. Buyers appreciate the salesperson's consideration in not wanting to interrupt them at inopportune moments. In addition, each buyer is allowed to get ready for a salesperson's visit. The buyer can do any surveying or checking needed, can have facts and questions ready, can confer and arrange. These advantages are particularly helpful when the buyer is already a customer of the salesperson.

The technique of making appointments does have some disadvantages. Perhaps the most significant is the risk of refusal when the salesperson asks for an appointment. It is easier for buyers to refuse to see a salesperson who is calling or writing for an appointment than it is if the salesperson appears in person and asks to see the buyer. A second drawback is the possibility of being late for an appointment or the possibility of not being able to keep the appointment at all.

Suggestions on How to Make Appointments. A salesperson who intends to make appointments for interviews must determine exactly how to do this. Direct mail, telephone calls, and face-to-face requests for future interviews are three ways of setting up appointments. One simple method of arranging appointments is to send an announcement card giving the buyer the date of the salesperson's forthcoming call; supplementary literature may accompany the card. In a few cases, a mutual friend may make the appointment, although friends normally prefer to limit their cooperation to an introductory card or even to an anonymous identification of prospects. Regardless of which technique the salesperson uses to make appointments, it should be realized that the further in advance appointments are requested, the more appointments the salesperson will succeed in getting.

If the salesperson can schedule the appointment for his or her office, this will be especially beneficial. There interruptions can be barred and the buyer can be introduced easily to products, individuals, and facilities. The salesperson may also derive a psychological advantage from arranging the appointment in this manner. If the interview is held at the salesperson's place of business, the buyer may be more inclined to join in the salesperson's way of thinking. The buyer's role as an invited guest may influence buying actions.

Handling Barriers

Barriers are people who have the responsibility of seeing that the prospect's time is not wasted. Barriers are supposed to stop salespeople when it appears that such salespeople will not be beneficial. Switchboard operators, receptionists, secretaries, junior employees, partners, and even members of families can be barriers. Frequently their excuses for not allowing the salesperson to see the prospect are that the prospect is not interested, not open to buy, or not available. They may or may not ask the salesperson to leave sales literature or to call again. The job of barriers is to bar only the salespeople who do not qualify for some of the prospect's time. They are instructed to admit any salesperson whose product or service would probably benefit the prospect.

Four techniques of handling barriers are (1) delivering a requested item, (2) depending on the company name, (3) revealing something of the mission, and (4) being confident in expecting cooperation. Although these techniques will be helpful, nothing is more basic or more effective than collecting and analyzing as much information as possible about the prospect. The more advance information the salesperson has, the better are the chances of seeing the prospect. No tricks are warranted in gaining admission to see the prospect. Such tricks are resented, remembered, and usually damaging to the salesperson's chances of making a sale.

Delivering a Requested Item. If the prospect has written to the salesperson's company for product information or product samples, the salesperson can deliver the requested item and use it to get in to see the prospect.

Depending on the Company Name. Some highly prestigious companies instruct their salespeople to start the request for the interview with a statement such as, "I'm Jeannie Jones with the XYZ Company." These companies feel that the mention of the company name frequently is sufficient to insure getting some of the prospect's time.

Revealing Something of the Mission. When a barrier is particularly difficult, a salesperson may find it necessary to reveal part of the sales mission to the barrier in order to see the prospect. However, the salesperson should guard against making too much of the sales presentation to the barrier.

Being Confident in Expecting Cooperation. One of the best ways of coping with barriers is to exhibit a good appearance and a confident, pleasant manner. If the salesperson looks and acts like the type of person that the prospect should see, the chances are that the salesperson will receive an interview. The salesperson's obvious conviction that the prospect will find the interview to be of value is the best assurance of admission.

THE APPROACH

In considering the approach to a sales interview, this section of the chapter will first consider a tailored approach versus a standard approach, discuss the basic principles of an effective approach, and then enumerate those items which should be checked just prior to opening the interview.

Tailored Versus Standard Approach

All salespeople should recognize the advantages and the limitations of both the tailored and the standard approach. There are strong arguments supporting the use of either technique. The *tailored approach* is generally favored because no single approach fits all prospects and all selling situations, particularly where there are considerable differences among prospect groups. Also, no single approach fits the personality of each individual salesperson.

Supporters of the *standard approach,* however, feel that it is more effective because it has been carefully developed, tested, and proved. The standard approach tends to give results that are more uniform and predictable. It is more beneficial to inexperienced salespeople because it prevents their making mistakes in attempting to tailor the opening of the interview.

Each salesperson will probably want to experiment with tailored and standard approaches to discover which will work best under certain conditions. It may be desirable to develop a single "best" approach for each prospect classification, or to experiment with approaches that tie in with current news events. If it is decided to use a standard approach, the salesperson should have ready at least one service approach and one selling approach. The service approach begins with the offer of a favor to the prospect in the hope of obtaining goodwill so that the main presentation can be made later. In the selling approach, the salesperson begins the presentation immediately after contacting the prospect. This procedure is most effective when the salesperson knows the prospect.

Principles of an Effective Approach

Regardless of whether a tailored approach or a standard approach is used, there are certain principles that it would be wise to follow. The salesperson should make maximum use of advance information, never call "just to be calling," ask questions if necessary, secure control at the beginning of the interview, keep in step with the prospect, observe the law of self-interest, promise a buyer benefit early, show sincere interest in the prospect's welfare, and be personable.

Making Maximum Use of Advance Information. A salesperson who knows the needs and goals of the prospect and skillfully recognizes these in the sales approach will be more apt to receive approval to tell the complete sales story. The prospect, seeing that individual buying circumstances have been considered, is inclined to listen to the entire presentation.

Never Calling "Just to Be Calling." The salesperson should never call "just to be calling." There should be a definite reason and a definite goal for each call, and the salesperson should start moving toward that goal from the first moment.

Asking Questions If Necessary. In many cases, the salesperson will need data that was unavailable prior to the interview. Thus, the salesperson will find it helpful to ask tactful questions.

Securing Control at the Beginning of the Interview. The salesperson wants to secure control of the interview and to hold that control throughout the visit. The approach should connote authority, but the salesperson must be subtle in attempting to lead the prospect to the desired way of thinking.

Keeping in Step with the Prospect. The salesperson should keep in step with the prospect. The salesperson's thinking and conversation must be synchronized with both the direction and the speed of the prospect's thinking.

Observing the Law of Self-Interest. All prospects are motivated by self-interest. For this reason, the salesperson should do and say those things which will appeal to the prospect.

Promising a Buyer Benefit Early. The salesperson will usually find it desirable to promise a benefit to the prospect within the first few moments of the interview. Prospects listen only to those salespeople who promise advantages to them, so the salesperson wants to appear immediately as one who will help the prospect in some way.

Showing Sincere Interest in the Prospect's Welfare. One of the best ways to gain acceptance is to have and demonstrate a sincere interest in being of assistance to the prospect. The salesperson can indicate by attitude and expression a desire to know the prospect better in order to be of greater assistance.

Being Personable. The salesperson should strive to be easy to talk to and pleasantly mannered throughout the approach and, later, the sales interview. The salesperson should be thoughtful of the prospect's feelings and ideas and should approach the prospect with understanding.

The Salesperson's Final Check

Four matters deserve a final check by the salesperson as part of the approach: physical appearance, mental attitude, equipment, and the plan for the interview.

Physical Appearance. The first 30 to 60 seconds of an interview often determine the outcome of that interview. Thus, it is essential that the prospect's immediate reaction to the salesperson be favorable. Everyone tends to judge strangers on the basis of first impressions; and if a salesperson's physical appearance does not impress the prospect, it is difficult for the buying proposal to do so.

Mental Attitude. The outlook the salesperson should maintain in leading up to the interview should be one of optimistic confidence. The salesperson must expect to be courteously received and listened to with interest. The prospect's business is very important to the salesperson; therefore, the prospect should be made to feel important.

Equipment. Whatever the salesperson needs in the way of equipment should be checked before the interview begins. This equipment may be comprised of vital facts and figures, diagrams, pictures, product samples, testimonials, price

THE APPROACH

The *approach* is of great importance, for it will determine to a great extent your future association with a prospect, including: (1) how receptive the prospect will be, (2) whether your close will be difficult or easy, (3) how welcome you will be on succeeding calls.

The objective of the approach is to determine who needs our service and to insure a presentation to an interested individual, or one who can become interested.

Many sales experts agree that the first thirty seconds are the most important part of the approach. In fact, sales managers believe that the first thirty seconds are the most important time you will ever spend with the prospect.

Before getting in to see the prospect, you must first "sell" yourself to the prospect's secretary or receptionist. This person must be on your side, or you will never see the prospect, and the more important the prospect's position with the firm, the truer the statement.

A good immediate impression can be made by a fine appearance and attitude. You must be appropriately and neatly dressed and convey a sense of poise and dignity. Your greeting should be warm and sincere, but not familiar or patronizing.

Introduce yourself and your company, present a *readily available* business card, and ask to see the prospect.

Remember, the way you impress the secretary or receptionist will make an invaluable ally or an adversary of equal import.

When you enter, the prospect must react favorably to your appearance and manner and be made to invite you to tell your complete story.

Do not sit down until invited to; if the invitation is not issued in a reasonable length of time, it is proper to ask if you may do so.

The approach must accomplish several things to lay a good foundation for a successful presentation. You must progress through the following steps in this order: (1) Neutralize the adverse thoughts which were in the buyer's mind. (2) Establish the idea you wish to sell. (3) Get the buyer interested in your proposition.

ILLUSTRATION 9-2. These ideas on the nature of the salesperson's approach are from the sales training material of a well-known company.

lists, an advertising portfolio, or contract forms. The salesperson will naturally want to have at hand all the equipment needed, yet will want to hold down the bulk as much as possible. All equipment should be arranged for quick reference and easy handling. If there is any special equipment intended for a particular prospect, the salesperson should give this special attention.

Plan for the Interview. A final item to be checked is the plan for the interview. The salesperson should intend to make every minute count toward achieving the objective of turning the prospect into a customer. The salesperson should review what seem to be the best buying motives to appeal to, the best procedure to use in doing this, the buying proposal to make, the points which should be stressed, the proof to be offered, the prices to be quoted, and the time to ask for the order.

SELLING IS SOLVING BUYERS' PROBLEMS

The salesperson who is planning how to conduct interviews should be thinking basically as a problem solver. Of fundamental concern should be identifying buyers' problems and then working with the buyers toward solving them. The salesperson should communicate this concern to buyers promptly.

The first step in problem solving is to wonder if (or sense that) something is not right. This leads to the observation of the present state of affairs, to the gathering of facts. The salesperson's first responsibility is to determine the nature of the problem about which the buyer makes buying decisions.

In Step 2, the problem solver studies the problem established in Step 1. The salesperson tries to analyze and classify the problem, to define, limit, and clarify it. The salesperson tries to estimate what the buyer will gain from solving the problem.

Creativity dominates Step 3. Here the salesperson accumulates a number of possible ways to solve the problem. The salesperson estimates the time each would require and its cost. Salespeople see many problems and many solutions tried.

Step 4 is a comparison-and-competition step. After comparing the solutions (maybe experimenting with two or three), the salesperson discards those solutions not worthy of consideration and, from the remaining, selects the best one as the winner.

Final Step 5 is a verification step. The selected solution is tested and results are evaluated.

THE FIRST MOMENTS OF THE INTERVIEW

The opening of an interview cannot be considered satisfactory unless the salesperson begins to achieve control of the selling situation within the first few seconds. The problem is one of leadership, guiding and influencing the prospect toward a purchasing decision. Control is most easily secured when the salesperson has made it obvious that the call is a gesture of sincere, personal interest.

Surveying the Selling Situation

The first phase of surveying the selling situation involves sizing up the prospect. This early appraisal will help to guide the rest of the interview. The salesperson observes the prospect to gain clues as to what type of person the prospect is and what the prospect is thinking. Throughout the entire call, the trained, alert salesperson will continue to follow the prospect's reactions as they are expressed in looks, tone of voice, and actions.

A second phase of the survey calls for the quick inspection of physical surroundings when the interview is held at the prospect's home or place of business. External elements can be indicators of such important matters as purchasing power, tastes, interests, and needs.

Another phase of the survey is to determine as quickly and accurately as possible what the prospect really needs. This will help in finding the prospect's buying problems.

The Salesperson's Attitude

A salesperson must be relaxed and confident. Good salespeople have many reasons for feeling confident. They know what their company has done and is doing. They know how their product has helped other buyers in the past. They know that they have made themselves authorities, experts in solving prospects' problems. There is no occasion for fear or timidity because they know more about their product than the prospects do. They have a sincere belief in the ability of their company, their product, and themselves to help their prospects.

Viewed from another angle, the attitude that good salespeople have is one that assumes that they will be welcome, that their story will be heard, that their prospects will realize the desirability of the product, and that a purchase will be made. These are the assumptions that prevent the salesperson from being defeated before going in.

By inviting and inspiring the confidence of prospects, the salesperson puts prospects in the mood to discuss and explain their problems. This frequently must be done before the salesperson can attempt to ascertain a prospect's needs. Prospects must have confidence in the salesperson and the salesperson's propositions before they are accepted. Prospects must feel that the salesperson is both honest and well-informed.

The Introduction

When first encountering the prospect, most salespeople state their own name together with the name of their company. This constitutes a formal introduction. In some selling situations, however, salespeople may give only their company's name and not their own. Salespeople making house-to-house calls, for example, might not use a formal introduction. The formal introduction can also be dispensed with when salespeople are calling to generate, retain, or increase goodwill or when their company's identity is more significant than their own. Every salesperson needs to establish a feeling of friendliness and confidence; if a formal introduction is suggested by the type of prospect, the type of sale, or the salesperson's company, that kind of introduction should be used. The formal introduction is straightforward and allows the prospect to concentrate on what the salesperson has to say instead of wondering who the salesperson is.

Capturing the Prospect's Attention

The prospect must be attentive to understand the full significance of the salesperson's presentation. The salesperson must have the prospect's undivided attention to obtain and hold control of the interview. If the prospect tunes in to the salesperson's message and grasps the meaning of what the salesperson has to say, then the salesperson has the prospect's attention.

The best technique of capturing the prospect's attention is to make a specific appeal to a specific need or want. References to an individual's desires and present circumstances are powerful attention-getters. A second possibility is to approach a person with some matter of universal interest. Because people are interested in other people, one may refer to other individuals who are prominent. Reference to current events and matters of common concern can also attract attention. Once the salesperson receives a prospect's attention, however, that attention must be directed quickly to the needs and wants which the salesperson's product will satisfy.

Having secured the necessary attention, the salesperson is next ready to gain the prospect's interest, and this is done by relating the product to one of the prospect's needs, problems, or hopes. The prospect becomes an attentive listener to the salesperson's story, becoming curious enough about the salesperson's product to hear the salesperson. Indeed, the prospect feels that both the visit and the salesperson's proposal are important.

Principles of Opening the Conversation

One of the first things to remember in opening the selling conversation is that it is generally undesirable to ask specifically for permission to tell the complete sales story. For example, a salesperson might need a minimum of 45 minutes to make a complete presentation, yet the prospect would refuse that amount of time if asked for it. The best procedure in most cases is to begin the sales story, then sell the prospect on the desirability of listening to the whole story only if the prospect tries to shut the salesperson off.

Here are some other sound principles for opening the sales conversation:

1. Reflect for a moment during the first few seconds of the contact to organize your thoughts and make sure that the opening remark will be appropriate.
2. Get down to business promptly and appeal to something the prospect consciously or unconsciously desires which can be satisfied by the product you are selling.
3. In the opening remarks, make maximum use of prospect information obtained in advance; state a definite, individualized reason—some kind of buyer benefit—why the call is being made.
4. Put yourself in the prospect's position; ask yourself, "If I were the prospect, what could this salesperson say or do to interest me?"
5. Accompany the spoken opening remarks with the most appropriate physical presentation.
6. If a question is to open the conversation, do not allow it to be abrupt, too personal, or of such a nature as to alert instinctive resistance.
7. Never open the conversation in such a way as to embarrass the prospect, put the prospect on the defensive, or allow the prospect to take a negative attitude toward buying.

After the first few sentences, the salesperson should pause to obtain the prospect's reaction. If there has been no comment or if the prospect has given a polite and obviously formal comment, interest has not been aroused. If the reaction is clearly good or bad, the salesperson can judge what action to take next.

Examples of Opening Remarks

Some salespeople have more or less standard opening remarks that they use with certain types of prospects. These standardized remarks are particularly helpful for cold calls when the salesperson has little or no information about the prospect. A refinement of this technique is to have a predetermined set of opening remarks for each prospect type and to vary these remarks only as suggested by the conditions encountered at the meeting. Here are some examples of ways to open a sales interview:

1. Show the prospect something immediately and begin talking about it. Example: "Have you seen this new material we're now using in our automobile seat covers?"
2. Render some free service to the prospect, and let that favor be the basis for opening a conversation. This can be done easily by salespeople who sell to retailers, and often no authorization or permission will be needed. Where the prospect must approve in advance, the offer of the service or favor can be the opener. Example: "I'll count your empties."

3. Point out current conditions which your product can be helpful in improving. Example: "I notice that juries around here have recently been awarding plaintiffs large damages in personal liability suits. You know, this could happen to you."

4. If a single buying motive is obviously predominant, appeal to it in the opening remark. Example: "We know that you fleet owners don't buy tires, you buy economy; my tire is the one that gives you the most transportation for your dollar."

5. Refer to some personal interest of the prospect. When the salesperson knows the prospect, the prospect's personal interests and aspirations can be mentioned. Example: "I believe I saw your picture in the paper last week—you pitched for the softball team that won the championship."

6. Locate something on which the prospect can be sincerely complimented, and use the compliment or congratulations as the opener. Example: "I'd like to be one of the first to congratulate you on your promotion."

7. Ask the prospect a question. Tactful questioning is permissible, particularly in ascertaining a prospect's needs; but if questions are to be used, certain rules should be observed. Do not apologize for asking the questions. Do not ask too many questions. Ask personal questions only when they are absolutely necessary. Do not ask for information the prospect can't supply. Do not collect vague, general information, because it is of little or no value. Example: "Have you checked on how the recent revisions in the social security laws affect you?"

8. Make a statement or claim. To business prospects, the claim will usually have to do with reducing expenses or increasing sales so as to make profits greater. If the salesperson prefers, the claim can be striking or challenging so as to jolt the prospect. Example: "A few minutes of your time could well be worth $400 to you."

9. Within a limited area, dramatic or curiosity-arousing openings are both permissible and effective. These have a dual value in that they usually secure complete attention from the prospect and also encourage the prospect to ask for more information. Example: Salesperson touches lighted match to material that looks flammable and asks, "Ever see anything like this before?"

10. Relate a case history which may point out either something the prospect wants or wants to avoid. Example: "If you've been in business long enough to have some inactive accounts, you'll be interested in what a similar manufacturer did about this problem."

11. Where the prospect has requested something from the salesperson's company or made a request of the salesperson on the last call, the conversation can be opened by saying, "Here's what you wanted."

Among the worst, absolutely inexcusable openers are these:

"Hot enough for you?" "About ready to give us some business?" "What's new?" "What do you know?" "How's business?" "I would like to interest you in a money-making proposition." "Just happened to be out this way and thought I'd drop in."

WHAT BUYERS DISLIKE

One salesperson was too darn nonchalant. His lounging, slouchy manner seemed to imply he didn't think I was a particularly important person.

Her eyes were shifty and evasive. I didn't like the way she kept them narrowly slitted.

One salesperson's eyes were unfocused and dreamy. I didn't like their blank stare. I didn't like the phony smile. It was either a forced smile. . . . or the kind of a half-smile you see on the face of a baby about to have a gas burp.

That particular salesperson's whole manner was that of an order hawk rather than of someone sincerely trying to help me. I got the impression that getting an order from me meant he was adding another scalp to his belt.

I didn't like the bored, impatient way the salesperson listened when I talked. Her manner seemed to say: "For heaven's sake, will you ever pipe down and let a *smart* person talk."

I didn't like the liberties he took, like placing a soiled hat on my papers, balancing a lighted cigarette on the edge of my desk. . . . and then, later on, knocking its ashes off into the little jar that holds my paper clips.

I didn't like the pompous, bombastic way in which he orated his sales talk.

He fingered his lips as he talked, so his words sounded like someone drinking coffee out of a moustache cup.

I didn't like the presumptuous, back-slapping way the salesperson breezed into my office and took the initiative in shaking my hand.

The salesperson's manner implied he was a wiser, better man than I.

She was full of nervous mannerisms that distracted my attention.

I didn't like the salesperson's obvious attempts at flattery.

The salesperson's manner was too oily, too clever. My reaction was: "I don't want to play poker with *this* city slicker!"

She was too synthetically pleasant. I like salespeople to be sunny . . . but I don't want to get freckled.

ILLUSTRATION 9-3. In a research study to find out more about how salespeople affect and impress buyers, one question asked buyers was, "What do you most dislike in the general manner of any salesperson who has called on you?" The above responses were among those given by the buyers surveyed.

After each interview, salespeople should evaluate how successful the opening remarks were. In this way, they can learn which openers were most effective and which should be avoided in the future.

COMMON FIRST CALL DIFFICULTIES

One difficulty commonly encountered in a salesperson's first call on prospects is that their natural fear of strangers may put them on guard. Uneasiness in the presence of a stranger may make prospects suspicious, particularly if they have been the victim of some unethical salesperson in the past.

A second difficulty is that of getting a full hearing. Thirty minutes may be needed to make the presentation yet only ten are granted. If the prospect specifically tells the salesperson that only so many minutes are allotted and if that amount of time is obviously insufficient, the salesperson may feel forced to spend at least part of the time allotment in "selling" the value of the longer interview. Seldom can a thirty-minute story be condensed into ten minutes and still be effective. If the needed time cannot be obtained at the moment, the salesperson should ask for another appointment. This indicates that the salesperson means business, and the prospect may reconsider and grant the full amount of time.

A third problem is that of prospects who say they are busy. This means that the salesperson must earn some of the prospect's time, and this is often best achieved by being able to offer some helpful ideas and suggestions. In selling to middlemen, offering merchandising ideas is especially helpful. Salespeople should check the displays, stock arrangements, selling techniques, advertising, and sales promotion of each merchant they call on in search of good ideas that they can pass along to other prospects.

Sometimes prospects who say they are busy are merely stalling. To minimize this, salespeople should have a businesslike manner which shows that they value both their own time and that of prospects. If a prospect really is too busy, the salesperson should try to obtain a later appointment. When the prospect is preoccupied, the salesperson's story obviously is not going to register. Thus, the salesperson should offer to return and should sell the prospect on the desirability of having proper conditions for the interview.

A fourth difficulty is that of prospects who sincerely claim that they are not interested. Here, the salesperson must remember that each prospect is interested in something and that the job is to find the prospect's most important buying motives. In cases of uncertainty, the salesperson can sometimes ask for a few minutes in which to determine whether the product can be of any aid and, consequently, of any interest to the prospect.

It is inexcusable to be arrogant or impertinent in the face of this obstacle of disinterest. Once in a while it might be permissible to meet this type of resistance with an aggressive, independent attitude, but that is a risky course to follow.

SUMMARY

The chance of securing a sales interview is maximized if the salesperson (1) contacts the proper person, (2) selects the right time, (3) considers the desirability of making appointments, and (4) knows techniques for handling barriers to securing the interview.

Identifying the proper person can sometimes be difficult, but the salesperson should try to see the person who is most influential in the purchase of the product. In determining the proper time to call for a sales interview, the salesperson must consider time of day, week, month, and year. The use of appointments depends on the salesperson, the product, the prospect, and the situation. Sometimes obtaining an appointment is advantageous, and other times it is not. Direct mail, telephone calls, and face-to-face requests are three ways to set up an appointment. Barriers are people whose responsibility is to see that the prospect's time is not wasted. Techniques for handling barriers are to deliver a requested item, depend on the company name, reveal something of the mission, and be confident in expecting cooperation.

Approaches can either be tailored or standard. The tailored approach is generally favored because no one approach fits all prospects. The standard approach tends to produce uniform and predictable results.

Principles of effective approaches include:

1. Making maximum use of advance information
2. Never calling "just to be calling"
3. Asking questions if necessary
4. Securing control at the beginning of the interview
5. Keeping in step with the prospect
6. Observing the law of self-interest
7. Promising a buyer benefit early
8. Showing sincere interest in the prospect's welfare
9. Being personable

Four matters deserve a final check by the salesperson as a part of the approach: physical appearance, mental attitude, equipment, and the plan for the interview.

Thinking as a problem solver is important in the interview. First, a problem must be recognized. Then, the problem must be analyzed. Next, a number of possible solutions must be generated. Then, the salesperson selects the best answer. This solution is tested and results are evaluated.

The salesperson must try to control the interview from the start. The selling situation should be surveyed. The prospect is sized up first. Then the physical surroundings are inspected. External elements can be used as indicators of purchasing power, tastes, interests, and needs. The prospect's needs should be ascertained as quickly as possible.

A salesperson must be relaxed and confident. This will encourage the confidence of prospects. A feeling of friendliness must be established also. A formal introduction may or may not be necessary or appropriate. The salesperson must gain the prospect's undivided attention. This can best be accomplished by making a specific appeal to a specific need or want.

Sound principles for opening the sales conversation include:

1. Organizing your thoughts
2. Getting down to business promptly
3. Making maximum use of prospect information obtained in advance

Common difficulties encountered in a salesperson's first call on prospects follow:

1. The prospect's natural fear of strangers
2. Getting a full hearing
3. Prospects' claims that they are too busy
4. Prospects that are not interested

REVIEW QUESTIONS

1. Which person in an organization should be sought out for an interview?
2. What elements go into deciding if the salesperson should call for an appointment?
3. List three advantages of appointments.
4. What is a barrier?
5. Why are tailored approaches generally preferable to standardized approaches?
6. Which salespeople are helped by a standard approach?
7. What is the law of self-interest, and why should it be observed?
8. What should the salesperson check before beginning the interview?
9. What are the five steps in problem solving?
10. What attitudes should the salesperson have going into the interview?
11. How can the salesperson quickly capture the prospect's attention?
12. List three principles for opening the conversation.
13. What are some typical first call problems?

DISCUSSION QUESTIONS

1. One of the best ways to handle barriers is to reveal something of the mission. Why is this method effective?
2. Describe the last tailored approach a salesperson delivered to you. Also describe the last standard approach a salesperson used to you. Which was more effective? Why?
3. Problem solving is an important aspect of securing and smoothly opening an interview. When should this process take place? When should the salesperson work at solving the prospect's problem?

4. Give three examples of prospects with whom it would be desirable to obtain an appointment. Give three examples of prospects with whom it would not be desirable to obtain an appointment. Explain why you put each prospect into its respective category.

CASE STUDY 9

Here are two telephone conversations. Both Salesperson A and Salesperson B ask the switchboard operator for John Williams, vice-president of manufacturing for a sportswear firm, and are connected with his secretary, Mary Parrier.

Conversation A

Secretary: Mr. Williams' office, Mary Parrier speaking.

Salesperson A: (briskly, trying to impress her with his importance) Mr. Williams, please.

Secretary: Whom shall I say is calling?

Salesperson A: (curtly, still trying to be impressive) Bill Bates.

Secretary: (apparently on guard now) For what company do you work, Mr. Bates?

Salesperson A: (recognizing that he is losing ground, he lets his irritation show) Just tell him it's Bill Bates.

Secretary: (definitely cool) What shall I tell Mr. Williams you want to talk to him about, Mr. Bates?

Salesperson A: Why don't you just let me tell him myself? It'll only take a minute or two.

Secretary: I'm sorry but I can't connect you with Mr. Williams unless I can tell him what the call is about.

Salesperson A: Well, if you must know, I want to make an appointment to show him our new laser-controlled pattern cutter.

Secretary: Oh, is that it? You should talk with Mrs. Byer, our purchasing agent. If you'd like I'll have the operator transfer your call.

Salesperson A: Now wait a minute! I need to talk to Mr. Williams. I know he'll want to give me an appointment.

Secretary: I'm sorry sir, but Mrs. Byer always handles these matters. If you don't want to talk with her, I'll mention you to Mr. Williams when I get the chance. Then, if he wants to see you, I'll be glad to call you back if you'll tell me your phone number.

Conversation B

Secretary: Mr. Williams' office, Mary Parrier speaking.

Salesperson B: Good morning, Miss Parrier. This is Art Sellers of the Custom Pattern Cutter Company. Is Mr. Williams' schedule pretty crowded for the next few days?

Secretary: It's always crowded, Mr. Sellers. Why do you ask?

Salesperson B: Well, several of your departments use machines like our laser-controlled pattern cutter. We now have a new model that I think will cut some of your costs and reduce manufacturing time. I'm planning to see Mrs. Byer, your purchasing agent, about it, but I hear that Mr. Williams is very interested in a cost reduction program, so I thought I'd give him a call to see if he'd like to sit in on a demonstration.

Secretary: (somewhat uncertainly) I see. Well, I'm sure Mrs. Byer will discuss it with Mr. Williams if she thinks Mr. Williams would be interested.

Salesperson B: Oh yes, I'm sure Mrs. Byer will. But if Mr. Williams would like to see the demonstration, I'll postpone talking to Mrs. Byer until it's convenient for Mr. Williams. In fact, maybe I should talk with Mr. Williams first so he can set up an appointment that's convenient for him, and then get Mrs. Byer and anyone else who might be interested to come.

Secretary: Oh, I see. Well, I believe I'd better let you talk to Mr. Williams about that yourself, Mr. Sellers. Just a minute—I'll connect you.

1. Why did Bates fail?
2. Why did Sellers succeed?

Delivering the Sales Presentation

Chapter 10

After studying this chapter you should be able to:

- Trace the advantage-proof-action sequence for telling a sales story

- Explain headlining

- Summarize six useful types of proof

- Demonstrate knowledge about the mechanics of delivering sales presentations

- Name and explain some difficulties which may be encountered when making sales presentations

- Answer questions about selling against strong competition

This chapter presents the advantage-proof-action plan for telling a sales story, makes suggestions about the actual presentation, identifies certain problems which may arise during the presentation, and suggests ways to handle strong competition.

THE ADVANTAGE-PROOF-ACTION TECHNIQUE

You have already learned that people do not buy merchandise but rather satisfaction, which is composed of many separate advantages. The way to attract a buyer's attention and interest in a sales presentation is to promise advantages or benefits. Because most buyers are somewhat inclined to doubt salespeople's promises, salespeople usually find that they must support their promises with proof. Then the salesperson tries to get action from the buyer in the form of a commitment to buy.

Stating Advantages

Stating an advantage to be gained from buying the salesperson's product is actually an appeal to a buying motive. For each buying motive to which the salesperson plans to appeal, it is necessary to have in mind several advantages to stress. The salesperson can isolate the specific advantages of a product by studying it, reading advertisements for it, reading material supplied by the company, and being alert for comments about the product from other individuals. By understanding the fundamentals of buying behavior and by placing special emphasis on the buying motives that are mainly responsible when a prospect investigates buying this type of product, the salesperson can isolate those advantages that will probably be most important to each particular prospect. The salesperson can also isolate advantages significant to a particular prospect by analyzing the advance data obtained on the prospect and by observing the prospect before and during the interview.

Suggestions for Stating Advantages. Here are some suggestions about how to state specific advantages in the sales presentation:

1. Relate what a person buys (advantages) to the reasons for buying (buying motives). The most effective way to do this is to match the most outstanding features of the product with the prospect's strongest buying motives in that product classification.
2. Make the advantage personal by fitting it to each prospect. Homemakers, for example, are members of a somewhat homogeneous group, but each homemaker wants the salesperson to personalize the presentation, not talk about homemakers in general.
3. Explain just how the prospect will actually receive the advantages. This may demand some description of technical phases of the operation of the product.
4. Do not depend on the prospect to translate the product into its benefits. Do not stop at merely pointing out the exclusive features of the product; instead, state the advantages and effectively picture what they mean to the prospect.
5. Concentrate on one buying motive at a time, and do not leave it until it has been covered satisfactorily. Under this one buying motive, do not move from one advantage to another until the first advantage has been accepted.
6. Show respect for competition. Never include in the stated advantage any reference to competition which might offend the prospect or work to a disadvantage.
7. Make no claims of advantages that cannot be proved.
8. Make the advantage specific instead of general. It is better to say, "You should net $38 a week more from this line," than to say, "This product will make money for you."
9. Use different methods of stating the advantage and be alert for new techniques of presenting advantages. For example, ask a question that challenges the prospect: "Did you know that you can arrange to receive

$600 every month after you are 60?" Or make a plain statement that promises the prospect something: "This plan will pay you $600 every month after you are 60." Or ask an "iffy" question: "If I could show you how you can get $600 every month after you're 60, you'd be interested, wouldn't you?"

Sources of Advantages. The prospect is the most productive single source of advantages the salesperson will need. Here, the first step for the salesperson to take is to study human behavior and motivation, placing special emphasis on the buying motives that are mainly responsible when a prospect thinks about, investigates, buys, and is happy with the salesperson's type of product. A second method of using the prospect as a source of advantages is that of analyzing the advance data the salesperson has on the prospect. The salesperson should look at the product from the prospect's point of view and then decide what motives will cause that particular individual to buy. A third and final way of learning from the prospect what advantages to use is through observation. Before and during the interview, the salesperson has a good opportunity to observe the prospect. The salesperson can talk with and even question the prospect, thus gaining much information about the prospect from what he or she has to say.

TRANSLATING FEATURES INTO BENEFITS

Here are a few quick translations of automobile features into benefits:

We don't sell brakes. We sell safer, surer, stops. We sell security. We sell ease of stopping.

We don't sell torsion bars. We sell smooth, controlled rides. We sell easy handling, even over rough roads. We sell "no-squat, no-dip, no-sway" in all kinds of driving and road conditions.

We don't sell insulation. We sell quiet rides. We sell protection from heat and cold.

We don't sell power steering. We sell ease of handling, the ability to park easily. We sell quick response steering in emergencies. We sell driving comfort without loss of "feel" of control.

We don't sell air conditioning. We sell driving and riding comfort. We sell clean traveling. We sell purified and filtered air—a protection against allergies.

Source: *Plain Talk About Automobile Selling,* Chrysler Corporation, pp. 46 and 47.

ILLUSTRATION 10-1. Don't depend on the prospect to translate the product into its benefits.

If the salesperson requests and gets permission to make a survey of the prospect's situation, observation identifies the advantages the prospect will enjoy if the purchase is made.

The product itself is the second source of buyer benefits. Other product sources of buyer benefits include advertisements, material supplied to the salesperson by the company, and comments from members of the distribution channel.

Headlining

Prospects are not equally interested in the same advantages or motivated by the same desires. Yet selling is easiest when it is based on the interests that are strongest for each particular prospect, when the salesperson can make major appeals to the prospect's dominant buying motives. Equipped with a large collection of product facts and buyer benefits, the salesperson feels the need for some method of selecting the major points and advantages which should be stressed.

The tactic known as headlining may often be what the salesperson is looking for. In headlining, the salesperson absorbs and masters a two- or three-sentence summary for each major advantage. The sales story is opened with a quick, impressive summary of the chief benefits of the sales proposal and a brief outline of the major reasons for buying. For example, the salesperson might give a thumbnail sketch of what the product will do in the areas of appearance, safety, and ease and economy of operation. As a product's major appeals are covered, the salesperson observes the prospect's reactions, listens to remarks made by the prospect, and analyzes the situation for clues as to which appeals to stress.

The salesperson hopes to strike a responsive chord or to draw a comment from the prospect. The salesperson wants the prospect to look at the headlined preview of the story and to respond in such a manner as to indicate the sections that he or she wants to know more about. The salesperson hopes that prospects will select the topics for the ensuing conversation just as they glance over the front page of a newspaper and decide, from the headlines, which story they will read first, which they will read next, and so on.

When the prospect responds with enthusiasm, the salesperson can emphasize those product features that tie in with this prospect's interest. The sales presentation should emphasize the services and benefits which have created the prospect's enthusiasm. The salesperson can point out advantages and offer proof relating to the prospect's individual buying motives.

Principles of Presenting Proof

The first step in the advantage-proof-action technique secures the prospect's attention, gains the prospect's interest, and kindles a desire for the product. The sole objective of the second step—giving proof for the advantages claimed—is to convince the prospect that a purchase should be made. Skepticism must be expected from prospects. They cannot be asked to believe without proof, and for this reason the salesperson must have proof for all product claims made. The salesperson must prove each advantage to the prospect until the prospect feels that it is possible to attain that advantage.

General claims of product excellence are weak and usually cannot be regarded by the prospect as legitimate grounds for buying. Concise facts are more interesting than are vague claims, and specific evidence is superior to generalizations. Prospects prefer to prove claimed advantages to themselves; but, where this is impractical, their second choice is proof from an authority. Here are six useful types of proof:

Logical Reasoning. Logical reasoning appeals to the prospect's judgment, common sense, and experience. It is a positive form of proof if the product does not lend itself well to demonstration. It can be forceful and easily grasped if it is kept simple and direct. Logical reasoning has two limitations: (1) it will seldom overcome prejudice, defective thinking, or emotion; and (2) its effectiveness is limited by the prospect's mental capacity.

The simplest and weakest form of logical reasoning used as proof is made orally by the salesperson. Oral statements may be somewhat stronger when they come from a salesperson who has extensive knowledge of and experience with buyers' problems. A second form of logical reasoning is printed. The prospect may accept this more readily than oral statements because of an inclination to believe the printed word more than the spoken. A third type of logical reasoning is found when the prospect and the salesperson sit down together and calculate on paper what will result if the prospect buys. This third form is superior to both the previously discussed forms of logical reasoning used to prove a sales point.

Company-Supplied Proof. The salesperson's company may supply a variety of types of proof. First, the company may have run tests, the results of which can be used to support the salesperson's claims. A product guarantee is a second type of proof that the product is a quality one. Third, in talking to middlemen, the company's advertising support of the product may be used as evidence of the market for the product. In discussing advertising support, the salesperson will find it desirable to know the number of dollars earmarked for advertising, the media to be used, and the total circulation of those media. A fourth example of company proof consists of statistics, such as data on dealers or consumers, supplied to the salesperson by the company. A fifth example of company-supplied proof could be the findings from a survey that the salesperson made of the prospect's circumstances.

Independent Research Findings. This third type of proof consists of data secured from impartial sources outside the salesperson's company. An example of such proof would be the results of an analysis of the salesperson's product, together with an account of the experiments conducted by an independent commercial testing laboratory. A second example would be the results of market studies made by some unrelated concern—consumer preference studies made by newspapers or magazines, for example. A third type might consist of related statistics a salesperson has acquired, such as the probability and expectancy tables of insurance companies, or the sales and expense figures for department stores collected by some impartial agency.

Testimonials. Although testimonials as a selling technique have been abused, they can still constitute an effective type of proof, particularly when the nature of the product does not allow demonstration. The person who delivers the testimonial may be: (1) an expert in some field whose position demands the prospect's respect; (2) a prominent person from the society, sports, or entertainment world; or (3) a so-called "ordinary" individual whose testimonial may be more acceptable because the individual is an everyday person like the prospect.

Case Histories. Case histories are quite similar to testimonials. The case history is built around a third party whose experience the prospect is inclined to believe because the third party is not biased, as the salesperson is, toward the product. In using case histories as a form of proof, it is generally best to build them around a customer as much like the prospect as possible. The ideal situation is to use a case history involving someone in the prospect's locality, perhaps even someone the prospect knows and can call for verification of the salesperson's statements.

Demonstration. The best type of proof that a salesperson can use is demonstration of the product. Demonstration shows how the product is constructed and how it will perform. Sometimes, of course, the nature of the product is such that it cannot be easily demonstrated. Kinds of demonstrations include that given by the salesperson during the sales interview, distribution of product samples, selling on approval, trial offers and trial orders, and placing the product in the prospect's hands to experience what it will do. Because the art of demonstrating a product effectively is so important in selling, the next chapter will be devoted to it.

Principles of Securing Action

In delivering the sales presentation, the action the salesperson wants is agreement. The salesperson wants the prospect to concur with the conviction that the prospect should have the product. Specifically, the salesperson first wants the prospect to agree with each point made and to accept each advantage presented and proved. Then the salesperson wants a "yes" to each of the five buying decisions—including, of course, the decision to buy immediately. If the salesperson is to succeed in achieving these decisions, each of the prospect's agreements must be voluntary and made without reservation. Getting some form of action early from the prospect helps to make the prospect "action-minded" from the start of the interview. Then the act of purchasing will not seem so much like a brand-new idea at the end of the interview. When a

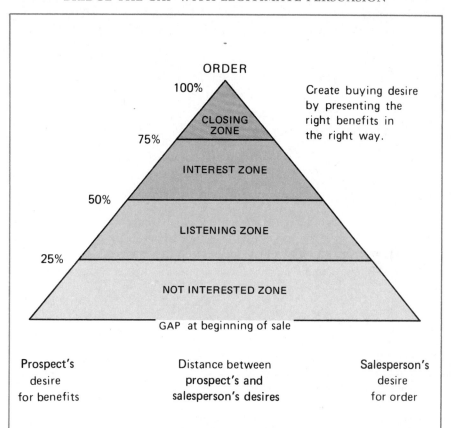

ORDER

100%

Create buying desire by presenting the right benefits in the right way.

CLOSING ZONE

75%

INTEREST ZONE

50%

LISTENING ZONE

25%

NOT INTERESTED ZONE

GAP at beginning of sale

| Prospect's desire for benefits | Distance between prospect's and salesperson's desires | Salesperson's desire for order |

There is an old legal phrase applying to contracts: "There must be a meeting of the minds." This applies to your sales too.

From a purely selfish standpoint, there is always an initial gap between your desire for the order and the prospect's desire for what he wants.

Maybe you like roast beef, but if you expect to catch fish, you feed them what they like to eat.

Successful salespeople avoid talking about what they want and emphasize instead what their prospects will get. That's how they bridge the inevitable and initial gap.

ILLUSTRATION 10-2. For its salespeople, the United States Gypsum Company describes the sales presentation as a pyramid.

prospect withholds agreement, the salesperson knows that more advantages must be presented.

Action is secured by asking questions throughout the interview—questions constructed so as to secure from the prospect a favorable commitment to each selling point and advantage. Even with difficult prospects, the salesperson will usually continue to ask questions until the prospect says something that can be interpreted as a "yes." By asking frequent questions, the salesperson observes one of the cardinal rules of selling: to take up a second point or advantage only after the prospect has accepted the first one. Occasional violation of this rule is permissible when a prospect feels lukewarm toward a particular advantage. In such cases, the salesperson will attempt once or twice to get a commitment and then will move on.

In periodic checks on the prospect, the salesperson is always alert for enthusiastic agreement on an advantage because that is a signal to try at once for a commitment on the buying decision. When there is enthusiastic agreement on one of the buying decisions, that may be a signal to try to close the sale.

Here are a few questions that can be used to advantage:

"Don't you agree?"
"You like that, don't you?"
"Isn't it?"
"Isn't that true?"
"That's worthwhile, isn't it?"
"That's what you want, isn't it?"
"You'll enjoy that, won't you?"
"Your friends will certainly enjoy this, won't they?"
"A 10 percent increase in sales sounds good, doesn't it?"
"You'd like to cut delivery costs 17 percent, wouldn't you?"

A salesperson should always be ready for unfavorable action by having some reserve selling ammunition ready. If beauty, comfort, performance, and economy fail to sell an automobile, for example, the salesperson can still talk about dependability and safety. Any attempt to get action must be so executed that a negative response will not bar the salesperson from continuing the sales presentation. In trying to achieve agreement, the salesperson should not try to trap the prospect. Instead, what is desired is the confirmation of a sound conclusion that two individuals have reached by a free discussion of mutually recognized facts. Agreement must be strong and sincere, especially in the case of the first buying decision, *need.* Until this type of agreement is secured, the salesperson must continue to add more advantages.

MECHANICS OF DELIVERING THE PRESENTATION

A sales presentation should be simple, yet complete, and should contain positive statements of what the product will do rather than negative statements of what the product will not do. A confident delivery is a valuable asset in the presentation. The poised salesperson makes a presentation that is characterized by assurance, smoothness, and finesse. The objective is to deliver successfully a presentation that will convince and persuade the prospect to make a buying decision beneficial to both parties.

Consideration for the Prospect

Because the prospect knows the caller is a salesperson from whom a presentation must be expected, the salesperson should start the sales story early in the interview. The prospect resents the salesperson's killing time on weather, sports, politics, and other unnecessary conversation. The salesperson should get down to business promptly and after making the presentation, leave promptly.

A salesperson must be careful not to offend prospects by the manner in which the presentation is made. It irritates the prospect to be interrupted while asking a question or making an objection. If the salesperson follows up by arguing or contradicting, this not only antagonizes the prospect but also makes the prospect defend any resistance. Any tactics that the prospect considers objectionable are to be avoided. That includes pestering, wisecracking, dictating, begging, or being too persistent. The salesperson should keep a respectful distance from the prospect. At the same time, the salesperson must not be the aloof type of person who talks *to* prospects rather than *with* them. Prospects do not care to be overwhelmed with the salesperson's personal opinions on products or such controversial subjects as labor unions, religion, politics, or the danger of war. Such opinions had best be expressed only when the prospect requests them. Attacking the prospect's present choice of product, or arbitrarily making a decision or selection for the prospect are unreasonable presumptions.

The salesperson's assumption in making the sales presentation should be that the main objective is to serve the prospect. This attitude will be reflected in a concern for the prospect and a sensitive response to the prospect's interests. Adopting the role of an interested friend, the salesperson will strive for the prospect's goodwill by being agreeable and by demonstrating courtesy and tact. Anything that annoys or upsets the prospect works against, rather than for, the salesperson.

Necessity for Social Interaction

Social interaction is the salesperson's most useful approach to influencing a buyer's opinions and purchase decisions. Social interaction takes place when the salesperson and the buyer exchange information, feelings, attitudes, and ideas; it is two-way communication. The superior salesperson is sensitive to and in harmony with each buyer's likes and dislikes. The salesperson can strengthen the social relationship by recasting the buyer's comments, asking the buyer questions, or soliciting the buyer's opinions.

The more satisfaction or value (appreciation, agreement) the buyer receives from a salesperson, the more the buyer is inclined to do what the salesperson wants done. When the salesperson and the buyer identify and interact with each other, they constitute, in a sense, a "we" unit.

A salesperson needs a large vocabulary, and must be able to use it effectively. With a generous command of words, the salesperson can choose from a wide assortment and select for use those that are most appropriate. Thus, expression can be more impressive as well as more precise. Concepts and suggestions can be expressed in a concise manner, and greater conciseness contributes to greater success in influencing the thoughts and actions of buyers.

WORDS THAT PEOPLE LOVE TO HEAR

Since a salesman's stock-in-trade is words, he ought to know which ones carry the most impact with prospects and customers. One salesman, over a period of time, has discovered that the following words—and phrases built around them—get the most attention—and action—from people.

Introductory words: *Phrases:*

You	You are the most important consideration . . .
Yourself	Treat yourself to . . .
Here	Here is a product you can . . .
This	This is the best product you can . . .
Easy	It's easy to own, to learn, to operate, etc.
Know	As you probably know . . .

Words leading into explanations: *Phrases:*

How	Here's how to get the most . . .
Why	Why is this the product for you . . .
Learn	Learn the secret of . . .

Trigger words: *Phrases:*

Test	Test it yourself . . .
Prove	Prove it to yourself . . .
Look	Look at it, try it . . .
Write	Write to us immediately for . . .
Call	Call now, don't wait . . .
Earned	You've earned it . . .
Owe	You owe it to yourself . . .

Source: Reprinted with permission of *The American Salesman,* 2/1978, The National Research Bureau, Inc., 424 North Third Street, Burlington, Iowa 52601.

ILLUSTRATION 10-3. The salesperson must not be the aloof type of person who talks *to* prospects rather than *with* them.

While it is true that a salesperson should appeal to more than just the buyer's sense of hearing, one can nevertheless contend that words are a salesperson's basic tools. They are depended on most heavily in communication with buyers.

In those types of selling where buyers' backgrounds, intelligence, and education are above the average, the need for an outstanding vocabulary becomes even more important. In those areas, salespeople must set themselves apart from ordinary salespeople because their buyers are not ordinary buyers. Instead, such buyers are highly sensitive to and respond to salespeople's speech. The better their mastery and use of words, the better the salespeople sell.

Voice and Rate of Delivery

A pleasing, effective voice is a valuable asset to a salesperson. It is a most important selling tool, and it increases both confidence and sales volume. Two common errors involve loudness. If the salesperson talks too loudly, buyers are irritated; if the salesperson talks too softly, buyers must strain if they are to hear, and the salesperson may not sound authoritative. Incidentally, salespeople should master the uses of whispers *and* shouts. They should be expert in the use of inflection (the changing of voice tone or pitch) so that important words will be emphasized. In general, voices pitched rather low are more pleasing than those pitched high.

SPEAKING PROBLEMS

The National Society of Sales Training Executives surveyed 200 purchasing agents to find out what they felt were annoying habits and problems in the speech of salespeople. Here are the most frequently mentioned problems:

Talking in a hesitating manner.	Talking with gum in the mouth.
Talking in an affected manner.	Talking with a stutter or lisp.
Talking in a mumble.	Talking too loudly.
Talking in a high-pitched voice.	Talking too fast or too slow.
Talking in a dull, colorless way.	Talking in a brash tone.
Talking with a nasal twang.	Talking indistinctly over the tele-
Talking with excessive saliva.	phone.

Source: R. M. Sandell, "Your Voice—A Valuable Asset As You Sell." Reprinted with permission of *The American Salesman*, 2/1979, The National Research Bureau, Inc., 424 North Third Street, Burlington, Iowa 52601.

ILLUSTRATION 10-4. A pleasing, effective voice is a valuable asset to a salesperson. It is a most important selling tool.

The rate of delivery of the sales presentation must be adjusted to the prospect's speed of thought and ability to comprehend. If the salesperson rushes the presentation by talking too fast, some points will not register and thus will not be understood. If the salesperson talks too slowly for the impatient prospect, the prospect's attention will wander. The more common error is for salespeople to talk too fast because they know their presentations so well.

The salesperson's delivery should be animated and not monotonous. By dramatic use of pauses, by executing accompanying gestures, and by changing the voice's pitch and volume, the salesperson is able to maintain a more interesting pace. Although speed of delivery should be varied for emphasis and variety, the flow of the story should be so smooth that salesperson and prospect stay mentally in step with each other.

Uses of Silence

Silence can be a great ally to the salesperson. Here are examples of its uses: (1) Silence gives the buyer an opportunity to make a comment, ask a question, or voice an objection; these usually signal the salesperson to resume selling. (2) Too many salespeople talk too much; some silence is a welcome change of pace to many buyers. (3) Silence establishes rapport and contributes to social interaction. (4) It can focus attention on a product or dramatize a product feature in certain product demonstrations. (5) A moment of silence emphasizes the last point the salesperson made, encouraging the buyer to accept it. (6) Silence can permit a hostile buyer to "talk away" some hostility. (7) It is a mild but effective influence toward purchase, letting the buyer think matters over and reach a decision to buy.

The Skill of Creative Listening

Most of the time the salesperson is not talking should be spent in creative listening. Talking is one phase of oral communication—listening is the other. Listening is a skill because it can be improved.

A salesperson should spend much time listening to buyers. Why? To get information, to bid for buyers' goodwill, and to compliment buyers are three examples. A salesperson who is to be an active listener, interested in and alert to buyers, must acquire the skill of listening; listening is hard work.

What do salespeople who are good listeners do? They maintain eye contact with the buyer, showing attention and interest. They permit themselves little relaxation of posture or facial expression. Good listeners concentrate attention on what the buyer says and does, never faking that attention; this is quite an achievement because, for most individuals, speed of thinking is much faster than talking speed. Good listeners note changes in a buyer's tone and inflection, and try to interpret what the buyer does *not* say. They hope to think ahead of the buyer, focusing on main ideas and striving to understand what the buyer is actually communicating.

Salespeople who listen well do not hesitate to ask questions for clarification and confirmation, but do not interrupt; do not run out of patience; do not reveal any lack of interest in what the buyer says; are not distracted by a buyer's personality, appearance, grammar, or delivery; do not harbor bias or prejudice; and do not allow themselves to react emotionally to "red flag" words such as taxes. The goal of creative listening is to assure effective two-way communication.

Assuring Two-Way Communication

Interviews are more satisfactory if both the salesperson and the buyer take part. Thus, it is desirable for the salesperson to encourage each buyer to enter into the interview and to contribute ideas, questions, and reactions. It is particularly wise for a salesperson not to monopolize the conversation when the buyer is expertly informed and qualified in buying, as many purchasing agents are. The salesperson may find that an interview with such a buyer is an excellent opportunity to acquire valuable information and that there is a much better chance of making the sale if the buyer is encouraged to talk.

The proper amount of buyer-participation is difficult to define and just as difficult to control. The buyer who talks too much is just as much a problem as the buyer who says little. Somewhere between these two extremes is a satisfactory balance. Even while listening, the salesperson's facial expressions, movements, and actions can, at least to a degree, influence how much the buyer talks and can guide what is said. What does a salesperson gain from seeing that buyers take part? Here are some of the more significant benefits:

1. The salesperson receives additional information that can be used to advantage because the buyer reveals the thoughts and feelings of the moment.
2. The salesperson can spot the buying motives and objections of the buyer and can proceed accordingly.
3. Buyers who take part in the conversation are more apt to lead themselves through the stages of interest, desire, and conviction.
4. Buyers who take part in the conversation are apt to disclose, intentionally or unintentionally, what they want in a given product and even how the salesperson can help them achieve it.
5. The salesperson gains goodwill because attempts to encourage the buyer to talk indicate interest in what the buyer has to say.

Not all successful salespeople encourage questions and comments from prospects, preferring to present their entire proposals without interruption. This does not seem to be so sound a policy as that of welcoming questions and objections from the prospect. When the prospect expresses his or her views, it gives the salesperson an indicator which measures the progress the salesperson is making because it shows what the prospect is thinking. The prospect who takes part in the conference generally has greater interest. Answers to the salesperson's questions supply needed information. These same questions can be used to challenge the prospect and to plant ideas. If the prospect is so agreeable as to make the salesperson suspicious about the penetration and actual acceptance of the story, such questions as these are helpful:

"Just where can my product help you most?"
"Which concerns you more, increased sales or reduced expenses?"

The fact that the salesperson arranges for and achieves dialogue gives variety to the presentation. Most important of all, dialogue makes it possible for the salesperson to get agreement as the interview progresses, leaving no gaps in acceptance.

Using Questions

There is an art to asking questions just as there is an art to listening to a buyer's conversation. Strategically, the salesperson can use questions to help discover what a buyer needs or wants from a product. Then questions can be phrased to help a buyer recognize these needs or wants. Questions can identify the topics which a salesperson can profitably discuss and the topics which should be avoided or at least handled cautiously.

There are also several tactical jobs that questioning can perform. First, it is the simplest technique for insuring two-way communication. Second, it can be used to recapture a buyer's attention and to create interest. Third, a salesperson can determine how well the sales story is being understood by asking questions. Fourth, buyers appreciate and are favorably impressed by questions about their ideas and attitudes. Finally, asking questions and receiving answers to them are ways of getting on record a buyer's agreement to portions of the sales proposal.

Rehearsing the Presentation

A quick and painless way to become proficient in presenting a sales story is to rehearse. Cheerleaders and members of the clergy, politicians and debaters, public speakers and actors—all know the value of rehearsals. These people will assure salespeople that running through a sales story aloud is the best preparation and training they know to acquire poise and confidence. Salespeople are advised to write out a sales story, and then read and reread it—editing, revising, and improving it on each trip through. Then comes the rehearsing. At first this can consist of nothing more than reading or speaking the story aloud. Next, the salesperson can talk before a mirror. After this, the presentation can be made to someone else, perhaps an accommodating friend. Or two salespeople can take turns playing the role of salesperson and buyer. Eventually, the salesperson will progress to the point at which a presentation can be rehearsed mentally; this permits rehearsal in a variety of places and circumstances.

Certain matters should get particular attention in the rehearsals. One such matter is the salesperson's manner of speaking. The objectives here should be correct pronunciation, pleasant tone of voice, clear enunciation, proper inflection, and a change of pace which lends variety and emphasis to the presentation. Another matter, closely related to speech, includes the key words and phrases which, after being tried and tested, prove to be effective. A third matter is that of the extremes which should be avoided. Anything overdone or underdone—whether it is emphasis, enthusiasm, contrast, speed, or length of story—handicaps the salesperson.

DIFFICULTIES ENCOUNTERED IN THE SALES PRESENTATION

Almost all salespeople encounter some difficulties or obstacles in any given sales presentation. The most common difficulties are external interruptions; interruptions by prospects; and difficult prospects who may be inattentive, silent, indifferent, undecided, skeptical, or hostile.

External Interruptions

One of the most troublesome experiences encountered by salespeople is external interruption of their presentations. The external interruptions a salesperson must cope with are usually of three types: the prospect may receive a telephone call, may be called away from the interview, or may be visited by someone else. These external interruptions break the prospect's flow of thought by calling attention to other matters. They reduce the cumulative force of the presentation, consume the salesperson's time, and give the prospect an excuse for ending the interview or for not buying.

The salesperson can use the break caused by an external interruption for a quick mental review of what has been done up to that point. This will enable planning the rest of the interview soundly. When the prospect resumes the interview, the salesperson should not act as though nothing has happened; that would be too abrupt, because the prospect has been away physically, mentally, or both. Instead, the salesperson should summarize the points made prior to the interruption to remind the prospect of the ground that was covered, and check for understanding and attention.

For lengthy interruptions, particularly those from which the prospect seems to return in a worried or distracted frame of mind, the salesperson should try to regain control and continue the presentation. If unsuccessful, the salesperson should make an appointment for an early return call. When external interruptions are either too long or too numerous, it is usually advisable to make a later appointment.

It is frequently possible to avoid or reduce external interruptions. The shorter the salesperson's presentation, the less time there is for interruption. Also, there will be fewer interruptions if the salesperson calls during hours that are not especially busy for the prospect. Sometimes a direct, courteous request to go to a quiet place is sufficient. Finally, if the salesperson can convince the prospect that this will be an important interview that should not be interrupted, the prospect is likely to cooperate.

Interruptions by Prospects

Every question that a prospect asks interrupts the salesperson's story, whether the question is a request for information, an objection, or a willful attempt to derail the salesperson from the sales talk. There are two broad methods of handling a question: to deal with it at once, or to postpone answering it. If the salesperson elects to handle the question immediately, he or she should do so with firmness and conviction. The reply should be brief, yet satisfy the prospect, and the salesperson should attempt to resume the story immediately.

If an instantaneous answer to the prospect's question would, for any reason, be awkward, then the salesperson should try to postpone handling the question. Particularly if the question is really an objection, the salesperson may find it desirable and possible to delay an answer with some such reply as:

"I'm coming to that."
"I'll take up that point in a minute."
"Yes, I can see your point."
"Yes, I'll cover that later."
"Perhaps you're right."

The salesperson will then resume the presentation.

We know that the sales story should be built about the product's advantages rather than the weaknesses of competitive products, for this construction makes it more persuasive. If the prospect insists early in the presentation that the salesperson's product be compared with a competitive brand, perhaps the brand the prospect then owns, the comparison should be executed immediately and fairly.

Prices should be kept in the background in the initial stages of the interview. Price is a relative factor that depends on what the buyer gets; it is important only in terms of value. A prospect cannot judge price fairly without knowing what the product will do. And a price quoted too soon always sounds high because the salesperson has not had time to establish the value. For these reasons, an early inquiry about price should be sidetracked, perhaps with such a diverting question as "Which model fits your needs?" or "What size are you thinking about?"

Chapter 12 is devoted to discussing the most troublesome form of interruption by prospects, the objection.

The Difficult Prospect

Sometimes a salesperson encounters a prospect who for some reason is difficult to handle. Six causes of such difficulty are now discussed.

Inattentiveness. When the prospect's attention wanders away from the presentation, the salesperson should try at once to determine the cause. It may be that the sales story is so vague that the prospect cannot or will not spend the effort required to follow it. It may be that the salesperson's method of presentation is failing to interest the prospect. It may be that the prospect's attention is intermittently yet irresistibly drawn to other matters.

One possible course of action is to mention the prospect's various wants, if the salesperson knows them, in the hope of finding a clue to the prospect's most powerful buying motives. A second and somewhat similar possibility is to summarize what the product delivers, all the while looking for clues. Third, the salesperson may need to startle the prospect and recapture the prospect's attention by enthusiastically presenting a new slant, a new case history, or a new advantage. Fourth, proof that is more meaningful than any yet given may be offered. Fifth, the salesperson may pause in the presentation until the prospect's attention returns. Sixth, in serious cases when the prospect is too inattentive, the salesperson may frankly ask for more attention. If none of these techniques succeeds in recapturing the prospect's attention, the only resort left is to ask for a later appointment.

Silence. Being met by silence is not so serious as it might seem because the prospect who listens can be sold. The proper procedure is to feed advantages and proof slowly to the prospect and to make sure the prospect is listening. If questions such as, "That's true, isn't it?" are frequently interspersed, the salesperson is taking positive action to draw out the prospect. An occasional question which cannot be answered by "yes" or "no" will help the salesperson check the progress being made.

Indifference. One of the most exasperating hurdles a salesperson must overcome is prospect indifference. The difficult job here is to convince the prospect of need, without the prospect becoming aware of being on the road to buying. To do this, the salesperson must keep the interview informal and frictionless. The salesperson must make the interview a casual dialogue and, ignoring the prospect's apparent indifference, must continue to add advantage to advantage.

Indecision. The salesperson confronts indecision where the prospect's uncertainty and hesitation cause postponement of the purchase. With this kind of difficulty, the salesperson must take the initiative by demonstrating friendly but firm guidance. By taking a positive, decisive attitude, the salesperson helps the prospect make a decision. Questions should be asked throughout the presentation to build up a series of commitments by the prospect, and the close should not frighten the prospect. Relating case histories can be an extremely effective method of dealing with the indecisive prospect.

Skepticism. Skeptical prospects are usually people who have been deceived by a salesperson or who know other people who have been deceived. Instead of making the skeptic back up claims, the salesperson should go ahead with the presentation and keep piling up facts backed by reliable proof. By being intentionally conservative, the salesperson makes it difficult for the prospect to voice disagreement. Above all, the salesperson must remain poised in dealing with the skeptical prospect and must refuse to argue.

Hostility. The salesperson who encounters a prospect who is decidedly antagonistic must try to change that attitude. Such an attitude can have far-reaching harmful effects on the salesperson's company and the salesperson. Also, a hostile prospect tends to become a good customer once an erroneous opinion of the salesperson and the salesperson's company has been corrected. The worst course of action the salesperson can take is to argue. The prospect will naturally become defensive, even if proved wrong, and will usually be too irritated to buy. Instead, the salesperson should listen sympathetically, thank the prospect for the information, and promise to investigate and try to remedy the cause of dissatisfaction.

SELLING AGAINST STRONG COMPETITION

To sell effectively in a competitive environment, a salesperson must (1) have the proper attitude toward competitors, (2) know who the competitive salespeople are and what their sales presentations are like, and (3) avoid unsound ways of handling information about competitors.

Proper Attitude Toward Competition

One feature of the salesperson's attitude toward competitors should be a respect for them and their products. In many lines, one brand of product is just about the same as other brands, and prospects know this. Furthermore, competition involves companies, salespeople, and products that have both good points and loyal supporters. A prospect may buy or use a competing product. In view of this, it is a mistake to show lack of respect for competition in front of the prospect. The wiser thing is to show respect for all competitors by giving them credit for their selling efforts and their products.

A second characteristic of a proper attitude toward competitors is fairness. Salespeople lower themselves in the prospect's estimation when they do or say anything that smacks of unfair treatment or unfair criticism of competition. Resentment may be particularly strong when no defenders of competitors are present or when a direct comparison requested by the prospect is not made fairly. All questions and comparisons call for an honest "Let's put all the cards on the table and see just what is what" treatment. Such fairness gives the salesperson two things: (1) the good feeling that results from operating ethically and (2) more enthusiastic customers.

Confidence is a final essential of a proper attitude toward competition. It is the comforting knowledge that the salesperson has nothing to fear from any fair product comparison. Some people feel that the new salesperson can know too much about the competition. This attitude is explained by two fears. The first fear is that if the new salesperson learns very much about the competition, a fear-of-competition complex may develop. The second fear is that the salesperson may do unwise things in the collection and use of these facts.

These fears are not sound. Success as a salesperson is in serious doubt if the salesperson is one who in learning about the competition will develop a fear-of-competition complex, will be unduly impressed by competitors' good qualities, or is apt to get an exaggerated idea of who the competitors are and what they are doing.

The second fear cannot correctly be charged against the salesperson's knowledge of competition, for what the critics refer to is the salesperson's misuse of time or selling efforts. They fear that the new salesperson may be inclined to spend too much time hunting for competitive weaknesses when that time should be devoted to studying the merits of the salesperson's own product. Selling efforts are misdirected if they are channeled into a condemnation of competing products for their weak points instead of into a positive explanation of what the salesperson's product does for buyers.

Instead of being frightened at the thought of learning too much that is good and bad about competition, the successful salesperson collects and uses information about competition in a purposeful manner.

Competitors' Selling Activities

In regard to competitors' selling activities, the salesperson will want to obtain information on competitive salespeople and on competitive presentations.

Competitive Salespeople. The first thing to know about competitive activities is who the competitive salespeople are. Personal facts about the people who represent competitors might include their names, backgrounds, where they live, their interests and tastes, their avocations, and the social circles within which they move. Business facts might include the length of time they have been with their companies, what they did previously, their various duties, and how long they have worked in their territories.

More specific and relevant information about competitors' salespeople concerns their sales personalities. Their personal characteristics are worth knowing. Their concepts of the duties of a salesperson and their patterns and methods of operation should be valuable. How their prospects and customers rate them as salespeople, what prospects like and dislike about them, and whether they are considered as personal friends as well as sources of supply are bits of information that can be used to advantage.

For example, if a salesperson relies too heavily on friendship to hold present customers, relationships with them are not secure. Such a situation invites another salesperson to move in with more quality, more service, lower prices, or better selling efforts because these are the things that will get and hold customers away from competition.

The more similar competing products are, the more the emphasis shifts away from merchandise features and toward the salesperson as an individual. In some lines, a given product can be bought on the buyer's specifications from two or more vendors of equally satisfactory standing and at the same or approximately the same price. In such cases, the purchaser has little on which to base a choice except differences in competing salespeople. Hence, a salesperson needs to know whom as well as what the competition is.

Competitive Presentations. As far as competitive presentations are concerned, a salesperson is particularly interested in two things: what was said and how it was said. The proposition offered by the competing representative is the "what" that our salesperson needs to know, and the first consideration is the product recommended to the prospect. Our salesperson must determine whether or not the item recommended adequately meets the prospect's requirements. The price quoted by the other representative, as well as terms and allowances, should be learned.

A second phase of the "what" of competitive presentations involves what is said about the competing product and about our salesperson's product. Particularly desirable is information about the selling points stressed. Which product features do competitive representatives emphasize? Which are not mentioned? What word-of-mouth publicity is being given to our salesperson's products? Do competing salespeople take a dim view of some of the features of others' products? If so, can that view be converted from a drawback into an effective advantage for the buyer?

A third phase of what competing representatives say is comprised of their most effective selling techniques. For each individual prospect, a salesperson benefits from knowing those features of competitive proposals that have strong appeal. Similarly, the features which most often impress prospects in general are good to know. Add to these persuasive features the closing appeals that frequently take away orders, and the result is a collection of data that better enables our salesperson to select and emphasize the features of the proposition which will counteract competitive features.

The second part of the competitive presentation concerns methods of presentation; these are important because the more a salesperson knows about the type of presentation made by each competitor, the stronger the salesperson's own presentation can be. The aids that are used, the models, samples, charts, catalogs, reports, and survey findings are all parts of the presentation. If demonstrations are used, especially when they are impressive, our salesperson cannot afford to be uninformed about them.

Handling Information About Competitors

Selling against strong competition takes tact, judgment, and control. Every product, salesperson, and company has its good points. Each salesperson will stress those points. The prospect buys the product the prospect believes will provide the greatest amount of satisfaction. Because selling against competition is, at best, a difficult matter, some suggestions about what not to do should be helpful. If the following errors are avoided, the handling of competition will be less risky and costly:

1. Do not include any reference to competition in constructing the sales presentation because it is not sound strategy to recognize it in that manner. In putting your presentation together, be like the runner who eyes the tape, not the other runners.
2. Never initiate the subject of competition. If it is to be mentioned, let the prospect make the first reference. Furthermore, do not compare your product with another unless the prospect demands it. Neither should competition be discussed except to answer a direct question.
3. Do not stray or be maneuvered away from the primary task, which is to explain what your product will do for the prospect. Do not be dragged into a discussion of competitive topics.
4. Have no ambitions to win mudslinging contests. Most prospects detect and resent any disparaging remarks made by competing sales representatives.
5. Never make a statement about competition before checking its accuracy.
6. Do not expose flaws in competition in the hope of making sales through this tactic.
7. Don't welcome gossip. If you must listen to it, don't repeat it.
8. Never criticize competition. Criticism evidences poor sales technique. Prospects know that you are not impartial and thus may have difficulty believing you. Prospects may like and have faith in the other brand, and they will resent any belittling of it.

SUMMARY

The way to attract a buyer's attention and interest is to point out advantages or benefits. This is the first phase of the advantage-proof-action technique. By understanding buying behavior and the motives buyers have when purchasing a given product, the salesperson can isolate the most desirable advantages of the product and develop ways to present them. The prospect and the product are the two major sources of advantages. Headlining is when the salesperson uses a summary for each major advantage. Then the salesperson looks for clues from the prospect as to which appeals to stress.

The second phase of the advantage-proof-action technique, giving proof for the advantages claimed, is to convince the prospect that a purchase should be made. Proof can be offered in the form of logical reasoning, company-supplied proof, independent research findings, testimonials, case histories, or demonstrations.

The action the salesperson wants is agreement that the prospect should have the product. Action is secured by asking questions throughout the interview. Agreement must be strong and sincere, especially regarding need.

A sales presentation should be simple and complete, containing positive statements of what the product will do. The salesperson should begin the sales story early in the interview, be careful not to offend the prospect, and show concern for the prospect, acting like an interested friend. Anything that annoys or upsets the prospect works against the salesperson.

Social interaction is the salesperson's most useful approach to influencing a buyer's opinions and purchase decisions. A "we" unit is most desirable in a selling situation.

A large vocabulary, appropriately used, is necessary. Concepts and suggestions must be expressed concisely. A pleasing, effective voice is an important selling tool. Appropriate volume and rate of delivery are necessary when presenting a sales talk. Silence can also be used effectively.

Listening is an important skill. Listening involves maintaining eye contact with the buyer, showing interest, and interpreting what the buyer is saying and not saying. Two-way communication makes interviews more effective. Getting the buyer involved helps the salesperson identify what the prospect wants in a given product.

Rehearsing is the best way to become proficient in presenting a sales story. Speaking manner, key words and phrases, and avoiding extremes are important areas for rehearsal.

Almost all salespeople encounter some difficulties or obstacles in any given sales presentation. The most common difficulties are external interruption; interruptions by prospects; and difficult prospects who may be inattentive, silent, indifferent, undecided, skeptical, or hostile.

Respect and fairness should be shown toward competitors and their products. Still, the salesperson must be confident. The salesperson should know who the competitors' salespeople are, their backgrounds, patterns, and products. Also, competitive presentations should be understood, specifically what was said and how it was said. Selling against strong competition takes tact, judgment, and control. Handling information about competitors in the proper way will reduce the risks and costs of selling in a competitive environment.

REVIEW QUESTIONS

1. What are the best sources of advantages?
2. How should salespeople determine which advantages to stress to a particular prospect?
3. Why is proof presented to buyers?
4. List three effective types of proof.
5. How is action best secured?
6. What actions do salespeople try to evoke from prospects?
7. Why is social interaction necessary in the sales presentation?
8. How can silence be used to help a sales presentation?
9. What do salespeople who are good listeners do?
10. How can salespeople minimize the effects of external interruptions?
11. What are some methods for dealing with inattentiveness?
12. Describe the proper attitude toward competition.
13. What should a salesperson know about the competition's salespeople and their presentations?
14. What are some effects of mishandling information about competitors?

DISCUSSION QUESTIONS

1. Assume that you are a salesperson using a canned approach. What specific concerns would you have about your presentation that another salesperson who was not using a canned talk would not have?
2. Assume that you are the sales manager for a home furnishings manufacturer. You have working for you a salesperson who operates on a very tight schedule, seeing more customers than any other salesperson each week. This salesperson's volume is about average, but the sales per customer are smaller than average. What would you say to this salesperson to help improve performance?
3. A cardinal rule of selling is never argue with a customer. How can a sales manager persuade an argumentative salesperson who has been complained about by a customer to stop arguing?

CASE STUDY 10A

Bruce Stuart has been selling carpets to home furnishings retailers for the two years since he graduated from college. He considers himself to be a better-than-average salesperson and is particularly proud of the tight schedule he maintains in order to cover his territory efficiently.

The tight schedule he keeps helps him sell more, he believes, because it allows him to see more prospects each day and because it wastes less of the buyer's time. To make sure of keeping a tight schedule, Stuart has memorized and practiced his sales presentations and knows exactly how long he can and should spend with each prospect.

He finds that he is usually quite successful in selling what he expects to sell to each prospect, so he was surprised last week to be criticized by his sales manager for missing out on some opportunities for several fairly large sales. He replied to the sales manager that he could hardly have been expected to make these sales because he didn't even know that the buyers were planning these major purchases. They must have been spur-of-the-moment purchases, Stuart suggested, because he felt quite sure that those customers would not have ordered from anyone else if they had planned their purchases and called him in advance.

1. What is Stuart doing wrong in his sales presentations?
2. What can he do to improve?

CASE STUDY 10B

Chris Armstrong is a young salesperson with the Global Life Insurance Company. One day a friend, Joe Craig, tipped Armstrong to the fact that Ed Carmichael had mentioned he was having trouble saving money. Armstrong discovered that Carmichael was a servicer with Monarch Electric, a combination electrical contracting firm and appliance store. Craig told Armstrong that Carmichael is just 22 years old, has a wife and infant, and has a trade school education. He has worked well for Monarch and is in line for promotion. With this information, Armstrong telephoned Carmichael one Friday at Monarch Electric.

Salesperson:	Mr. Carmichael, I'm Chris Armstrong. Joe Craig and I were talking earlier this week. Joe said something that led me to believe you might be interested in a plan to save some money. I know a good way to save money and would like to tell you about it. May I drop by your house tonight—about 7:30?
Prospect:	We'll be real busy tonight packing for a two-week vacation which starts tomorrow.
Salesperson:	I wish you would spare me a few minutes tonight. It could be well worth your time.
Prospect:	No, I can't, and I've told you why.
Salesperson:	Then after you get back?
Prospect:	Maybe.
Salesperson:	Today is Friday, July 8. How about three weeks from tonight, July 29 at 7:30?
Prospect:	Oh, all right.
Salesperson:	Fine. See you then.

On Friday, July 29, Armstrong knocked on Carmichael's door at 7:20 P.M.

Salesperson:	Mr. Carmichael? I'm Chris Armstrong. Three weeks ago I phoned you at work and set up an appointment for tonight to talk about saving money.
Prospect:	What's this? Who are you? I don't remember any appointment.
Salesperson:	We set this up the day before you went on your vacation.
Prospect:	Well, maybe so. Come in.
Salesperson:	I hope Mrs. Carmichael is here.
Prospect:	She went out a few minutes ago to see a neighbor.
Salesperson:	Mr. Carmichael, if a person earns $9,000 a year on the average from age 25 to age 65, that's a total of $360,000. A lot of money, isn't it? What do you think your average earnings will be from now to the age of 65?
Prospect:	I don't know. Maybe $10,000.
Salesperson:	$10,000 multiplied by 40 years equals $400,000. Part of that should be yours to keep. But, too often, the size of the savings account goes up and down like a yo-yo. Ed, just how much do you think you could save each week—$6? $5? $4?
Prospect:	I guess I could save $4 a week.
Salesperson:	Here's a plan where you save only $3 a week. It covers all three possibilities: first, that you live and complete the plan; second, that you die before reaching your goal; and third, that you quit the plan somewhere along the way before completing it. At 65, you can have $10,450 in a lump sum, or you can choose to get a monthly check for life to supplement your other retirement income. If you should die before reaching your goal, $10,000 will be paid to your beneficiary.
Prospect:	Wait a minute! What you call a savings plan sounds like life insurance to me. Is it?
Salesperson:	Well—uh—it's both. But let me finish. If you quit the plan somewhere along the way, the policy will provide you the cash value it has built up or an amount of fully paid-up insurance. So, you see, this plan takes care and provides if you live, if you die, or if you quit. Now, how would you prefer to make your premium deposit? (At this moment Mrs. Carmichael enters the front door.)
Prospect:	Beth, this is Chris Armstrong. I think he's been saying we should save money and then spend it for insurance.
Mrs. Carmichael:	Hi. We must tell you, Mr. Armstrong, we won't be buying any insurance now.
Salesperson:	Well, thanks for your time. See you later. Goodnight.

What errors did the salesperson commit?

Demonstrations 11

After studying this chapter you should be able to:

- Indicate the psychological value of demonstrating
- Recognize when and what to demonstrate
- Argue successfully that advance preparation is necessary
- Outline the principles of effective demonstrating
- Describe the use of showmanship in demonstration

Demonstrations can be used for many purposes. They can be constructed to capture the interest of the prospect and move the prospect toward desire, conviction, and, hence, action. They are particularly effective in achieving conviction. They show what the product will do for the prospect. They prove that the product is the solution to one of the prospect's problems. They prove the salesperson's points by presenting external evidence to back up assertions. They make the story sink in and stick. They translate words into action. They can be used to teach the prospect how to use the product or the merchant how to sell it. Finally, they can be real time-savers because one simple demonstration can often be the equal of a flood of oral elequence.

PSYCHOLOGICAL VALUE OF DEMONSTRATING

When a salesperson delivers only an oral sales presentation, prospects may instinctively adopt a defensive role and confront the salesperson as an opponent. But when the salesperson demonstrates, prospects feel involved. The prospect no longer sees the salesperson as an adversary; instead, salesperson and prospect are joint participants in a situation or an exercise.

"Seeing is believing" is psychologically sound. Truly, to see, smell, touch, or taste is to accept and believe—to learn—because your senses report to you. The more complicated the subject, the more demonstration facilitates learning.

To get the maximum psychological impact from a demonstration, the salesperson must do some research. The salesperson must identify the major benefits to demonstrate and must devise the most persuasive way to communicate those benefits. The demonstration must be as simple, clear, and dramatic as possible. Prospect participation is essential. If these requirements are met, rapport will be maximized and the demonstration will be psychologically strong.

Why Prospects Like Demonstrations

Prospects like demonstrations because they prefer to trust their own senses rather than a salesperson's promises. They would rather taste than be told how something tastes, rather touch than be told how something feels, and see how a product works than hear a description of the process. When prospects take part in the demonstration, their participation gives them something to do for themselves. Prospects learn by experience what the product will and will not do, and how to operate and use it properly.

Demonstrations are popular because they permit prospects to understand the salesperson's product and proposal quickly. They convert talk into action, translating general concepts into specific, concrete form.

Why Salespeople Like to Demonstrate

Salespeople like to demonstrate because demonstrations are helpful both in starting prospects out on the road to buying and in carrying them well down that road. They reach out and grab the prospect's attention, quickly develop it into interest, and usually increase the prospect's desire for the item. This is true because for many products the demonstration is one of the quickest and surest ways to prove need. Demonstrations also are effective in achieving conviction. They convince better than words because they are a much stronger form of proof. The sense of sight is an especially powerful channel through which to communicate. Some authorities have claimed that the eye is 22 to 25 times as powerful as the ear in transmitting impressions to the brain.

Demonstrations make presentations more effective. Clearly, when the salesperson makes contact with a prospect through two or more of the prospect's senses, the chances of selling are greater than if the prospect is reached through only the sense of hearing. The impressions the salesperson makes are deeper and more vivid. The points made are remembered longer because they penetrate further. Belief is more likely because the prospect's grasp of the product and its advantages is firmer.

Opposition to buying is reduced by effective demonstrations. Attention is focused on the benefits that are to be had. The prospect cannot deny what the salesperson is demonstrating. The salesperson does not seem to be selling—just operating, explaining, and showing. The prospect and the salesperson are partners in executing and watching the demonstration. As a result, there are fewer interruptions of the troublesome, unwelcome type.

Finally, demonstrations make for strong, effective selling. They simplify the salesperson's job, giving the salesperson more time and confidence. Not only can they be used to impress, startle, and even amaze, but they also can steer prospects whose attention is prone to wander. It is difficult to quarrel with the claim that every sales story ever composed can be strengthened by the addition of demonstrations.

WHEN AND WHAT TO DEMONSTRATE

Demonstration can be used by the salesperson at any time. The salesperson may use demonstration to open the interview. Usually those openers are only partial demonstrations and are employed only to get the prospect's complete attention. The demonstration most often follows some introductory selling talk and is usually accompanied by its own oral presentation.

Salespeople must be able to demonstrate every product feature that a prospect finds interesting. In addition, salespeople must master several methods of demonstrating the outstanding points of their products. This is not to say that salespeople should go through their entire assortment of demonstrations on every call. In using a more effective plan, the salesperson learns the prospect's exact needs and interests, then concentrates the demonstration on the features of the product that most closely relate to those needs and interests.

To demonstrate every feature with equal emphasis ignores two basic truths: (1) product features are not of equal importance, and (2) prospects are not alike. If Prospect A is mainly interested in safety while Prospect B is more influenced by comfort and a salesperson embarked on a long demonstration of comfort, Prospect A would become restless and irritated and probably voice objections to buying.

THE NECESSITY OF ADVANCE PREPARATION

Considerable advance preparation is needed if demonstrations are to be powerful and persuasive. The demonstration must be constructed carefully and thoughtfully. Planning the demonstration is just as important as planning the sales story.

The salesperson's first responsibility, then, is to have a plan. This involves deciding what features to demonstrate, what features to omit, and the most effective sequence for these points. The salesperson will also want to find the best standard sequence of steps to be followed when able to learn little or nothing that would aid in tailoring the demonstration to an individual prospect. The amount of emphasis each step deserves must be determined, and the timing of each must be scheduled. If prospects are to take part in the demonstration, how and when they are to participate must be determined.

Any products that are to be shown, operated, or used in any manner should be inspected before they are exhibited. If a product is supposed to function in a certain way yet fails to do so, this failure can ruin the chances of making a sale. If some items are exposed to the prospect's view often or under harsh conditions, their appearance should be periodically checked to make sure they look as presentable as possible. Even the best salesperson cannot sell a product that has a poor appearance.

Often prospects must be prepared in advance for what is to take place in the demonstration. If possible, their curiosity should be whetted until they are eager to see at least certain phases of the demonstration. They should understand what is being done or what is to be demonstrated.

The usual demonstration is accompanied by some explanation and description, so a sales talk should be composed prior to the demonstration to point out the benefits being shown. Such a talk not only informs prospects but also helps persuade them to buy.

Time and place of demonstration are frequently left to the salesperson's choice. The salesperson hopes that both hour and site will work for his or her purposes.

In the automotive field, by way of example, planned demonstrations are far superior to unplanned ones. The rule is to give only a brief demonstration in the showroom before the main demonstration, the ride. The car used as the demonstrator should be immaculate and in perfect condition.

Finally, the salesperson sometimes wants to make use of other people. The salesperson wants them present, would like to use products they bought earlier, or prefers to use their experiences. In such case, arrangements should be made well in advance.

PRINCIPLES OF DEMONSTRATING A PRODUCT EFFECTIVELY

The all-encompassing principle of effective demonstration is that the salesperson should not tell a prospect something when the prospect can be shown the same thing. Showing includes sending messages to the prospect's senses of sight, touch, taste, and smell. Demonstrating to senses other than the sense of hearing should be done as often as possible. Appealing through them is more subtle in that sometimes prospects can be shown what they would resent being told. Demonstration allows the product to do its part of accomplishing the selling by appealing to whichever sense or senses are most appropriate.

Using Visual Aids

The product is not the only item the salesperson can show to the prospect. Maximum use should be made of visual aids that help to picture the sales proposition. Examples of visual aids include advertisements, cross-sections of the product, models, and samples. See Illustration 11-1 for a more complete list.

Covering Vital Product Features

The standard demonstration should include vital features of the product. Three specific dangers of omission are worth mentioning. First, the feature omitted may be of particular interest to the particular prospect. Second, competitors may be stressing their comparable feature in talking to that prospect.

Examples of visual aids include:

1. Accessories	9. Figures	18. Portfolios
2. Advertisements	10. Graphs	19. Posters
3. Booklets	11. Letters	20. Recordings
4. Cartoons	12. Lights	21. Samples
5. Chalkboards	13. Manuals	22. Signs
6. Charts	14. Maps	23. Slides
7. Cross-sections	15. Models	24. Sound films
of the product	16. Movies	25. Swatches
8. Drawings	17. Pictures	

ILLUSTRATION 11-1. Maximum use should be made of visual aids.

Third, competitors may be telling the prospect that this particular feature of their product is more outstanding.

Those who sell to merchants need to demonstrate all the benefits that will accrue to the retailer as well as the benefits that will accrue to the retailer's customers. In other words, the salesperson's demonstration to the retailer is not complete unless it demonstrates how to demonstrate.

Making the Sales Talk Interpret the Demonstration

One of the first things a salesperson must learn to do is to synchronize a spoken message with each phase of the demonstration. An accompanying sales talk is necessary primarily because it permits the salesperson to continue his or her selling efforts. This is particularly desirable because prospects may not be able to interpret the demonstration for themselves. A second purpose served by this sales talk is to prevent awkward periods of silence.

The initial part of the talk normally precedes the demonstration itself. The purpose of this preliminary part of the talk is to build up the demonstration in the prospect's mind, selling the idea of a demonstration. The body of the talk takes product features and converts them as they are demonstrated into advantages of owning and using the product. These advantages can make a strong impact on the prospect because any spoken claim is instantly backed up by product performance.

Making the Product Look Its Best

In all demonstrations, both the salesperson and product must make a good impression from the first moment. The product must be displayed in its best possible light, and this calls for staging the demonstration when and where it will be most effective. Every distraction that will compete for the prospect's attention should be eliminated. The merchandise should, of course, be tested in advance to see that it will work perfectly.

Nothing is more basic to showing a product off to best advantage than that the salesperson's performance be of professional quality. Salespeople should practice giving demonstrations phase by phase and point by point until everything is done perfectly and naturally.

Making the Demonstration Clear

Because one purpose of the demonstration is to clarify what the salesperson says, care must be taken to see that it fulfills this function. The salesperson begins by making sure that the prospect understands the purpose of the demonstration. Then the salesperson demonstrates one point at a time so that the prospect can completely absorb each one. Brevity aids in making the demonstration clear, provided completeness is not sacrificed. Do not attempt too much in any one demonstration; displaying too many products or making too many points often results in confusion. Clarity sometimes demands that the salesperson perform some activity rather than depending on the prospect to perform it, for example, figuring out costs or savings. In some circumstances, it may be desirable or even necessary to repeat a demonstration several times.

Making the Demonstration True to Life

It is not enough for the salesperson just to point to each part or accessory of the product and name it. Instead, the salesperson must show why each was provided and what each means in the day-to-day use and operation of the product. This can best be done if the product is demonstrated in circumstances of actual use. When conditions and atmosphere are realistic, the prospect's feeling of confidence in product and salesperson is increased.

Tailoring the Demonstration

The salesperson fits the demonstration to the prospect by dwelling on features which seem to be of particular interest to the prospect. In other words, the salesperson adjusts the demonstration by dramatizing those buyer benefits that fit each prospect. When any installation is to be used for the demonstration, the one selected should be as nearly like the prospect's circumstances as possible.

In some ways, the salesperson prepares for the demonstration exactly as for the sales story: plans it in advance and then modifies it only when such modification will make it better fit the individual prospect. The job of tailoring the demonstration also includes such matters as scheduling it to suit the prospect's convenience, determining its length in the light of the same consideration, and executing it at the proper rate of speed for the prospect.

Encouraging Prospect Participation

A basic feature of demonstrating is to let the prospect take part as much as possible in the demonstration. Product and prospect working together can often do more to bring about a purchase than can the salesperson just by talking to the prospect. The prospect becomes better acquainted with the product's features and remembers them longer. In handling the product, the prospect experiences the feel of ownership.

Achieving Prospect Agreement

After demonstrating each product feature, the salesperson should check to see that the prospect has absorbed what was being shown and accepted the demonstration as satisfactory proof. This is the same principle that is followed when the salesperson delivers the presentation. Agreement on all points as the demonstration proceeds puts the prospect on record as finding in the product the qualities needed and wanted.

Maintaining Control

Control must rest with the salesperson during the demonstration. It is unwise to turn the product or any visual aid over to the prospect if such a step gives up control of the course of the demonstration. An example of this is the prospect who is allowed to leaf through a portfolio or catalog while the salesperson is talking.

By maintaining control of the situation, the salesperson can also prevent the prospect from making mistakes which might be embarrassing. An illustration of this might be the prospect who accidentally breaks the product sample.

Occasionally a salesperson wanders away from the planned sequence of the demonstration and its objectives. It is not wise to digress from the demonstration and interject such things as local gossip or opinions on matters not connected with the sales interview and demonstration. Instead, conversation should relate to the advantages being shown by the demonstration.

Demonstrations Involving Present Customers

Sometimes a salesperson of installations will demonstrate the merchandise using units that have been bought by and installed for satisfied buyers, previous prospects that have been converted into buyers. This might be true, for example, of a heating and air conditioning system for a house. When the salesperson's demonstration involves present customers, several rules should be kept in mind. First, those customers should be inconvenienced as little as possible. The salesperson should call them well in advance, choose a satisfactory time for the visit, and not stay too long. Second, the customer should be put to no expense. Third, the salesperson should do as much as possible to get things ready for the demonstration and should later put things back as they were. Fourth, the salesperson should express appreciation for any testimony the customer gives the prospect and for answers the customer gives to the prospect's questions.

Following up the Demonstration

There should be no hesitation at the conclusion of the demonstration. In most cases, the salesperson will sum up the demonstration and try to complete the sale at that point. If the prospect hesitates, the salesperson should return to the sales story.

DEMONSTRATION INSTRUCTIONS

If the salesperson's company provides an outline of a suggested demonstration, it probably omits nothing important. Company plans are usually well tested, usually represent the organized experiences of the company, and often are the cream of successful field trials. Illustration 11-2 gives the general suggestions one company makes for any demonstration by its salespeople.

USING SHOWMANSHIP IN THE DEMONSTRATION

If the demonstration is the dramatization of the sales story, showmanship can be considered to be dramatization of the demonstration. Showmanship makes the demonstration picturesque instead of allowing it to be commonplace. A salesperson who jumps up and down on a suitcase to prove its durability is using showmanship. The salesperson who does no more than list reasons for buying in black ink and list the buyer's objections in red is using showmanship. Handling the product with obvious respect is also showmanship.

The purpose of showmanship is to make the demonstration more effective. Showmanship enables facts to be presented or actions to be executed in such an unusual way as to secure attention, increase prospect receptivity, make proof more spectacular, and bring about conviction. Showmanship makes a definite impression on the prospect's emotions. Because the prospect buys on both emotion and reason, a message with emotional appeal can often be just as persuasive as a statement of fact.

Two additional and minor uses of showmanship are to entertain prospects while prescribing for their needs, and to demonstrate to merchants the showmanship they can use to secure sales.

Much of the salesperson's thinking and talking—and use of showmanship—must be tailored to the prospect, but the major tailoring job in the area of showmanship is fitting it to the salesperson. Two salespeople can be quite successful and yet not be able to use the same types of showmanship. Instead, each salesperson must experiment to identify what can be used in the area of showmanship that will be in harmony with his or her own personality.

DEMONSTRATION INSTRUCTIONS

Here are the general suggestions the J. I. Case Company makes for any demonstration. All sales personnel are expected to study these ideas and to discuss them in sales meetings scheduled for that purpose.

1. Inspect the work to be performed prior to agreeing to demonstrate.
2. Arrange for a specific time for demonstration and see that the maximum number of interested prospects and personnel will be available at the specific time for the demonstration.
3. Lubricate, adjust, and work the equipment before the demonstration without any prospects or interested people observing.
4. Have a skilled, experienced, and qualified operator to demonstrate the tractor and equipment, an operator who knows the equipment and knows what it will do.
5. Actual demonstration:
    A. Have two participants in attendance:
        (1) The operator (qualified).
        (2) The salesperson, who will direct the demonstration and explain the various features and advantages of the equipment and its performance.
    B. The initial part of the demonstration is the unloading of the tractor or equipment from the trailer. If a Case trailer is being used, do not do this until the group is assembled.
    C. Give a short explanation of the features of the tractor such as:
        (1) Its weight in relation to power.
        (2) Its clearance.
        (3) Power on both tracks when turning and our Terramatic Power Shifting Transmission in those models which have them.
        (4) The advantages of the antifriction lower track wheel bearings.
        (5) The advantages of the method of mounting our dozers and loaders.
        (6) The advantages of our unitary loader frame—direct pushing cylinder.
        (7) The advantages of having a dozer or loader close to the tractor.

(8) The advantage of our torque tube in the tractor and how we push or pull from this torque tube, the backbone of the tractor.

(9) The advantages of our pushing position and our powered bucket.

(10) Our cylinder design, packings, etc., interchangeability.

(11) Terratrac Backhoe—foot swing strength, alloy pins, bushing quick removal.

D. Both participants should have a card with each operation listed on it in the sequence in which they are to be performed. The salesperson should tell the operator what to do and direct the demonstration, and when any particularly outstanding feature of work is performed, the demonstration should be stopped and this explained. At some time during the demonstration, the operator should be told to proceed for five minutes without stopping. This should be announced to the crowd. At the end of the five-minute interval, he should stop so that the crowd can see the work performed in this interval, whether it be loading trucks, bulldosing, or digging a ditch with a backhoe. During this operation, the operator should make every move count. Take a full cut, all the tractor will handle without slowing down excessively. It is better to take a shallow cut, make a complete pass without stalling and clutching than it is to try to take too big a bite and then to stop in the middle of the pass.

E. The concluding demonstration (particularly with loaders) is the loading of the tractor onto the trailer, showing how easy and simple it is. The tractor should then be left on the trailer.

6. Length of demonstration.

A half hour should be adequate for the demonstration. The success of the demonstration depends on knowing what you're going to do and doing it. Do not allow anyone else on the tractor until after the first fifteen or twenty minutes and you have definitely and effectively shown the outstanding performance of the equipment. Never allow operators who are not familiar with the equipment to operate it without first explaining the operation and the handling of the controls. It is good and desirable to have operators sit in the seat of the tractor and turn the tractor slightly from side to side so they can see how easily it steers and handles, but inexperienced people or smart alecks should not be turned loose with the tractor.

A half hour of properly prepared and conducted demonstration will show more and be equal to a day of disorganized work. Customers who want to see the tractor work a week or so are more interested in getting work done than they are in seeing the equipment work.

ILLUSTRATION 11-2. Companies may provide an outline of a suggested demonstration.

Where Showmanship Is Most Useful

Some form of showmanship can be used with almost any product and almost any salesperson. There are, however, certain areas in which showmanship is more suitable and effective than in others. First, new products will benefit more from showmanship than will established products. The sale of a new product demands a change in the prospect's thinking pattern before the buying pattern will change, and showmanship can help accomplish this big task. Second, specialty products offer more and better opportunities for the salesperson's imagination to be translated into showmanship than do staple items. This must not be interpreted, though, as meaning that the selling of staple products disallows the use of showmanship. Third, intangibles need showmanship more than do tangibles. Fourth, as price and quality increase, so does the possibility for using showmanship. Finally, there is greater use of showmanship in selling to ultimate consumers than in selling to purchasing agents and middlemen, and more opportunities for showmanship in selling to retailers than in selling to wholesalers.

Cautions About Using Showmanship

Salespeople should remember a number of important cautions about the use of showmanship. First, it is no substitute for a thorough preparation for selling that includes product information, prospect information, and the principles of selling. Second, showmanship must not be gaudy, insincere, or undignified because this not only fails to make a sale but also gives a bad impression of the salesperson and the product. Third, showmanship must be used only to get sales and not to show off. A salesperson's showmanship must not call attention to itself or distract the prospect's attention from a product's advantages.

Attitudes Toward Showmanship

Sales managers have conflicting attitudes toward showmanship; based on these attitudes, sales managers might be classified into three groups. The first group consists of those who do not want their salespeople to use any showmanship. They want a sound, businesslike presentation and want a salesperson to appear to the prospect as an earnest individual who knows the business thoroughly and is keenly interested in customers' welfare. Some of these managers feel that both advertising and sales promotion need showmanship, but personal selling does not.

Sales managers in the second group feel that showmanship can be helpful but is not essential and argue that some salespeople cannot develop the art of showmanship, no matter how hard they try. These sales managers prefer that their salespeople work on developing a forceful personality instead of a knack for using showmanship.

The third group of sales managers considers showmanship an essential ingredient in a good salesperson. They consider the use of showmanship one of the most important phases of a salesperson's presentation, largely because advertising in magazines and on radio and television has accustomed people to expect dramatic presentations. They contend that prospects respond more readily to showmanship and that dramatized selling is thus essential.

SUMMARY

Demonstrations can be used for capturing the prospect's interest, achieving conviction, providing information, making the sales presentation sink in, and saving time.

Demonstrations have psychological value. They involve the prospect and make the prospect a partner in the sales presentation. To get the maximum psychological impact, the salesperson must identify the major benefits to demonstrate and devise the best way to present those benefits. Prospects like demonstrations because they prefer to trust their own senses rather than a salesperson's promises. Demonstrations permit prospects to understand the product quickly. Salespeople like to demonstrate because demonstrations make presentations more effective. They gain attention, increase prospect belief, and reduce opposition to buying.

Demonstrations can be used at any time. Salespeople must be able to demonstrate every product feature that a prospect finds interesting. In addition, salespeople must master several different methods of demonstration. Advance preparation is a must. The demonstration must be planned carefully. A standard sequence should be established. Then, any products that are to be shown must be inspected before they are exhibited. Prospects can be partially prepared for what they will see. Sometimes a salesperson may want to have other people present. In such cases, arrangements must be made in advance.

The most important principle of effective demonstrations is that the salesperson should not tell a prospect something when the prospect can be shown the same thing. Demonstration to senses other than hearing should be done frequently.

Visual aids should be used if they can help the demonstration. The vital features of the product should be included in the demonstration. The salesperson's spoken message should be synchronized with the demonstration to increase the effectiveness of both. A preliminary talk can build up the demonstration. The product must be made to look its best. The salesperson's performance has to be of professional quality, so practice is essential. The demonstration must be clear. The prospect has to understand the purpose of the demonstration and every important point made. A demonstration under conditions of actual use is most effective in increasing the prospect's feeling of confidence in the product.

Every demonstration should be tailored to the prospect. The demonstration must be planned, scheduled, and executed at the proper pace for the prospect. Prospect participation should be encouraged to help the prospect experience the feeling of ownership. After demonstrating each feature, the salesperson should check to see that the prospect has absorbed what was being shown and has accepted the demonstration as satisfactory proof. Control must be maintained by the salesperson. Making sure the prospect is paying attention and keeping the preplanned demonstration sequence are important.

Sometimes a salesperson will demonstrate an installation belonging to a customer. The salesperson should not inconvenience the customer or cause the customer any expense. The salesperson should prepare the presentation thoroughly and thank the customer for any testimony given to prospects.

Showmanship can make the demonstration more effective, securing the prospect's attention and making a definite impression on the prospect's emotions. Showmanship must be tailored to both the prospect and the salesperson.

Showmanship is effective in selling new products, specialty items, intangibles, and high-priced goods. Showmanship is no substitute for thorough preparation. It must not be gaudy, insincere, or undignified. Showmanship must not call attention to itself or distract the prospect's attention.

Sales managers have conflicting attitudes toward showmanship. Some do not want it used. Others feel it can be helpful but is not essential. Still others consider it an essential ingredient in any sales presentation.

REVIEW QUESTIONS

1. To get the maximum psychological impact from a demonstration, what kinds of things must a salesperson research?
2. What advantages do buyers get from demonstrations? How do salespeople benefit?
3. Should all product features be stressed equally? Why or why not?
4. What kind of preparation should salespeople make in advance of their demonstrations?
5. How should prospects be prepared for a demonstration?
6. Why should a sales talk interpret the demonstration?
7. What should the salesperson do to make the demonstration clear?
8. Why should the salesperson try to make the demonstration true to life?
9. How can a demonstration be tailored to each individual prospect?
10. What advantages are there to encouraging prospect participation in demonstrations?
11. What are some signs that the salesperson has lost control of the demonstration?
12. List four important elements of demonstrations involving present customers.
13. When is showmanship most effective?

14. How can showmanship hurt a presentation?
15. Describe three possible attitudes of management towards showmanship.

DISCUSSION QUESTIONS

1. What would you include and exclude from a talk preparing a prospect for a demonstration?
2. Assume you are selling stereo systems in a stereo shop. How would your demonstration to a young adult differ from one to a middle-aged couple?
3. It has been suggested that a good salesperson involves the prospect in the demonstration whenever possible. Would it be even more beneficial if the prospect was just given the product to try for awhile without a normal demonstration?

CASE STUDY 11

Sensormatic Electronics makes electronic surveillance systems for retail stores. The systems use large plastic tags that will sound an alarm if a shoplifter tries to take tagged merchandise out of the store. The tags and scanning devices act to deter shoplifters. This means that retailers won't have to risk angering customers or spend valuable time in court.

Sensormatic salespeople sketch a pyramid to illustrate three factors that contribute to shoplifting: frustration, opportunity, and low risk.

The surveillance systems eliminate low risk, the base of the pyramid, and thus act as deterrents.

Sensormatic salespeople can quote the following case history to prove that their system deters shoplifting. When one department store in San Francisco put in the Sensormatic system, potential shoplifters chose another store nearby rather than risk getting caught in the store with the Sensormatic system. The second store reported indications of a 200% increase in shoplifting.

Source: *Sales and Marketing Management* (February 4, 1980), pp. 13 and 14.

1. What makes the Sensormatic sales presentation work?
2. What else would you include in a presentation for a product of this type?

Answering Objections 12

Main Question: So much money: don't have it!

After studying this chapter you should be able to:

- Show why buyers offer opposition to buying
- Discuss the proper attitudes toward objections
- Differentiate between excuses and objections
- Summarize the principles of handling objections
- Name ten techniques for handling objections
- Explain how to prevent objections

Because an individual's purchasing power is limited, a salesperson meets resistance from prospects. This resistance may be active or passive, expressed or implied. Regardless of which it is, prospect resistance is of significance to the salesperson because it is a test of skillful, effective selling technique. In everyday selling, salespeople encounter resistance which acts as a bar between them and sales.

By opposing purchase suggestions, prospects hope to get rid of the salesperson without buying. Or they may hope to avoid an obligation which will lead to a purchase. An objection does not mean that prospects do not need or want the product involved. In the majority of cases, prospects object because they lack information. They may not be conscious of a need that the salesperson's product will fill, or they may need help in justifying the purchase, either to themselves or to others. Furthermore, they want assurance that what they are doing is correct, and this frequently means that a doubt must be dispelled by the salesperson.

THE ART OF FRICTIONLESS DISAGREEMENT

Disagreement between salesperson and prospect is understandable, universal, and inevitable. Objections are both evidence and causes of disagreement. Because the salesperson must be able to disagree without being disagreeable, we must preface our study of objections with a look at some facets of disagreement. Here are some guidelines on disagreement for salespeople:

1. Establish what the facts are. Should the prospect be in error, establish the facts with tact and diplomacy. Show that *you are right, not that the prospect is wrong.* Give the prospect every opportunity to save face.
2. Agree with the prospect on as many points as possible, introduce them into the dialog, and get the prospect to acknowledge them as points of agreement. Examples include experiences, hobbies, and backgrounds. When the prospect learns that the two of you have much in common, hostility begins to wane and rapport begins to develop.
3. Disagreement must not be allowed to lead to argument nor to a tense, emotional confrontation. Remember, "Lose the argument and you lose the sale—win the argument and you lose the customer."
4. Often you can reword the prospect's statement of disagreement so as to show that your recommendation and the prospect's best interests are in harmony, not in conflict.
5. Sometimes you can switch the conversation smoothly to a topic on which you both agree.

COPING WITH PROSPECT HOSTILITY

Some prospects are hostile and become antagonistic as they discuss certain objections with salespeople. This demands careful treatment by the salesperson. If a hostile prospect is not handled properly, it can really hurt the salesperson, the brand, and the company. The salesperson's interests are to avoid generating hostility, and to handle hostility satisfactorily when it is encountered. Suggestions about coping with hostility follow:

1. Above all, listen courteously and sympathetically without interrupting. Try to remain poised, to be friendly, and to stay in control of yourself.
2. Explore to see if the prospect has any justification for belligerence. If you, your product, or your firm is at fault, agree to that fact, apologize, and try to right what is wrong.
3. Ask the prospect questions. Then sit tight and listen to the prospect's gripes and resentments. Indulge the prospect by being an attentive and interested audience.
4. On extreme occasions, end the interview on some pretext (you need to get additional information, for example) and schedule a future call.
5. If the prospect's hostility is aimed at *you,* stop calling. You cannot afford to yield and defer beyond the limit of your self-respect.

WHY PROSPECTS OFFER OPPOSITION

All salespeople meet resistance and opposition. Success in selling consists of disposing of resistance. There is nothing more basic in selling than for the salesperson to acknowledge resistance in the forms of silence, questions, and objections. Since opposition will be a problem as long as a salesperson sells, a salesperson should learn as much as possible about it and become skillful in handling it.

Much resistance is the result of prospects' not knowing enough about their needs and the products that might answer those needs. They must have more information before they can grasp the salesperson's ideas about need and product. They need more understanding of their needs and of the benefits the salesperson promises before they can appreciate the salesperson's product for what it really is and does. Sometimes the information a prospect has is not accurate. Sometimes there is not enough of it.

When a prospect does not understand the sales story, that prospect will probably offer opposition to buying. Such difficulty is clearly the salesperson's fault. The salesperson should have held the prospect's attention and should have presented such a clear sales story that the prospect easily understood it.

Prospects are reluctant to change their habits. They tend to adopt a way of life and to stick to it, repeating the same actions time after time. They are not interested in making a change. For some prospects, the voicing of objections has itself become a habit. These prospects give all salespeople at least some token opposition, whether or not they are going to buy.

Some opposition is presented in order to check on the salesperson's knowledge of the product and ability to answer objections. Sometimes prospects are really asking for justification for the purchase they want to make. Or, at the other extreme, they may be trying to justify not buying now.

Personal preference and prejudice can cause resistance. Differences of opinion exist in prospects' minds about the quality and suitability of various products. Some prospects believe that certain competing products are superior to the one the salesperson is selling, and such beliefs cause opposition.

Finally, prospects are often afraid to buy. They fear that the product may not perform as the salesperson claims, or that the salesperson will benefit more from the transaction than they will. They fear that soon after the purchase they will see a new product which they should have waited to buy.

THE PROPER ATTITUDE TOWARD OBJECTIONS

Instead of fearing objections, the salesperson should welcome them and encourage the prospect to speak up. The objections a prospect voices can be helpful to the salesperson. Viewed in one light, they are the prospect's way of asking for more information and of pointing out areas that need more coverage by the salesperson. As requests for information, prospects' objections give the salesperson opportunities to explain what the product will do for the prospect and why the prospect should have that product immediately.

Selling is made easier when the prospect objects, because the prospect who talks is easier to deal with than the silent prospect. When a prospect refuses to take part in the conversation, the salesperson is in the dark about what the prospect thinks, about points that need amplification, and about the buying motives to appeal to. Objections throw light on the prospect's thinking. By underlining the buying decisions that are missing, they indicate what is needed before the attempt to close the sale can be made. The most dangerous objections are those that are not disclosed.

Objections indicate that the salesperson is making progress toward completion of the sale. The prospect who objects in some way is generally one who is giving some thought to the salesperson's presentation. It is fairly safe to say that almost all sales are made after the prospect has voiced some objection.

The salesperson's proper reaction, then, is to welcome objections. All questions and negative statements should be treated as requests for information, and objections should be used to plan the future course of the sales presentation. In handling objections, the salesperson should be courteous so as not to antagonize the prospect. The salesperson should be poised and tactful and should have a sympathetic understanding of what an objection really is.

EXCUSES VERSUS OBJECTIONS

Before a salesperson can close a sale, real obstacles that stand between the prospect and a purchase must be identified and removed from the prospect's mind. The hostile statement or objection the prospect makes may or may not be the real barrier preventing the purchase. Frequently, apparent objections are only excuses. Rather than admit feeling unable to afford the product, the prospect may tell the salesperson that the color is wrong; or rather than admit to being a procrastinator, the prospect may ask to talk things over with his or her spouse. Thus, one of the salesperson's first objectives is to identify and isolate the real reason why the prospect refuses to buy. Those obstacles that are really excuses merely waste the time of a salesperson who handles them in detail. If one excuse is answered sincerely, the prospect merely thinks up another.

The Difference Between Excuses and Objections

An excuse is any insincere resistance offered by a prospect; it is not a real obstacle to buying. Sometimes it is an attempt to dismiss the salesperson. Sometimes the prospect is rationalizing resistance to buying, as, for example, the prospect who buys a lower-priced item and hates to admit it, does not have the authority to buy, or is not carrying enough money to buy. Sometimes the excuse is only a buying defense erected by the prospect who feels obligated to offer some resistance even when planning to buy. Stock excuses are often voiced by prospects, many of whom tend to repeat what they have heard from someone else.

An objection is the real reason the prospect has not said "yes" to one of the five buying decisions. It points to the buying decision still missing. The objection represents valid resistance, and it must be handled before the prospect will buy.

There is no sure method which will quickly and accurately separate excuses from objections. Two different prospects could indicate resistance to purchasing by making exactly the same statements, yet in one case the resistance would be an excuse and in the other an objection. To detect excuses, a salesperson must depend on observation, interpretation of each prospect's words and actions, and experience. There are two techniques which can help a salesperson cope with the problem of separating excuses from objections. The first technique is that of tactful questioning; the second makes use of what is best described as the parallel track answer.

Tactful Questioning. The salesperson's use of questions was recommended earlier in connection with the delivery of the sales presentation. The same basic tactic is just as useful in the handling of opposition or resistance, and particularly in the salesperson's attempts to determine what is an excuse and what is a sincere objection. Often a prospect sets up a smoke screen by voicing some token of reluctance to buying in order to save face, feel important, or help rationalize some other purchase to be made soon. Questions help the salesperson penetrate this smoke screen and probe for any serious objection the prospect has concealed. When they are asked skillfully, questions can help prospects resolve their thinking and arrive at sound decisions. By phrasing questions so that they will result in affirmative answers, a salesperson sometimes can help a prospect realize that what seemed to be a valid reason for not buying is nothing more than an excuse. Answers to questions give the salesperson facts, and no salesperson can deal successfully with resistance without adequate and correct information about the nature of the prospect's resistance.

The "Why" Question. The word *why* is one of the salesperson's strongest allies. It is absolutely essential in the salesperson's vocabulary. This one-word question helps clear up the issues between the salesperson and the prospect. It gets prospects to indicate where they stand. It recommends to prospects that they think more seriously about the salesperson's proposals. Qualified prospects may be trying to mask their real convictions when they make such statements as:

I'll talk it over.	I'm satisfied.
I'm not interested.	I'll think it over.
I can't afford it.	I'll let you know.
I'm too busy to talk.	I'm well fixed just now.

By asking a *why* question, the salesperson often learns why prospects feel as they do or answered as they did. The salesperson must identify the real barriers before deciding intelligently how to proceed.

The Additional Question. If a salesperson strongly suspects that the voiced resistance is a mere excuse, there is much merit and little risk in asking the prospect to reveal the real reason for not buying. A prospect may, for example, be using a respectable excuse to hide a prejudice or an attitude he or she prefers not to reveal. On the other hand, the prospect may be raising a dummy barrier to cover ignorance or inertia. In such cases, the salesperson is not interested in the prospect's feeling or belief as expressed in the excuse, but must change the prospect's thinking on the hidden objection. So the salesperson asks, "Is there any other reason in addition to the one you mentioned—any additional reason for your wanting to wait?" or "Isn't there something else, too, holding you back?" Prospects do not seem to resent such questions. In many instances, they will reveal their real explanation for refusing to buy.

The Parallel Track Answer. The other method of separating excuses from objections can also permit a salesperson to make some strong sales points. Suppose that a prospect asks a hostile question or makes an unfavorable comment about some specific matter. If the salesperson believes this resistance to be an excuse and choses to reply with a parallel track answer, the salesperson will not comment on the exact resistance voiced by the buyer. Instead, commenting on a sales point closely related to the opposition, the salesperson answers on a parallel track, not the same track. Three examples of parallel track answers follow:

1. A prospect complains about a product's design, and the salesperson answers by talking about the raw materials that were used in making the product.
2. A prospect disapproves of the stand the salesperson's company takes on labor unions, and the salesperson answers by describing the company's labor force—how skilled the workers are and the quality they build into the company's products.
3. A prospect finds fault with the price of the salesperson's product, and the salesperson suggests that they review what goes on back at the factory where the matter of price actually starts.

PRINCIPLES OF HANDLING OBJECTIONS

The basic principles of handling objections which a salesperson should learn and remember are: (1) clarify the objection if necessary; (2) classify the objection; (3) maintain control at all times in handling the objection; (4) don't argue with the prospect; (5) be diplomatic in answering the objection; (6) fit the answer to the prospect; (7) minimize, not maximize, the objection; and (8) capitalize on the objection if possible.

Clarifying the Objection

Before attempting to answer any objection, the salesperson must have a clear understanding of just what the prospect means. A difficult problem is presented when the prospect hides behind such excuses as "not interested," "not in the market," or "no time to see you." One way to find the objection is to urge prospects to discuss fully what they have on their minds. Another resort is to diplomatically ask what, where, who, how, and why concerning the objection. A third course consists of alert observation until the real objection is identified. In clarifying the objection, it is often desirable for the salesperson to restate the objection. This assures the prospect that the difficulty is understood and gives the salesperson a few seconds in which to analyze the objection and determine what might be the best method of answering it.

Classifying the Objection

The act of buying requires that the buyer make five affirmative decisions, and objections point out negative buying decisions. The salesperson can thus tell from the type of objection which buying decisions are still to be made favorably.

Some objections clearly indicate that the prospect does not recognize any need or does not want to admit the existence of need. In other cases, the objection implies a belief on the part of the prospect that no personal needs demand immediate attention.

Some prospects show through their resistance that they believe competing products are better than the salesperson's product. Or the prospect may decide that the services accompanying competing products are superior. Resistance of this nature indicates that the salesperson has not successfully established need and matched the product or service to that need.

Opposition to source usually implies a lack of confidence in the seller. Perhaps the prospect does not have complete confidence in the salesperson as an individual, or perhaps the prospect has doubts about the salesperson's company.

Objections to price mean that the salesperson has not built up an acceptable amount of value or satisfaction for the price quoted. More selling efforts may be needed on the buying decisions of need and product.

When a prospect objects to the decision concerning time, it means only one thing: the salesperson must obtain more enthusiastic agreement on the first four buying decisions.

Maintaining Control

Every salesperson needs to acknowledge that there are some prospects who will hide behind a host of objections. These objections must be treated calmly, necessitating control. The salesperson who stops talking after answering an objection, or worse, asks if there are any other questions or matters causing the prospect difficulty easily loses control. Instead of pausing, a better course of action is to resume selling immediately. This does not, however, forbid the practice of checking with the prospect to determine understanding and agreement.

Not Arguing

A salesperson should never argue with a prospect. If the salesperson wins the argument, the prospect's goodwill is lost; if the salesperson loses the argument, the sale is lost. Because it is hopeless to antagonize someone and at the same time try to gain influence, it is never wise to take issue with prospects. Even when the salesperson is right, contradicting the prospect is running a great risk. Rebuttal by the salesperson intensifies opposition. Blanketing the prospect with questions so as to divert negative thoughts and to bring out the weakness of the objection is more effective than arguing.

Being Diplomatic

Challenge, contradiction, or direct attack increase prospect opposition, no matter how sound or logical the salesperson's answer is. The salesperson should never disagree with the prospect in such a way as to cause offense. A flippant or belittling answer, a blunt statement that the prospect is wrong, and a condescending attitude are all likely to cause unfavorable reactions from the prospect. Diplomacy demands that the salesperson tactfully remove incorrect beliefs and replace them with accurate ones.

Fitting the Answer to the Prospect

The salesperson must give the objecting prospect a new concept to accept as a substitute for a former opinion. The salesperson's chances of success are increased if the answer is molded to fit the prospect. This task has two phases. In the first phase, the salesperson makes certain that the prospect's real difficulty is understood and convinces the prospect of that understanding. The second phase consists of phrasing the reply in whatever manner seems most appropriate to the prospect's nature. Answers will be more persuasive if they are constructed in accordance with the prospect's own personality. The prospect's attitudes and not the salesperson's should be the guide in shaping the reply.

Minimizing Objections

Objections should be minimized, and to accomplish this, the salesperson should go to no greater length than is necessary in handling an objection. The salesperson should make sure that the prospect understands and agrees and should then immediately leave the objection. In saying just enough to dispose of the objection to the prospect's satisfaction, the salesperson avoids dwelling on it and thereby exaggerating its importance.

An attempt to avoid an objection completely tends to magnify its importance. The prospect may attribute undue significance to an objection that the salesperson does not answer.

SOME TECHNIQUES FOR HANDLING OBJECTIONS

The following ten techniques are frequently used in handling objections:

1. *Product comparison.* When the prospect is mentally comparing a product being used now or a competing product with the salesperson's product, the salesperson may make a complete comparison of the two. The salesperson lists the advantages and disadvantages of each.

2. *Relating a case history.* Here the salesperson describes the experiences of another prospect similar to the prospect to whom he or she is talking.

3. *Demonstration.* A product demonstration gives a quite convincing answer to a product objection because the salesperson lets the product itself overcome the opposition.

4. *Giving guarantees.* Often a guarantee will remove resistance from the prospect's mind. Guarantees assure prospects that they cannot lose by purchasing. The caution, of course, is that guarantees must be meaningful and must provide for some recourse on the part of the prospect if the product does not live up to the guarantee.

5. *Asking questions.* The "why" question is of value in separating excuses from genuine objections and in probing for hidden resistance. The same question is useful in disposing of objections. Probing or exploratory questions are excellent in handling silent resistance. They can be worded and asked in a manner that appeals to the prospect's ego. In making the prospect do some thinking to convince the salesperson, questions of a probing nature get the prospect's full attention.

6. *Showing what delay costs.* A common experience of salespeople is to obtain seemingly sincere agreements to the buying decisions concerning need, product, source, and price, only to find that the prospect wants to wait some time

before buying. In such cases, the salesperson can sometimes take pencil and paper to show conclusively that delay of the purchase is expensive.

7. *Admitting and counterbalancing.* Sometimes the prospect's objection is completely valid because of some limitation in the salesperson's product. The only course of action in this case is for the salesperson to agree that the product does have the disadvantage to which the prospect is obviously objecting. Immediately after the acknowledgement, however, the salesperson should direct the prospect's attention to the advantages which overshadow the limitation of the product.

8. *Hearing the prospect out.* Some prospects object mainly for the opportunity to describe how they were once victimized. The technique recommended for this type of resistance is that of sympathetic listening.

9. *Making the objection boomerang.* Once in a while the salesperson can take a prospect's reason for not buying and convert it into a reason for buying. This takes expert handling. Suppose the prospect says, "I'm too busy to see you." The salesperson might reply, "That's why you should see me—I can save you time."

10. *The "Yes, but" technique.* The best technique for handling most resistance is the indirect answer known as the "Yes, but" method. Here are two examples of what salespeople might say when using this technique: (1) "Yes, I can understand that attitude, but there is another angle for you to consider." (b) "Yes, you have a point there, but in your particular circumstances, other points are involved, too." The "Yes, but" method avoids argument and friction. It respects the prospect's opinions, attitudes, and thinking, and operates well where the prospect's point does not apply in a particular case.

ILLUSTRATION 12-1.   The salesperson must be able to disagree without being disagreeable.

Capitalizing on the Objection

Every objection should be used constructively to bring out as many benefits as possible. The salesperson can capitalize on an objection by translating it into a justification for purchase. Each objection can thus be used to bring the purchase closer.

In taking advantage of an objection, the salesperson may find it wise to clarify some or all of the sales points that have already been made. A second thing that might be done is to review all the advantages the product offers that are related to the particular objection. For example, when a prospect complains of high price, the salesperson points out all the product features the buyer will enjoy for that price. A third method of capitalizing on the objection is to offer more facts to the prospect. A fourth technique is to isolate the buying motive that gave rise to the objection and then build up as many benefits as possible for that one motive.

To capitalize effectively on an objection, the salesperson should never hesitate after answering the objection; the salesperson should never invite the prospect to voice another objection. Instead, the salesperson may attempt to complete the sale at once. A return to constructive selling is needed if a trial close is attempted and does not succeed or if the salesperson feels that it is too early to attempt to close.

WHEN TO HANDLE OBJECTIONS

Just as there is no single, speedy test which will separate objections from excuses, there is, likewise, no single technique for coping with either. In one sense, every excuse or objection should be handled. This does not mean that each should be answered, and most certainly it does not mean that the excuse or objection should be featured. Each of the general methods now listed will be effective in some situations. Unless otherwise specified, throughout the rest of this chapter the word "objection" will be used to include both real objections and excuses.

Future Handling

It is not always necessary to answer an objection immediately. Instead, the salesperson may choose to *disregard* the objection the first time it is made. In passing up the objection, the salesperson can make no comment at all, simply appearing not to hear it, or the salesperson can say "yes" with no change of facial expression and continue the presentation.

Ignoring the objection is one way of separating the real from the artificial. If the prospect's objection was an excuse used just to change the subject or just to interrupt the salesperson's story, it probably will not be mentioned again. Indeed, if it was phony, there is no reason for the salesperson to answer it.

In some cases, the prospect gets the idea that the objection was not important enough to have any impact on the salesperson. By not stopping to handle it, the salesperson keeps the objection from appearing to be a big issue and thus tacitly suggests that it not be brought up again.

Sometimes when an objection is raised, the salesperson can ignore it and immediately make recommendations on the quality and price for the prospect to order, being careful to suggest larger amounts or higher price lines than the prospect will buy. This encourages the prospect to switch from the first objection to objecting to the quantities and prices recommended. However, sometimes this technique antagonizes the prospect, which can result in a lost sale.

There is one thing the salesperson can count on when an objection is ignored; the prospect who is serious will repeat the objection.

Postponing the answer to an objection may help the salesperson in more ways than one. Resistance, when set aside for a few moments, often evaporates. Also, the delay allows the salesperson to establish more benefits before taking up a negative matter, thus reducing its significance. Finally, by postponing the handling until some later moment, the salesperson maintains control of the interview and is confronted by the obstacle at the time of his or her own choosing. As has been mentioned, postponement must not resemble evasion.

Immediate Handling

For some salespeople, for some prospects, for some objections, and for some situations, an immediate, *direct* answer is the proper method of handling. One big advantage of this technique is that it convinces the prospect of the salesperson's sincerity. In addition, it prevents any inference of evasion or inability to answer. A third advantage is that quick, deft handling, accompanied by courteous and intelligent consideration, frequently kills objections before they establish themselves in the prospect's mind. Another point is that once prospects realize that the objection was really no objection at all, they can concentrate completely on the rest of the salesperson's story. Lastly, quick and final handling keeps the salesperson off the defensive. However, smiles and tact are essential to success.

The *indirect* answer is probably the most widely recommended, the most widely used, and the most effective method of handling objections. It is versatile, flexible, and safe. Basically, it involves two steps. The first is for the salesperson to agree with the objection with some such remark as "That's true" or "Yes." The second is to follow up with "but" or "however" as a point of departure into a different area for consideration, an area that leads right back into the selling story.

The salesperson's "yes" implies an attitude of respect for the prospect's viewpoint, and the "but" suggests that the salesperson has certain related facts which may not have come to the prospect's attention. The salesperson agrees with the prospect as far as possible, admitting that there may be some truth in what the prospect says, and then points out some other factors which must be considered. After giving some ground in opening the reply, the salesperson then tactfully proceeds to show the prospect how this particular case is different.

The principle of this technique is, naturally, that concession on the salesperson's part will influence the prospect to be more receptive. By expressing an understanding of the prospect's position, the salesperson encourages the prospect to listen.

EXAMPLES OF HANDLING OBJECTIONS

This section of the chapter consists of examples of objections that are frequently encountered and answers that will, at times, be appropriate and successful. The objections are divided evenly among the five buying decisions.

Objection to Need

Example No. 1.

Prospect:	"I'm not interested in a new furnace."
Comments:	This can mean that the prospect is not willing to make the sacrifice that buying would demand. It may mean being unaware of needs, or uninformed about what the salesperson's product will do. Often it is a mere excuse. The "I'm not interested" comment definitely cannot mean that the prospect is not interested in health, wealth, popularity, economy, comfort, safety, and convenience. So the salesperson's job is to find where product-satisfaction touches and stimulates one or more of the prospect's buying motives.
Technique:	*Relating product to the prospect's buying motive.*
Salesperson:	"Of course you're not interested in a new furnace—but you are interested in economical heating, aren't you?"

Example No. 2.

Prospect:	"Really, I don't need to handle another line of canned soup."
Comments:	Prospects often do not know that they lack something. It is risky to take issue with them over whether they need the salesperson's product. Instead, the salesperson should feed examples to the prospects, relating the experiences and case histories of impartial, similar third parties. Prospects can be counted on to recognize the similarity between their own needs and those of the salesperson's satisfied customers. Need must be established before any other consideration can be discussed seriously.
	If an individual cannot use the salesperson's product to advantage, that person does not need it and, hence, is not a prospect. When a salesperson has the misfortune to spend time

on a person only to find that need does not exist, then the only thing to do is to start a search for a person who *is* a prospect.

Technique: *Case history.*

Salesperson: "Before you make that decision a permanent one, let me tell you about another grocery store very similar to yours. Its owner decided to take on our line, even though she, like you, was not certain she was doing the right thing. Today, she is enthusiastic over our line because of the profit it nets her."

Example No. 3.

Prospect: "My customers don't ask here for toys."

Comments: When retailers tell a salesperson that they will handle the merchandise only after there is a demand for it, they are usually just trying to get rid of the salesperson. It may not be too far from the truth to say that no retailer has, or can become, a successful merchant by waiting to get calls before stocking a product. More progressive and aggressive competitors would take and hold too much of the local market. Because of the influence they enjoy with their customers and because their advice is asked, retailers can and do move new items.

The "boomerang" technique converts an objection into a reason for buying. It demands skilled handling and a friendly manner. It should be used sparingly.

Technique: *Boomerang.*

Salesperson: "No demand? Of course not. You get no calls for toys because your customers know your drugstore does not stock them. They'd ask for them if you carried them. There's no demand because you don't have toys."

Example No. 4.

Prospect: "I'm not in the market for any more insurance."

Comments: A buyer who takes this position sees no reason to take any buying action. The implication is that the circumstances have been examined and all requirements are covered.

Technique: *Agreement and diversion.*

Salesperson: "Of course not. If you were, you would have come to my office instead of my coming to yours. But you have been thinking some about retirement, haven't you?"

Objection to Product

Example No. 1.

Prospect: "I don't have much confidence in this stepladder. It's so light I don't see how it could be safe."

Comments:	Frequently, all a prospect needs is proof. Logical proof is of certain value; testimonial proof is usually more effective; demonstration proof of what the product will do is an even better answer where practicable. Almost nothing removes doubts so completely as letting the product itself answer an objection, particularly if a test can be designed in which the prospect participates.
Technique:	*Demonstration.*
Salesperson:	"You stand on any rung, and then I'll add my weight to yours. It will easily support the two of us."

Example No. 2.

Prospect:	"Don't talk to me about that make of car. The last one I had was a complete lemon. I'll never buy another one."
Comments:	When a prospect is bitter toward the salesperson's make or brand, the salesperson has a difficult job. The salesperson must be conciliatory and in harmony with the prospect, yet dare not appear disloyal to the company represented and its merchandise. Sometimes the salesperson can point to product changes which make the prospect's criticism no longer valid. Sometimes the changes have been not in product but in circumstances, with the same result. Sometimes the salesperson should encourage the prospect to get rid of resentment by letting off pressure and to unburden personal feelings before an audience by airing the complaint completely. At the same time, this performance aids the salesperson in two ways. It obligates the prospect to listen to the salesperson's reply, and it provides tips and clues as to what that reply should be.
Technique:	*Sympathetic listener.*
Salesperson:	"Tell me all about it."

Example No. 3.

Prospect:	"Radio is okay, but I prefer newspapers."
Comments:	The indirect answer technique was mentioned earlier in the chapter. The salesperson agrees, then goes on to point out differences. The salesperson gives ground, then brings in a new thought.
Technique:	*Yes, . . . but.*
Salesperson:	"Yes, I agree with you and the many other retailers who feel that newspapers are a good advertising medium. However, in radio, you won't be competing with another ad on the same page, you can schedule your message for any hour of the day, and radio reaches people that newspapers don't."

Example No. 4.

Prospect: "I don't know why I should buy parts from your company when I can get parts cheaper from someone else."

Comments: Trucks and farm equipment are two product lines in which the manufacturer's parts encounter competition from parts made by other firms. Often the equipment manufacturer is at a competitive disadvantage as far as price is concerned.

Technique: *Implying that price reflects quality.*

Salesperson: "What kind of a guarantee do the makers of off-brand parts give you? Are they as interested in quality and performance as they are in sales volume? Are their engineering standards as high as ours? Has a defective part ever failed and caused you an expensive repair job?"

Objection to Source

Example No. 1.

Prospect: "Your company is too small."

Comments: Sometimes a diverting move benefits the salesperson. One way to switch the prospect's mind away from the objection is to pass the conversational ball back in the form of a question. The salesperson can use the question to be certain to have a clear understanding of the nature of the prospect's resistance and, thus, know where more selling is needed. It makes the prospect make a commitment, and that can be revealing. If the objection was only an impulse, the salesperson's question will discourage any more opposition of that type. Sometimes the salesperson finds rumor, envy, or propaganda back of the objection. Tact will be needed in cases where the prospect finds that a statement was foolish or pointless and not a valid objection.

Technique: *Question.*

Salesperson: "Too small for what? How is it too small? Why?"

Example No. 2.

Prospect: "I'm going to add a line of electric razors, but I don't know which make it will be. I can't see much difference in razors, prices, or margins."

Comments: What a manufacturer does to win new customers is always good news to retailers.

Technique: *Merchandising aid.*

Salesperson: "Rather than talk about selling my brand *to* you, let me describe the advertising and merchandising aid my company supplies to sell my line *for* you."

Example No. 3.

Prospect: "I've been giving all my business to the ABC company for years and see no reason to change now."

Comments: Prospects who are fiercely loyal to their present suppliers are excellent customers because of just that characteristic. Friendship between buyer and seller can be a very difficult factor for the salesperson who is hunting for concrete, clear proof that the prospect should take on a new vendor. The problems involved in buying from friends, the healthful effect of competition on present suppliers, the importance of not being dependent on a single source of supply, the desirability of a wider inventory, and the relatively greater importance of product over maker are possible lines of approach. Intelligent selling technique demands that the salesperson find why the prospect is so loyal and prefers to deal with the ABC company.

Technique: *Advantages of diversification.*

Salesperson: "That's fine, because ABC is a good company. You might find, however, that if ABC had a bit of competition, you would stand to benefit. And the danger of putting all your eggs in one basket is something to think about."

Example No. 4.

Prospect: "I've heard that your company is going to lose the XYZ account over in Charlotte, and that the XYZ folks don't think much of what's happening. Is that true?"

Comments: If what the prospect thinks or claims is completely untrue, if the destruction of the objection can be done quickly and to the complete satisfaction of the prospect, and if the salesperson takes pains to remain pleasant and controlled, then a diplomatically executed correction may be the right answer. Salespeople who immediately show the prospect to be in error prove their own sincerity, but encourage argument.

Technique: *Immediate refutation.*

Salesperson: "Just a minute there, please. Someone has misinformed you. We are as solid as ever with XYZ. If you care to, call them up at my expense and ask them about it right now."

Objection to Price

Example No. 1.

Prospect: "That is entirely too much money to pay for a vacuum cleaner."

Comments: It is always good for the salesperson to build up, as early as possible, a large mass of value against which the prospect can measure price. The larger the mass and the lower the price, the more attractive the ratio seems. The salesperson should never apologize for a high price. Instead of taking the defensive, the salesperson should point out how modest the price is in relation to what it buys. Some prospects relax a bit when they are told that instead of spending money, they are making an investment. Other prospects like to be told that what they will save will pay for the item. Purchase price is often minimized when reduced to small amounts by, for example, spreading the cost over the life of the product.

Technique: *Spreading the cost over the life of the product.*

Salesperson: "You can count on using this machine for a minimum of ten years. This means that the cost to you is the very modest sum of forty cents a week."

Example No. 2.

Prospect: "I'm afraid I'll never have $1,200 to spend for a fur coat."

Comments: So-called "easy" terms of payment need no comment as an exceedingly effective answer to large price. Features stressed are low down payment, small periodic payments, long pay period, low charge for the privilege, and, in general, the philosophy of paying out of income.

Technique: *Installment terms.*

Salesperson: "You don't need $1,200. You can buy on our liberal budget plan and pay only a small amount each week while you are wearing and enjoying your coat."

Example No. 3.

Prospect: "Before we use up any of each other's time, how much will a cash register cost?"

Comments: It is neither desirable nor possible to ignore the fact that price is a tremendous obstacle for higher-priced products. The sooner the salesperson has to take up the topic, the greater the handicap is. When the salesperson has to quote a rather high price early in the interview, it seems all the higher because there has not been time to describe all that the product will do for its user. The more firmly the salesperson establishes the benefits before referring to price, the more price becomes merely a detail.

Technique: *Postponing.*

Salesperson: "I have them from $300 to $2,000, so I can't quote a price to you until we see what model you need."

Example No. 4.

Prospect:	"The price of your tire is just too high."
Comments:	Every price is high until related to the benefits, advantages, and satisfaction it represents. Assume that Brand A costs twice as much as Brand B. That makes Brand A seem high, but what if it delivers three times more than does Brand B?
Technique:	*Talking overall cost instead of initial price.*
Salesperson:	"Let's look at it this way. If tire cost is to be determined accurately, it must be in terms of performance—in terms of service received. The price of a tire when you put it on one of your wheels does not mean much. That price is high or low only when compared to total wear."

Objection to Time

Example No. 1.

Prospect:	"Check with me 30 to 60 days from now."
Comments:	Several replies may be made to the prospect who hopes to minimize risks by postponing a decision. In the past, the prospect has undoubtedly delayed buying, sometimes regretting it. Perhaps assortments are widest now or prices are apt to rise soon. The prospect's judgment is best when facts are freshest. Indeed, will things be any different 45 days hence?
Technique:	*Anticipating a price increase.*
Salesperson:	"At this moment you have our entire Christmas line in mind more completely than will be the case later on when business becomes hectic. You can order this far in advance with perfect safety, and you won't have to worry about a future price increase."

Example No. 2.

Prospect:	"I guess I'll have to wait till next year to have my house insulated."
Comments:	One way to try for an immediate purchase is to describe and emphasize the enjoyment that begins with possession. This enjoyment usually consists of added satisfaction, added savings, or both. By comparing costs now with what they would be if the product is bought later, the savings can often be used to justify the purchase. The line of reasoning that "You're paying out enough to have it, so you might as well get it" can be effective. Whenever possible, specific figures in dollars and cents should be used instead of generalities.

Technique:	*Showing what waiting would cost.*
Salesperson:	"That means six months of winter between now and the time you insulate. If we take the minimum saving figure we agreed on, $22 a month, the delay will cost you not a cent less than $132—even more if fuel prices keep moving upward."

Example No. 3.

Prospect:	"It might be nice to install a new lighting system, but I guess we'll have to make out a while longer without it."
Comments:	This type of resistance is very close to that found under Buying Decision No. 1—need. The prospect may not be convinced of the desirability of the salesperson's recommendation. "You have a problem and I the solution" talk from the salesperson may be needed. The inadequacy of the present circumstances must be stressed, together with what the product will do for the prospect.
Technique:	*Proof obtained from survey.*
Salesperson:	"I would not feel right if I left you without emphasizing that each year my company's engineers examine hundreds of retailers' lighting facilities. The survey we made of your store convinced us that your lighting requirements should have immediate attention."

Example No. 4.

Prospect:	"I'd better think this over."
Comments:	This may come from a postponer of decisions. It may come from one who was not actually sold on need for the product. Some of the salesperson's points may not have been clear to the prospect, or they may have been misinterpreted. Technically, the objection is more of an evidence of inadequate interest than it is a real objection. The salesperson may elect to move for an immediate close by finding out what it is the prospect wants to think about and handling it then and there. In this event, the advantages of buying now will be stressed. If unsuccessful in this attempt to close the sale, the salesperson may choose to leave with the prospect a checklist against which the prospect can test the brands under consideration. Because the list is drawn up for comparison purposes, it will certainly include every characteristic or feature that is exclusive with the salesperson's product.
Technique:	*A review of plus points.*
Salesperson:	"Okay, here are the main facts you will want to remember about my offer."

PREVENTING OBJECTIONS

Preventing objections keeps the prospect from doing any negative or unfavorable thinking and talking. Second, voicing of an objection at an awkward moment is avoided. Third, prevention makes more time available to the salesperson for use in presenting a complete sales story. Fourth, the salesperson appears completely fair in cases where objections are both raised and answered by the salesperson or the answer is woven into the presentation. Fifth, and most important of all, the prospect is prevented from taking a position. Once an individual states a position, there is pressure to stick to this commitment and to defend it. Most people hate to appear easily influenced, to allow their minds to be changed with little trouble; that is close to admitting they were wrong.

The best plan to keep out objections calls for constructing and telling a complete sales story, one that includes all the information the prospect will need. Then in telling the story, the salesperson should check with the prospect to make sure that each point is clear.

The salesperson should note and list the most frequent and most troublesome objections encountered in interviews. The salesperson should then work into the sales presentation the most effective answers to these most common questions, complaints, and criticisms. The answers should be in the form of positive selling points. Especially to be included in the sales story are strong points about product features which competitive salespeople discount. When competition indicates to the prospect that it fails to be impressed by some aspect or characteristic of the salesperson's product, competition is probably planting an objection, or at least a doubt, in that prospect's mind. It is this type of product feature which must be covered fully and favorably in the sales story.

The clearer, more logical, and more complete the sales story, the less important a prospect's objections become. If the prospect's attention is monopolized by a mountain of positive points and a small pile of negative points, the prospect will be inclined to consider the objections planned as too insignificant to mention.

SUMMARY

Prospect resistance occurs because an individual's purchasing power is limited. Disagreement between salesperson and prospect is inevitable. Objections are both evidence and causes of disagreement. Frictionless disagreement should be strived for.

Some buyers are hostile when objecting. Courteous listening, exploration, questioning, and avoidance are ways of dealing with hostility.

Buyers offer resistance when they do not know enough about their needs. They are reluctant to change habits, and they resist products that will lead to such changes. Resistance is sometimes offered as a test of the salesperson's knowledge or abilities. Personal preference, prejudice, and fear can also cause resistance.

The salesperson should encourage the voicing of objections, because the salesperson will then know what information to offer or what points to clarify. All questions and negative statements from buyers should be treated as requests for information, and objections should be used to plan the future course of the sales presentation.

Frequently, apparent objections are only excuses. One of the salesperson's first objectives is to identify and isolate the real reason why the prospect refuses to buy. An excuse is any insincere resistance offered by the prospect. It is not the real obstacle to buying. Tactful questioning and the parallel track answer are two effective ways to separate excuses from objections.

The basic principles of handling objections are: (1) clarifying the objection if necessary, (2) classifying the objection, (3) maintaining control at all times, (4) not arguing with the prospect, (5) being diplomatic in answering the objection, (6) fitting the answer to the prospect, (7) minimizing the objection, and (8) capitalizing on the objection if possible. The following ten techniques are frequently used in handling objections: (1) product comparison, (2) relating a case history, (3) demonstration, (4) giving guarantees, (5) asking questions, (6) showing what a delay costs, (7) admitting and counterbalancing, (8) hearing the prospect out, (9) making the objection boomerang, and (10) the "Yes, but" technique.

Objections can either be given future handling or be dealt with immediately. The salesperson can disregard the objection until it comes up again. This is one way of separating the real from the artificial. When an objection is put aside for a while, its significance may be greatly reduced. Finally, by postponing the handling until later, the salesperson maintains control of the interview.

Sometimes an immediate, direct answer is appropriate. This technique convinces the prospect of the salesperson's sincerity. The indirect answer is the most widely used and effective method of handling objections. The salesperson acknowledges the objection, and then goes on to another area for consideration that leads right back into the selling story.

Preventing objections keeps the prospect from doing any negative or unfavorable thinking and talking. A well-constructed and complete sales story that includes all the information the prospect will need is the best technique for preventing objections.

REVIEW QUESTIONS

1. Why is frictionless disagreement desirable?
2. List three ways to deal with buyer hostility.
3. List four reasons why buyers offer objections.
4. Why should the salesperson welcome objections?
5. What is the basic difference between an excuse and an objection?
6. What is a parallel track answer?
7. How can the salesperson use objection classification as a sales tool?
8. Why shouldn't a salesperson ever argue with a prospect?

9. How can salespeople capitalize on objections?
10. What are the advantages of a direct answer?
11. What is the best way to prevent objections?

DISCUSSION QUESTIONS

1. Assume that you are the sales manager for a large industrial distributor. Your most successful salesperson is retiring in three months. You have selected a replacement who is a young, aggressive salesperson. What objections is the replacement probably going to face because of replacing an old, popular salesperson? What would you do as a sales manager to limit these objections?
2. It has been suggested that one of the best ways to handle objections is with an indirect answer, and that using direct answers may be a risky approach. Is the reverse ever true?
3. React to this statement: "Sales talks should always be prepared in such a way as to anticipate all major objections before they occur."
4. How can the Socratic Method be used to advantage when answering objections?

CASE STUDY 12

Jim Balsam, a salesperson for a large industrial distributor, has been selling in his present territory for two years. Balsam started in this territory upon the retirement of his predecessor, a salesperson who had spent 15 years building up the area's volume to a high figure. One of the predecessor's strengths was his contacts with plant personnel. For example, in the Epic Manufacturing Corporation the former salesperson had many long and close contacts with operating and production personnel. Those contacts, of course, helped explain his large sales volume to Epic. At the time of his retirement, Balsam's predecessor had virtually the run of the Epic plant; the Epic purchasing agent had seen this freedom develop, had approved of it, and had even encouraged it.

On Balsam's first call, the Epic purchasing agent told him that he was to stay out of the plant for the time being. He indicated fear that Balsam might waste the working time of the plant personnel; he commented, with both humor and seriousness, that he did not want Balsam "bribing" his operating personnel.

During his first two years on the job, Balsam asked several times for permission to consult with plant personnel about various technical matters. Such permission was not granted. Toward the end of the second year, Epic placed a very large order for a certain item with Balsam's firm. Balsam just happened to learn that an engineer in the plant had specified the brand of this type of product on which Balsam's firm had a franchise. This made Balsam more eager than ever to make contacts in the plant.

What can you say about Balsam's problem?

Chapter

Closing the Sale 13

After studying this chapter you should be able to:

- Point out how prospects feel about attempts to close sales
- Indicate when salespeople should try to close sales
- Relate closing clues to trial closes
- Describe various techniques of closing sales
- Compare activities after successful sales calls with those after no-sale calls
- Discuss the scheduling and handling of call-backs

The close is the final stage of the sales interview proper. The salesperson has told the sales story, has demonstrated the product, has disposed of resistance, and wants the prospect's commitment to purchase.

Sometimes difficulty is experienced at the close, caused by circumstances prior to the close. If the opening of the interview and delivery of the presentation are not adequate, closing will not be easy. The presentation may be weak because the salesperson lacks sufficient information about the prospect. The weakness may be in the sales story. Sometimes the salesperson's handling of objections or the demonstration is faulty.

Sometimes the salesperson is unsuccessful in obtaining an affirmative buying decision because of flaws in the close itself. If a ceremony is made out of the close, it tends to frighten the prospect. If the salesperson seems awkward or anxious during the closing, this can cause resistance. Successful closes are jeopardized if the salesperson fails to steer a middle course between too much and too little aggressiveness. If the close is unfortunately worded or ill-timed, the sale is not likely to be completed.

PROSPECTS' ATTITUDES TOWARD THE CLOSE

Usually the thought of buying has both positive and negative aspects for prospects. They would obviously not be prospects unless they could somehow benefit from buying. On the other hand, they cannot have all the things they want, and they cannot prove in advance that they will not regret their decision to buy the particular product under consideration. Reluctance to buy, then, is normal and expected. Prospects feel the urge to conserve their purchasing power and avoid making a commitment.

It would seem, then, that what prospects need most in the close is assurance. Confidence in their decision to buy must be great enough to override their doubts. To convey this assurance adequately, the salesperson must show the proper amount of self-confidence. The negative feelings which invade the thinking of some salespeople as they prepare for the close are contagious. They can ruin the closing because they influence the prospect's attitude and ultimate decision.

What the salesperson tells prospects is as important as attitudes and actions in assuring the prospect. Prospects want to hear statements that will dismiss their indecision. They want to be told that they are doing the correct thing in buying. In the closing remarks, then, the salesperson should remove from the shoulders of prospects as much decision making as possible. The salesperson should make positive, constructive recommendations instead of provisional suggestions. The salesperson should describe what is going to happen after prospects have bought, and not what will happen if they buy. The salesperson strengthens prospects' resolution to purchase by telling them that they are demonstrating common sense, that they can feel proud of their action, and that they can feel confidence in the salesperson and the company represented. In some situations, the prospect will feel a need for reasons that can be used in justifying this purchase to others. These reasons can be an important part of the close.

WHEN TO CLOSE THE SALE

Actually, the major part of a successful closing is the preliminary work done in the early stages of the sale. If a sound presentation is made from the outset and the prospect gives complete assent to the points the salesperson makes, the close will almost take care of itself. Thus, the salesperson should consciously start moving toward a close the moment the interview is opened.

Understanding and agreement should be secured from the prospect as the salesperson makes various selling points. This practice should be continued throughout the close. Unless the prospect concurs with the salesperson's analysis and recommendations, no attempt at closing will be successful. If prospects go along with each benefit as it is presented, they must logically accept the aggregate of the benefits at the end by agreeing that the only thing to do is to buy immediately.

Specifically, the salesperson sprinkles the presentation with questions which can hardly be answered sensibly by any response other than a "yes." Nearing the close, the questions tend to be separated by shorter and shorter time intervals. Sample questions are:

1. It would be a shame to let all this basement space of yours go to waste, wouldn't it?
2. This item certainly will reduce your fuel bill, won't it?
3. Ours is the most liberal guarantee you've seen, isn't it?
4. Beautiful, isn't it?

The use of such questions is helpful because each earlier agreement reduces the magnitude of the final agreement—the final decision becomes just one (the last) of a number of decisions. The prospect will not be surprised and shocked by an attempt to close.

Closing Clues

Closing clues are the signals indicating that a close should be attempted by the salesperson. They alert the salesperson to the fact that the prospect may be ready to buy. The salesperson who studies the prospect's reactions can learn to spot closing clues, although, of course, this diagnosis can never be completely accurate.

Prospects give some indication when they are near the act of buying. As a matter of fact, there may be several of these clues or signals in a single interview. This is possible because a prospect can get near buying, draw away, and then once again be on the verge of making a purchase—all in the same interview. Because reactions show when the prospect is ready for the salesperson's attempt to close, they are extremely valuable to salespeople. Nothing is more important in closing than for the salesperson to learn to spot these signals and to act on them.

There are physical closing clues. Examples include when the prospect smiles in agreement, the prospect's attention returns time after time to one model, the prospect stands up, and the prospect operates one product several times.

Verbal closing clues may be comments or questions. Several examples follow:

1. Your brand has always been good to me.
2. This chair is certainly attractive.
3. I'd have to have it by Friday.
4. And your guarantee is for two years?
5. Do you accept credit cards?
6. What colors are available?
7. Do you charge for installation?
8. Which model do you think best for me?

Trial closes are attempted by the salesperson to see if the prospect is ready to make a purchase; they sound the prospect out. If the prospect's response to the trial close is favorable, the salesperson goes ahead at once and tries to complete the sale. If the prospect's reaction clearly shows that the prospect is not yet ready to buy, the salesperson continues the sales presentation.

The trial close serves two purposes. First and foremost, it is a safe and simple way of asking the prospect to buy. If it succeeds, it can result in an immediate purchase. Second, it is an inoffensive check on how prospects are thinking. Are they reacting favorably? Are they convinced yet? Are they ready to buy? The trial close sheds light on these matters.

Verbal trial closes are usually phrased in the form of questions which call for decisions on minor points. A verbal trial close customarily asks the prospect to make some choice. Some sample questions for a trial close are:

1. Will there be a trade-in?
2. When do you need it?
3. Will six be enough?
4. Will you want this sent to your home or to your office?
5. Do you prefer to pay cash or use credit?

It takes only a glance at these examples to see that the prospect who gives a direct answer to the question has in effect agreed to make the purchase.

Physical trial closes are those in which the salesperson starts to execute the physical phases of the sale without asking permission to do so. For example, the salesperson could pick up an order book and start to write out the order. When a trial close, either verbal or physical, fails to complete the sale, the salesperson analyzes why the prospect is not ready to buy and then works on the difficulty.

A salesperson does well to execute trial closes in these situations:

1. When the prospect gives a closing clue
2. When the prospect gives enthusiastic agreement on one of the selling points or one of the salesperson's leading questions
3. When the prospect accepts proof of the product's advantages in a convinced manner
4. When the salesperson has just completed an effective demonstration of the product
5. When the salesperson has disposed of some objection in an effective way.

In the use of trial closes, the salesperson must not stimulate the prospect's buying defenses. Instead of asking for a decision on the major issue at that time, the salesperson will bypass it in favor of a lesser decision. Also, the salesperson must never close the door to more discussion or make it possible for the prospect to do so. If the salesperson detects a closing clue, executes a trial close, and then finds that it was not a clue, it should be possible to resume the sales story.

When to Attempt the Close

A sound rule for closing is to do it as early as possible, for more sales are lost by trying too late than by trying too early. A salesperson's objective is to close a sale—not to present a complete sales story just because one is prepared. A closing attempt made too early will find one or more of the five buying decisions missing. However, the salesperson who talks past the first closing opportunity may lose the sale by not having tried to close when the prospect was favorably inclined toward buying.

Salespeople used to think that only one moment for closing ever occurred during any one interview and that the salesperson had to make an attempt to close at exactly that moment if a sale was to be made on that call. Authorities on selling now believe that this so-called "psychological moment" is a myth. They believe that there may be several high spots of conviction during the selling conversation and that purchase might easily be made at any one of them. Resistance and opposition are at a minimum at these points, objections are not raised, and the prospect seems sold on the salesperson's proposal. The salesperson might even miss on the first, second, and third high spots but be successful in closing the sale on the fourth one. The general rule, then, is for the salesperson to make an attempt at closing whenever it appears that the time to close is right. Obviously, experience is a great help in learning to sense when the conditions for closing are most favorable.

TECHNIQUES OF CLOSING THE SALE

No salesperson closes every sale. It must be pointed out, however, that one mark of a successful salesperson is the high percentage of sales made in difficult situations. Mediocre salespeople get orders from prospects who are ready and waiting to buy; the expert salesperson can succeed in selling to almost anyone who qualifies as a prospect.

No specific technique of closing is effective in all cases. No matter how logical and usually successful is the close first attempted, the salesperson may be forced to use others before finally making the sale. A number of methods of closing that have proved valuable to salespeople will now be discussed.

Closing on a Choice

The technique of closing on a choice is probably the most often used closing technique because it is the most versatile and the most likely to be successful. This technique is also referred to as the technique of closing on a minor point, the double question method, the selection close, and the split decision close.

The salesperson takes for granted that the prospect is going to buy; but at the same time, knows that the prospect is reluctant to concede, in effect, "Yes, you win—you've sold me—I'll buy." So what the salesperson does is ignore and avoid the major buying decision, which is to buy or not to buy, by posing a minor decision for the prospect to make.

Closing on a choice is particularly appropriate when the prospect is having trouble deciding because it narrows the choice down to two. This makes the process of choosing less complicated, and hence, less confusing. The device is also good when a new salesperson is reluctant to press for a close.

In using the technique of closing on a choice, the salesperson asks the prospect which of the two products is preferred. The difference between the two may be a matter of model, color, size, material, or some other product feature. The salesperson frames the choice by asking such a question as, "Do you prefer the full-color assortment or the single-color assortment?" The prospect makes the choice, and either alternative chosen represents a closing of the sale. The question the salesperson asks should be framed so that the choices offered will be of equal utility and suitability, so that either choice will be satisfactory to both prospect and seller.

The Assumption Close

In the assumption close, both salesperson and prospect have a single specific product in mind; both are thinking about the same model, color, size, material, and price. The prospect may have narrowed the field down to the one product, or the salesperson may have selected the most appropriate item for that particular prospect.

The assumption close is a result of the salesperson's doing and saying things throughout the presentation which indicate that the major buying question is settled. The closing question assumes the prospect's acceptance of the salesperson's recommendations and inquires only about some minor point. The question asked and the choice presented are quite similar to those used in the choice close, except that the question now concerns an auxiliary matter and not the product itself. Thus, the salesperson may ask questions such as these:

1. How do you prefer to pay?
2. How much do you want to pay as a down payment?
3. How do you want this shipped?
4. When do you want this to become effective?

The Single Feature Close

Sometimes a prospect will be particularly anxious to obtain one special feature in a product, or sometimes a product will have a feature that competition cannot match—perhaps a matter of design, a method of operation, or a manner of construction. In any of these situations, the single feature close may be the best method for the salesperson to use. If the prospect does not fully appreciate the feature, then the salesperson highlights it and relates just what the feature will mean to the prospect. The aim is to persuade the prospect to buy solely because of this one feature. If the prospect does appreciate the feature, the salesperson agrees with the prospect, emphasizes how this brand excels on that score, and then attempts a close centered around that one feature.

Disposing of the Single Obstacle

Sometimes a prospect gives honest agreement to every point the salesperson makes except one, and that one obstacle prevents the purchase from being made immediately. Perhaps everything is satisfactory except price; perhaps the prospect feels obligated to buy from some other vendor; or perhaps the prospect fears the cost of operating the product.

The first thing the salesperson should do is to get the prospect to agree that the objection raised is the only thing holding up the purchase. The salesperson may ask: "Is that the only reason we can't do business? There's nothing else standing in the way?" Otherwise, answering the specific objection satisfactorily will not close the sale. The true barrier to buying will still remain in the prospect's mind. The salesperson must dispose of the single obstacle conclusively. When the objection has been handled, the next step is the closing of the sale.

Reviewing the Five Buying Decisions

As you have learned, no one makes a purchase until positive that there is a need for something, that a certain product will fill that need, that a particular salesperson or company is the proper source, that the price is satisfactory, and that the time to buy is now. One course the salesperson can follow in closing the sale is to review these five decisions and obtain the prospect's approval on each one. Until the prospect actually buys, only one conclusion can be drawn: agreement is still missing on one or more of the five decisions. If this is true, the salesperson brings in additional facts and supplies more convincing proof until the missing decision is made affirmatively.

Summarizing the Benefits

After covering most of the benefits which the salesperson thinks will appeal to the prospect, the moment has come to try to close the sale. A method of closing that may be effective—especially when the prospect will have to defend the purchase to family, friends, or employer—is a review of each advantage the salesperson has mentioned. The collection of advantages may be impressive enough to persuade the prospect to buy immediately. If any one or two of the benefits seemed to be of particular interest to the prospect as they were initially described, they should be stressed in the summary.

The summary should be made simply and without formality and may be prefaced by some remark such as, "Let's review the benefits I've mentioned so we won't forget any that might be of special interest to you." The salesperson will ask the prospect for agreement on each benefit so that if there is an objection to one, it can be disposed of immediately. When there is complete agreement, the salesperson assumes that the prospect is ready to buy and goes through the mechanics of closing. The salesperson may or may not ask for instructions or information on some detail.

CLOSING THE SALE

DO'S

Do display a friendly manner at the close, even though there is disagreement. This helps to avoid arguments.

Do be sure to have all materials and equipment that will be needed. Misplaced order blanks, obsolete price lists, and faulty pens can lose sales.

Do realize that begging for a sale makes you and your offer look bad; it also disgusts the prospect.

Do ask the prospect to "OK" or approve the order rather than sign it.

Do make buying as easy and painless as possible.

Do try for privacy at the close. Telephone calls and third parties distract.

Do study each prospect as a baseball pitcher studies each batter. Then pitch to the prospect's weakness.

Do lead the prospect to think as the owner of the product from the very beginning of the interview.

Do put the order book and pen in a conspicuous, convenient spot long before attempting a close.

DON'TS

Don't be apologetic, particularly in quoting price.

Don't make written or even oral promises unless authorized to do so.

Don't make a ceremony out of closing lest the prospect become frightened.

Don't give the prospect an excuse or an opportunity to back away from the purchase.

Don't ever ask the prospect for the buying decision in such a way that it is possible to answer with a "no."

Don't make it difficult for the prospect to complete the purchase quickly if desired.

Don't let the prospect miss seeing that you expect a purchase.

Don't make it easier for the prospect to refuse than to buy.

ILLUSTRATION 13-1. Here are some do's and don'ts for the salesperson to remember in preparing to close a sale.

The Emotional Close

Sometimes the sales interview progresses satisfactorily through the first four buying decisions but encounters difficulties with the fifth. This is quite understandable; the first four decisions are easy for the prospect to make because no final action is required. The fifth—decision to buy now—is more difficult. When the salesperson reviews and obtains agreement on the questions of need, product, source, and price, yet cannot close the sale, the emotional close may be effective.

In using the emotional close, the salesperson tries to produce an impulsive buying reaction, having been unable to persuade the prospect to take calculated buying action. The salesperson stimulates such buying motives as those resulting from the desires for affection and self-esteem.

The "Standing Room Only" Close

People want what other people want and what other people have. They want anything that is hard to get. This is the reasoning back of the "standing room only" close.

A salesperson who tells a prospect that a price increase is due next week, that the doctor turned down one of the prospect's friends when he applied for insurance, that the supply of a product is limited, or that a premium offer expires soon is using the "standing room only" close to stimulate the prospect to buy. This device should be held in reserve until late in the interview because it can weaken the presentation. There is often a temptation to use this close unethically to get rid of slow-selling merchandise.

The Direct Appeal Close

Because the direct appeal close can be somewhat risky, it should generally be used only as a last resort. If a direct appeal fails, the salesperson will find it awkward if not impossible to return to the sales presentation. In using the direct appeal close, the salesperson says, in effect, "I've explained this product and how it will benefit you as best I can. You understand the product and what it will do for you. You need it. You have safely followed my recommendations in the past, and you can do so now. If there are any questions remaining, let's clear them up now. Otherwise, suppose we go ahead."

Before the direct appeal close is used, the prospect should obviously be interested in buying and expect to benefit from the purchase. The salesperson and company must also enjoy an established standing with the prospect.

Here are sample wordings the salesperson might use:

1. Shall I draw up the contract now?
2. When shall I send my assistant over to take the measurements?
3. I'll send your order in today.

4. I'm glad you appreciate what my product will do for you; now I need some information for my report.

The Special Concession Close

In using the special concession close, the salesperson offers the prospect some special inducement for acting at once. The most common inducement is a cut in the price originally quoted. For some product lines, the salesperson might offer something free to the buyer; for example, a retailer might be given one dozen free items for each ten dozen bought immediately. In selling to wholesalers and retailers, there may also be some allowance—such as an advertising allowance equal to 5 percent of the merchant's purchases—which can be given if certain minimum quantities are purchased immediately. The trial order can also be a form of concession because the salesperson agrees to settle for the purchase of a smaller, trial quantity instead of the quantity originally suggested.

There are other types of special inducements. A trade-in allowance can be revised upward, or down payment reduced. A manufacturer may offer PMs (push money) to a retailer's salespeople to push the manufacturer's brand or might offer the retailer more elaborate POP (point-of-purchase) displays than the retailer has been getting. Premiums, free accessories, extra discounts, and longer pay periods are other examples of special inducements that might be offered.

Special concessions should not be offered until the last moments of the interview, and even then there are dangers in using this technique. The prospect may keep pressing for more concessions once the salesperson starts offering them, or the prospect may begin to wonder about the product's value and desirability if concessions must be made to sell it. Concessions also reduce the seller's profits. And finally, the salesperson must not play favorites among buyers.

The T-Account Technique

The T-account can be an effective closing device. The salesperson draws up a large T. On the left side the salesperson lists reasons for the prospect to buy and on the right side lists reasons for not buying. Obviously, there must be more weight on the left side than on the right, for example:

PRO (Buy)	CON (Don't Buy)
Save $100 per month	Large investment required
Less duplication	Prices have been dropping
Reduce overtime	
Better control	
Salesperson's machine works faster	

The Request for an Order

When a salesperson has recommended a sound solution to a problem and the prospect seems to be in agreement, the salesperson is entitled to ask for an order. The salesperson can do like the political candidate who asks a voter, "Will you vote for me?" When the time has come to write up an order, the salesperson may say:

"I'll appreciate your business. Will eight dozen be about right for you?"
"Fine. Then let's go right ahead. How many do you want and when do you want them?"
"Approve this order and you'll get delivery by Wednesday of next week."

THE SALESPERSON'S POSTSALE ACTIVITIES

Whether or not the prospect buys, the salesperson always thanks the prospect at the end of the interview for the consideration given and tries to leave the prospect kindly disposed toward the product and the company represented. The salesperson makes certain that the prospect has his or her name, address, and telephone number, as well as some literature or other material about the product. There are also more specific activities that the salesperson will perform depending upon whether the prospect buys or does not buy.

Activities Following a Successful Sale

If a seller is to avoid ill will, complaints, demands for adjustments, cancellations, and unfavorable word-of-mouth publicity, customers must use the products they buy, like them, and continue to buy them. The time to start converting a first-time customer into a regular, satisfied one is just after the first sale has been made.

The first thing, of course, is to thank the prospect for becoming a customer. This should be sincere, yet crisp, and must never be allowed to become casual. A compliment can be paid to the prospect's good judgment, and assurance given that the product will live up to expectations.

A second thing is to try to make certain that the prospect will use the product to maximum advantage. The prospect should understand the operation and care of the product in order to benefit most. If appropriate, the prospect should be impressed with the importance and necessity of following directions and with the continued service the seller makes available.

A third thing is to see if any other sales possibilities are at hand. If the salesperson is handling a family of products, perhaps there are other items that might benefit the customer. It may be observed that opportunities for more business will be coming up in the future. The customer may allow the salesperson to take before and after pictures to use in other solicitations. The new customer may be asked to help the salesperson by agreeing to be a source of testimonials. Or the customer might be able and willing to supply the names of, and other facts about, people who are prospective buyers.

Extreme care should be used in writing up the order. Errors are bad, particularly on the first order. Omissions are bad, too; for example, forgetting to obtain any data that will be called for by some department of the company, such as the credit department. In writing up the order, the salesperson may ask several questions, even though the answers to them are known. This helps to keep the buyer from being idle and wondering if the purchase was wise. As a matter of fact, it lets the buyer help close the sale. The salesperson might repeat the terms or figures being written on the order blank or sales contract. This prevents awkward periods of silence and eliminates the possibility of misunderstanding between seller and buyer over quantity bought, price, delivery date, method of shipment, and such. This time of writing up the first order is most suitable for making certain that the new customer knows the terms of the seller and also understands why they are important.

After making the sale, there are certain mistakes the salesperson should avoid. The salesperson should not:

1. Talk too much, especially about the purchase, or talk down to the buyer.
2. Stay too long, wasting both parties' time. This is very important if the buyer is a purchasing agent.
3. Act like the "winner," for that implies that the buyer lost.
4. Thank the buyer too profusely.
5. Give the impression that sales are novel and infrequent.
6. Relax too obviously.
7. Be casual to the point of appearing indifferent.
8. Leave so abruptly that he or she forgets to compliment the buyer.
9. Fail to assure the buyer of the salesperson's availability and continuing interest.

The time immediately after the first sale is the right time to begin to learn as much as possible about the former prospect who is now a customer. Hence, just as he or she keeps a file on all prospects, the salesperson must also keep an individual, detailed record of each customer. All transactions should be noted on the record as should a list of all products bought. These records should be studied thoroughly, systematically, and often. They reveal which items the salesperson sells with ease and which with difficulty, indicate what buying decisions have been troublesome, and supply clues as to what revisions or adjustments are needed.

Activities Following No-Sale Calls

When the sale is not closed on a particular call and the prospect is to be visited again, the salesperson should spend the final moments of the interview in building up goodwill and paving the way for a return visit. Any needed information is secured so that a more appropriate and beneficial proposal may be presented later. The salesperson inquires whether there are any facts to be obtained or any favor that might be done for the prospect before the next call. Sincere appreciation is expressed for the time the prospect has given.

Immediately after leaving the prospect, the salesperson begins to prepare for the return call. Everything learned about the prospect is jotted down so that the salesperson will have a record to review before calling again. What took place in the conference is summarized. Any mistakes made are listed with possible means of correcting them. A matter that must not be overlooked is that of the objections encountered; while the call is still fresh, thoughts may come to mind about how to handle such obstacles better. Buying decisions should be classified into two groups, those made in the affirmative and those still missing. The salesperson must note and file away information on prices quoted, deliveries promised, or any other commitments. These notes should be made to avoid possible misunderstanding in the future or failure to fulfill promises. Finally, the salesperson must enter the call-back date in his or her calendar.

The causes of failure to sell must be handled in some systematic fashion if the number of failures is to be reduced. Some companies require that a lost order report be filed with the sales manager. Illustration 13-2 shows a typical lost order report.

Another method is for the salesperson to start a checklist which will indicate the deficiencies that resulted in an incomplete sale. The assumption is, of course, that the salesperson's product and its price are satisfactory and that the prospect has a real need and can afford to buy. Items such as appearance, product knowledge, and approach may appear on a checklist. See Illustration 13-3 for an example of such a checklist.

Scheduling and Handling Call-Backs

There will be times when prospects refuse to commit themselves, either because they are actually unable to buy or because they are unwilling. It may be that before giving a final decision, someone else's permission for the purchase must be secured or certain matters that are involved in the transaction must be arranged. Regardless of the reason, prospects may postpone buying for what to them is a real and justifiable cause. When the salesperson is certain that the prospect is determined to delay the purchase, the only thing to do is to suggest a later visit.

By recognizing that many sales require more than one call, the experienced salesperson leaves gracefully as soon as he or she is positive that another call will be necessary. This avoids antagonizing the prospect by pressing for an immediate decision and also minimizes the time the salesperson spends in ineffectual conversation. The best plan is to agree at once on a definite time for the next meeting in which the salesperson hopes to review the buying decisions

Lost Order Report   BOUNTIFUL
                                                     BASICS

1. Name of sales representative _____
2. Name of prospect/buyer _____
   Address _____
   _____
   _____

   Has the above firm ever bought from us? _____
   If so, when? _____
   Was the firm satisfied with our product(s) and service? _____
   If not, why not? _____
   _____

3. Product(s) quoted on:
   Product   Quantity   Unit Price   Total Price
   _____
   _____
   _____
   _____

4. To what company was the order given? _____
5. Did you see the competing product(s) the company is now using? _____
   If yes, name the product(s) _____
   _____

6. State your reasons for losing this order _____
   _____
   _____

7. How can we help you with this account? _____
   _____
   _____

8. When do you expect to make another call? _____
9. Date report filed _____
10. Signed _____

ILLUSTRATION 13-2. Some companies require that a lost order report be filed with the sales manager. By analyzing why an order was not obtained, both the salesperson and the company benefit.

LOST ORDER CHECKLIST

Check YES or NO to diagnose why your order was lost. The more NOS, the harder it was for the prospect to say YES.

	YES	NO
1. I prepared for the interview	___	___
2. My appearance was good	___	___
3. I felt confident	___	___
4. I was enthusiastic	___	___
5. I showed sincere interest in the prospect	___	___
6. My approach was well chosen	___	___
7. I inspired the prospect's confidence	___	___
8. I awakened the prospect's interest	___	___
9. I concentrated on the sales points that most interested the prospect	___	___
10. I made the prospect realize his/her needs	___	___
11. I questioned the prospect intelligently	___	___
12. I could answer the prospect's questions about the product.	___	___
13. I was careful not to interrupt	___	___
14. I anticipated the prospect's objections	___	___
15. I handled objections well	___	___
16. My talk was arranged in logical order	___	___
17. I stuck to the facts	___	___
18. I demonstrated my talk	___	___
19. I backed up what I said with examples, figures, and visible proof	___	___
20. I boiled everything down to a few definite, simple sales points	___	___
21. I tested the prospect's agreement on one point before going on to the next one	___	___
22. My sales presentation was a good length	___	___
23. I used showmanship	___	___
24. My interview was free of argument	___	___
25. I asked for an order	___	___

ILLUSTRATION 13-3. The salesperson may use a checklist to indicate the deficiencies that resulted in an incomplete sale. Items such as appearance, product knowledge, and approach may appear on a checklist.

already made, obtain favorable decisions on the missing ones, and close the sale. Making a specific appointment for the call-back has a number of advantages. First, it avoids wasting the salesperson's time because it assures that the prospect will see the salesperson on the second call. Second, the salesperson can suggest a date for the call-back which will fall as closely as possible to the next time the prospect will be in a position to buy. Third, this technique calls the prospect's attention to the salesperson's interest, expectation of getting the order, and desire to be of service. Fourth, the prospect can look forward to a second, scheduled visit from someone who wants to be of assistance. Finally, arranging an appointment may mean that the prospect can arrange to block out interruptions during the next conference, thus giving full attention to the salesperson.

Call-backs demand special preparation. In getting ready for the next visit, the salesperson should carefully review the prospect card and what took place at the previous meeting. The salesperson who promised to bring something back to the prospect, such as information or samples, should be sure to have them. Because the prospect's attention has been called to many matters in the interim between the two calls, the salesperson must be prepared to revive the prospect's interest and reestablish contact; the salesperson cannot expect the prospect to remember all that was said on the last call. In some instances, the prospect may have taken a negative attitude toward the sales proposal. Pressure, then, is on the salesperson to have some message for the prospect that is new and important.

In executing the call-back, the salesperson must offer a justification for the repeat visit. Whenever new facts of value to the prospect are used as an introduction to the call-back, the chances of a friendly welcome are good. Whatever introduction is used, the salesperson must quickly capture the prospect's interest and place the interview on firm ground. The salesperson should personalize the conversation, show particular interest in the prospect's problems, and offer definite advantages to the prospect just as would be done on any first call.

SUMMARY

The close is the final stage of the interview. Prospects usually want the product, but they resist because they want to conserve their purchasing power. It is the salesperson's job to show the prospect that a purchase now is more valuable than that conserved purchasing power.

Closing clues, either verbal or physical, must be noted by the salesperson. Trial closes are attempted to see if the prospect is ready to make a purchase; they sound the prospect out. If the prospect's response to the trial close is positive, the salesperson tries to complete the sale. Closing should be attempted as early as possible.

Closing on a choice is the most often used closing technique. The salesperson takes for granted that the prospect will buy, asking the prospect which of two products is preferred.

In the assumption close, both salesperson and prospect have a specific product in mind. The closing question assumes the prospect's acceptance of the salesperson's recommendations and inquires only about some minor point.

Sometimes a closing attempt will resolve around a single product feature. This is called the single feature close.

Frequently only a specific objection prevents a purchase from being made immediately. The salesperson then gets the prospect to agree that only one objection is preventing the sale. When the objection is handled, the closing takes place.

The salesperson can review the five buying decisions and add convincing proof until any missing decision is made affirmatively. Summarizing product benefits is another useful method. An emotional close may be used when the first four buying decisions have been made but the fifth one is lacking. The "standing room only" close is an appeal showing that a great opportunity will be lost if a purchase isn't made immediately.

The direct appeal close is risky and should be used only as a last resort. The special concession close offers bonuses as inducements for making purchases. The T-account technique lists the pros and cons of a purchase. When a salesperson has recommended a sound solution to a prospect's problem and the prospect seems to be in agreement, the salesperson is entitled to ask for an order.

Whether or not the prospect buys, the salesperson should thank the prospect for the consideration given. The salesperson should also make certain that the prospect has his or her name, address, telephone number, and some product information.

If a sale is made, the salesperson must sincerely thank the buyer, and make certain that the product will be used to maximum advantage. Then the salesperson should see if there are any other sales possibilities. Careful writing up of the order and the recording of customer information are next.

If a sale is not closed, the salesperson should build up goodwill and pave the way for another visit. Prospect information is recorded, and reasons for the failure to secure a sale are analyzed.

When the salesperson is certain that the prospect is determined to delay a purchase, a later visit should be suggested. A definite time and place for the next meeting should be agreed upon.

Call-backs demand special preparation. In executing the call-back, the salesperson must justify the repeat visit. Information or samples that have been promised should be delivered.

REVIEW QUESTIONS

1. What are closing clues?
2. What is the purpose of a trial close?
3. When is the best time to try a trial close?
4. What is meant by closing on a choice?

5. When is an emotional close useful?
6. List four things that a salesperson should do after a sale has been made.
7. When does preparation for a return call begin?
8. What information should be generated and recorded after an unsuccessful call?
9. What are the advantages of making a specific appointment for a call-back?
10. How should a salesperson arrange and prepare for a call-back?

DISCUSSION QUESTIONS

1. How might team selling improve the seller's chances of completing a sale?
2. In most instances, the direct appeal close is considered risky. Are there ever any circumstances when it should be attempted early in the sales presentation?
3. Frequently, the final agreed upon price is lower than the initially requested price for a product. Are all of these sales the result of special concession closes?
4. Assume that you are sales manager for a furniture distributor. It has come to your attention that one of your salespeople has been unsuccessful because he seemingly is intent upon playing out his entire presentation rather than closing the sale. How would you try to help this salesperson?

CASE STUDY 13

The Brunswick Jewelry Store is located in the downtown area of a large city and handles merchandise of medium to high quality. One of the store's salespeople has just noticed a prospect enter the store.

Salesperson: Good afternoon. May I help you?

Prospect: I hope so. I lost my regular watch a few days ago, and this old one I've been trying to make do just isn't dependable enough. My regular watch was such a good one.

Salesperson: Well, we have a wide assortment of fine watches. (Takes five watches from the display case and sets them on the counter for the prospect to see.) Which do you like best?

Prospect: I don't know.

Salesperson: (Picks up one of the watches.) This is the Supreme 400. Stainless steel case and back. Because it's electric, it never needs winding, on your wrist or off. This watch is completely dependable. It's shock-resistant, antimagnetic, waterproof, and fully adjusted. Cleaning, regulating, and servicing requirements are absolutely minimum. It will run up to two years before you will have to replace its tiny power plant.

Prospect: It's a nice-looking watch. How much is it?

Salesperson: $85.

Prospect:	Oh, that's too much. What do you have that is less expensive?
Salesperson:	(Returns Supreme 400 to the counter and picks up another watch.) Here we have the Acme Ambassador. The gold-filled sells for $75, the stainless steel for $59.95. You can have your choice of a black dial or a white one. Personally, I prefer the white. Handsome styling, isn't it?
Prospect:	That's still pretty high.
Salesperson:	Then take a look at this Chronos. This is a new model that just came in. Seventeen jewels; self-winding; antimagnetic. It has an unbreakable mainspring, too. Comes in a 14-karat gold-filled case with a stainless steel back.
Prospect:	May I try it on?
Salesperson:	(Hands watch to prospect who puts it on, checks the fit of the band, and studies the watch.) How does it feel?
Prospect:	Awkward. It's round, whereas my old watch had more of a square case.
Salesperson:	(Picking up another watch.) Here's one with a square case. This is the Imperial Deluxe. Seventeen jewels. Note how thin this one is. Notice, too, that the dial is luminous. Retails for $65.
Prospect:	What's the difference between this Imperial and the Supreme 400 you showed me first?
Salesperson:	$20.
Prospect:	What about guarantees?
Salesperson:	All our watches are guaranteed for one year. Parts and work-manship are warranted against defects.
Prospect:	If I brought a watch back for service during that first year, would I have to pay anything?
Salesperson:	If you had abused the watch, yes. Of those you've looked at, which do you like best? I strongly recommend the Supreme 400. It's not just a teller of time, it's a piece of fine jewelry. (Displays her own watch.) Look, I've been wearing one for two years, and it's never given me any trouble.
Prospect:	Is Supreme a reliable manufacturer?
Salesperson:	We don't carry watches made by unreliable makers. You can take my word for that. Have you made your selection?
Prospect:	No. Let me look around and think it over. (Starts to leave.)
Salesperson:	Sure thing. Glad to see you any time.

Why did the salesperson fail to make a sale?

BASIC SELLING RESPONSIBILITIES

part V

Building Sound Customer Relationships

After studying this chapter you should be able to:

- Suggest guidelines for scheduling calls on established customers

- Understand how salespeople build repeat business and increase the volume bought by customers

- Argue that salespeople should try to secure customer support and influence customers' merchandising policies

- Answer questions about salespeople's meetings with customers

- Outline what salespeople can do when dealing with customers' complaints, cancellations, and returned goods

- Show a grasp of credit and collection problems

When a salesperson's selling activities are viewed over the long run, two stages become apparent. In the first stage, the salesperson deals with prospects —individuals who can advantageously use the product but do not buy it. This first stage ends when a prospect makes the first purchase and becomes a customer. The second stage concerns the salesperson's dealings with customers. Just as the salesperson drafted a program to make a customer out of a prospect, a program must be drafted for serving and selling to that customer.

THE IMPORTANCE OF BUILDING SOUND RELATIONSHIPS

The salesperson who works constantly to see that each customer derives the maximum benefit from purchases lays the foundation of a sound customer relationship. The salesperson should be guided by the customer's circumstances and make only sound purchasing recommendations. A sound relationship means that the customer respects the salesperson both personally and as a merchandise adviser.

The rewards of working systematically with customers in order to build sound buyer-seller relationships are many. Repeat sales which lead to increased sales volume represent perhaps the most obvious reward. Satisfied customers are also valuable sources of a number of kinds of information: case histories, solutions to common business problems, testimonials, suggestions of new uses for the salesperson's products, and names of new prospects. Finally, satisfied customers provide favorable word-of-mouth publicity.

There are many specific activities which can help salespeople build sound relationships with their customers. In this chapter we will consider the problems of scheduling calls on customers; building repeat business, increasing the volume of accounts; handling inactive accounts; securing customer support; profitably influencing customers' merchandising policies; aiding customers by holding informative meetings with them; dealing effectively with customer complaints, order cancellations, and merchandise returns; regaining lost customers; handling the problems of credit and collection; and building goodwill.

SCHEDULING CALLS ON ESTABLISHED CUSTOMERS

After the first purchase that makes a prospect a customer, the salesperson should schedule an early return visit to see that the new customer is satisfied with the purchase. On this visit, the salesperson should make sure that the order was filled correctly and that the customer is using the product properly. Instructions about use and maintenance may be repeated, and any questions that have come up since the initial sale should be answered. If anything has gone wrong with the purchase, the salesperson can use this early return visit to find out what happened and take appropriate action. The call can also be useful in continuing to sell the customer on the benefits which may be derived from the purchase. Finally, the visit may help prepare the ground for future purchases and may result in obtaining a testimonial for the product or some leads and preapproach information about new prospects.

After this early return call, the salesperson is faced with the problem of deciding how often to visit the new customer. Calling too frequently wastes selling time and money and may irritate the customer. Informed customers recognize that too many calls are being made, and this tends to make them question the salesperson's judgment and managerial ability. If the calls are scheduled too far apart, there may also be difficulties. The customer resents being given inadequate service and thus begins to wonder about how much dependence can be placed on the salesperson. Furthermore, infrequent calls are an invitation to competition to move in and steal the account.

Classifying Customers for Scheduling Purposes

No one interval between visits will fit all customers; some demand a short interval between calls, while others require fewer calls. Perhaps the most efficient solution to this problem is to classify customers according to their importance in terms of sales volume. Three or four classifications should be adequate for most selling situations, and the classifications below are typical:

1. Group A: Most important customers; called on once a month; entitled to attention of high executives when necessary.
2. Group B: Good, substantial customers; called on every other month; expect and should get considerable attention from salesperson.
3. Group C: Less profitable customers; many are small; many spend more with the salesperson's competitors; called on twice a year; some mail and telephone solicitation.
4. Group D: Least valuable customers; small, weak, and expensive to handle; no calls, handled entirely by mail and telephone.

Problems in Handling Small Accounts

What is sometimes called the "80-20 principle" operates in connection with the just-discussed classification of customers: 20 percent of the customers account for about 80 percent of the sales. For the salesperson, the problem is what to do about scheduling calls on the 80 percent of the customers who account for only about 20 percent of the sales volume.

Some small accounts will eventually grow into Group A accounts, and some, of course, will become even smaller and eventually disappear. No seller wants to cut off a small account just because it is small and perhaps is being handled at little profit under current conditions. The seller who does will have

HANDLING SMALL ACCOUNTS

Here are some specific suggestions for handling small accounts:

1. Service no account buying less than a certain amount. (While this may work toward eliminating unprofitable customers, it will drive some customers to competitors.)
2. Adopt a service fee for small orders. (Both establishing and collecting such a fee is difficult.)
3. Establish a system of quantity discounts.
4. Educate small customers about the costs of handling small accounts.
5. Raise the size of the average order through better selling.
6. Classify small customers into two groups, the promising and the unpromising, and give the former most of the time and attention available for small customers. This time will be determined by such factors as how many of these customers the salesperson has, how often they are in the market to buy, and how often they need merchandising assistance.

ILLUSTRATION 14-1. For the individual salesperson, the best policy is probably to work with small customers in an effort to develop them into large ones and to continue this practice until convinced that it is not possible to effect this growth.

an almost impossible task trying to recapture it later. But regardless of the potential growth of a small account, its profitability at the moment must be considered. No salesperson can continue indefinitely to call on a small customer whose patronage does not result in some profit. So, the salesperson must evaluate its present volume and future possibilities versus the present cost of handling the account. For the individual salesperson, the best policy is probably to work with small customers in an effort to develop them into large ones and to continue this practice until convinced that it is not possible to effect this growth. Illustration 14-1 offers some specific suggestions for handling small accounts.

Handling Group B and Group C Accounts

Group A accounts should not be serviced to the neglect of Group B and Group C accounts. Almost all Group A accounts were at an earlier time Group C, then Group B accounts. The salesperson who wins out over competition at the B or C level will be better able to maintain this position when the buyer becomes an A account.

In servicing Group B and Group C accounts, the salesperson must do everything possible to insure ease of buying for the ultimate consumer. The salesperson tries to persuade the B or C customer to do those things that will enable the merchandise virtually to sell itself. Thus, the salesperson tries to see that the merchant has a balanced stock and that products are displayed so as to invite consumers to examine them.

Specific selling techniques that have proved effective elsewhere are passed on to the merchant and the sales force. Periodic reference to customer records will show how well the salesperson is succeeding with any customer and guide the salesperson in allocating time to that customer in the future.

BUILDING REPEAT BUSINESS

Frequently a salesperson spends much time and money in calling on a particular prospect before obtaining an order. Just as frequently, the first order is not large enough to equal the expenses incurred up to that time; in some cases, three, four or even more orders will be required to equal the development cost of the account. A customer who switches to a competitor must be replaced at the further expenditure of the salesperson's time and money. Thus, a salesperson must not let accounts slip away. Except for the relatively few salespeople who sell products that are purchased infrequently (houses, for example), the salesperson looks to repeat orders for the bulk of sales volume.

Because satisfied customers are hard to take away from their present source of supply and personal standing with customers is so important, the salesperson should be careful in handling all transactions and contacts with customers. The salesperson should win and keep their complete confidence concerning honesty, judgment, and discretion. The salesperson should not ask favors of customers except in emergencies.

The salesperson must be alert for any signal that might indicate a deterioration in the buyer-seller relationship. Such a signal may be financial: a customer's sales may drop or some change may be made in financial policy. A second signal is of a personal nature: the customer may be increasingly influenced by someone hostile to the salesperson, may pay less attention to business matters, or may allow associates to handle more business responsibilities than they formerly did. Finally, outside events may change good customers into poor ones: legislation, product obsolescence, and physical changes such as the rerouting of traffic flow are examples. Any one of these signals demands the salesperson's examination because they could affect the amount of repeat business obtained from any one customer.

As part of an annual analysis of their own performance, salespeople should study each account acquired during the previous year and make definite plans for holding it. Each account retained and each account lost during the period should also be examined in detail. In determining the cause of the loss, it may be found that the merchandise did not sell well in a certain area, that the dealer failed to handle the line properly, that the dealer's margin was inadequate, that the salesperson's company gave poor service, or that the salesperson was somehow at fault. Once the cause has been identified, an appropriate program to regain desirable accounts should be started.

INCREASING THE VOLUME OF ACCOUNTS

It is not enough for the salesperson to acquire and then hold an account; it must be built up to its full potential in sales volume. The aim is to develop the account until the customer is buying and selling or using as much of the salesperson's product as can be expected. Among the more important reasons for increasing the volume of an account are:

1. Additional volume means additional income for the salesperson's company.
2. Less time is required to build up the volume of established customers than to obtain the same dollar amount by converting prospects to customers.
3. The customer who ought to be buying the salesperson's complete line but buys only part of it is not completely supplied. This customer should appreciate suggestions regarding how better to provide for requirements.

Obstacles to Increasing the Volume of an Account

Certain obstacles make increasing accounts a challenging job. A quite serious obstacle is the reluctance or even refusal of a buyer to change buying habits. Some buyers divide their purchases among vendors to keep a close check on the prices of various vendors. Others do this in an attempt to insure a source of supply in case something should happen to any one supplier. Reciprocity influences still others. There can be powerful pressures on buyers not to switch their patronage from current sources of supply, because other salespeople are working just as fiercely.

Sometimes, for one of the reasons just mentioned or because of some other influence, the salesperson is never able to secure as great a share of a customer's total business as desired. This still does not excuse the salesperson from estimating a realistic share in each case and then making appropriate plans to obtain it.

Suggestions for Increasing the Account

It is a mistake to be either too conservative or too aggressive in trying to increase the customer's volume of purchases. Overly conservative salespeople give competitors an opportunity to pursue and obtain orders that they could have had. Overly aggressive salespeople, in their haste to effect changes and realignments, can close doors in their own faces permanently. Too often salespeople are determined to write up a large order without proper consideration of the customer's needs. The best strategy is to follow a moderate course by holding onto current business while gradually taking over other items and other lines.

The following methods may prove helpful in increasing the dollar volume of a customer's purchases. All of the methods mentioned will not be appropriate in every situation, but each will be effective for certain customers on certain occasions.

A Systematic Development Program. Be systematic about the development program. A carefully thought out master plan is needed to increase sales volume. This broad program should consist of definite plans for building up the business of each individual customer.

Identifying Merchandise for Balanced Stock. Identify merchandise that the customer does not carry but should carry for a good balance of stock. Then talk about the popularity of your line in that area, how rapid its turnover is, and the size of the potential market.

Replenishing Stock. Keep alert for signs that the customer needs to replenish the stock of an item which is now bought from someone else. A customer who is in danger of running out of that particular product, with the resulting cost or loss, is most apt to listen to your warning and to act on it by letting you rush an order through so that the stock will not become exhausted.

Special Concessions. Whenever there is a special concession that can be made, use it to enlarge the customer's order by pointing out the lower price per item and the greater discount resulting from a larger order.

Relating New Items to Current Stock. When a new item is placed in your line, relate it to what the customer is currently buying. Show the new product and what it will do for the customer.

Stressing the Desirability of Handling a Single Line. If the customer is a split dealer, handling competing brands or buying from competing vendors, stress the desirability of handling a single line. Then point out ways in which your line is superior and why it deserves to be chosen as the line for concentration.

Cementing the Buyer-Seller Relationship. Do something on each call that will better cement the buyer-seller relationship. While the nature of this action may be suggested by referring to the customer's record, probably the most important type of favor is the imparting of some valuable merchandising information.

INACTIVE ACCOUNTS

The kind of inactive account about which the salesperson can do little or nothing is the former customer who ceases to be a prospect; for example, the industrial firm which begins to manufacture all it requires of some part it used to buy from the salesperson. But customers are lost who still buy, but from a competitor. A customer may become inactive (lost for the short run) for various reasons, such as misunderstanding, sellers' mistakes (especially in order filling, delivery, and billing), weak selling, a specific product complaint, and lower prices offered by competitors.

To prevent inactive accounts, the salesperson should achieve effective communication, watch each customer's order size, and stay sensitive to any hint of customer dissatisfaction. When trouble develops, the salesperson should determine the facts promptly, usually in person. It is important to correct misunderstandings and remove causes of friction. The salesperson should be as generous as possible. Point-by-point comparisons against competition may be helpful. In addition, the salesperson may look for some unique benefit to offer.

SECURING CUSTOMER SUPPORT

Up to this point we have been discussing aid and assistance in one direction —from seller to buyer. Now it is time to examine and evaluate the customer as a possible source of help to the salesperson.

The phrase "customer support" is used to describe the most desirable and sought-after service the buyer can render the seller. At the start, the individual is a prospect and nothing more. The prospect places the first order and becomes a customer. Only one further step remains in the process of development, and that step is taken when the customer becomes an enthusiastic and loyal supporter.

In this relationship, the customer is actively and enthusiastically in favor of the salesperson, company, products, and service. The retailer customer sees that the salesperson's line of merchandise is always stocked in adequate volume, is favored in the display treatment given it, and is pushed by personal selling as much as practicable. In one sense, the customer actually sells for the salesperson. Most important of all, the customer looks on the salesperson almost as a partner. The customer asks the salesperson's opinions on a variety of matters, some broader than just the salesperson's line, and often relies on the salesperson's judgment. Because the salesperson is regarded as an expert, the customer relies on his or her advice.

How to Obtain Customer Support

There are several possibilities for obtaining support from customers. Develop an agreeable, pleasant personality, and then use it. You want to be on a friendly basis with the customer and with the customer's employees. A friendly relationship, not undue familiarity, is the goal.

Frequent contact, even if only a reminder postal card, is desirable. Make each visit an occasion by always having a good, new reason for calling, such as a new product, model, sample, plan, or bit of information. Don't ever give the customer the impression that you "just happened by," or "just dropped in to see how things are going." By indicating that a special call is being made, you flatter the customer and encourage cooperation.

Be more than just a salesperson. Never stop accumulating knowledge, particularly about your products and the art of selling. Be posted on your field not only locally, but also nationally and internationally. Be able to interpret and justify your company's decisions and policies. Your grasp of general business conditions, causes, and trends must expand continuously. To the maximum extent, be a dependable source of current information about such matters as collections, advertising, and legislation.

Serve the customer's best interests by providing wise guidance and helpful service. The customer should never have to ask about something new or wait for something due. No customer should ever be given cause or opportunity for losing enthusiasm. Don't allow anything to happen which would encourage questioning of any buying decision.

Do as many favors for the customer as possible. Any help, sound advice, valuable information, or personal assistance obligates the customer just that much more and by implication asks for reciprocation by increased patronage and support. Whenever practicable, locate customers and prospects for your customers.

Show the customer the benefits of giving you support and loyalty. It may be that some policy of your company helped the customer to weather a price war, to maintain a certain margin, or to cash in on a special event. Or you may show actual figures that prove how other customers have increased sales in the

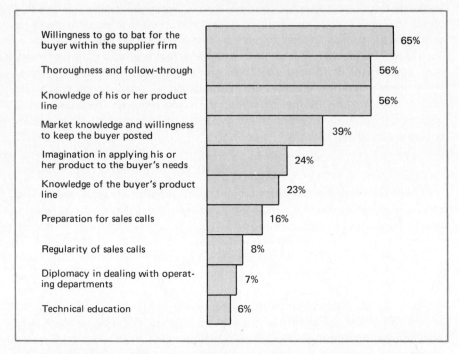

QUALITIES THAT MAKE SALESPEOPLE TOPS

Willingness to go to bat for the buyer within the supplier firm	65%
Thoroughness and follow-through	56%
Knowledge of his or her product line	56%
Market knowledge and willingness to keep the buyer posted	39%
Imagination in applying his or her product to the buyer's needs	24%
Knowledge of the buyer's product line	23%
Preparation for sales calls	16%
Regularity of sales calls	8%
Diplomacy in dealing with operating departments	7%
Technical education	6%

Note: Percentages for each year total 300 because respondents were asked to check three outstanding characteristics.

Source: *Sales and Marketing Managment* (August 20, 1979), p. 38.

ILLUSTRATION 14-2. Readers of *Purchasing* magazine, mainly industrial buyers and purchasing managers, were asked to choose the three traits that make top salespeople. Their answers for 1979 are summarized above.

past by tying their efforts in with those of your company. Finally, always point out how the customer will gain by cooperating in the future.

How Customers Help Salespeople

We mention here six types of assistance that customers can give salespeople. The first is case histories—experiences customers have had which are of interest or value, but which did not involve any particular problem. One merchant put Brand X tires on his delivery trucks, got exceptionally good mileage out of them, and was delighted. Or an individual provided for her child's education through insurance. Or a retailer installed a certain system of lighting with gratifying results.

Second, solutions to common problems may be passed along. A retailer revised business hours, a wholesaler installed a new system of stock control, and each change was an improvement.

Testimonials are a third type of assistance. The customer may describe the benefits of air conditioning. The salesperson may write a conservative, appropriate statement for use over the customer's signature on the customer's letterhead. A slightly different kind of testimonial, one that salespeople can construct without having to obtain anyone's permission, is a list of their customers.

Fourth, a list of references may consist of customers. Prospects sometimes like to talk to individuals who have bought and used the item under consideration, feeling that this source may be more unbiased and impartial than the salesperson. Many customers enjoy having their names given as references.

Fifth, new uses for the product may be furnished or pointed out by customers.

Finally, customers may supply the names of new prospects for the salesperson to investigate and cultivate. In some instances, background information may supplement a name and address. Or a letter of introduction may be volunteered by the customer in special cases. Once in a while, the customer will even make an appointment for the salesperson with the prospect.

INFLUENCING CUSTOMERS' MERCHANDISING POLICIES

In this section, the word "merchandising" means advertising, display, and personal selling. Good salespeople are able to help shape and guide the merchandising activities of their retail customers and, by doing so, ultimately help determine retail merchandising policy.

It must be emphasized at this point that the job of influencing a customer's policies requires skill and tact. In an overall way, the object of such influence is to maximize dollar profits for customer and salesperson. In more detail, the salesperson wants the customer to handle the full line and to maintain adequate stock at all times. This permits balanced sales, including sales of higher-priced, high-profit items. The salesperson would like every customer's place of business to be a model of enthusiasm and efficiency. In this atmosphere the salesperson's merchandise would be the most preferred, favored, and pushed—to the extent that a retailer can afford to push a single line.

Customer buying patterns may be influenced. A starting point is a study and analysis of a customer's orders. Once a pattern has been identified, it can be compared with that of the most outstanding customer in order to locate weak spots. Advertising policies can be influenced, too. One approach is for the salesperson to persuade the customer to plan and schedule merchandising activities to tie in with the complete promotion program of the salesperson's company. Along this line, the salesperson should convince the customer of the desirability of using all available company promotional material that is suitable.

The salesperson may get the retailer to encourage suggestion selling and trading up, increasing the amount of the average sale and the average selling price per item. The salesperson tries to get the customer to do an effective advertising job, both for the customer's entire business and for the salesperson's own merchandise. Salespeople should never be too important or too busy to lend a hand in setting up displays, dressing windows, or doing other merchandising jobs. Finally, the salesperson needs to make constructive suggestions that will help insure profitable operation.

Influencing Advertising Activities

Before attempting to influence a retailer's advertising policies, salespeople should clearly understand (1) the general nature of advertising, (2) the more specific nature of their companies' advertising, and (3) their customers' advertising problems.

In regard to the first point, salespeople need an appreciation of the role advertising plays in the distribution process and an awareness of its potential achievements and its limitations. Sometimes they will have to defend advertising as a selling tool, especially as it is used by their companies, and explain to nonadvertising customers how they may be handicapping their business operations by not advertising. An effective strategy to use in convincing the nonadvertising customer to use advertising is to show the total potential demand which could be reached within the trading area by advertising.

As far as their companies' advertising efforts are concerned, salespeople must first know what company policy is and how to justify it to customers. Smaller customers may criticize a company that advertises extensively, claiming that those dollars should instead be spent in giving greater discounts to dealers. Salespeople who have a sound understanding of their companies' advertising policies should have little trouble in satisfactorily answering these objections. They should also have complete information about their companies' current and future advertising efforts: what campaigns are running, which media are being used, how large the advertising budget is, what the results of a particular campaign were, and what new campaigns are scheduled. They should know what their companies will do for customers in the way of advertising. If the company identifies its dealers in certain of its advertisements, if advertising materials are supplied to them, if a cooperative arrangement operates between company and customer, if direct mail pieces with or without the dealer's imprint can be obtained, these facts will all be of interest to customers.

The third part of influencing a customer's advertising activities concerns the customer's advertising problems. The usual sequence in planning advertising goes like this:

1. Setting up an advertising budget and advertising objectives
2. Identifying prospects and trading area boundaries
3. Media selection

4. Selection of messages
5. Informing personnel of advertising plans
6. Execution of the plan
7. Evaluation of the advertising effort

On each of these phases, the salesperson must be willing and competent to advise the customer. Then and only then is the salesperson in a position to encourage the customer to use advertising in adequate volume. The plea will be for a well-balanced, continuous program. Until the retailer realizes that advertising is not a luxury to be denied when volume drops, that it must not be scheduled according to whims or to the persuasiveness of advertising salespeople, and that it must be undertaken with full knowledge that its effectiveness is reduced when turned on and off like an electric light, the retailer is not ready to advertise.

Influencing Display Activities

Salespeople have two definite obligations in promoting the use of display. One is to keep the retailer completely informed about what is available from their company and on what terms, what display materials the retailer should use, and how these materials should be used to get the best sales results. The second obligation is to know at all times what their retailers are actually doing about general display and the display of their products.

With the growth of self-service merchandising, retail merchants necessarily must use display as effectively as possible. The importance that manufacturers attach to good display is indicated by their competition for prominent positions for their respective brands, positions that will increase sales and profits. Many prefer favorable store position to mention of their products in local newspaper, radio, or television advertisements.

Salespeople should check continuously to see that their retailers are using display as an extra sales force—first, in a storewide way, and second, for the salesperson's line of products. This frequently means that the salesperson must first sell the retailer on the general idea of planned display, then on the use of particular material, and then on placing it in a preferred spot. The salesperson may point out how attractive the display is, how well it was rated when tested, and how it will increase sales and stock turnover. These points may be especially useful if the retailer is asked to defray part of the cost of the display piece or asked to buy a minimum amount of goods in order to obtain the display item.

Influencing Personal Selling Activities

Manufacturers are quite concerned about the quality of selling that ultimate consumers encounter in retail stores. Manufacturers must depend on retail salespeople to handle their interests at this final stage of the distribution process. In this sense, retail salespeople are representatives of manufacturers and are so regarded by at least some of the buying public. If it were practical, manufacturers would have their own employees present to handle each purchase of their products by ultimate consumers; but since this is obviously impossible, they try to obtain the kind of representation from retailers' employees that most nearly approximates the ideal.

There is a second, broader phase of the manufacturer's interest in retail selling. Manufacturers want their retailers to be profitable so that they qualify as excellent outlets for their merchandise. The progressive, prosperous merchant is the one who will probably sell a better-than-average amount of the manufacturer's merchandise. Thus, the manufacturer's first step is to influence the merchant to raise the quality of selling in a general way so that the store becomes a better store. The second move is to help get more sales power for the manufacturer's own lines from the retailer's sales force.

Salespeople must be extremely tactful in trying to upgrade retail selling. An effective method of bringing to the minds of retailers the significance of their employees' selling activities is to ask about the training program in operation, thereby calling their attention to the subject and setting the stage for further discussion of it. A second method is to note what happens when a retail salesperson meets a retail prospect in an actual sales situation and then to use these observations to open the conversation. Salespeople may also show retailers or their salespeople how the product should be demonstrated. Still another possibility is to pass on to retailers ideas about selling techniques that have proved effective in other stores. If the salesperson's company provides training materials, the task is to see that they are used in retail stores.

HOLDING MEETINGS WITH CUSTOMERS

Some salespeople will never have occasion to hold a meeting in connection with their selling activities because of the nature of their sales transactions, as, for example, those selling automobiles, insurance, or home insulation. Other salespeople will conduct meetings, but before doing so, will be trained specifically and thoroughly for that job, and will then be supplied by their companies with everything they need. This section on holding meetings is included not particularly for the benefit of these two groups of salespeople, but instead to help the salespeople who, when they begin selling, need to work with customers by scheduling and conducting meetings without much assistance from any source.

Purposes of Meetings

Holding meetings with customers can be an extremely worthwhile undertaking, but this project demands time, patience, and thorough planning from the salesperson. The overall purpose of any meeting is to increase profits for the salesperson and the company by increasing the customer's volume of sales and profits on the salesperson's products. The purpose of any single meeting, however, is much more specific. Here are some topics the salesperson might choose to discuss in a meeting:

1. Customer matters: how to get new customers, how to hold customers, how wholesalers build up retail accounts, what to do about small orders, or how to revive dormant accounts.
2. Product matters: how merchandise should be demonstrated, the manufacturer's support and promotion plans, how to launch a new product, or a study of the advantages of the salesperson's product.
3. Selling matters: how to prove product claims, how to handle objections, how to obtain the five buying decisions, or how to close the sale.

In most cases, the salesperson's audience will be composed of either a wholesaler and staff, a retailer and staff, a group of wholesalers, or a group of retailers. When the meeting is with a wholesaler or retailer and staff, the staff may be limited to sales employees. Meetings should obviously be scheduled when and where they will do the most good. The better accounts—those which do the most outstanding selling jobs—are the ones entitled to benefit from the time and money spent on meetings.

Principles of Conducting Meetings

Here are some principles concerning the holding of meetings which have proved to be effective:

1. Have a definite reason for the meeting and publicize the reason beforehand. Describing in advance how the meeting will be of value to customers helps sell all prospective attendants on being present.
2. Schedule only one topic for each meeting. This will assure shorter meetings, more complete treatment of a certain subject, and increased understanding on the part of customers.
3. Have a definite timetable for the meeting. Start it on time, run it according to schedule, and do not allow the tempo of the meeting to drag.
4. Stay in control of the meeting, but make provisions for group discussion.
5. Make it as easy as possible for the audience to understand and retain the message by distributing printed material—such as an outline of the meeting and summary of the major points to be made—and by making maximum use of audiovisual aids and props.

Preparing for the Meeting

Thorough preparation is always needed for the scheduled meeting. Meeting groups quickly recognize whether or not time and thought have been spent by the salesperson in getting ready for the gathering. A definite written schedule of a complete program should be made in advance. It should name a specified day, place, and hour so as to maximize the chances of success. The written schedule will outline what matters are to be treated, how much time will be devoted to each phase, and the method of treatment, including the props to be used.

Particular preparation is needed for meetings where group participation will require some flexibility in handling and fitting the meeting to the time schedule. If a schedule is not established and agreed to prior to the meeting, the salesperson will frequently experience postponements, absence of key individuals who were to take part in the program, lack of coordination, and even failure. The junior salesperson may be more relaxed with prepared opening remarks, questions for discussion, and closing thoughts. While in the presence of the audience, the salesperson should do no more reading from notes than is absolutely necessary.

If it appears that a considerable amount of time will be required, several short sessions should be scheduled rather than a few long ones. To maintain a high degree of interest throughout a long meeting is difficult.

Before the meeting, a collection should be made of case histories, experiences, and other happenings from the locality where the meeting is to be. For instance, a new sales technique that was originated nearby, or the experience of some local merchant who successfully tied promotion efforts in with those of the manufacturer, gets and holds the interest of the group. Facts, figures, impartiality, and tact are needed in using such information.

DEALING WITH CUSTOMER COMPLAINTS

All salespeople can expect some complaints from dissatisfied customers, and the effective handling of complaints can do much to build sound customer relationships. Some companies have a separate division to handle all complaints; they adopt such a procedure because they feel that harmonious salesperson-customer relationships are too valuable to be exposed to the risks encountered when the salesperson is the first person to handle a complaint. For example, it is awkward for a salesperson to have to turn down a customer's request for an adjustment when company policy clearly dictates such a refusal, and then try to sell later to that same customer. In many companies, however, the salesperson is required to handle complaints because this is the individual who comes in contact with the customer most frequently, knows the most about the customer and the buying circumstances in question, and is the person to whom the customer looks for satisfaction.

The salesperson must, of course, prevent complaints to the maximum extent possible, and must handle those that are voiced as skillfully as possible. The first step in prevention calls for sufficient knowledge about the product and the customer's needs so that the salesperson can guide the customer in buying, recommending only appropriate items and even refusing to sell if only disappointment and dissatisfaction can result. A second step is to make certain that customer and salesperson think alike about the product to be purchased and what it will do, the two of them being in agreement as to just what the other expects and believes. Third, the salesperson should describe, in whatever detail is needed, the policies and procedures of the company. The customer should know in advance how inquiries are handled, how mail orders are treated, the specific procedure for dealing with complaints, and what the company's position is on such matters as claims, allowances, damaged merchandise, credit terms, and returned goods. Finally, much will be done toward holding complaints down to a minimum if the salesperson carefully keeps all promises. The salesperson who promises to pick up merchandise that does not sell should pick it up with no hesitation. If delivery is promised by Wednesday, the goods should be there by Wednesday.

If a complaint cannot be prevented, then it must be handled by someone, and a delicate treatment is usually necessary. For example, the salesperson will be trying to hold the customer's patronage even if the complaint is perfectly justified, and will try to keep both goodwill and business if the requested adjustment is refused.

At the very start, the customer must be made to know that the salesperson is determined to be completely fair and to give every courtesy and consideration. There must be no indication of doubt or suspicion in the salesperson's mind. At the same time, the salesperson must reaffirm the customer's faith in the company, thus encouraging the customer to accept the company as one that does the right thing by its customers. When the salesperson or the company is at fault, admission of that fact should be made at once, followed by a promise of prompt and satisfactory adjustment.

Another helpful measure is to act as a sympathetic audience while the customer lets off steam and demands satisfaction. All the while, the salesperson is collecting information, saying nothing until all the facts are in.

Still another principle is that the salesperson should handle the complaint immediately, if possible. Correspondence, offering the customer a chance to get angry all over again, is avoided. Furthermore, the salesperson makes a favorable bid for increased confidence by taking hold and handling it. Referring the matter to some company official tends to magnify its significance.

If the salesperson is unwilling or unable to handle the complaint, the reasons should be explained clearly to the customer. The salesperson should review company policy with the customer and outline company procedure for handling complaints, assuring the customer of prompt and proper attention, and following it up so as to know at all times where the matter rests.

In some instances, complaints can work in the salesperson's favor. The technique calls for representing the salesperson and the company as being fair and reliable, convincing the customers that they have received and will always get honest treatment and a square deal. A particularly fine opportunity to increase goodwill presents itself when the adjustment made is more liberal than the customers expect or would have made to one of their own customers.

DEALING WITH CANCELLATIONS AND RETURNED GOODS

Closely related to the problem of customer complaints are the problems of cancellations and returned goods. The handling of these two problems increases a seller's expenses. Their presence means that the original selling job was a failure and that the same merchandise must be sold a second time, sometimes at a lower price. If the seller was at fault, loss of reputation results.

Buyers cancel orders and return merchandise for several reasons. A salesperson may have sold the wrong quantity or the wrong quality. The buyer may have been oversold on the privileges of cancelling orders and returning unsatisfactory goods. Sometimes an order is filled incorrectly, or the merchandise is defective or damaged when it arrives. Sometimes the shipment does not arrive by the promised date. Prices may drop, or a competitor may make a more attractive offer. The buyer's need may disappear. Sometimes the person who placed the order is overruled by someone else, and the purchasing decision is cancelled.

Salespeople obviously must not contribute to these causes of cancellations and returns. They must always try to raise the quality of their selling efforts, work especially hard to identify need accurately, and then sell the buyer completely on the product to fill that need. They must be careful to recommend exactly the quality and quantity the buyer should order, and they must stay away from unrealistic promises. Usually the salesperson should go over the order and terms with the buyer so that the buyer understands them clearly, particularly in regard to the conditions under which orders can be cancelled and goods returned. If two or more people have a voice in the final buying decision, the salesperson should usually talk to them as a group and sell all of them on the soundness of the sales proposal. The same thing is true if there is a strong buying influence in addition to the buyer.

REGAINING LOST CUSTOMERS

Customers who used to buy, but who do not buy at the present time, may well be good prospects. Of course, if their needs or conditions have changed so as to make a product no longer of use to them, they are not prospects. When customers discontinue buying because of dissatisfaction or because a more persuasive competitor took them away, it may well be worthwhile to try to get them back as customers. Each case should be examined to see why, how, when, and to whom the account was lost. The answers to these four questions will point out the techniques that should be used in attempting to regain the account. Usually, many of the techniques of handling complaints are equally appropriate and effective here.

HANDLING CREDIT AND COLLECTION PROBLEMS

Companies differ in their methods of dealing with credit and collection activities, some making extensive use and others making little use of their salespeople. Salespeople should be informed about credit management, regardless of the extent to which they are involved in their firm's credit and collection activities.

Credit Information Needed

For the following treatment of credit and collection, let us assume that the buyer is a retailer and that the purchase involves merchandise for resale. Before a seller opens a credit account for a retailer, these questions must be asked:

1. Can that retailer pay for the merchandise?
2. Will that retailer pay for the merchandise?
3. What maximum credit limit should be given?

These questions must be answered for each retail account because retailers vary in their ability to pay, in their determination to pay, and in the limit they should be allowed to owe the seller at any one time. Before these questions can be answered, the seller must have facts.

The seller needs information about the retailer's capital circumstances—financial situation and strength. The seller needs a picture of the retailer's assets, liabilities, and net worth. No retailer is solvent unless assets are greater than liabilities; no retailer is liquid unless there are dollars today to pay tomorrow's bills.

The seller needs information about the retail firm's capacity, its ability to sell a satisfactory amount of merchandise at satisfactory prices. The sales and earnings records of the store can suggest what future sales and earnings may be. Respectable capacity reflects sound, able management.

The personal character of the retailer can be an important credit factor. Sellers prefer to deal with merchants who are honest and trustworthy. They hope their credit customers have a fierce determination to pay their debts because they think it is right to pay what they promised to pay. The greater a buyer's sense of obligation and integrity, the less moral risk is involved.

These three credit influences—capital, capacity, and character—must be considered in the light of current circumstances. For example, competitors' policies and practices of the moment affect a seller's policies and practices. The present stage of the business cycle, too, must be known and respected. In bad times, one can defend certain actions which would be difficult to defend in good times. A third consideration is the safety-risk standard the seller is observing for credit sales. Here the seller determines the minimum safety standard—the maximum acceptable risk limit. A fourth and final matter is current policy on collection. The stricter the seller is in collecting what is owed, the lower the safety-risk standard can be set.

Sources of Credit Information

The retail firm itself is a prime source of information about its own credit rating. The National Association of Credit Management has designed a financial statement form that sellers can ask retailers to fill out. This form supplies a vast amount of credit information, and features the balance sheet and the income statement.

Many manufacturers ask their salespeople to collect certain credit information on prospective retail customers and on present customers. By nature, of course, the typical salesperson is not a credit reporter. However, salespeople have a vital and continuing interest in retailers' credit and in their firm's credit management. In the process of collecting credit information, the salesperson gets to visit with the retailer, know the manager personally, see the store in operation, and sense how business is going.

A seller's own records contain valuable credit information about present customers and former customers. This information is contained in the file set up every time a new account is opened. Prominent in this file is the customer's ledger record.

Then, of course, there is Dun & Bradstreet, Inc., the organization which reports on the credit standing of retailers. Twice a year the agency issues credit reference books, state by state, in pocket size. Credit managers and salespeople make much use of these handy and informative reference books.

As for miscellaneous sources of credit information, there are banks, attorneys, public records, references supplied by retailers, and other (usually noncompetitive) sellers.

Three Credit Management Suggestions

Credit information has both quality and quantity. *Quality* asks how good the information should be; it asks if the information is accurate, current, and basically relevant. *Quantity* asks how much information one should collect. Collecting a large amount of information can demand much time and money and can cause retailer resentment. Collecting less information is more speedy and economical but more risky.

A second suggestion is that credit management be seen as having two major objectives. One is to maximize sales; the other is to minimize credit expenses. Credit expenses include clerical costs, interest on capital invested in accounts receivable, collection costs, and bad debts. If credit management is too lax, the seller maximizes sales volume, but reduces the percentage of accounts receivable collected. If credit management is too strict, sales volume and earnings suffer.

Finally, the seller must recognize that credit and credit management demand continuous attention and analysis. The management of a retail store can change. Market potentials sometimes increase, sometimes decrease. The business cycle is often going up—or down. Any one retailer can improve or slip as a credit risk as time passes. So, each credit customer's credit rating must be checked regularly and credit limit revised if needed. Sellers should try to anticipate changes in a customer's credit condition before they take place.

Collection

Because a period of time passes between the date of a credit sale and the scheduled date of payment, some credit customers will not pay all they owe when they owe it. Credit sales become actual sales only when the buyer pays for the merchandise bought. Unless the seller gets the money due, merchandise is not being sold—it is being given away.

When does the collection period start? The moment the credit period runs out. If a retailer agreed to pay on or before May 10 but does not, the collection period starts May 11 because the account becomes past due on May 11.

Why Credit Customers Don't Pay

Time explains why cash selling poses no collection problems, whereas credit selling does. Time means changes, uncertainties, faulty predictions, risks, mistakes, and disappointments. Here are seven situations.

1. The retailer does not understand the seller's credit terms. The best way to prevent this is to see that all details are clear to the buyer at the time of the first sale.
2. Because the balance owed is small, the retailer prefers to postpone payment until it is larger. This is a tough one for which there is no magic answer. Vigorous collection attempts would be costly and would irritate the customer. Maybe this is one that the seller simply has to learn to live with.
3. The retailer is slow in paying because of habit. Seldom does this retailer pay any supplier before receiving one or more collection notices. This situation calls for considerable and firm collection effort. The seller may be wise to check the expense of selling to this account against the gross margin made. This type of retailer can easily be unprofitable as well as unpleasant.
4. Some customers are merely careless. When customers overlook or forget, they should be reminded that their accounts are overdue.
5. Every now and then buyers run short of cash for the moment. Maybe they overbought, their accounts receivable paid below expectations, or they suffered some accident. The first move in this type of situation is

to verify the tight condition. The next step is to adjust the debt and to extend the pay period, if at all justifiable.

6. What about the store that is experiencing rough going? Maybe the management has deteriorated. Maybe the market has shrunk. Maybe the retailer is experiencing trouble because of other causes. The basic question here is whether or not the retailer can become profitable in a reasonable period of time.

7. If retail customers turn out to be dishonest, turn them over to a lawyer or a collection agency.

BUILDING GOODWILL

Salespeople need and want the goodwill of their customers. Salespeople enjoy the goodwill of their customers when they have their customers' faith and confidence and when their competence and integrity as advisers are respected. Salespeople enjoy goodwill when their customers like them, think well of them, and broadcast these complimentary opinions.

It is clear why salespeople work so hard for the goodwill of their customers. The first sale is often made only after goodwill has been won. Repeat sales will not be forthcoming unless the customer feels goodwill toward the salesperson. A customer's account cannot be increased to its maximum potential without goodwill. Then, finally, the customer's continuing support, loyalty, and cooperation will not be so great as they might have been unless there is goodwill.

To get goodwill, nothing is so essential as a program of helping customers. Helping them in business ways will increase the customer's sales, reduce the customer's expenses, or both. Helping them in personal ways results in the customer's securing more personal satisfaction.

Goodwill is invited when salespeople let themselves be guided by their customers' interests and goals. The salesperson learns the customer's circumstances and takes a position in sympathy with them. The salesperson makes sound recommendations and then takes pains to see that the customers understand fully what the results will be if they buy and if they do not buy.

Salespeople invite goodwill by their ethical conduct. They keep promises; they are fair and honest, they demonstrate the fact that the Golden Rule is good business as well as good behavior.

Finally, salespeople invite goodwill by liking each of their customers personally. They learn to do this by knowing and understanding customers and by being a real friend to them. Salespeople show this liking in many ways. They appreciate any favors done by a customer and are prompt to repay in generous measure. They ask their customers for advice, opinions, and suggestions. They take the time and effort to adopt the customer's mood of the moment, respecting the customer's right to feel differently on different calls. They supply the customer with related information, keeping the customer well posted on the latest happenings in various fields. They may entertain certain customers on special occasions. At Christmas, birthdays, and anniversary times, salespeople will certainly remember customers in appropriate ways. They will congratulate the customer on the birth of a baby, and will mail a get-well card when the customer is ill. All this takes time, but it is well worth the effort.

SUMMARY

Salespeople's selling activities are divided into two stages: (1) dealing with prospects and (2) dealing with customers. Salespeople who work constantly to see that each customer derives the maximum benefit from purchases lay solid foundations for sound customer relationships. Repeat sales, important and useful information, and favorable word-of-mouth publicity are some of the rewards of good customer relationships.

Soon after a first purchase, the salesperson should visit the customer and make sure that everything has gone well with the product. Further return calls should be scheduled appropriately. No one interval between visits will fit all customers, so a classification system is helpful.

Usually 20 percent of the customers account for about 80 percent of a salesperson's sales. Problems arise when scheduling the 80 percent of the customers who account for only 20 percent of the sales. The best policy is probably to work with small customers in an effort to develop them into large ones and to continue this practice until convinced that it is not possible to effect this growth.

Repeat business is usually the most profitable, so repeat business must be built up. The salesperson should be alert for signals that may indicate a deterioration in the buyer-seller relationship.

After an account has been acquired, efforts should be made to increase its volume. Buyer reluctance to change habits is an obstacle to increasing volume. Methods used to increase volume include persuading the customer to designate the salesperson's company as the regular source of supply and doing something on each call that will better cement the buyer-seller relationship.

Inactive accounts may be caused by misunderstandings, sellers' mistakes, weak selling, specific product complaints, and lower prices elsewhere.

Customers can be helpful to salespeople. In one sense, the customer may actually sell for the salesperson.

Customer support can be obtained in many ways, including the following: frequent contact, making each visit an occasion, and doing as many favors for the customer as possible. Case histories, solutions to common problems, testimonials, new product uses, and suggested prospects are types of assistance customers can give to salespeople.

Good salespeople are able to influence the merchandising activities of their retail customers. This requires skill and tact. Customer buying patterns may be influenced. Advertising policies can be influenced also. Salespeople must understand advertising in general, the specific nature of their firm's advertising, and their customers' advertising problems before offering suggestions. Salespeople can help with advertising objectives, media selection, and other phases of advertising.

Salespeople have two definite obligations in promoting the use of displays. One is to keep the retailer informed about what is available from their company. The second obligation is to keep abreast of what the customer is doing about displays.

Manufacturers are interested in the performance of their retailers' sales forces. Training programs and product demonstrations are two areas that can be helpful to salespeople.

Holding meetings with customers can be productive. Customer matters, product matters, and selling matters are three areas usually discussed. Principles of conducting meetings include:

1. Have a definite reason for conducting the meeting.
2. Keep meetings short and limited to one topic.
3. Have a definite timetable.
4. Stay in control of the meeting.
5. Make audience understanding easy.

Thorough preparation for every meeting is necessary. A program must be developed and mastered, and a schedule has to be prepared and sent to everyone concerned. Case histories and other facts must be assembled into a complete presentation.

All salespeople must expect to deal with complaints. The salesperson must try to limit complaints, and must handle skillfully those that are voiced. Fair treatment, a show of sympathy, and immediate handling are important principles for handling complaints. When handled well, complaints can sometimes work in the salesperson's favor.

Handling cancellations and returned goods is expensive and may result in a loss of reputation. Wrong order quantities, incorrect order filing, damaged goods, and late deliveries are some causes of returns. Salespeople must not contribute to these causes of cancellations and returns.

Customers who used to buy, but who do not buy at the present time, may well be good prospects. Depending on the circumstances of each case, it may be worthwhile to try to get them back as customers.

Companies differ in their handling of credit, and the use of salespeople in this area varies widely. Ability to pay, willingness to pay, and credit limits are three basic credit questions. The seller needs information that will help answer these questions before any credit is granted.

The proper quality and quantity of information should be generated. The objectives of credit management are to maximize sales and minimize credit costs. Credit records must be kept up to date to deal effectively with changing conditions.

The reasons customers don't pay include: (1) the customer doesn't understand the seller's credit terms, (2) the balance owed is small, (3) habit, (4) carelessness, (5) cash shortages, (6) the customer is experiencing rough going, and (7) dishonesty.

Salespeople need and want their customers' goodwill. With goodwill, sales come easier, and customers' accounts are more easily increased.

REVIEW QUESTIONS

1. What is the 80-20 principle?
2. How can salespeople economically handle small accounts?
3. Why is repeat business the most profitable?
4. List three obstacles to increasing the volume of an account.
5. Why do accounts become inactive?
6. How can salespeople gain the support of customers?
7. List four ways customers can help salespeople.
8. What must the salesperson understand before trying to influence customers' advertising?
9. What two obligations do salespeople have in regard to displays?
10. How can salespeople assist their customers in improving the effectiveness of their personal selling?
11. List five principles of conducting meetings.
12. How can salespeople limit complaints, cancellations, and returned goods?
13. What must the seller know about a customer before granting credit?
14. List four reasons why customers don't pay their bills.
15. How can salespeople build customer goodwill?

DISCUSSION QUESTIONS

1. What should be the ultimate consideration when formulating a credit policy?
2. What is the difference between customer support and customer goodwill?
3. What are the possible consequences of a firm's turning a large number of customers over to collection agencies because they did not pay debts?
4. Respond to the following: "Fancy lunches and customer conventions at exclusive resorts cannot be justified as anything other than bribes for the firm's business."

CASE STUDY 14

Donna Grayson sells for an industrial distributor. Her customers are the purchasing agents of manufacturing companies in several different industries. The Williamsville Furniture Company is one of Grayson's customers. Each year Williamsville buys about $50,000 worth of items of the kind sold by Grayson's wholesale firm. Grayson, however, gets only about $5,000 of this volume.

Grayson's predecessor did no better, although the salesperson he replaced had sold the company considerably more.

For ten years, Grayson's firm has not been getting what it considers to be a decent share of Williamsville's total business. When Grayson asked the Williamsville purchasing agent about this matter, she was told that her firm was getting a respectable share, that spreading the volume of purchases over several suppliers was a desirable form of protection, and that Williamsville was obligated to be loyal to suppliers of long standing.

How can Grayson obtain a larger share of the Williamsville Furniture Company business?

Chapter 15
Self-Management

Self-management is essential to profitable selling. There are really only two ways to increase sales volume: the salesperson can do more selling, and the salesperson can do more effective selling. Self-managed salespeople succeed in both these areas. They arrange to put in more hours each week and month talking with prospects than do other salespeople, and they are always trying to raise the quality of their selling efforts. The objective of all self-management activity is to spend as much time as possible in face-to-face selling, and this objective can be gained only if all selling efforts are directed most effectively. The efforts salespeople exert must be soundly planned and their work must be systematically performed according to a program or schedule.

ESSENTIALS OF SELF-MANAGEMENT

All salespeople want to call on as many promising prospects as they can. In addition, they want to spend the maximum amount of time possible in face-to-face selling and the proper amount of time in nonselling business activities. Many companies ask and expect their salespeople to average a minimum number of calls each day or each week. One very large company, for example, wants its salespeople to average twelve interviews each complete working day. These objectives cannot be reached without planning; salespeople must organize their work in advance.

Here are some benefits enjoyed by salespeople who plan their work:

1. Systematic planning helps salespeople become more familiar with all aspects of their jobs, because planning starts with a study of their problems and objectives.

2. By directing their efforts, salespeople can concentrate on the most promising prospects and markets to do more thorough, more successful jobs. They do not spend time on people who cannot use their product to advantage, and this results in seeing five buyers three times each rather than seeing one buyer fifteen times.
3. Planning minimizes lost time, and lost time makes it easier for competing salespeople to take over a salesperson's accounts. Mistakes and oversights are also reduced by systematic planning.
4. Planning provides consistency of action.
5. Planning helps improve the quality and effectiveness of the actual sales presentation.

Salespeople should always have a plan for their work, and it should be followed in most respects and in most situations. However, no plan can replace judgment and common sense.

Handling Selling Duties

In contacting prospects and customers, a salesperson is thinking primarily of making a minimum number of calls and of achieving at least a satisfactory sales volume. A salesperson will always be contacting members of three different groups: present customers, prospects who have been contacted but who have not yet bought, and new prospects who have just been located but who have not yet been contacted. Because the salesperson's main concern is usually to make large customers out of medium-sized ones and medium-sized customers out of small ones, more time should properly be spent with the customer group than with either of the prospect groups. The second group contains prospects on whom time, thought, and money have been spent, yet who have placed no orders. The salesperson's objective here is to devote the most attention to the most promising prospects. A definite amount of time should be spent each week working with the third group and scouting for future business. Members of this third group replace customers who are lost each year for various reasons. Only by setting up goals for each group and then scheduling calls in line with those goals can the salesperson be sure the proper amount of time is being devoted to each group.

The second element with which the salesperson is obviously quite concerned is sales volume. This is expressed in terms of a quota which may be set up in dollars or in merchandise units. The best quota is one that forces the salesperson to work in order to reach it, yet is attainable if he or she does work. Such quotas can be established only after the market potential in the salesperson's territory has been evaluated. Because conditions change, continuing flexibility is an essential feature of any sound quota.

The most precious time a salesperson has is that spent helping prospects buy in face-to-face conversation. Yet, surveys show that many salespeople spend more time in traveling, doing paperwork, or even in waiting to see prospects than they spend in actual face-to-face selling. In most areas of selling, only about one-sixth of the working day is spent with customers. If face-to-face time with prospects and customers can be increased, sales can also be increased. One of the salesperson's most important functions, then, is to identify just how much time is devoted to selling and to nonselling activities. The objective is to minimize the time spent on nonselling duties.

Nonselling activities vary depending on the kind of selling that is being done, but most salespeople are involved with the following nonselling duties: traveling; waiting to see prospects or customers; giving service to customers, such as setting up window displays; handling adjustments; public relations work; market research; prospecting; planning; paperwork, including correspondence

HOW SALESPEOPLE SPEND THEIR TIME

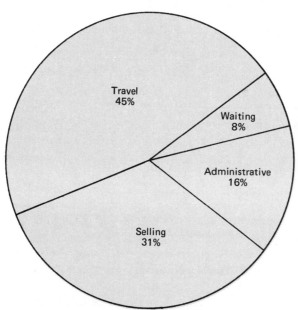

ILLUSTRATION 15-1. Above is what one company discovered when it investigated how its topflight salespeople spent their time. The company clocked those salespeople from the time they left their homes in the morning until they returned at night.

and recordkeeping; and self-development. Some companies prescribe in detail the nonselling duties they expect their salespeople to assume. For the non-supervised salesperson, experience should dictate the choice of nonselling activities.

It is not difficult for the salesperson to keep a reasonably accurate record of how much time is spent on each of the nonselling duties. Such a record will quickly point out areas in which too much or too little time is being spent. Nonselling functions can be justified only if they allow the salesperson to spend more time with prospects or if they lead to increased future sales through goodwill. By selecting the nonselling duties carefully and devoting the proper amount of time to each, the salesperson achieves the optimum ratio of selling time to nonselling time.

What salespeople do with time that is spent in neither selling nor nonselling activities is, in one sense, their own business. As is true of many types of career, however, most of those hours will influence a salesperson's selling career at least indirectly. Most sales managers are convinced that a salesperson's private life can have an important bearing on success. Thus, during off-the-job time, sales-people should not conduct themselves in such a way as to damage either their personal standing or their company's standing with customers.

Good salespeople have their automobiles serviced outside selling hours. They make no personal telephone calls and do no personal shopping during selling hours. They reduce their personal time enough to make one more call a day, outside regular selling hours, and they make no phony excuses for not making calls that should be made, even on difficult buyers.

As for matters concerning buyers, good salespeople budget for each account the amount of time appropriate; some may deserve more, some less than in the past. They either remind buyers with whom they have appointments with a mailing just before the appointment date or confirm them by telephone. They shorten sales presentations, perhaps using direct mail to presell in advance of their calls. They do not spend too much time socializing merely because visiting with some buyers is pleasant, but may, as a rule, invite to lunch people who can do them some good.

As for in-the-field matters, they call on only those buyers who are genuine prospects, keep a record of each working day to spot time leaks, and allow no one to raid or steal any of their selling time. They restrict coffee breaks, knowing that an extra cup of coffee can cost selling time. They use waiting time by doing paperwork, reading business publications, checking stock, or such.

TECHNIQUES FOR ROUTING

Systematic physical scheduling is called *routing.* Well-planned routing raises both the number of calls the salesperson is able to make and the ratio of selling time to nonselling time. The salesperson who uses well-planned routing sees the maximum number of buyers when they are most ready to buy; works the territory in a logical, planned, and controlled manner; and covers the territory thoroughly.

Geographic Considerations in Routing

Whatever programs and timetables salespeople establish to attain their objectives can be constructed only in terms of the geographic area covered and what it contains. The boundary lines must be clear in the salesperson's mind, for they embrace both problems and possibilities. They specify the exact area in terms of which the salesperson must plan and operate.

Virtually all salespeople have clearly delineated sales territories assigned to them. Some of the factors that influence the size of the territory are the total number of prospects within a certain area, the buying habits of the prospects, the location of the prospects in relation to transportation facilities, the best frequency-of-call schedule, how often the salesperson is to be called back to the home office and for how long, the competition present in a given area, and the potential dollar demand present in various markets.

Salespeople who cover a number of cities or states face the problem of organizing their sales territories in the most manageable, profitable manner. When the territory is divided into smaller sections, the salesperson's responsibility is for a number of individual markets or trading areas. The salesperson thinks, plans, and works in terms of the several trading areas that make up the whole territory. Even a city or local salesperson is forced to think of a single city market as being made of different sections or districts.

When the salesperson analyzes and operates in terms of smaller, more convenient units, the need for the salesperson's products can be more promptly and accurately estimated. The salesperson can also be more sensitive in detecting the appearance of any new market or of any new market conditions. Because the territory is organized as a collection of separate trading areas, it is possible for selling activities to be adapted to each area.

Principles of Routing

Good routing insures that the salesperson covers the territory according to plan. It permits the salesperson to strike the desired balance between intensive and extensive coverage, and it helps reduce traveling costs. When routing permits the prospect to anticipate the salesperson's call, there is more chance that the prospect will be ready to see the salesperson and will require less of the salesperson's time. Routing also helps the salesperson make a better showing against company performance standards.

There are several principles to follow in establishing the most efficient routing plan. These principles concern geographic area, face-to-face time, future planning, optimum coverage, scheduling next calls, prospect and customer convenience, and experimentation.

Geographic Area. Study the geographic area thoroughly. Plot the cities or markets on a map and trace the most economical ways to get to each. Then do the same type of mapping for all prospects and customers to be contacted within each city or market.

Face-to-Face Time. Routing should provide the greatest amount of face-to-face time with the most profitable buyers; therefore, routing in a straight line is usually desirable because it shortens distances and permits more calls. In determining methods of transportation to be used, strive to conserve time, money, and energy reserves.

Future Planning. Make up the routing plan for the most suitable future period, often for the coming week. This permits the designation of a mailing or telephoning point for the company, prospects, and customers.

Optimum Coverage. A valuable concept is that of optimum coverage of each trading area. The salesperson moves toward this by asking, "What else can I possibly do on my way to, while in, or on leaving that particular district or town?"

Scheduling Next Calls. In some lines, buyers should be able to count on a salesperson's calls on a certain day or perhaps even at a certain hour. This demands the establishment of a routing sequence that will be repeated at regular intervals. When leaving a buyer, the salesperson should indicate approximately when to expect the next call.

Prospect and Customer Convenience. To whatever extent possible or necessary, plan the route to suit the convenience of prospects and customers. If the day or hour of the salesperson's call is inconvenient, additional resistance is faced. This means that in some cases it might be possible for a salesperson to spend more time traveling, see fewer prospects and customers, yet find that the time spent has increased in effectiveness.

Experimentation. Experimentation is essential to successful routing. Only through trial and error can the best routing plan be determined.

TECHNIQUES OF SCHEDULING

Salespeople who route themselves carefully but do not follow up by mapping out a program for each day's activities stop short of a necessary step in self-management. If the salesperson is to spend the greatest possible amount of time in the presence of buyers, each selling day must be a scheduled day.

Elements of the Schedule

Four basic elements determine the makeup of the daily schedule: (1) the number of calls the salesperson hopes to make that day on present customers, old prospects, and new prospects; (2) the expected sales volume in dollars or units for that day; (3) the number of hours of work planned that day; and (4) the salesperson's own energy and industry.

Salespeople should start with the amount of time they consider available for budgeting. Then they can list all the demands that will be made on that time. They think of how much time they should allot for selling and how much for each legitimate nonselling function. They think of how much time they should spend on each market covered and how much on each prospect and customer in that market. They earmark the best hours during the day for selling and earmark night or weekend hours for paperwork and other nonselling duties. Successful salespeople demonstrate their superior ability to spend time wisely and profitably by spending more time in the presence of buyers. They assume that the activities planned will produce the sales volume budgeted for that day.

The calls that salespeople make are, thus, planned calls. They know specifically what they hope to accomplish on each; they have a plan or outline for each interview; and they have all the material they will need packed in prospect folders that are arranged in the order of the planned calls. In addition to the selling calls, the day's schedule will include any "in-between" contacts with customers and prospects. These are calculated contacts that are sandwiched between selling calls and may be made by mail, telegram/Mailgram, phone, or even in person.

Principles of Scheduling

The schedule for each day should be constructed around the most important prospects and customers for that day. The following principles will prove helpful in setting up a practical and efficient daily schedule.

Setting Times for the Most Important Calls. Set a time for each of the most important calls for the day. These important calls may be on buyers who are ready to buy, buyers whom you know to be accessible during this particular trip but who may be out of town or otherwise unavailable during another trip, buyers with whom you have appointments, and buyers whom you were instructed to see. Minor calls should be spotted around the major calls.

Setting a Time to Begin Work Each Day. Have a definite time to start each day's work, and do not stop until the jobs scheduled for that day have been completed. Plan a full day's work for each working day.

Laying Out More Than a Day's Work. Lay out more than the usual day's work, if necessary, to stay busy and meet the quota. Some salespeople schedule one-third more calls than they expect to make. If they hope to make nine calls, a satisfactory quota for the day, they put twelve on the schedule. Then if interviews go faster than usual or if some of the buyers are unavailable, the salesperson still keeps busy.

Allowing Enough Time for Each Call. Allow enough time for each day and call so as to minimize departures from and disruptions of the schedule. Lay out the calls in sequence.

Reducing Wasted Time with Appointments. Appointments, where practical, are worthwhile because they reduce pointless calls, waiting time, and the average length of the call. Appointments made for an early hour, 8 to 9 A.M., and for the late afternoon hour, 4 to 5 P.M., help keep the salesperson on the job all day.

Devoting the Most Productive Hours to Selling. Devote the most productive hours of the day to selling to buyers. Schedule routine jobs, paperwork, and service functions for other hours.

Scheduling According to Routing and the Needs of Customers. Prepare the preliminary draft of the schedule for each day of the coming week or two weeks as a part of routing for that period. The final version of each day's schedule should be written out on the preceding night. Construct the schedule as much as possible according to the needs and wishes of buyers.

Substituting Mail or Telephone Contacts for Personal Contacts. Sometimes the salesperson will find that each day can be made more productive by substituting mail or telephone contacts for personal contacts. Duties must obviously not be slighted by depending upon the telephone or mail to do things that should be done in person. It is possible, however, for the salesperson to use direct mail to hold and even to obtain some business while visiting other trading areas. It is also possible to make good use of the telephone or mail to deliver advance notice of calls in cases where such notification would increase the effectiveness of interviews.

Flexibility in Routing and Scheduling

There must be a certain amount of flexibility in a salesperson's routing plans and daily schedules. Changes and cancellations in both travel arrangements and appointments, often on short notice, are inevitable. Schedules must be revised to fit emergencies, and lost time must be made up. No salesperson should adhere to a plan blindly, regardless of developments. Transportation delays, broken appointments, and inability to get away from buyers on schedule are typical causes of changes in plans.

There are several ways of achieving the needed flexibility. One is for the salesperson to have the right attitude toward unavoidable revisions. Flexibility is partially a frame of mind, and one begins to achieve it when one starts cultivating the ability to improvise. A second step toward flexibility is the realization that minutes can be moved about within a time budget in the same way that dollars can be shifted around in a financial budget. Minutes can be temporarily borrowed from today's paperwork allowance, used for selling to buyers, and replaced tomorrow. A third method of achieving flexibility is for the salesperson always to be easily accessible to prospects, customers, and the salesperson's own company.

Another suggestion is that alternate plans be established in case there is unexpected spare time. By having a second choice of activities if a certain prospect is out of the office the salesperson can avoid wasting time. Second choices might be such activities as canvassing for new prospects, calling to see whether a dormant account can and should be revived, making call-backs, or catching up on paperwork.

THE TELEPHONE AS A TIME-SAVER

Because salespeople must work toward a certain degree of economy both in time budgeting and expense budgeting, they should experiment with using the telephone as a supplementary selling tool. Certain buyers, particularly retailers, like to order by telephone for reasons of speed and simplicity; certain products, especially staples, can be sold successfully by telephone.

The salesperson can call a buyer anywhere, at any chosen hour. Because geography is no limitation, the number of calls possible during a day is high. Contact by telephone is almost instantaneous. This means that salespeople can send urgent information to whomever they need to reach.

Sometimes the salesperson will find it easier to get through the switchboard operator than through a receptionist-barrier of some sort. Some prospects will talk on the telephone when they will not see a salesperson who calls in person.

Even though few salespeople find telephone calls a complete substitute for face-to-face calls, most are well advised to remember the difference in costs between the two. For some salespeople, the typical personal call costs 20 times as much as the typical telephone call. Telephoning permits the salesperson to get in touch with important buyers often, particularly between personal calls, and permits more effective market coverage.

Uses of Telephone Calls

Salespeople find that telephone calls can be time-savers in making sales, making appointments, delivering news, cultivating buyers' goodwill, handling customer problems, and doing prospecting and preapproach work. Each of these uses will now be briefly discussed.

Making Sales by Telephone. Salespeople can obtain regular orders by telephone; can call buyers to increase mail orders by trading up or by suggestion selling of related or timely merchandise; and can make telephone calls to land follow-up orders and to move odd lots, job lots, end-of-season merchandise, and discontinued items. Salespeople can also sell hard-to-see buyers and impulsive buyers by telephone. After a first personal call which went well but did not result in a purchase, they may telephone buyers to encourage them to take immediate buying action. In these calls, the salesperson can repeat and support what was said in person.

Making Appointments by Telephone. A major use of the telephone by salespeople is for making, confirming, and rescheduling appointments. By making appointments, the salesperson is able to cover more territory, make more calls on buyers, and give more service to customers. Sometimes some buyer information can be obtained when phoning for an appointment, but the salesperson should not try to do any selling at that time. The telephone call requesting an appointment may be preceded by a mail communication. After the appointment has been made, the salesperson may send a confirming note, reminding the buyer of the date of the appointment.

Using the Telephone to Deliver News. Because it permits instant contact, the telephone helps a salesperson keep buyers posted on matters involving products, their prices, promotion efforts, and company policies. Perhaps a manufacturer is launching a major advertising campaign in which retail customers will be interested. Perhaps a price rise is in the offing, but buyers can place orders immediately at the present price. Perhaps delivery can be made to an impatient buyer earlier than originally promised. If certain ordered items cannot be shipped, the salesperson may telephone to tell the buyer that they have been back-ordered and when to expect them.

Using the Telephone to Cultivate Buyer Goodwill. The telephone can be used to keep the buyer-seller relationship on a personal, friendly basis. For example, a call can introduce a salesperson to a new purchasing agent before the salesperson's first visit in person. Salespeople can telephone to congratulate buyers on promotions and achievements. They can call to thank buyers for first interviews, first orders, testimonials, referrals, and case histories. Telephone calls let the salesperson keep in touch and check up on customer service. The fact that a salesperson is concerned enough to take the time to telephone is flattering to most buyers. Of course, telephoning can be overdone; it then becomes annoying to buyers.

Using the Telephone to Handle Customer Problems. In handling customer problems, the personal touch of a telephone call can often give quick and satisfactory results. When a written complaint or a cancellation reaches the salesperson, a telephone call may be appropriate. Certain collection matters can also be better handled by telephone than by letter. Calls can reveal why a good customer quit buying; they can be effective in reviving dormant accounts; and they can be used to obtain approval for a substitution in an order.

Using the Telephone for Prospecting and Preapproach Work. Cold canvassing from a directory is possible by telephone. Customers can be asked for leads. Salespeople telephone to qualify prospects, to build a prospect list, and to obtain the data needed for evaluation of buyers. Calls can identify the real

DON'T TRAVEL 400 MILES ON GUT FEELING.

Qualifying prospective clients can waste too much time, money and energy—if you try to rely on office visits alone. With Long Distance, you can select the best possibilities and the right contacts before you go on the road.

You can plan trips with more confidence. And greater efficiency. That way, your valuable travel time can be spent properly... on serious selling instead of blind searching. Phoning first with Long Distance really pays off.

FIND OUT FIRST WITH LONG DISTANCE.

Long Distance. It's the way to get things done. Today.

 Cincinnati Bell

Source: Cincinnati Bell

ILLUSTRATION 15-2. Salespeople telephone to qualify prospects, to build a prospect list, and to obtain data needed for evaluation of buyers.

prospects on a company mailing list, the buying influences, and those who are open to buy or are seriously considering a purchase.

How Telephoning Affects Routing

Some salespeople have incorporated the use of the telephone into what they call *skip-stop* routing. Suppose that a salesperson has 20 markets in which some personal calls must be made. The salesperson numbers each market and constructs two circuits. On the first circuit, the salesperson visits all odd-numbered markets and telephones certain buyers in even-numbered markets from the closest odd-numbered market. On the other circuit, the salesperson visits all even-numbered markets and from them telephones buyers in the odd-numbered markets.

Other salespeople build their routes on key towns. Under this plan, a salesperson divides markets and buyers into two groups: those deserving personal calls and those who must be handled in a more economical manner—

namely, by telephone. Individual customers in the second group are reached by telephone when the salesperson is in the closest key town. It is not unusual for a salesperson to telephone certain small buyers who reside in key towns, or to alternate telephone calls with personal calls in handling certain accounts of modest size.

Suggestions for Conducting the Telephone Conversation

The salesperson should generally open the call with identification by name and company and should then follow with the justification for the call. The salesperson should immediately give the buyer a reason for staying on the phone rather than ending the conversation; this reason may be based on curiosity or on information of interest and benefit to the buyer. It is virtually impossible for the salesperson to get to the point too quickly because revealing the goal of the call may prevent the buyer's losing interest and hanging up. Sometimes there is something to which the salesperson can tie the call: a letter sent to the buyer earlier, some communication from the buyer, the last personal call, the buyer's last order, or even an earlier telephone contact.

A pleasant, courteous manner from the outset of the conversation helps make a favorable impression. Most principles that are effective in face-to-face selling are equally effective for telephone communication. Here are some of them:

1. Telephone calls should be made at times convenient to the buyer.
2. Buyers should be addressed by name and made to feel important.
3. Salespeople should refrain from interrupting the buyer, arguing, and monopolizing the conversation.
4. Salespeople must make every word contribute to their goals as they convert product features into buyer benefits.
5. They must not be so aggressive and push so hard as to close the door on a subsequent call.
6. They should experiment with various presentation plans and should also keep records on the calls they make.
7. They should not let the buyer feel that the call is a routine one and that the salesperson is unwilling to call in person.

For most salespeople, telephoning can never replace personal calls. Use of the telephone should increase, not decrease, the number of personal calls made; and it clearly is not as effective as a personal visit.

RECORDKEEPING

Even the best methods of obtaining information on buyers and on selling techniques and the data accumulated by using these methods are of limited value until they are organized into readily usable records. The amount of time that is required in keeping records is justified by the improvement that results in the quality of the salesperson's selling. Records enable salespeople to organize their work. Salespeople lean heavily on them in managing themselves. Daily accomplishments must be known if they are to make their quotas.

As an example of the tactical use of records, the salesperson can use them to shorten calls, thus permitting more calls to be completed each week. For instance, on call-backs, records relieve the salesperson of spending time in finding out at what point the last visit ended. The salesperson can stress only those points that need stressing and thus avoid needless repetition in the sales presentation.

Mechanics of Keeping Records

No record is worth keeping unless its information can be used to advantage. Records that demand too much paperwork generally contain much useless detail. Records that are complete, yet simple, are the ones that should be kept up-to-date and used.

If possible, the salesperson should fill out any daily reports immediately after each call. By following this practice, the records will contain fewer mistakes, fresher facts, and more complete information. This practice also saves time, permits earlier mailings to the home office, and means that the salesperson is reasonably caught up with paperwork if any emergency should arise. If orders can also be written up on the spot, time will not have to be spent at night or on weekends processing them. Orders and reports should be mailed to the company promptly after they have been checked for clarity and completeness.

Records That Should Be Kept

This section will point out the major areas in which most salespeople will need some form of records. Obviously, the salesperson will keep whatever records his or her company requires, whether the information is for the use of the sales department or for other departments such as credit or advertising. In addition to those required, any other records that contribute to the salesperson's success are worth keeping and using.

Prospects and Customers. These two sets of records are commented on together because they are so similar, each consisting of a card which contains a complete history of the salesperson's attention to and experience with each individual buyer. Each card will contain the prospect information the salesperson collected about the buyer, any other facts the salesperson finds useful, an account of the salesperson's work on and progress with the buyer, and plans for the next interview. Time spent in keeping these records is extremely well invested.

Daily Calls. The daily call record is a basic record because it shows the number of attempts to sell. It notes any prices quoted and any promises made; shows the results of each call; and when sales are lost, gives a brief reason for the failure to sell. Any suitable facts can be transferred from the daily call record to prospect and customer records.

Sales. There are many breakdowns for sales volume. The total dollar figure may be classified according to product line if the salesperson handles more than one product, or to price line if more than one price line is sold. The breakdown may be by day, week, and month. It may be by size of order. It may be by type of buyer or by type of sale. These are only a few examples of the breakdown possibilities. Each salesperson must select the ones to compile and maintain.

Expenses. If expenses are to be kept in a healthy ratio to sales volume, they need to be carefully controlled. This demands records. Considerable itemization is needed so that the total figure will be complete and so that the various items can be analyzed and compared with common or control figures. If the salesperson's expense groupings are too detailed, they require too much time; if the groupings are too broad, control and comparison are difficult.

Time. Time records are designed to log hour and minute expenditures for each day. The immediate result is that the salesperson learns just how much time is being spent on each activity. The long-range result of time records should be more time spent in the presence of buyers. Illustration 15-3 shows the differences in value of an hour depending upon annual income. Analyzing your time records will enable you to eliminate wasting time on unimportant activities.

Tickler File. A date tickler file is particularly valuable in bringing to mind whom to see and what to do on each day of the month. By referring to prospect

WHAT'S YOUR TIME WORTH?

Annual Earnings	Value of an Hour[1]
$ 10,000	$ 5.21
20,000	10.42
30,000	15.63
40,000	20.83
50,000	26.04
75,000	39.06
100,000	52.08

[1]Assumes a 240-day work year and an 8-hour work day.

ILLUSTRATION 15-3. The more sales you make, the greater is the value of each hour of your time.

and customer records, the salesperson knows what each prospect should be told about and how that prospect should be approached.

SELF-EVALUATION OF SALES PERFORMANCE

Plans, sales objectives, and records are of little value unless salespeople check the results of their selling efforts against what they had scheduled for themselves. The basic question is: "What do I have to show for my management of myself and my territory?" Only by answering this question frankly and accurately in terms of each day's performance measured against that day's plans can salespeople determine the kind of job they are doing and how they can improve.

To measure their accomplishments, salespeople must have certain performance standards. When they undertake the task of measuring their productive effort, they automatically assume that standards of activity and achievement can be set. Yet, the very nature of selling makes the establishment of absolute standards of achievement difficult. For example, how can missionary salespeople or other "goodwill" representatives of a manufacturer tell how good a job they are doing? Despite this, salespeople are still under pressure to check their accomplishments.

Quantitative Standards

Quantitative standards are not difficult to construct; standards for volume of sales, for number of calls, for new customers, and for expenses are examples. In operation, quantitative standards are based on a comparison of the salesperson's current performance with previous performance or with some budget figure or quota. The standards can be used for both control and incentive purposes.

If the question is raised of how many quantitative checks are necessary to measure a salesperson's performance, an argument for having only one check might be made. This one standard would be net profit from the salesperson's selling activities. The reasoning behind it would be that this single yardstick is adequate, since everything the salesperson does in selling activities is reflected in the net profit figure. But because there is need for more detail, a double check consisting of gross margin and expenses might be recommended. Or three checks, consisting of gross margin, expenses, and sales volume, might be suggested.

There is no sacred number of quantitative criteria by which the salesperson's effectiveness should be measured. Some of the more common and more revealing standards are:

1. Time: number of days worked; number of hours worked; number of hours spent selling to buyers; average length of call.

2. Calls: number of calls per day; number of demonstrations made; number of calls per sale; cost per call.
3. Sales: sales per week or month; percent increase in sales; average size of order; percent of quota sold; number of new accounts added in relation to number of old accounts lost; degree of balance in sales (including number and size of customers, frequency of purchase by customers, composition of orders, average size of orders, unit of sale, seasonal fluctuation, relation of sales volume to cost of sales, and proportion of new accounts to old).
4. Profit: ratio of expenses to sales, ratio of expenses to gross margin, and dollar profit on sales.

Qualitative Standards

Qualitative standards are more difficult to construct because of their subjective nature. Examples of these somewhat inexact standards are those for goodwill, customer loyalty and esteem, planning ability, and industry. Outstanding or unsatisfactory performance in these areas soon shows up in matters that can be quantitatively measured, such as sales.

Qualitative evaluation of a salesperson's performance also involves matters that influence net profit; but these matters are more elusive than are the quantitative gauges. Here are some fairly typical questions that may be used as qualitative standards:

1. How much growth has the salesperson shown in ability to plan and to administer?
2. How much goodwill does the salesperson create, and how much is it worth?
3. How does the salesperson react to the creative phase of the job and the demands for imagination, tact, and versatility?
4. How much allowance should be made for changing conditions in evaluating job performance—changes in sales potential, the business cycle, competitors' activities, or the policies of the salesperson's own company?

Because the salesperson will no doubt find it impossible to do an objective job of evaluating his or her performance on such scores, an unbiased third person should be asked for an impartial rating.

Personal Rating Chart

Beginning salespeople sometimes find that they can benefit for a considerable period of time from daily use of a personal rating chart. The purpose of the chart is to enable the salesperson to check quickly on points of personal strength and weakness so that steps can be taken to maximize strengths and minimize weaknesses.

While it is true that each chart must be built to fit the particular salesperson, the elements of such a chart will probably follow a consistent pattern. The specific items can be just a one-word characteristic or quality, or they can be structured in the form of a question. Qualities that might be included on a personal rating chart are appearance, alertness, courtesy, enthusiasm, honesty, loyalty, obedience, and tact.

Examples of questions that might be included on a personal rating chart are:

1. Did I make today's decisions on the basis of facts?
2. Did I follow up today's leads promptly?
3. Did I spend some time hunting for new prospects?
4. Did I organize my hours and duties and then follow my plan?
5. Did I waste any time?
6. Did I waste any of the company's money or my money?
7. How can I do more and better tomorrow?

The salesperson can use percentages, letter grades, numbers, yes and no answers, or any other system that seems appropriate.

After-Call Analysis

Regardless of whether or not a sale was made, the salesperson should analyze the conduct of each interview in a critical fashion. This can best be done if an account of each call is faithfully kept, each call being one chapter in the case history of that particular buyer. As these case histories grow, the salesperson will find them extremely valuable sources of information about buying motives, objections, the effect of different sales approaches, and other vital matters. The record should be made as soon as possible after the salesperson leaves the buyer, while the details of the call are still remembered and a note can be made of each important aspect. The main concern of the salesperson is what was well done, what was done badly, what changes of a general nature should be made, and what should be done the next time that buyer is called on.

The novice is not the only one who needs to ask why the interview turned out as it did. More experienced salespeople can keep out of undesirable ruts and avoid forming bad habits only by giving careful scrutiny to their performances.

Selling Slumps

Every salesperson knows periods of success and periods of slumps. The smart salesperson accepts periodic slumps as normal and universal and does not make alibis for them. What should be done about slumps?

Because of the relationship between health and energy, *health* deserves a check. A salesperson is under strain that makes good health absolutely essential. Health includes mental, emotional, and physical dimensions. The salesperson needs a tranquil mind and emotional reserves in a healthy body. Good physical condition requires regular medical exams, recreation, rest, exercise, and a proper diet. The golden mean of centuries ago, *moderation,* is still the soundest way to obtain and maintain good health. Moderation should govern recreation, rest, exercise, and diet.

A *positive attitude* is needed to come out a slump because attitude affects selling performance. Negative thinking, doubts, worries, fears, and self-pity consume energy and emotional resources, and they cannot be tolerated. Enthusiasm is contagious, and thinking success encourages success. Salespeople must have belief and pride in themselves. They need confidence, affirmative feelings, and solid convictions about their company, their buyers, and their products.

Most important in working out of a slump is *action.* The salesperson must do something. The salesperson may hurry to see the next buyer on the call schedule, may visit with the sales manager, or may make notes on the services that can be rendered to buyers. The salesperson checks and improves plans, then carries out those plans.

The Experimental Attitude

The same questioning search that salespeople make in their effort to increase the effectiveness of their calls must be translated into their complete operation. If there is a better way to make their sales presentations, then might there not also be a better way to route themselves? This determination to seek and find better ways of doing things can best be described as an experimental attitude.

Thought and study highlight this attitude. Well-managed, self-managed salespeople ponder their problems and speculate about solutions. They encourage their minds to demonstrate independence by daring to think new, constructive, creative thoughts. They study what they do and the results they get day by day and week by week. They make tests and experiments as part of their self-management, learning what needs revising, and using what has been found to be best. They recognize that change will always be present and provide for ease in adapting to change by refusing to outgrow the habit of study. Finally, they obey the most fundamental commandment in all selling: "Never think you are so good that improvement is impossible." Maintaining the successful salesperson status requires continual effort.

SUMMARY

Self-management is essential to profitable selling. It helps salespeople do more selling, and do more effective selling. Maximizing the time spent in face-to-face selling and spending the right amount of time on nonselling activities are goals of self-management. Planning helps salespeople concentrate on the most promising prospects and markets, minimizes lost time, and provides consistency of action. Travel, waiting, and recordkeeping time should be minimized and used as efficiently as possible. Personal time must also be properly managed, since what salespeople do outside work will influence their selling activities and performance.

Systematic physical scheduling is called routing. The salesperson who uses well-planned routing sees the maximum number of buyers when they are most ready to buy; works the territory in a logical, planned, and controlled manner; and covers the territory thoroughly. Factors influencing territory size include the number of prospects in a certain area, buying habits, and the location of buyers in relation to transportation facilities. Sometimes it is useful to break a territory into a number of districts.

Once routing has been determined, scheduling must be arranged. Elements built into a schedule include the desired number of sales calls, the expected sales volume, the work hours planned, and the salesperson's own energy.

The calls that salespeople make should be planned calls. Salespeople should set a time for each of the most important calls. Appointments help greatly in scheduling. It is important to build flexibility into the schedule. Schedules must be revised to fit emergencies, and lost time must be made up.

The telephone is a great time-saver. In addition, telephone calls are much less expensive than face-to-face calls. The telephone can be used for making sales, scheduling appointments, delivering news, cultivating buyer goodwill, handling customer problems, and prospecting and preapproach work. Skip-stop routing is an effective routing technique using the telephone. Principles for conducting effective telephone conversations include convenient calling times for the buyer, addressing the buyer by name, not interrupting or arguing with the buyer, economizing on words, not being too aggressive, experimenting with different telephone presentations, and making each call special to the buyer.

Recordkeeping is an important nonselling activity, increasing salespeople's efficiency and effectiveness. Records should be kept only when the information will be used. Information that should be kept includes prospects and customers, daily calls, sales, expenses, time, and a tickler file.

Both quantitative and qualitative standards of self-evaluation should be constructed. A personal rating chart is a useful tool for self-evaluation. After-call analysis should be carried out in a critical fashion.

Every salesperson goes through periods of success and slumps. A positive attitude and action are needed to come out of a slump. Good salespeople constantly experiment with their sales presentations, routing, and every other aspect of their sales operations. Maintaining the successful salesperson status requires continual effort.

REVIEW QUESTIONS

1. What is the objective of self-management?
2. Why is careful routing important?
3. List four factors that influence the size of a sales territory.

4. List three elements involved in creating a schedule.
5. List four uses of the telephone in selling activities.
6. Describe skip-stop routing.
7. What areas of information should salespeople keep in their records?
8. List three quantitative and three qualitative standards that a salesperson might use to measure effectiveness.
9. What factors should a salesperson consider in after-call analysis?
10. How can selling slumps be broken?
11. What is meant by an experimental attitude?

DISCUSSION QUESTIONS

1. Should sales calls be made on customers only when you expect to make a sale?
2. React to the following: "Paperwork should be done in the evenings and on weekends."
3. Suggest some guidelines concerning travel, time allocation, and approaches to prospects when developing a new territory.
4. How can a salesperson build up the self-confidence that is vital for successful selling?

CASE STUDY 15A

Jim Chang is a salesperson for an office equipment and supply firm in a major midwestern city. His customers are insurance firms, loan companies, banks, and savings and loan institutions. He recognizes the value of budgeting his time well, but he feels somewhat uncertain about *how* to budget his time. Several more experienced salespeople have suggested the following rules.

1. Avoid nonessential sales calls.
2. Never call on a customer unless you expect to make a sale.
3. The amount of time you allocate for a sales call should depend on how much the customer has purchased from you in the past.
4. Minimize the amount of time you spend entertaining customers.
5. Servicing is as important as selling.
6. Paperwork should be done in the evenings and on weekends.
7. Always eat lunch with a customer (if there's one nearby); never eat lunch alone.
8. Help your customer and yourself by checking his stock.

As he looks over this list of rules he's jotted down, Chang is a bit concerned: some of these rules seem to conflict with each other. Some seem shortsighted. How could this be when all of these suggestions have been used successfully by more experienced salespeople?

How would you answer Chang's question and resolve his doubts?

Rosa Ramirez is a relatively new salesperson for a manufacturer of office equipment. Customers tend to be small to medium-sized businesses, including retailers, professional groups, service firms, and some manufacturers. Ramirez shares a territory in Western Pennsylvania with four other salespeople. The five are free to call on any *prospects* they can identify, but they are not allowed to call on each others' *customers.*

Each month a "report card" is produced for each salesperson, showing how each performed compared with the other salespeople in the territory and the nation. According to the report card, Ramirez has been putting in more hours per day, but is making fewer (albeit longer) sales calls.

She is discouraged by the relatively low sales during her first eight months on the job. She has very little time to study new product information. In addition, she has received two traffic tickets, one for speeding to get to an appointment on time, and the other for an expired auto inspection sticker.

List the actions that Ramirez might consider to improve her sales performance.

Chapter 16
Legal, Ethical, and Social Responsibilities

After studying this chapter you should be able to:

- Describe the major laws affecting a salesperson
- Show how these laws apply to pricing and other selling practices
- Identify behavior by salespeople that could be considered unethical
- Tell how the ethics of salespeople could be improved
- Comment on the social responsibilities of salespeople

Of course the salesperson must sell, but he or she has other responsibilities as well. Each must obey the laws that govern company policies and the salesperson's actions. Each should have a strong sense of what constitutes ethical conduct. And, finally, there is growing recognition that the sales force plays an important role in helping the company fulfill its social responsibilities.

LEGAL RESPONSIBILITIES

Salespeople must know what laws prohibit and require and how laws apply to their actions. The salesperson, however, is not expected to be a lawyer. A cardinal rule is: *when in doubt, don't.* Consult your supervisor or your legal department.

Laws Affecting a Salesperson

A salesperson is affected by federal legislation and by state and local laws.

Federal Legislation. The major federal legislation affecting selling activities includes the Sherman Act (enacted in 1890), the Clayton Act (1914), the Federal Trade Commission Act (1914), and the Robinson-Patman Act (1936). Although none of these laws are new, their interpretation by the courts and their enforcement by administrative agencies have expanded their impact on selling activities.

The Sherman Act. The Sherman Act is the oldest of the anti-trust laws. One major purpose was to outlaw monopolies or attempts to monopolize. This rarely applies directly to the sales force. A second major purpose was to outlaw actions that were in "restraint of trade." That is, it sought to prevent activities that lessened competition. Price-fixing is the best-known activity in restraint of trade, but agreements not to sell, to sell only in certain markets, or to sell only to certain customers are also included within this act. Except in seeking remedies in court cases, it makes little difference whether the agreements are written or oral, explicit or implicit, intentional or accidental.

The Clayton Act. The Clayton Act had the same intent as the Sherman Act, but tried to clarify the Sherman Act by pointing to specific practices that were illegal. Of particular concern to a sales force are provisions restricting exclusive dealing and tying arrangements. *Exclusive dealing,* which is illegal, involves requiring buyers of one product not to buy certain products from another seller. A *tying arrangement* is the practice of requiring the buyer to purchase one product in order to be allowed to buy another.

The Federal Trade Commission Act. The Federal Trade Commission Act extended the Sherman Act by outlawing unfair methods of competition and deceptive practices. It also established the Federal Trade Commission (FTC), whose job it is to see that all of these laws are observed. In 1938, the Wheeler-Lea Amendment to the Federal Trade Commission Act was passed. This allowed the FTC to take action against deceptive practices regardless of whether competition had been harmed.

The Robinson-Patman Act. The Robinson-Patman Act, passed during the Great Depression, grew out of concern that large and rapidly-growing chain retailers would demand and get price discounts which would allow them to drive small retailers out of business by underpricing them. Thus, the Robinson-Patman Act was passed to outlaw price discrimination between buyers for products "of like grade and quality" if the price discrimination tended to harm competition. Price differentials are permitted for products of different quality, when costs of doing business with certain buyers can be proved to be less, in order to match competitors' prices, or when the buyers are not in competition with each other. It is not easy for a firm to interpret how the law applies to it because it can never be sure what a judge will accept as evidence of justifiable price differentials.

The Robinson-Patman Act also outlaws providing various merchandising and promotional aids and allowances in a discriminatory manner if this would tend to harm competition. Instead, these aids and allowances must be provided in a "proportionately equal" manner. It is often the salesperson's responsibility to inform customers of the availability of these aids and allowances.

Other Laws. The range of legislation dealing with contracts, consumer protection, and personal selling is wide.

The Uniform Commercial Code. The Uniform Commercial Code, which deals in part with the laws of contracts, may treat a sales representative as an agent of the company, authorized to make commitments for the company. Thus, an offer made by a salesperson and accepted by a customer could, in effect, bind the salesperson's company to a contract the company may not have intended. Similarly, comments made by a salesperson about the suitability of a product for certain purposes may be construed by the courts as the equivalent of warranties or guarantees.

Consumer Protection Legislation. Some state and local governments have passed what are known as Green River Ordinances (after one of the places where they were first passed—Green River, Wyoming). These laws restrict the activities of certain types of salespeople (notably door-to-door salespeople) by requiring that they apply for and receive a license before they can sell in that area.

Door-to-door selling (and sometimes telephone selling) is often restricted in other ways by state and local laws. Salespeople may not get a foot in the door by claiming that they are taking a survey when the survey is only incidental to their real purpose—to sell. Salespeople must also inform customers who have signed contracts about any cooling off period, a time (often three days) during which the customer can reconsider and cancel a contract.

Truth-in-lending legislation requires that the seller inform the buyer of the effective rate of interest and the amount of the carrying charge for any credit purchase. The intent of the law is to inform the buyer of the costs being incurred when buying on credit.

Applying the Laws

The laws affecting selling are complex, and their interpretation is difficult. Nevertheless, some actions are illegal, while others are merely unethical. Some of the problem areas are discussed below.

Pricing Actions. Pricing actions such as price-fixing, predatory pricing, and discriminatory pricing are illegal. Paying bribes and accepting kickbacks are also unethical and can affect prices.

Price-Fixing. Price-fixing is a civil and a criminal offense. The company can be sued and a salesperson can go to jail for participating in price-fixing. In fact, even the appearance of price-fixing may be illegal. Thus, a salesperson must be careful not to agree with a competitor's salesperson to charge a certain price to a customer. And the salesperson must even avoid exchanging price information with a competitor because it may appear that there was some unspoken agreement to fix prices.

How does this translate into action? Don't discuss prices with competitors at a trade association meeting. Don't respond to questions about price from a competitor, even if your prices are published in price lists and are common knowledge to your customers. If, by chance, you overhear a competitor's salespeople discussing their own prices, there is nothing wrong with listening, but you may not join the conversation. In addition, it must be clear that their allowing you to overhear the pricing information was not intended to be a way of communicating the information to you. There is, however, nothing wrong with getting information about competitors' prices from a customer as long as you haven't arranged to use the customer to transmit information about price.

Requiring that your distributor or retailer charge certain prices to their customers is illegal. The salesperson must be careful not to give the impression that the distributor or retailer must charge a certain price.

Price-fixing is rarely a concern of retail or direct-to-home salespeople. For advice about a specific situation, you should always rely on your company's lawyers.

Predatory Pricing. The opposite of price-fixing is predatory pricing. This practice, also illegal, involves intentionally lowering prices below costs so as to drive a competitor out of business. Thus, price competition that is too vigorous may be as bad as agreeing not to compete on a price basis. The outcome of a lawsuit charging predatory pricing may depend on the perception of a judge or jury of the company's intent. Statements made at a sales meeting or to a customer may provide evidence of intent. "We're going to drive _____ out of business" or "the way we're pricing, they don't have a chance" may build morale at a sales meeting or impress a customer, but they may also impress a judge or jury—in the wrong way.

Price Discrimination. Price discrimination is also illegal under the Robinson-Patman Act. The safest way to avoid legal problems is to sell at the same price to everyone. You cannot sell at a lower price to a customer you like or to one who is important to you. Therefore, you must know when charging lower prices to certain customers is legal and when it is not. (Once again, when in doubt, consult your company or its attorney.)

Price discrimination is not an issue when the product you are selling to a customer is not of like grade and quality to that which you are selling to other customers. In other words, if you sell custom-made products or services, you are probably safe. Nor is price discrimination an issue if the customer to whom you are planning to sell at a lower price is not in competition with those customers to whom you sell at a higher price. This may occur when the customer is in a different industry or a different geographical area.

You can justify different prices to customers in the same industry for your standardized product when it is less expensive to sell to certain customers; that is, there is a cost basis for the price differential. You can also justify different prices when your customer can show that a competitor is selling at a lower price. You can meet the prices that your competitor is charging, but you cannot reduce your prices to a lower level.

Quantity discounts, a popular way of encouraging and rewarding large orders, must be justified in the same way as any other price differentials. In addition, a buyer who encourages or knowingly accepts a price that is lower than appropriate can be guilty of price discrimination.

Free goods or product displays as allowances for promoting a product are governed by the Robinson-Patman Act. These are not illegal, but because they offer the possibility of discriminating on the net cost to a customer, they must be made available on a "proportionately equal" basis. You must inform all your customers, large or small, of their availability.

Paying bribes and accepting kickbacks are as much ethical matters as they are legal ones. Bribes are money or valuable gifts given to a buyer to obtain business. Kickbacks occur when a broker working for and paid by the buyer receives a payment from the seller for making the decision to buy from that seller.

Channel/Market Restrictions. Channel/market restrictions are illegal. The first of these channel/market restrictions involves deciding not to sell to certain customers. Often the idea is to avoid head-to-head confrontations. A competitor may say, "If you don't leave my customers alone, I'll come after yours." If you agree, you may be part of channel/market restriction. Channel/market restrictions occur when competitors agree to split up the market, one selling in one area and the other selling in another. Restriction may also be initiated by a customer who says, "I'll buy this product from you if you'll agree not to sell it to my competitors."

When you are selling to a distributor who will resell your products, the legality of certain actions is less clear-cut. For example, it may or may not be illegal for that distributor to ask you not to sell to another distributor. You will have to consult your lawyers for advice.

Nothing said so far implies that you cannot refuse to sell to a customer who has proved unsatisfactory to deal with. Such actions are usually viewed as a perogative of the selling company.

Exclusive dealing and tying arrangements are other channel/market restrictions. Both are specifically outlawed by the Clayton Act. You may not require a customer to buy only from you or not to buy a competitor's products (exclusive dealing), although the customer may make that decision independently. You may not force a customer to buy a product that is not wanted in order to get one that is wanted (tying arrangements).

Reciprocity may also be considered a channel/market restriction. It violates both the Sherman Act and the Federal Trade Commission Act. You may not suggest that the buyer will lose sales of a product (business machines, for example) to your company if the buyer does not buy your product (electronic parts, for example). Similarly, you cannot promise that your company will buy a product if the seller agrees to buy from you.

Other Illegal Practices. Other illegal practices include disparagement of competitors, harassment of competitors, and misrepresentation of your company's products and policies.

Disparagement. Disparagement is criticizing a competitor's product without proof that what you are saying is true. To avoid being charged with this practice, some companies go so far as to require that their salespeople not even mention competitors' products in their sales presentations.

Harassment. Harassment takes various forms. It occurs when a grocery products sales representative takes a competitor's products off the store's shelves or moves them to a less desirable location without the store manager's approval, lets the air out of a competitor's tires, and persuades friends to complain to the store manager about the quality of the competitor's products. Taken individually, these actions are unethical, but together they may be an unfair method of competition under the Federal Trade Commission Act.

Misrepresentation. Misrepresentation involves telling a lie or hiding the truth. It may be intentional or the result of oversight. In any event, it is illegal and to be avoided. The salesperson may be viewed as a legal agent for the company and, therefore, must be particularly careful about making commitments that the company does not intend to make. For example, promising a delivery date or guaranteeing the performance of a product may create a legal commitment for the selling company. Thus, knowing the company's policies and products is important not only for effective selling, but also for legal selling.

ETHICAL RESPONSIBILITIES

Although legal responsibilities may seem unclear, a salesperson's ethical responsibilities may be even more so. Sometimes unethical practices are also illegal, but sometimes they are not. Business firms and their salespeople must frequently decide what constitutes ethical behavior. This text can, however, suggest areas where behavior is often viewed as unethical.

Unethical Behavior

To discover what unethical behavior is, we must first consider what ethical behavior is. Dictionaries can help. A look at several of them produces phrases like the following for the word "ethics": "rules or standards of a group or profession"; "moral principles"; "actions based on conscience, or a sense of right and wrong"; and "codes of behavior." Thus we might say that *unethical behavior* for salespeople is behavior that violates the rules or standards of a firm or selling profession, or it is behavior that goes against one's conscience.

The concept is still difficult to grasp and apply. To help, we can look at an example drawn from the insurance industry, where most salespeople are ethical, but a few have become the focus of concern for industry leaders and legislators. An article in *Sales and Marketing Management** listed the following malpractices found in selling health insurance to the elderly:

1. Twisting—The agent persuades customers to cancel current policies and buy a new one when the new policy is not, considering costs and benefits, an improvement over the current policies, but the salesperson represents it to be.
2. Clean sheeting—The agent fails to report to the insurance company a customer's health problems. This makes it more likely that the company will issue the insurance policy and the agent will receive a commission but very unlikely that the company will pay a claim to the customer when it discovers hidden, previously-existing conditions.
3. Stacking—The agent sells the customer more coverage than can be afforded or more coverage than needed. The article reports one instance of a 76-year-old woman who had sixty insurance policies with annual premiums of $15,000.
4. Scare tactics—The agent suggests unreasonably that the customer buy immediately because the customer may not be able to qualify for insurance later. However, there can be an element of truth in a suggestion of future uninsurability, so such a suggestion may actually constitute proper advance warning.
5. Free checking—The customer is asked to make the check payable to the agent, who does not send it on to the company. Unknowingly, the customer may still be uninsured.
6. Pie-in-the-sky—The agent misrepresents the policy in some other way, for example, by promising higher than actual benefits, broader than actual coverage, or lower than actual costs.

Now, consider three general areas where salespeople have the opportunity to behave unethically: high-pressure selling, conflicts of interest, and confidential information.

High-Pressure Selling. This, unfortunately, is what many people think of when they think of effective selling technique. They view selling as high-pressure practices that manipulate individuals by playing on their fears and unrealistic desires, or practices that sell customers something they do not need or cannot afford. High-pressure selling (not to be confused with factual and persuasive selling) is as unnecessary as it is undesirable. Properly qualified prospects have the need for your product and the ability to buy it.

---

*Martin Everett, "The Dark Side of Insurance Sales," *Sales and Marketing Management* (February 5, 1979), pp. 25–29.

Conflicts of Interest. A conflict of interest exists when a salesperson must choose from two or more courses of action and the course of action that will benefit the salesperson most is not the one that will benefit the buyer most.

Bribes and kickbacks are conflicts of interest, and even the appearance of a bribe or kickback is to be avoided. Most companies suggest that accepting things of value is unethical except for low-cost gifts and entertainment (a country ham or an appointment book as a Christmas gift, a business dinner, or tickets to a World Series game) that are commonly found in the industry. The ethical dilemma usually occurs for most salespeople when they are trying to determine when a gift is too expensive or entertainment is too lavish. Timing is also an issue. A gift received just prior or subsequent to a sale seems suspicious. Similarly, most companies suggest that offering bribes or expensive gifts is equally unethical. (Bribes and kickbacks may, of course, be illegal as well.)

Confidential Information. Salespeople are often in situations which expose them to confidential information. They know about their firm's marketing plans before they are implemented. They may be told about or allowed to observe a customer's manufacturing process or see financial records of a company. They may be exposed to confidential information at trade association meetings, during calls on customers, when changing jobs, or even in an elevator. Because they also come in contact with individuals and firms who would like to have this information, salespeople may be asked to pass this information along. In an effort to maintain or raise the ethical standard throughout the industry, more and more companies are instructing their employees not to pass along such information.

Improving the Ethics of Salespeople

The pressure to be unethical grows when you or your company is not doing well. Then it may seem that personal or corporate survival takes precedence over ethics. For this reason, and because there will always be unethical persons in any profession, it is unlikely that unethical conduct can ever be eliminated. But unethical conduct can be reduced, and the solution starts with individuals who make or influence selling-related decisions or carry them out. Reduction has at least three stages: (1) increased sensitivity, (2) development and strengthening of a personal code of ethics, and (3) more responsive, responsible interactions with other members of the sales team, customers, and competitors.

Sensitivity. Increased sensitivity leads the way to heightened awareness of the ethical dilemmas facing salespeople. A salesperson seeking to be ethical should identify possible ethical dilemmas and consider in advance what actions are appropriate. Salespeople should seek out and be open to the opinions of others in these matters.

Codes of Ethics. In developing a code of ethics, the individual should consider not only what not to do, but also what actions should be taken. To accept responsibilities is a part of ethical conduct. You owe your company certain things (loyalty, hard work, and such) and your customers other things (honest advice, good service, and such), and if you fail to provide them, you have acted unethically.

A code of ethics may be informal; it need not be written down or framed on a wall. A code is necessary even if it is incomplete and a bit unclear. Difficulties will always exist when trying to be specific, but it should be possible, at least for the experienced salesperson, to develop guidelines for behavior by looking at many possible situations. Illustration 16–1 suggests some broad areas that might be used as a starting point for a code.

In order to judge ethical implications, it may be necessary to ask questions about any course of action. Your list of questions may be different, but those that follow are worth considering:

1. Would I want someone else to act this way toward me? (The Golden Rule)
2. What do I owe my company in this situation?
3. What do I owe my customers in this situation?
4. How would I explain my actions to someone else?
5. What are the long-run implications of this action?

Actions which pass the test implied by these questions are likely to be ethical. Those which do not pass the test are not ethical.

CODE OF ETHICS

As a sales representative I have an obligation to uphold the standards of my profession;

To always conduct myself in an acceptable professional manner;

To endeavor, to the best of my ability, to serve my employer's best interest;

To realize that it is not good business to recommend a product for a purpose for which it is not suitable;

To keep myself fully informed about the latest technology in my field;

To deal fairly with my customers and prospective customers;

To render service to my customers—to serve as I sell.

ILLUSTRATION 16-1. A typical code of ethics for a salesperson might include these items.

Responsive, Responsible Interactions. Salespeople don't have to stop with personal codes of ethics. They should work hard to see that their companies and industry have sound codes of ethics, too. When all salespeople act in an ethical manner, the temptation to be unethical is reduced.

SOCIAL RESPONSIBILITIES

Social responsibility is a controversial topic. It includes being legal and ethical, but it is often taken to mean something more—that salespeople will consider the impact of their actions not only in a narrow context (company, competitors, customers, themselves) but also in a broader context, a social context that considers the impact of the salesperson's actions on many elements in society.

In viewing a firm's social responsibility, some suggest that the social responsibility of a firm is to make a profit for its stockholders. Viewed in a similar manner, a salesperson's social responsibility would really be an economic one —to make sales, to hold down expenses, to sell products with good gross margins. Others suggest that the enlightened self-interest of firms and their employees, including salespeople, requires that they do what they can to consider the impact of their actions on the larger environment in which they work.

Thus, what constitutes socially responsible behavior and the reasons for being socially responsible may rest on pragmatic and more noble grounds. Pragmatically, acting in a socially responsible manner will likely minimize government intervention. More nobly, businesses and their representatives are powerful forces in society, and power implies responsibility. In either event, the salesperson can have much to say and do that will influence the way the company is perceived.

We can divide the possibilities for acting in a socially responsible manner into three categories: actions taken as a good company representative, actions taken as a good company citizen, and actions taken as a good community citizen.

The Company Representative Role

Here we include the responsibility to avoid the possibly unethical and illegal actions mentioned previously. We also include the salesperson's responsibility to use energy resources wisely; to avoid discrimination on the basis of sex, race, or age; and to build good public relations for the company.

The Company Citizen Role

As a salesperson, you must also take a look at your company's policies and practices. Those that are socially irresponsible should not be ignored if there is a chance to improve them. This does not mean that you should become a reformer to the detriment of fulfilling your selling responsibilities to the firm. But it does mean that you should use appropriate opportunities to raise the sensitivities of your colleagues, to question socially irresponsible policies, and to suggest ways to improve them, such as biodegradable packaging or encouraging the hiring of minorities as sales representatives.

The Community Citizen Role

Last, but certainly not least, is the role that the salesperson plays in community organizations, such as civic clubs, political groups, and community service organizations. Activity in these organizations may not be a requirement of the job, but this activity does affect the image others have of salespeople and the companies they represent.

SUMMARY

Salespeople must know what laws prohibit and require, but they are not expected to be lawyers. These laws include federal legislation and many state and local laws.

The Sherman Act outlawed monopolies and actions that restrain trade, including price-fixing. The Clayton Act clarified the Sherman Act, specifically restricting exclusive dealing and tying arrangements. The Federal Trade Commission Act outlawed unfair and deceptive practices and established the Federal Trade Commission. The Robinson-Patman Act prohibited price discrimination between buyers for products of like grade and quality. In addition, the Uniform Commercial Code and consumer protection legislation affect salespeople.

Applying these laws to specific actions is difficult, but it is possible to make some generalizations. A salesperson should avoid exchanging price information with competitors, avoid any indication of pricing to harm a competitor, be sure not to quote different prices to different customers unless there is a cost basis for the different prices, neither offer bribes nor accept kickbacks, be careful about deciding not to sell to certain customers, avoid any hint of requiring a customer to buy products the customer doesn't want to buy, make sure not to disparage or harass competitors, and never misrepresent his or her company's policies or products.

Although a salesperson's legal responsibilities may not be clear, ethical responsibilities are even more ambiguous. Unethical behavior for salespeople is behavior that violates the rules and standards of a firm, the selling profession, or one's own conscience.

One area of possibly unethical behavior is high-pressure selling, that is, manipulating people by playing on their fears and unrealistic desires. Conflict of interest exists when a salesperson must choose from two or more courses of action and the course that will benefit the salesperson the most is not the one that will benefit the buyer the most. Passing along confidential information is another behavior that may be viewed as unethical.

The pressure to behave unethically is greatest when personal or corporate survival is at stake. To reduce unethical practices, individual salespeople can increase their awareness of the ethical dilemmas they may face and consider in advance what actions would be appropriate. The salesperson should develop a code of ethics containing guidelines for behavior. The salesperson should work hard to see that the company and industry have solid codes of ethics, too.

Social responsibility is a controversial topic. Like a firm's social responsibility, a salesperson's social responsibility rests on both financial and environmental grounds. The possibilities for being socially responsible involve a salesperson in three roles: as a representative of the company, as a part of the company, and as a public-spirited citizen in the community.

REVIEW QUESTIONS

1. What should salespeople do if they are in doubt about the legality of a certain action?
2. What law is the oldest of the anti-trust laws?
3. How did the Clayton Act clarify the Sherman Act?
4. What law was passed to outlaw price discrimination?
5. How does the Uniform Commercial Code affect the salesperson?
6. How can a salesperson avoid charges of price-fixing?
7. What is predatory pricing?
8. List several circumstances in which different prices may be justified.
9. Define unethical behavior.
10. What steps can salespeople take to reduce unethical behavior?
11. List five questions that can be used to test whether a course of action is ethical.
12. What roles can a salesperson play in order to be socially responsible?

DISCUSSION QUESTIONS

1. Make a chart of the federal laws that affect salespeople, and identify the actions they restrict or prohibit.
2. If you were a member of your local government, what selling practices would you like to make illegal? Why? (Do not include practices that are already illegal.)
3. Would a code of ethics for an insurance sales agent be different from a code for a detailer or an industrial sales representative? Give reasons for your opinion.
4. What do you think are the social responsibilities of a salesperson?

CASE STUDY 16A

A manufacturer of electronics components (Elekco) was actively seeking a major order from a calculator manufacturer (Calco). Before submitting his bid, the Elekco sales manager sent one of his salespeople, Marshall Mason, to call on the purchasing agent at Calco to see whether he could find out some additional information that would help Elekco prepare the bid.

In the course of his conversation with the purchasing agent, Mason hoped to get some hint about what the other bids were. The purchasing agent wasn't very helpful, but she did indicate that all the other bids were in, pulled them out of the drawer where they were kept, and spread them out on the desk in front of her.

After this conversation, the purchasing agent excused herself and left the office, shutting the door behind her. Slowly it dawned on Mason that the purchasing agent meant for him to have an opportunity to look over the competing bids. He thought hard for a minute, then quickly leaned over the desk, looked at all the bids, and memorized the lowest one. After the purchasing agent returned, they talked about a number of trivial matters and then Mason returned to his office at Elekco.

Mason helped prepare the bid that was sent to Calco and was pleased to learn that Elekco received the order at a price just $150 below the next lowest bid.

1. What are the ethical issues involved in this situation?
2. If you were Mason and you truly believed that the purchasing agent intended for you to see the competing bids, what would you have done? Why?

CASE STUDY 16B

Elbert Hubbard was a classic salesperson at the end of the 19th century. In 1894, at the age of 35, he retired as a soap salesperson. He later became successful as a magazine publisher; a marketer of books, furniture, and other products; and a direct mail specialist. He was also a popular writer and lecturer.

Read Elbert Hubbard's business credo. Do you agree with his philosophy? If so, explain why. If not, explain why not, and indicate what changes you would make.

ELBERT HUBBARD'S BUSINESS CREDO

I believe in myself.

I believe in the goods I sell.

I believe in the firm for whom I work.

I believe in my colleagues and helpers.

I believe in American Business Methods.

I believe in producers, creators, manufacturers, distributors, and in all industrial workers of the world who have a job, and hold it down.

I believe that Truth is an asset.

I believe in good cheer and in good health, and I recognize the fact that the first requisite in success is not to achieve the dollar, but to confer a benefit, and that the reward will come automatically and usually as a matter of course.

I believe in sunshine, fresh air, spinach, applesauce, laughter, buttermilk, babies, bombazine and chiffon, always remembering that the greatest word in the English language is "Sufficiency."

I believe that when I make a sale, I make a friend.

And I believe that when I part with a man, I must do it in such a way that when he sees me again he will be glad—and so will I.

I believe in the hands that work, in the brains that think, and in the hearts that love.

Amen, and Amen.

—Excerpted from *Elbert Hubbard of East Aurora* by Felix Shay.
By permission of Wm. H. Wise & Co., Inc., publishers.

SPECIAL TYPES OF SELLING
part VI

Selling to Organizational Buyers

> **After studying this chapter you should be able to:**
>
> - Name and explain the features of organizational selling
> - Identify the nature of organizational buyers
> - Present a picture of what purchasing agents buy
> - Explain Value Analysis
> - Make suggestions about securing and opening organizational sales interviews
> - Contrast selling to a group with selling to an individual

Both products and services are sold to the organizational market. The product may be an entire plant, such as a factory or warehouse; heavy equipment, such as a loom or press; light equipment, such as typewriters or hand tools; raw materials, such as cotton or tobacco; processed materials, such as flour or steel; fabricating materials, such as batteries or packages; operating supplies, such as stationery or soap; and services, such as transportation or insurance. Typically, the products are used in the manufacture of other products or in the firm's operation. They differ from consumer products more in use and procedures for buying them than in physical features.

Organizational buyers of products and services are usually found in three groups: business firms, institutions, or governmental units. Wholesalers and retailers make two types of purchase. One is the purchase of merchandise for resale; the other is the purchase of operating supplies or light equipment, such as a cash register or a delivery truck. When wholesalers and retailers make this second type of purchase, they are considered to be organizational buyers.

FEATURES OF ORGANIZATIONAL BUYING AND SELLING

The first step toward an organizational buyer's purchase, as is true of all purchases, is the recognition of a need. For example, a firm may realize that it must replace obsolete machinery or expand its plant facilities. It is quite possible, however, that as many as one half of all organizational purchases fill needs that were unsuspected until salespeople pointed them out.

The next step in the procurement sequence is a tentative decision on the type of product to fill the need. Sometimes the buying firm will draft specifications for the product it has decided to buy. More often, though, the purchasing office will select several potential sources of supply and begin negotiations. The purchasing agent may even keep lists of approved suppliers for various products the firm buys.

Once the source of supply has been selected and negotiations completed, the buyer issues a purchase order and thus makes the transaction official. Next, the goods are received; inspected for correctness, quantity, and quality; and checked into inventory. When the seller's invoice has been checked and found in order, payment is authorized and made, and the transaction is completed.

Marketing Channels in Organizational Selling

In the marketing of organizational products, there is much direct selling from manufacturer to user. Sometimes the product involved must be tailored to a specific buyer's needs and is bought on the buyer's specifications, thus eliminating the need for any middleman. Sometimes the buyer needs technical advice which can come only from the manufacturer of the product, or sometimes a small manufacturer needs technical advice from a larger firm that will be using the product. The large amounts of money involved in many organizational transactions make direct selling most practical.

There is, of course, some indirect selling—used mainly when the product involved is low in price, standardized, and widely used by buyers who are small and geographically scattered. The middlemen may be merchant middlemen, such as industrial wholesalers and mill supply firms; or they may be agent middlemen, such as brokers, manufacturers' agents, and sales agents. Organizational middlemen operate only at the wholesale level.

Special Features of the Organizational Market

Like all salespeople, organizational salespeople must always convince the organizational buyer that the product will be suitable for the buyer's needs, that supply will be dependable, that service will be outstanding, and that price will be acceptable. Certain special features of the organizational market, though, make it different from other markets for products and services. Here are some of these special features which will be of particular interest to people in organizational selling:

1. The typical unit of sale in the organizational market is much larger both in dollars and in units than is the typical sale in the consumer market.
2. Organizational demand is derived, fluctuating, and often postponable; it is much influenced by the business cycle.

3. Unlike consumer markets, organizational markets ignore population distribution; they may be concentrated geographically and may consist of relatively few buyers.
4. Purchasing agents, in contrast to ultimate consumers, are trained, professional buyers. They indulge in little or no emotional buying because they are spending money which belongs to someone else.
5. Often the purchasing agent is not the only buying influence affecting purchasing decisions, and the identification of those other individuals can be a real challenge. Selling to a group can be quite different from selling to one individual.
6. Some prices in organizational selling are negotiated by the buyer and vendor together. Some orders go to the lowest bidder, and often a comparison of prices can be difficult.
7. Brand names play a lesser role in organizational buying than in consumer buying because of purchasing on specification and on the basis of performance.
8. Much time may elapse between a salesperson's first call on an organizational buyer and the first sale to that buyer. In some cases, the salesperson must first sell the buyer on a survey of the buyer's operations before purchasing recommendations can be made.

The Nature of the Organizational Salesperson's Job

The organizational salesperson's duties differ in several respects from those of most other salespeople, particularly those who sell merchandise to middlemen for resale and those who sell to ultimate consumers. It is common for a manufacturer of organizational products to have fewer salespeople than does a manufacturer of consumer products. Organizational salespeople make fewer calls per month than do consumer-goods salespeople, and each call is longer because they usually must see several people in each company contacted. Because these individuals are often located in different departments and on different management levels, great demands are made on the salesperson's ability in human relations. The organizational salesperson is responsible for fewer buyers or accounts than is the salesperson of consumer products, and few organizational salespeople are supported by the advertising and sales promotion campaigns that stand behind many other salespeople.

Organizational selling requires a high degree of creative selling, particularly when the salesperson must uncover a need or problem of which the buyer is unaware in order to sell a new product or the new use of an established product. The organizational salesperson must be a competent, honest consultant to purchasing agents. A great store of technical information about his or her own products or services and about the requirements of customers is also needed.

The salesperson needs accurate and complete information about products and how they can solve buyers' problems more profitably for both parties. Specific items of product data include: materials; specifications; manufacturing processes; sizes; designs, features; dangers; limitations; performance under different operating conditions; service or maintenance required; prices, credit terms, and discounts; contracts used; and policies of product specialization or diversification. The salesperson must be especially effective in making comparisons with other products the purchasing agent's firm may buy or even make. Such a comparison would certainly include prices, physical features, performance, vendor's reputation for quality, accompanying services, net cost, and value contributed.

Salespeople cannot know too much about their products because they never know just what questions will be asked by influential members of the purchasing agent's company. Salespeople must also have a great deal of information about their own company. In organizational buying, the nature of the vendor-company is an important factor in purchasing agents' buying decisions. Organizational salespeople should know the background of their company and its position in its industry. They need to be informed about company organization and about all company policies and procedures affecting them and the buyers they contact. Purchasing agents are also concerned about a vendor's previous performance, research activities, financial stability, capability to serve customers, and amount of service given to customers. Because the salesperson is the main contact purchasing agents have with their supplier companies, purchasing agents judge a salesperson's company to a considerable extent by the impression the salesperson makes.

THE NATURE OF ORGANIZATIONAL BUYERS

Organizational salespeople locate customers in several ways. Sometimes a buyer directs an inquiry about some specific product to that product's manufacturer or to its salesperson; the buyer's communication is occasionally nothing more than a description of a problem on which assistance is needed. Sometimes satisfied customers refer salespeople to prospects who later become customers, and often satisfied customers are good prospects for other products the salesperson handles. These sources, however, must be supplemented by what is probably the greatest customer-producing activity of all: the discovery by a salesperson of a need, a problem, or a use for which the product represented can be successfully recommended.

Buyer Information Needed

Organizational salespeople are under pressure to know as much as they possibly can about the operations of their prospect's company. They benefit from knowing what goals that company seeks to attain and what plans and problems are involved in reaching them. Because the product that they sell must contribute to or sometimes become a part of what the purchasing agent's firm sells, they must acquaint themselves with a prospect company's marketing efforts as well as with its production efforts.

Salespeople need to know the size of a prospect's company, its financial standing, and the location of its plants and buying offices. Knowledge of purchasing policies, procedures, and personnel is also valuable: how the company buys, who does the buying, who influences the buying, when and where key people can be seen, and what their backgrounds are. Prerequisite to making a sale is learning what the prospect currently does about the problem which the salesperson's product can solve; this concerns what the buyer thinks about the salesperson's particular product and competing products.

What sources of buyer information are useful to organizational salespeople? A study of the buyer's end product—done perhaps by the research staff of the salesperson's company—can be revealing, especially to sellers of raw materials and fabricating parts. If retailers handle that end product, their opinions can be helpful, and advertising for the end product can also supply useful information. Sometimes firms related in some way to the buying company can contribute to the organizational salesperson's information about a buyer; so can noncompeting salespeople.

A particular problem is caused by the presence of a need in the buyer's company that is unrecognized by the buyer, or a need existing in a department not visited by the salesperson. This suggests that the salesperson would benefit from a tour of the buyer's facilities. Talks with production personnel might reveal an impending product or plant change, production improvements needed, or troublesome problems. By examining, listening, and questioning, salespeople can often identify specific requirements which might lead to sales.

Buying Influences

Buying influences are those people in the buying firm whose attitudes carry some weight in the firm's buying decisions. These buying influences range from users and operators all the way through top management. The participation of top management in buying decisions is most common as the size of a contemplated purchase increases and as the size of the buying firm decreases. Supervisors are between users and top management, as are the operating managers in production, research, and engineering departments. The purchasing agent usually issues the purchase orders and has great authority in the purchase of some items but less in the case of others. In a real sense, the sales manager in the purchasing agent's company has much to say about what quality to buy because price usually reflects quality, and cost to the buyer must be recovered when the end product is sold. Thus, organizational salespeople selling a fabricating part may quickly find themselves selling sales managers on incorporating their products into what the sales managers sell.

A salesperson of plastics would want the approval of people in design, research, purchasing, production, and sales; the blessing of some members of top management might also be needed. What about a salesperson selling a new packaging material? The product development, sales, advertising, production, purchasing, legal, and customer service departments are all involved. One selling roofing, flooring, or plumbing faces the same complex pattern. Architects, owners, builders, engineers, specification writers, designers, and drafters must be convinced.

In each of their prospect companies, organizational salespeople need to know the names and titles of the buying influences who can help or hurt their cause, and this can be quite a challenge. The responses to business-paper advertising help to identify some unsuspected prospects and even to identify some unknown buying influences. Sometimes, perhaps after a salesperson has offered some very technical information to a purchasing agent or has asked a highly technical question, the purchasing agent refers the salesperson to some of the firm's technical personnel who are buying influences. When in doubt, the salesperson can simply ask the purchasing agent or even the receptionist for the names of individuals who would be interested or involved in a certain purchase. A complication, of course, stems from the fact that a job title—plant engineer, for example—does not mean the same thing from company to company. In fact, a person's name and title constitute minimal information. Actually, the salesperson would like to know the interests and motives of each buying influence and how best to cultivate them.

Another difficulty is caused by the continuous changing which takes place among the buying influences within each company. People are promoted and transferred; their titles and duties change; they join other firms; they retire; they die. It is quite possible that fewer than 50 percent of key buying influences stay put throughout one year.

In many companies and for certain products, the purchasing agent is not the most powerful buying influence; instead, that individual is a higher executive. In such circumstances, the purchasing agent would probably be most active early in the buying process and then at the end when a purchase order is to be issued. If a salesperson must sell three buying influences in a company and if, in that same company, two thirds of all buying influences seldom or never see salespeople (and these assumptions are realistic), then we understand why some salespeople feel they have done a very good job if they get in touch with one third of the buying influences in the organizations they visit.

Sometimes a team, a buying group, or a committee is set up to make a large purchase. Getting in touch with each member is not easy, especially if all members are not in the same locality. Another group not easy to see consists of the operating and technical advisers. Typically, the organizational salesperson does not know them because he or she does not see them.

Most writing on the subject of organizational procurement pictures purchasing agents as buying quality, service, and price—generally in that order. Each of these topics will now be briefly discussed.

Quality. Unless a product is correct for the use to which the buyer will put it, it should not be purchased. In this sense, quality refers to technical suitability. Just as a superior tool can do a better job in the production process, a superior package can increase the dealer and consumer acceptance of a brand. Evaluation of quality also involves the salesperson and the salesperson's company. For example, the purchasing agent wants to deal with reputable salespeople and companies that are financially responsible.

Service. Just as they must buy satisfactory products from vendors, purchasing agents must buy satisfactory service. Suppose that a particular transaction involves the purchase of heavy equipment. Prepurchase service could start with a survey of the buyer's needs. Survey findings would then be studied and, after thorough analysis, become the basis for a report and recommendations which constitute a purchasing proposal. If a purchase results, postpurchase service might consist of installation of the equipment and then lead to the training of those employees who will be using or operating the equipment. Other postsale activities could include maintenance and repairs.

Another feature of service that purchasing agents buy is dependability of supply. Organizational buyers must be able to count on a vendor's delivering exactly what was ordered when it is scheduled to be delivered. Buyers also welcome services which help them sell their finished products. Service of this sort is especially appropriate when the seller's product is an identifiable part of the buyer's end product.

Price. Obviously, the firm buying a salesperson's product or service is in business to sell some other product or service at a profit; and the price charged for that product or service influences the dollar volume of sales and the gross margin. Certainly, purchasing agents want to buy at low prices—at the lowest prices, under most circumstances. The qualification "under most circumstances" must be included because a purchasing agent can be too powerful in prevailing upon sellers to cut their prices. A purchasing agent who pressures a supplier to cut price to a point where the supplier loses money on the sale almost forces the supplier to skimp on the quality of the product in the hope of breaking even. The purchasing agent may also force the supplier to quit selling to him and this means a new source of supply will have to be found.

An organizational salesperson must be extremely effective in getting buyers to see that quoted prices are meaningless apart from other considerations, such as suitability of the product, quality of the product, service, and nature of buyer-vendor relations. In attempting this, many salespeople shift the buyer's attention from price and focus it on long-run cost, including such considerations as cost of storing, cost of handling, cost of rejections, and cost of use.

Other Considerations. In addition to quality, service, and price, purchasing agents have other interests in mind when they evaluate a particular product. One is the total cost to their companies of each alternative purchase. Flexibility in buying is another important factor, as are delivery dates and delivery methods. Most purchasing agents watch closely what competitors are buying and are sometimes apt to follow their lead. The sales manager and staff want whatever makes the product or service more marketable and superior to competitors' offerings. Engineers want the purchasing agent to buy high quality so that high quality can be built into their end products. In striving both for increased production and for less costly production, the production manager tries to reduce time, labor, stores, space, machine downtime, and rejections of finished products.

What Buyers Demand of Organizational Salespeople

Buyers make certain demands of organizational salespeople, and some of the more important aspects of their demands will now be discussed.

Thorough Product Knowledge. Purchasing agents obtain much of their product knowledge from salespeople. Quite naturally, they come to depend on all salespeople to a degree and on some salespeople most heavily as sources of information about new products, improved products, and new uses for established products. The purchasing agent's main interest, of course, is in receiving the greatest product benefits. In this way, organizational salespeople function as product consultants and experts, supplying accurate, helpful product information. Because they know a product's limitations and its merits, they can make recommendations with confidence. If the salesperson delivers enough product information, the purchasing agent will be able to explain and defend purchases should this become necessary.

Outside Ideas. Because of their many diverse contacts, organizational salespeople can and should bring ideas to purchasing agents and report to them on changing conditions and new developments outside their firms. Salespeople can describe what is going on within their own companies, in companies which compete with their firms, and in retail stores if the end product of the purchasing agent's company is sold by retailers. They can even report on what the purchasing agent's competitors are doing, provided they do not reveal anything told to them in confidence.

Ideas from the outside may pertain to economic conditions, pricing practices, trends within the industry of which the purchasing agent's company is a part, and even business trends in that company's market. It would not be improper for an outstanding salesperson to recommend new markets for the products made by the purchasing agent's firm or even to recommend new products that the firm might consider producing.

Assistance on Problems. The problem on which a salesperson works most quickly and with the greatest concern is a problem the customer has in using the product, but purchasing agents also welcome help on other problems. These problems include those which the purchasing agent may not recognize. The salesperson who is interested in buyers' problems, who acquires an intelligent understanding of them, and who takes the initiative in hunting for better solutions is particularly appreciated. Such a salesperson is always looking for cost-cutting steps that purchasing agents can take, and is always alert to see that customers receive all the service to which they are entitled. For example, the conscientious salesperson following up a customer's order involving a series of deliveries would make sure that exactly what was ordered was delivered on schedule.

Considerate Treatment. Purchasing agents expect organizational salespeople to be thoughtful, proper, and understanding. Because they must budget their time carefully, they do not have time to listen to idle chatter and cannot treat themselves or salespeople to much general conversation at the beginning or end of sales interviews. They want salespeople to become informed about the needs, personnel, procedures, and concerns of their company. Ideally, from the purchasing agent's point of view, no salesperson would call without some specific bit of helpful information.

Salespeople must keep confidential any information acquired about the classified activities of competing companies. They must also understand that most purchasing agents do not want to become obligated to salespeople by accepting substantial gifts, lavish entertainment, or expensive favors.

Most purchasing agents expect salespeople to get in touch first with purchasing office personnel. Contacts with other production and engineering personnel can then be made through the purchasing agent, who should, of course, be kept informed of calls made on other people in the company.

VALUE ANALYSIS

Value Analysis, pioneered by the General Electric Company, is a problem solving technique for reducing unnecessary costs without decreasing a product's usefulness, appeal, or sales. Value Analysis (VA) is a systematic analysis and evaluation of products and their component parts to see if changes in design, materials, or construction will reduce the cost but not the performance of a product. Basic assumptions of VA are (1) a high-priced product *may* be the best value and (2) a low-priced product *may not* be the best value.

VA is done by a team usually headed and coordinated by the purchasing agent, who frequently must sell the idea of VA to people in other departments.

Other members of the team may include the executives heading engineering, research and development, production, and sales.

If the firm is to maintain and even increase a product's utility while decreasing its selling price, it must ask questions, accumulate existing information, brainstorm for worthwhile ideas, settle on one course of action, execute that program, then evaluate the results. Sample questions are (1) Just what jobs does this product and each of its component parts do; does it have any unneeded features? (2) Can we combine several parts into one and, in this way, reduce assembly cost? (3) Which special component parts now specified can be replaced with standard parts? (4) Should we switch from making a part to buying it—or vice versa?

Most organizational salespeople must understand the basics of Value Analysis and be able to deal with purchasing agents who use it. Such buyers are always asking salespeople how costs can be reduced—and expecting salespeople to have suggestions. When creative, imaginative salespeople build into their presentations helpful answers to VA questions, the rewards can be great.

SECURING AND OPENING ORGANIZATIONAL SALES INTERVIEWS

Most purchasing agents are readily accessible to those salespeople who deserve to see them. It is not uncommon for a purchasing agent to contact two or three salespeople when searching for a source of supply for a soon-to-be-made purchase. Many organizational selling calls are made on an appointment basis. Both letters and telephone calls are used to make appointments; the letters can be sent by the salesperson or by the salesperson's company. Sometimes a salesperson can schedule the next call when leaving an interview, and sometimes appointments can be arranged at trade shows. Appointments are particularly appropriate if the salesperson's presentation is long, if he or she calls on others in the purchasing agent's company, or if the purchasing agent involved prefers interviews by appointment.

Unless the salesperson and the purchasing agent have known each other for some time, the salesperson should open the interview with personal and company identification. The salesperson should do this in successive calls on the same purchasing agent, remembering that that individual may have seen scores of salespeople since last seeing this one. From that point, the organizational salesperson conducts the interview in a fashion similar to that of any other salesperson. When the salesperson knows that the buyer is not ready to buy, the interview may be opened with information helpful to the buyer or with questioning which the salesperson intends to develop in a way that will benefit the agent and the agent's company.

Frequently, the first call an organizational salesperson makes on a prospective customer is not opened by an attempt to sell a product. Instead, the objective is to sell the buyer on giving the salesperson permission to make a survey of the buyer's circumstances. A life insurance salesperson might offer to examine the policies held by a company; a cash register salesperson might offer to study how cash sales, credit sales, payments on accounts receivable, and payouts are now being handled in a retail store. Usually the survey is free and does not obligate the prospective customer; occasionally the buyer will help defray the costs of the survey.

The purpose of the survey is to obtain current, correct, and complete information about the buyer. Salespeople must be particularly alert to spot any problem for which their products or services will be solutions. They want to determine whether buyers can make advantageous use of their products and, if so, exactly how the buyers can use the products. While the survey is being made, the salesperson may draw on the personnel and facilities from his or her own company, particularly if the survey is extensive and quite technical. In addition, the salesperson usually works with people other than purchasing personnel in the buyer's organization because their participation in the survey may be mandatory.

Once the survey has been completed, its findings are analyzed and then interpreted. If the buyer has no problem requiring action, there is no second step in that particular instance. Most of the time, survey findings constitute a sound foundation for a sales presentation. By knowing how things stand, the salesperson can make an effective comparison between present conditions and better conditions which will exist once the buyer has followed the salesperson's recommendations. The next step, then, is selling the proposal to the buyer.

SELLING TO A GROUP

Many organizational sales presentations are made to groups of individuals who constitute a buying committee. Most sales presentations to a group start with the salesperson's making the presentation to one person, a presentation which has as its purpose getting the one person to approve and schedule a meeting between the salesperson and the group. In some ways, the group behaves as a unit; at the same time, each member is an individual buying influence. A four-member group might consist of the vice-president for production, the general superintendent, the general supervisor, and the purchasing agent. Presentations to groups are made in various places. Perhaps most are made in a conference room in the buyer's quarters, but sometimes the seller designs and equips a vehicle to accommodate the buying influences and provide for product displays and demonstrations.

General Suggestions for Group Selling

Let us examine how a typical organizational salesperson might go about the task of selling to a buying group. Before meeting with the group, the salesperson is quite busy. The salesperson would like to do a preapproach on each member of the group to determine needs, preferences, prejudices, plans, and interests. The salesperson would like to discover what each member likes and dislikes about this product and competing products. If there is one person who is clearly a leader, and this is typical of most groups, the salesperson may be wise to try to see that person before the group meets in the hopes of making an ally ahead of time.

The salesperson then goes about constructing the presentation. As the sales story is drafted, advantages and proof are stressed and backed up with appropriate visual aids. Organizational salespeople have found the following visual aids to be particularly effective: samples, models, sketches, slides, photographs, movies, testimonials, advertisements, and performance records. Thorough rehearsal of the sales story and the use of visual aids is strongly recommended.

The final plan can then be drawn. The salesperson knows what will be needed in a physical way and assembles these items. The salesperson lists the questions and the most probable objections, with answers for each, and sets up in order the steps or phases of the presentation. Finally, each step or phase of the presentation is clocked and a timetable is established.

Once the presentation starts, the well-rehearsed salesperson should maintain almost continuous eye contact with the group, watching facial expressions and movements in order to sense reactions. If at all practicable, the salesperson will encourage members of the group to interrupt with comments and questions, once again alert to how developments are going. Seldom, however, will the salesperson ask for agreement as when selling to an individual. Nor will one advantage be stressed so much that benefits are not fully explained, because the various buying influences comprising the group have different interests and operate under different pressures. Benefits should be presented in a thorough manner.

During the presentation, the organizational salesperson has a difficult job in respect to the leader of the group. The salesperson wants to win the leader, but at the same time, no other member of the group should be given cause to feel slighted. The salesperson hopes to appear impartial even though referring and deferring more to the leader than to any other one member. Perhaps it is wise for the salesperson to remember that the leader can be influenced—even won over—by the rest of the group.

When responding to member A's question, comment, or objection, the salesperson must answer in a manner which includes members B, C, D, and E, too. This helps all members feel that they had a part in shaping the ultimate decision. The salesperson tries to avoid arguments, including arguments among members of the buying group as well as between the salesperson and one of the group. Control of the session may be more easily maintained if a top official of the prospect company shares the stage with the salesperson. In some situations the salesperson will want to arrange for the members of the group to talk among themselves privately. If literature or other printed material is to be distributed, this is best done after the salesperson has made the presentation and just before the question-and-answer period, if one has been scheduled.

Problems in Group Selling

When the buying group is made up of persons from different levels of management, the salesperson faces the problem of communicating with individuals who differ in background, training, personality, and goals. Each member has a motivation pattern, which may differ from the others. A complete sales story is probably the best solution to this problem.

Another problem, as has been mentioned, is that of identifying the leader of the group. The leader may be the oldest person, the one with the most impressive title, the one who asks the best questions, the one with the most definite ideas, or the last person to join the group. Sometimes the salesperson must simply try to sense who the leader is; the leader is not always the most vocal, the most active, or the most prominent person.

Should the organizational salesperson selling to a group bring in one or more people to help make the presentation? Sometimes there is no choice: a demonstration may require more than one person, or sometimes the buying group requests the presence of an additional person. A two-person selling team has certain merit. Salesperson A can interrupt Salesperson B, ask questions, or take over occasionally. One salesperson can take notes or just observe the group while the other is making the presentation. Of course, the selling team ought not be so large that it appears to overwhelm the buying group.

Questions directed to the salesperson before the scheduled question-and-answer period pose another problem. Premature questions should be discouraged, and any treatment of them should be brief. Closing, too, can be awkward. Seldom can it be attempted at the end of the presentation as it normally is in selling to one person. Seldom is it practical to ask an entire buying group for the order.

Team Selling

Team selling is one result of buying groups or teams, each member of which has particular interests and asks special questions. Specialization and projects have both been growing. The vast size and great complexity of some projects and contemplated purchases involve several specialized departments within the firm. Such projects and purchases are too big for one salesperson to undertake, too broad for one salesperson to master, too varied for one department to handle.

The captain of a selling team is an executive salesperson or sales engineer who coordinates the team. The team may include technical specialists from marketing, production, purchasing, finance, and accounting. Frequently, if there is a production specialist on a buying team, that person is matched by a production specialist from the selling firm, and so on. The captain serves as a communication channel between the buying and selling teams. This person designs the selling effort and directs the presentation.

The selling team permits the seller to make a strong selling effort. The prospect gets a great amount of information about the aspects of the seller's proposal from a group of experienced specialists. Analyses, solutions, and recommendations are sound, being made by a balanced team of experts.

SUMMARY

Both products and services are sold to the organizational market. Organizational markets are made up of business firms, institutions, and governmental units. Organizational buyers purchase goods for use in operations.

The first step in an organizational purchase is the recognition of a need. Next, a tentative product decision is made. Once the source of supply has been selected and negotiations have been completed, the buyer issues a purchase order, and thus makes the transaction official.

There is much direct selling from manufacturer to user. Tailored products, a need for technical assistance, and large investments make this necessary. Other special features of organizational markets include fluctuating demand and selling to trained purchasing agents.

Organizational selling differs from other selling in the following ways: (1) manufacturers of organizational products usually have smaller sales staffs; (2) their salespeople make fewer calls; (3) the calls of organizational salespeople are longer; (4) much creativity is necessary in organizational selling, and (5) the information requirements in organizational selling are greater.

Buying influences are those people in the buying firm whose attitudes carry some weight in the firm's buying decisions. Top management's involvement increases as the size of the purchase increases and the size of the buying firm decreases. Supervisors, operating managers, and sales managers are other examples of buying influences. Salespeople need to know who the relevant buying influences are and should speak with as many as possible.

Purchasing agents buy quality, service, and price. They strive to maximize these three criteria as well as flexibility and productivity. They demand thorough product knowledge, outside ideas, assistance on problems, and considerate treatment.

Value Analysis is a problem solving techique for reducing unnecessary costs without decreasing a product's usefulness, appeal, or sales. It is a systematic analysis and evaluation done by a team.

Most purchasing agents are accessible to deserving salespeople. Appointments are used frequently. Often, survey findings serve as a foundation for a sales presentation.

Many organizational sales presentations are made to groups of individuals who constitute a buying committee. Perhaps most presentations are made in a conference room at the buyer's quarters, but sometimes the seller designs and equips a vehicle to accommodate the buying influences and provide for product displays and demonstrations.

While the salesperson should give special attention to the group leader, no other member of the group should be given cause to feel slighted. Because each member of the group has a different background, training, personality, and goals, a complete sales story is needed.

Specialization sometimes is necessary when projects become quite complicated, and team selling is an answer to the need for specialization. The team usually consists of an executive salesperson and technical specialists to form a balanced team of experts.

REVIEW QUESTIONS

1. What groups make up organizational buyers?
2. Why is there direct selling to organizational buyers?
3. List three special features of organizational buyers.
4. How do the duties of an organizational salesperson differ from those of most other salespeople?
5. What kinds of information should organizational salespeople have?
6. What is a buying influence?
7. What is Value Analysis?
8. What are some difficulties often encountered with selling to groups?
9. When is team selling likely to be necessary?
10. What are some advantages of team selling?

DISCUSSION QUESTIONS

1. Are the interpersonal skill requirements higher for a salesperson selling to a group than are the requirements of one selling to a single buyer?
2. Why must organizational salespeople be expert problem solvers?
3. React to the following statement: "Because organizational demand is derived and postponable and there may be hidden buying influences, the organizational salesperson has less control of the factors that lead to sales than does a salesperson selling to wholesalers or retailers."
4. Assume that you are an organizational salesperson selling cardboard cartons to a large printing firm. What information should you research before making your first sales call, and what information would you gather in the first sales interview?

CASE STUDY 17A

Sandy Craig is talking with his sales supervisor about a problem that seems to be occurring more and more often.

Supervisor: I hear that you lost some new business with Armorseal this month. Aren't they good customers of yours?

Salesperson: You're right. Armorseal *is* a good customer of mine, or at least I thought it was. It opened up a new department that would be

	needing about $600 worth of lubricants each month, and I really thought I had a super chance of getting the business. Three other departments there already buy their lubricants from me.
Supervisor:	Well, what happened?
Salesperson:	As you know they used to have two supply sources, including us, but now they've added a third supplier and they seem to want to spread their business among the three of us. Since they were satisfied with the lubricants they were getting from us, they decided not to cut back on their current purchases from us. Instead they're planning to fill most of their new needs by buying from this new supplier.
Supervisor:	Didn't you point out the quality and price of our lubricants and the good service you've been providing them?
Salesperson:	Certainly. I've even stepped up my calls there to once a week so they're getting more attention than ever before. But the purchasing agent said that it wasn't a question of *our* performance at all. Because their company was growing they thought it wise to protect themselves by buying from more sources. And he said I should be happy with the current orders I'm getting.
Supervisor:	Are you?
Salesperson:	Of course not! And I said to him in the long run I hoped his choice would be governed by the best quality and service he could get, since this would be far better protection than several sources just for the sake of having them.
Supervisor:	Is this happening with any of your other customers?
Salesperson:	Unfortunately, it is. The bigger they get the more likely they seem to be to want to spread their orders around. That's why I wanted to talk to you. What can I do when purchasing agents have this kind of attitude?

1. As Craig's supervisor, how would you answer him?
2. What types of customer might create this kind of problem for a salesperson?

CASE STUDY 17B

XYZ Company is a conglomerate with three major divisions, each with its own purchasing manager. Division X has been, over the years, the most successful division in the company. It is the dominant producer in its industry, but its sales are increasing at a slow rate because industry growth is slow. The products produced by this division are fairly old and the technology to produce them is well-known, making price an important selling point. Division X fights hard to maintain its share of the market.

Division Y has a small share of a large, stable market. Its share has been declining recently, and the management of XYZ is known to be considering selling the division.

Division Z has a small but growing share of a rapidly growing market. XYZ is investing substantial sums of money to increase the sales of Division Z. Equipment and employees are being added. XYZ is pinning its hopes for the future on this division.

Suppose you are an industrial sales representative with the opportunity to sell products to all three of these divisions.

1. Which do you suppose would be the best prospect? Why? What additional information would be useful in helping you decide?
2. What are the motives that the managers of each of these divisions would probably have? How can you appeal to these motives in your sales presentations?

Chapter

Selling to Ultimate Consumers

18

After studying this chapter you should be able to:

- List the duties and responsibilities of retail salespeople
- Classify and comment on the information retail salespeople need
- Trace the steps in retail selling
- Compare trading up, substitute selling, and suggestion selling
- Make suggestions about postsale behavior
- Show how retail salespeople can build sound customer relationships

Although the fundamentals of selling are universal, the job of selling in retail stores differs from other kinds of selling in several respects. In retail selling, potential buyers come to the salesperson. These buyers are thus physically, financially, and emotionally closer to buying than are most of the buyers contacted by other kinds of salespeople. Buyer attention and buyer interest in some type of merchandise are strong enough to have stimulated the visit to a particular store. Even though retail customers are not usually so well-informed as the buyers whom organizational salespeople visit, they generally know something about the store they choose to visit, about the merchandise they are seeking, and perhaps even about the salespeople themselves.

The retail salesperson is typically responsible for selling many more different products than is the organizational salesperson. The number of buyers encountered is also considerably greater. Yet, the retail salesperson does not have the organizational salesperson's range of choices of when, where, and to whom to sell. Another difference between retail and organizational selling is that retail salespeople do little prospecting for customers. Their stores' advertising, displays, and reputations perform this function of drawing people into the stores.

The ultimate consumer is obviously the person most dependent on the retail salesperson. The retailer is dependent to a great degree on that same salesperson. Customers judge a store largely by its sales staff, and the customer who makes a purchase is really buying a package comprised of product, salesperson, retailer, and manufacturer. Finally, wholesalers, manufacturers, and facilitating firms are quite dependent upon retailers' sales forces. Most of their merchandising efforts mean little unless retail salespeople succeed in their selling efforts.

DUTIES OF RETAIL SALESPEOPLE

Retail salespeople have three principal types of duty or responsibility. The most important, obviously, is the duty to sell. Salespeople sell merchandise to the mutual benefit of the customer and the store, write up sales slips, wrap merchandise, operate cash registers, and make change. Satisfactory performance in this area depends on the salesperson's knowledge of the merchandise, customers, the techniques of selling to those customers, and store procedures.

Retail salespeople have various nonselling duties. Some receive and mark incoming merchandise and participate in taking inventory. Most are responsible for getting their departments ready for the selling day and closing them at closing time. They make sure their department stock is adequate and neat. Some build counter, floor, or window displays. A few compare merchandise in competing stores. Senior salespeople may act as sponsors and instructors for new employees. Other nonselling duties involve customer service, which often includes giving merchandise instructions to the buyer, helping the customer when a purchased item needs servicing, handling customer complaints, handling merchandise exchanges or returns, and giving directions to customers within the store.

Finally, salespeople have certain responsibilities to their employers. They should think and plan how to make a maximum contribution to the store's profitable operation; determine to minimize mistakes, waste, and expenses; make constructive suggestions to store management; and reflect to customers a loyalty to and a pride in the store.

THE SALES PERSONALITY

Retail employers and their customers unite in expecting store salespeople to exercise good manners. Practically all the research studies made in the field of customer-salesperson relations point up the demand for courtesy. Customers in retail stores prefer salespeople who take a genuine, understanding interest in them. Buyers want the salesperson to become their ally immediately. They expect a sincere desire to help to be present in the way they are served by the salesperson. Buyers insist that all claims and recommendations made to them be honest and sincere. If they are not, customers will take their business elsewhere, and the retailer as well as the customer knows this. So the retailer wants salespeople to show real interest in their customers and to guide those customers to the best purchases possible. Otherwise, patronage is lost, and it can be lost for an immediate gain to the store that is pitifully small.

Finally, customers expect salespeople to have competence in their analyzing and recommending. This competence rests on the correct diagnosing of

Here is a retail job specification from one of the country's best-known and most respected department stores.

Division: Apparel.

Job Title: Sales—Women's and Misses' Dresses.

Duties: (A) Sales—Sell dresses through intelligent use of size, style, and fashion information; must explain washability, cleaning requirements, advantages through certain design features which tend to enhance the customer's figure; meet objections to certain competitive stores' claims and price advertisements; be familiar with sizing by manufacturer so as to provide merchandise which will fit well with a minimum of alteration. Try to be certain when selling merchandise that the item is one that will not be returned because of a hasty decision, that the item is tried on so that the customer will have an opportunity of seeing as well as feeling the fit and style advantages.

(B) Stock—Fill in sizes as required, help keep section stock in order by replacing in proper racks and in correct size sequence items which have been shown but not sold. Assist in maintaining section orderliness, straightening chairs, picking up hangers, etc.

Previous Experience Requirements: At least six months dress or similar selling experience.

Educational Requirements: High school minimum.

Working Hours: Regular store hours of 40 hours a week.

Overtime: None except for 48-hour weeks, 4 weeks a year.

Physical Demands: Standing, walking (to fitting rooms, stockrooms) with the usual seasonal rush pressures.

Machines and Equipment: Cash registers.

Method of Compensation: Straight commission with guaranteed minimum.

ILLUSTRATION 18-1. By being qualified and competent, a salesperson avoids being classed with the lowest classification of sales personnel, the order-takers, who do no more than make change and wrap merchandise.

customer wants and then the proper prescribing for them. By being qualified and competent, a salesperson avoids being classed with the lowest classification of sales personnel, the order-takers, who do no more than make change and wrap merchandise.

INFORMATION NEEDED BY RETAIL SALESPEOPLE

To be considered competent as a merchandise advisor, a retail salesperson must be informed about certain aspects of the store, merchandise, and the kinds of customers that may be encountered.

Store Information

The most important information a salesperson needs about the store relates to *policies* and procedures of the store. One of the more significant policies concerns the *merchandise* the store stocks. The salesperson needs to know what types of products are carried by the store, in what price ranges, and of what general quality.

A second basic policy involves the *services* the store makes available to its customers. For each service there is a small but essential fund of facts without which the salesperson cannot function satisfactorily. For example, the store will or will not make credit sales; in either event, the salesperson will need to be able to explain the policy and, in certain cases, to justify it. Delivery is another service that is or is not offered. Its frequency and its cost to customers, if any, are necessary information to the sales staff. A third service is that of adjustments, and here the salesperson must know what the store does about refunds, exchanges, returns, and complaints. A fourth service, quite important in stores selling appliances, can be termed product service. As an example, a store selling washers and television sets must have policies about installation, repairs, service calls, and guarantees.

A store's *promotion* is a third vital policy about which the salesperson must know. Retailers, like other sellers, combine the basic marketing forces of personal selling, advertising, and sales promotion into what they believe to be the most profitable combination. Selling employees must have some conception of the relationships among these three factors. In regard to more immediate concerns, the salesperson should always keep informed about what items are currently being promoted and with what forms of promotion.

The second area of necessary information for a salesperson is *procedures* or store system, sometimes referred to as the mechanics of selling. Knowledge of merchandise location within the store is a basic element here. Another essential element is knowing how to make a charge sale, a task which calls for credit clearing and the writing of a sales ticket. For cash sales, the salesperson must be able to operate the cash register and to make change. Finally, some salespeople in stores must be able to wrap a neat, safe package.

Merchandise Information

Customers expect the sales staff of a retail store to know the merchandise the store carries. Nothing seems more natural than to look to the salesperson for answers to product questions. Most buyers are willing—even eager—to become better informed about merchandise. Many buyers go even further than that when making certain purchases, asking a salesperson for personal views, preferences, or convictions. In instances such as this, the buyer is assuming that the salesperson is an authority on merchandise.

What does the retail salesperson need to know about the merchandise? Specific product facts include the identity of the manufacturer, composition of each product, construction, finish, style, price, size, color, and model. The salesperson should also know what the product is used for, how it should be used or operated, its performance and its limitations, the care it requires, and the services—if any—available with its purchase. It is particularly important that the salesperson be able to compare a given product with its closest competitors and to highlight its various points of superiority. While the general rule is that the amount of product information needed increases as price rises, retailers hope that each salesperson will know one or more influential facts about as many of the products as possible.

Several productive sources of merchandise information are available to most retail salespeople. Many product facts can be found on the product's label, and the package can be as informative to those who sell the item as it is to those who buy. Some kinds of products—such as food, clothing, and beverages—can be tried under conditions of everyday use. All products can be carefully examined by the salesperson. Salespeople representing manufacturers and wholesalers who sell to the store can be valuable sources of information, as can their product literature, visual aids, and any plant tours made available by manufacturers. Advertising is another source of product information—the manufacturer's advertisements, those of competing manufacturers, those of competing retailers, and those of the salesperson's store. The individuals with whom the salesperson deals are still another source. One group, prospects, can tell why they do not use the product; the other group, users, can tell why they do use it. A final major source is the buying personnel of the store. They can make available to the selling staff valuable product information such as merchandise manuals, product specifications, and results obtained from testing bureaus.

Customer Information

The sales forces in retail stores do not have much of a prospecting job to do; their stores do the job for them. Advertising is one of the forces used by stores to attract buyers. The store's windows issue another invitation; they entice sidewalk traffic into becoming aisle traffic. Inside some stores are customer services or facilities such as telephones, post offices, and lounges. These bring individuals into the store, and some of those individuals become shoppers and customers. A few stores that can be termed prestige stores are found in most large markets. They are so widely and favorably known that they pull buyers in because of their reputations. Finally, some stores are adroit at obtaining considerable amounts of publicity—good publicity that recommends, even if subtly, the store as a place to shop.

Because the retail salesperson does not know who the next customer will be, a personalized preapproach is almost impossible. The salesperson can only assume that the next customer is in a buying mood and is curious about and interested in merchandise because of some need or want. The majority of shoppers do not enter stores unless these conditions exist. The salesperson must identify customers' buying motives quickly because contacts are of short duration. Instead of a preapproach, the salesperson is forced to rely on observation and experience. It is particularly helpful for salespeople to note the treatment *they* get in various stores when they are buying, and to analyze their reactions to it.

STEPS IN RETAIL SELLING

Selling in retail stores consists of several standard steps. The customer is approached and greeted. The salesperson learns what the customer needs or wants. Suitable merchandise is selected from stock, and it is then shown and described to the customer. Buyer-benefits are stressed. After handling objections, the salesperson closes the sale and attempts some suggestion selling if this seems desirable. A sincere desire to serve—to help customers buy what they should have—is the most important factor. It separates the salesclerks from the merchandise advisors. It is essential to retailing success, which has been described as "selling products that won't come back to customers who will."

Greeting the Customer

Before examining certain greetings, it is well to realize that the salesperson's manner of speaking and acting is really more significant than the particular words used. Customers demand much. They are in the store because of an invitation that, if not direct and specific, was clearly implied. Thus, customers want salespeople to be alert to give quick service when they are ready to buy. If salespeople are talking to each other, or if they are concentrating on other duties—such as stockkeeping—this essential promptness is lacking. Salespeople should always be friendly and polite, and their actions should recommend them to the customer as expert merchandise advisors whose major interest is in the customer's welfare.

When the salesperson approaches, the customer is usually either looking for assistance or looking at merchandise. In the first case, these greetings are acceptable: (1) "May I help you?" (2) "Are you being served?" (3) "How do you do?" and (4) "Good morning (or afternoon)." When the customer is looking at merchandise, the salesperson has two choices. One is the silent approach in which the salesperson steps up, obviously at the customer's service; the customer will almost always make a comment or ask a question to start the interview. The other choice is to use a merchandise greeting, such as: (1) "Very attractive, aren't they?" (2) "This is one of our new spring colors." (3) "These came in just last week from Ireland." or (4) "This item makes a most appreciated gift." When salespeople know their customers, they can call them by name and perhaps ask a casual question or make some informal remark as part of the greeting.

Determining Customer Wants

One handicap in retail selling is the impossibility of learning in advance what each customer needs and wants. The preapproach work that organizational salespeople perform simply cannot be done for retail customers. Yet, if a sale is to be made, the salesperson must determine fairly accurately what customers want. How can customer wants be determined? Several suggestions follow.

Observing. If the salesperson studies the apparent needs of all customers, observes each individual customer's interest in merchandise, and watches closely the customer's reactions to various products, some indications of customer needs and wants will be found.

Listening. Customers' comments may be vague or inaccurate, or they may be so rationalized that they camouflage the customer's real need. Even so, what the customer says must be analyzed and used. The sooner the salesperson places merchandise in the customer's hands and stimulates the customer's thinking about specific merchandise, the sooner there will be reactions to observe and comments to hear.

Headlining. While the customer is examining a particular product, the salesperson can quickly mention the three or four most outstanding benefits the product offers and then watch and listen for reactions.

Questioning. Restrained, tactful questions can be used to point up the customer's buying problems. Questions about material, style, and intended uses desired by the customer are appropriate. Questions about size are risky, as are questions about price. Answers to questions about price may commit the customer to a price level the store does not have in stock and may handicap attempts at trading up. The smaller the retailer's stock, the fewer questions that a salesperson should ask. Salespeople should not ask too many questions early in their dialog with shoppers. To do so reduces their options.

Serving Customers

At this point, we introduce some problems that the retail salesperson may encounter in the first stages of the retail sales interview. The most important problems concern how to handle decided and undecided customers, how to handle casual lookers, how to handle several customers at once, and how to handle groups of customers.

Serving Decided and Undecided Customers. In dealing with customers who know what they want, the salesperson should strive for a short sales interview. The salesperson should quickly place some merchandise before the customer, should avoid making a lengthy sales presentation, and should make answers to questions specific and brief. If the customer has decided to buy some product that would not be suitable, all the salesperson can do is to recommend a more suitable product and urge the customer to make a careful comparison of the two items before buying.

Undecided customers who want to buy something, but don't know just what, need considerable help from salespeople in pinpointing their problems and in selecting merchandise which will solve those problems. Perhaps the soundest suggestion to the salesperson dealing with such customers is to begin showing merchandise as soon as the customer is approached. From the moment he or she is shown merchandise, the customer can hardly avoid revealing information about prices, uses, colors, and product preferences. While showing the merchandise, the salesperson must attempt to analyze the customer's appearance and manner so as to determine real needs and wants.

Serving Casual Lookers. In many stores, well over half the customers are "just looking"; as casual lookers, they pose a difficult problem to salespeople. Salespeople can logically make four assumptions about casual lookers: (1) these people are not consciously planning to buy now; (2) their immediate wish is to be left alone to look at and perhaps price merchandise; (3) in all probability, the looker really wants to buy something and can finance the purchase or would not be looking; (4) it is the salesperson's duty to discover what the looker needs.

Several courses of action may be taken in dealing with casual lookers. One is to leave the customer alone, hoping that examination of the merchandise will sell it; many customers raise their buying defenses if they are immediately approached by a salesperson. Another course of action is to offer to help the looker inspect merchandise; this is particularly appropriate when products need to be demonstrated and when the salesperson is not busy with other customers. A third possibility is for the salesperson to brief the looker on the general location of merchandise, issue an invitation to feel completely at home, and assure prompt service just as soon as it is desired. A fourth technique is to refer the looker to some specific merchandise with a remark such as, "Take all the time you want; you may be interested in seeing our new collection of scarfs, right over there." Special sale items, products featured in the day's advertisements, products being pushed by the store's sales staff, and merchandise in window or interior displays may all be referred to.

Regardless of which method is used in dealing with a casual looker, it is the salesperson's duty to work toward achieving the goodwill of every looker. When goodwill is achieved, the salesperson may make a serious attempt to close a sale. Whether the immediate goal is achieving goodwill or making a sale, the salesperson should observe the looker closely and be ready to give service.

Dealing with Several Customers at Once. During store rush hours, there may well be several customers needing the attention of the same salesperson at the same time. This creates a problem involving promptness in approaching customers and the sequence in which customers are to be served. The most important principle for the salesperson to follow is that the first customer on the scene has top priority and that other customers must be served in turn. Sometimes the first customer will tell the salesperson to wait on another customer; in other situations, the salesperson may ask if it is all right to wait on someone who is ready to buy. The first customer must not be given cause for feeling neglected, discriminated against, or rushed into buying.

When additional customers approach, the salesperson should at least acknowledge their presence and promise prompt attention with a phrase such as, "I'll be right with you." At times the salesperson can permit a looker to examine merchandise alone, take care of the customer who is ready to buy, and then return to the looker. Sometimes, it is possible to give an item to the second customer for examination and return to the first customer.

Dealing with Groups of Customers. Often the retail salesperson is approached by several customers shopping together. Typically, the group will be composed of a customer and one or two friends, or a customer and one or more members of his or her family. The best thing is for the salesperson to try to determine which member of the group is the dominant one and what merchandise interests are involved. If the leader can be identified, the major sales efforts can be aimed at that person. As a shopping group is served, the salesperson must remember that people in the group must think highly of their companions' opinions, or they would not have come shopping with them. Members of the group should be given the opportunity to talk among themselves if they desire. If the group members cannot agree on merchandise, the best course is for the salesperson to recommend the item he or she sincerely believes to be the most appropriate.

Selecting Merchandise to Show Customers

Having greeted the customer and made a start at determining what the customer wants, the salesperson must select what merchandise to show and recommend. If the customer made a specific request to see a certain product, that, of course, is the one the salesperson will show first. If the customer was somewhat vague, then the salesperson must bring out what the customer might like. Here the salesperson is well advised not to lead off with either the highest- or the lowest-priced items. The safest as well as the most ethical guide in selecting merchandise to show is that of customer satisfaction. If a customer later regrets a purchase, the natural reaction is to blame the store. This usually results in buying less at that store and in unfavorable word-of-mouth publicity for it.

Trading Up. In selecting the merchandise to show, the salesperson must decide whether to attempt *trading up.* A salesperson succeeds in trading up when the customer buys a better quality item than the customer was planning to buy. Another version of trading up is selling a larger quantity of the product.

The customer who trades up and buys the better quality of a suit, for example, gets greater economy, or greater satisfaction of some other kind.

Salespeople should practice until they can show their superior lines of merchandise smoothly and recommend them naturally.

Substitute Selling. Sometimes the store will not have in stock the item a customer requests. Sometimes the salesperson may try to redirect the customer's interest to some other product or brand, even though the requested item is in stock. In either case, *substitute selling* is the result. No matter what the reason for substitution, there will be bad aftereffects if either the salesperson or the customer successfully insists on the purchase of a product the customer should not buy.

If the store does not have the requested product in stock, the customer should be told this immediately. If the store has a comparable product in stock, this item should be quickly given to the customer for inspection. The not-in-stock item should not be criticized, nor should the item shown be directly referred to as a substitute. The salesperson can question the customer tactfully while showing the substitute item.

If the store does have the requested item, there must be a sound reason for any attempt at substitution. If the customer intends to buy a product that would be entirely inappropriate, it is the salesperson's duty to try to prevent an unsatisfactory purchase and to recommend a more suitable one in its place. Often the salesperson is wise in showing the more appropriate product along with what the customer asked to see; many customers will immediately realize that their original preference was not sound.

Delivering the Sales Presentation

Retail salespeople deliver somewhat different sales presentations from those delivered by organizational salespeople. One difference is in length. Because the store presentation is shorter, the salesperson must make the strongest and most persuasive points at the beginning, or the opportunity to make them may be lost. Another difference is that the retail salesperson cannot plan the sales presentation in advance to the degree that the organizational salesperson can. Standard or canned presentations are almost impossible for retail salespeople to use because they sell many different kinds of products, but key words and phrases can be effectively used.

Most of the important principles of delivering a sales presentation that were discussed in earlier chapters can be effectively applied in retail selling. Customers do not buy until they are convinced that the purchase will be of benefit to them. The customer is entitled to the salesperson's complete attention, and the salesperson can in turn hold or recapture the customer's attention by directing it to the product or by asking the customer to do something with the item. Agreements on small matters should be obtained, and value should be established before price is discussed. If the customer asks the price of an item, the salesperson should quote the price immediately, but should also tell the customer about buyer benefits that justify the price. As the sales interview progresses, the presentation should become more specific and more emphatic.

Demonstrating Merchandise

In retail selling, as in outside selling, the salesperson should show the products when explaining how the buyer can use them. Because the item the customer buys is practically always in the store at the time of purchase, there is rarely an excuse for not demonstrating.

How much merchandise should be shown? This decision must be left up to the salesperson. If not shown enough merchandise, the customer may feel not well enough informed to buy. If shown too much, the customer may become confused. Customers ought to be shown all the items they wish to examine. The customer wants to see what is deemed to be a minimum assortment for making an intelligent, sound purchase. In every case, the customer should feel that the salesperson has shown, or will gladly show, every bit of the store's merchandise that is suitable. The demonstration phase of the sale rarely lasts very long, although there is usually time to repeat a demonstration, even in greater detail, if necessary.

The rules for product demonstration are applicable in retail selling. Customer participation is desirable and can be obtained by asking the customer to do something or to watch something. Whenever practical, the product should be handled or operated by the customer just as it will be used after purchase. For example, the customer can try on clothing or write with a pen. While this is being done, the salesperson should describe the buyer benefits that the customer is experiencing.

Merchandise should be displayed in its best light and in an impressive yet believable way. Demonstration should be designed to prove the advantages promised by the salesperson. Throughout the sales presentation, the salesperson should remember that the manner in which the merchandise is handled is quite revealing. Respect for the merchandise should always be evidenced; nothing must destroy or damage the customer's respect for the goods.

Handling Objections

Most buying resistance that retail salespeople meet stems from the customer's uncertainty about the buying decisions relating to product, price, and time. Few objections are based on need, although need must always be established. Obviously, even fewer objections concern source. Thus, the salesperson can expect to deal with customers who are not completely convinced that the product under consideration is the best buy, customers who feel that the price is really more than they can afford to pay, and customers who feel that they must think the prospective purchase over or shop around a bit more before making a final selection.

The general rule here, as in outside selling, calls for the avoidance of objections by explaining them away before the customer raises them. When the salesperson selects the most appropriate merchandise to show, the amount of product objection encountered is reduced. When the salesperson points out all the outstanding satisfactions to be obtained from the product, the likelihood of price objections is decreased. Difficulty with the time decision will be less frequent and troublesome as the salesperson does a more thorough job of achieving sincere agreements on product and price.

Sometimes a customer sincerely feels a need to think over or talk over a prospective purchase with someone. In these circumstances, there are several actions that the salesperson may take. He or she may agree with the customer that deliberation is desirable before making the purchase. The salesperson may offer to show even more merchandise to the customer before the customer leaves; and if this offer is not accepted, the customer can be given a summary of the most important benefits involved so that they can be thought about or relayed to the absent person who must be consulted. The salesperson may indicate that the item can be put aside for the customer until the customer has made a decision. The salesperson may give the customer literature on the product or a business card in an effort to get the customer to return to complete the sale later.

The concealed or camouflaged objection poses the same difficult problem in retail selling that it does in other selling. For example, after a presentation or demonstration, the customer may say, "I'm afraid that isn't exactly what I had in mind." The salesperson has little recourse in such a situation except to observe the customer's actions, comments, or facial expressions in an attempt to determine what affirmative buying decision is missing or to ask tactfully just what the shopper did have in mind. Meanwhile, the salesperson can repeat the most persuasive buyer benefits the products offers; this may cause the real objection to disappear. In some cases, the salesperson may directly ask the customer, "What have I failed to make clear?" Once the objection has been identified, it should be handled quickly and completely.

Closing the Sale

There are closing clues in retail selling just as there are in outside selling. Verbal closing clues can take the form of questions relating to price, size, or terms or can take the form of a statement such as, "It *would* save me time each week." Closing clues may also take the form of changes in facial expression that indicate interest or decision, reading of the product's label, or the movement to one side to see the product from a different angle.

As the salesperson senses the approach of the end of the sales interview, his or her manner should become more positive and forceful. The customer must feel the salesperson's confidence in the product and in the buying recommendation. No new merchandise should be brought out at this stage, and other items no longer under consideration should be removed. The salesperson should concentrate on the two or three items of particular interest to the customer and should review the merits of each. The salesperson should ask for customer agreement more often during this stage and should be ready to suggest a buying decision to an undecided customer, but never should the salesperson make it seem that the customer is being rushed into buying.

When a retail salesperson cannot close the sale to a certain shopper, often because of a personality conflict, he or she may call in a sales supervisor or another salesperson. The second salesperson and the shopper may be more compatible, and the shopper may feel a bit flattered by this treatment.

Suggestion Selling

No treatment of closing sales in retail stores is complete if it omits the topic of suggestion selling. The objective of suggestion selling is getting the customer to make unplanned purchases. It is the sale of items over and above those the customer requested and bought. It is additional sales volume, and that, of course, explains the store's as well as the salesperson's interest in it.

It can be said correctly that customers want suggestions from the sales staffs of retail stores. One explanation of this attitude is that suggestions can remind customers of products they need. Another explanation is that consumers will run out of products less often if they replenish their stock more often. Suggestions can also help consumers identify actual needs of which they were not aware. When made in a tactful way, suggestions are received by customers as favors and, hence, are appreciated. Suggested purchases can save both time and money and can increase the customer's personal satisfaction.

When should suggestion selling be attempted? It is usually best for the salesperson to care for the customer's requests first and to have this purchase agreed on before suggesting other products. Then, before going through the mechanics of completing this sale physically—writing up the sales ticket, wrapping the merchandise, or making change—the salesperson can make suggestions. Once in a while the salesperson can make use of the ensemble technique before the first purchase is made in the customer's mind. Here, for example, the salesperson might bring out a tie to show with a shirt the customer is examining. The tie often helps to sell the shirt; the purchase of the shirt recommends the purchase of the tie.

Because suggestion selling can be executed in such a way as to irritate or even drive customers away, certain rules or principles which have proved sound should be observed. The salesperson's ideal suggestion should prove to be a solution to a customer problem. If the suggested merchandise is something that will benefit the customer, the salesperson is well on the way to customer acceptance of the suggestion. Furthermore, the suggestion should be realistic and suitable. This rules out products that would not be appropriate for the customer's needs. Then, too, if the customer is in a tremendous hurry the salesperson would be wise to avoid suggestion selling. If the salesperson uses a tone of helpful concern and interest, it helps give the suggestion the appearance of a service to the customer.

Another rule is that suggestion selling must be moderate in intensity, in the amount of the recommended purchase, and in the number of items mentioned. A salesperson can easily be too aggressive in trying to increase the amount of the sale. If the salesperson sells too hard, the result will be customer resentment. If the salesperson tries to make too large an additional sale, the attempt smacks of overloading the customer. If the salesperson suggests too long a list of products, it certainly irritates and may even infuriate the customer.

Still another guide is that suggestions must be definite. The salesperson should not make the mistake of using any of the following questions: Now what else? Will that be all? Anything in socks today?

Merchandise best suited to suggestion selling includes: (1) related items (suits call for shirts, socks, and ties; gasoline calls for oil); (2) "specials" of the day, which may be new products or old products for which new uses have been found; (3) items currently featured in display and advertising; and (4) merchandise that is timely because of its relation to holidays or seasons.

POSTSALE BEHAVIOR

Immediately after making a sale, the salesperson should record it, demonstrating skill with arithmetic and the necessary mechanics. As the purchase is wrapped, the salesperson can at the same time assure the customer that he or she made an intelligent decision. A warm "thank you" should always be voiced to let the customer know that the purchase was appreciated, and a sincere personal invitation to return should be issued. If appropriate, the customer's name should be learned and associated with his or her appearance for possible future use. If appropriate, the customer should be told the salesperson's name or given a business card.

Regardless of whether or not the interview ends in a purchase, the salesperson must make the best possible selling attempt. When the customer postpones a purchase, the salesperson should continue to be just as courteous and friendly as before the decision. The salesperson should not disclose any irritation, disappointment, hurt, or resentment. Instead, excellent public relations will build goodwill for the store and the salesperson by the way the customer who did not buy is treated. The salesperson should let the customer know that visits to the store are and will continue to be appreciated. Customers should be encouraged to return by the salesperson's manner.

The customer has two undeniable rights—to postpone a purchase decision, and to shop further before buying. Any attempt to curtail these rights can be damaging to a store. If, therefore, a customer insists on asserting one or both of these rights, there is nothing to do except cooperate. Salespeople can summarize the advantages of their merchandise and ask the customer to investigate competing products on those points. It is clearly the salesperson's responsibility to see that the customer knows thoroughly and completely before leaving what the store can supply in the product lines being considered. The salesperson should assume that the customer will return and will then buy; he or she might even try to make a definite appointment for the return visit. In some cases, the salesperson can give a memo, a sketch, some literature, or a business card to the customer in an effort to increase the chances of the customer's return.

BUILDING SOUND CUSTOMER RELATIONSHIPS

Retail stores feel the necessity for continued patronage. Similarly, each salesperson has a strong desire to have regular, steady customers. Stated simply, customers return to and buy repeatedly from those stores which satisfy and please them. Customers want good values, accurate and adequate information about products, speedy service, and polite treatment. The customer especially wants to feel that each purchase and each return visit are appreciated by the store. Sound selling, plus sincere appreciation for each sale, build a loyal clientele whose esteem and goodwill are invaluable assets to a store.

No thorough attempt at working with customers can be made without reviewing the reasons why customers quit buying at certain stores and from individual salesmen and saleswomen. The indifference of salespeople always ranks high on lists of causes of customer loss. Selling tactics that smack of pressure, or of too much aggressiveness, can drive customers away. If too many attempts at substitution are made, or if the attempts are too crude and obvious, customers are going to take their patronage elsewhere. Customer complaints include the charge that some salespeople are haughty instead of friendly, while others are discourteous instead of well-mannered. Also included is the accusation that some salespeople are not well enough informed about their merchandise to supply the product information required by customers. A more disturbing charge is that some salespeople actually misrepresent their goods. When a salesperson promises something to a customer, such as a delivery date and hour, but fails to comply, the effects are not good. Finally, the mistakes of salespeople may discourage return visits and purchases.

There are certain steps that salespeople in some stores can take in their determination to build sound customer relationships. One of the simplest yet most rewarding is learning the names of as many customers as possible and addressing those individuals by their names. Another habit well acquired is that of remembering the preferences and prejudices of regular customers. In the higher-priced merchandise lines, some salespeople find it practicable and worthwhile to keep an individual record on some of their best customers. Such a record might include the customer's name, the date of the last visit, the items last bought, and any other significant facts about the customer. These customer records can be reviewed frequently, permitting the salesperson to give more tailored and personalized treatment to any of the recorded customers who drop

E. R. Squibb & Sons lists fourteen reasons why sales are lost.

1. *Disinterest*—Don't conduct a conversation with a fellow employee or another customer while waiting on someone. Give the customer your complete attention. Deadpan expressions, daydreaming, or "take it or leave it" attitudes leave unsold merchandise.
2. *Mistakes*—If you show the wrong item or make a mistake in change, acknowledge it and make the customer feel you are genuinely sorry.
3. *Appearing too anxious*—Show customers you want to serve their interests. Overinsistence and high-pressure tactics are objectionable to customers.
4. *Talking down other brands*—Talk up the brand you want to sell. Do not make unfair remarks about a competitive brand.
5. *Arguing*—Never argue with a customer. If it appears that an argument might develop, shift the conversation to another topic. There's little profit in winning an argument and losing the customer. If a customer makes an absurd statement, don't laugh or argue. You may anger the customer, and an angry customer is a lost customer.
6. *Being too long-winded*—A flood of words doesn't make many sales. Some people take time to make up their minds, and silence at the right time allows the customer to think and decide. Being a good listener often makes more sales than being a fast talker.
7. *Lack of courtesy*—Discourteous salespeople rarely last long on a job; they lose too many customers.
8. *Showing favoritism*—Never wait on your friends or favorite customers before taking care of customers who were there first.
9. *Being too hurried*—Take time to find out what a customer wants and then take time to show the merchandise properly.
10. *Embarrassing the customer*—Never laugh at a person who speaks with a foreign accent or correct a person who mispronounces words or product names.
11. *Misrepresenting merchandise*—Never guarantee any cures or make any claims for products that cannot be backed up by facts.
12. *Lack of product information*—Salespeople who are not well informed cannot expect to build a steady clientele for their store.
13. *Wasting customers' time*—When a customer is in a hurry, finish the sale as quickly as possible.
14. *Getting too personal*—Assume a professional attitude. Be sincere and friendly, but keep a touch of dignity and formality in all customer contacts. Never let familiarity creep into the conversation, for it is usually resented.

ILLUSTRATION 18-2. Often retail sales are lost through carelessness or indifference on the salesperson's part.

in. The records also serve the salesperson as a mailing list or as a telephone call list. Where installment credit is available, a salesperson can keep posted on customers' balances and recommend additional purchases at the appropriate times.

THE PROBLEM OF RETURNED GOODS

A retail problem of obvious interest to retail salespeople is that of merchandise bought by customers but subsequently returned to the store. Returned goods are a significant element in a retailer's expenses. Returns must be handled, and this involves cost. An item being returned may show evidence of use, abuse, or deterioration. Markdown may be necessary. Then, for the time the merchandise was out of the store, it was neither "sold" nor available for sale. Unless the retailer is to lose sales, inventory must be large enough to allow for this out-of-stock time. In addition, some returns reflect an increase in customer ill will. Finally, the volume of returns may suggest that buying or selling is less efficient and more expensive than it should be.

Retail salespeople are often responsible for a significant proportion of returned goods. Sometimes a salesperson makes a mistake unknowingly. Sometimes there is a misunderstanding between customer and salesperson involving just what is being bought or its price. An ignorant, poorly trained salesperson can expect returns; the same holds for the careless, indifferent salesperson who does not bother to tailor merchandise recommendations to individual shoppers. The high-pressure salesperson may as well brace for returns; so may the weak salesperson who urges shoppers to take goods home on approval instead of *selling* goods to those buyers. Equally guilty is the casual salesperson who allows customers to do a poor job of buying. Customer disappointment over merchandise performance—whether this is a matter of operation, fit, color, or size—often leads to the return of the item.

Of course, some causes of returned goods do not relate closely to the personal selling done by retail salespeople. For example, the reason could be a mistake in order filling, damage en route, or delay in delivery. The item might be inherently faulty. Or the customer may buy, then find the same item available in another store at a lower price.

Retail salespeople have an interest in the returned goods problem—a considerable interest if they work in department, clothing, or furniture stores. Their earnings are usually affected directly because they are determined by their sales volume. There are more than a few cases where a salesperson made a big sale, spent the commission, and then found the commission account charged because the merchandise was returned. In addition, returns can take up a salesperson's selling time when stores ask their sales staffs to handle returns. Then, too, there is often a makeup or replacement sale which must be made.

If the store has a liberal policy about returns, the retail salesperson has cause to be pleased because such a policy works in the direction of greater sales. New customers are more easily attracted, and present customers are more easily held. If the store's policy is generous, the salesperson should not fail to emphasize this fact. But, at the same time, this fact does not relieve the salesperson of the responsibility of helping customers make purchases that will not come back.

TECHNIQUES OF SELF-MANAGEMENT

Self-management is not nearly the complicated, challenging, and difficult matter for retail salespeople that it is for outside salespeople. Typically, the store schedules salespeople as to how many hours a week they will work and establishes their duties.

What, then, can or should store salespeople do about managing themselves? It would seem that they should concern themselves mainly with attitudes and activities. As to attitudes, the starting step is to recognize that training and modification must go on indefinitely because improvement is always possible. Salespeople must realize that their present as well as their future depends in large measure on how well they get along with three groups: customers, associates, and the store's executives. Further, they must remember that few customers who quit buying at a store do so because of the store's merchandise, its prices, or its customer services. Most quit because they find the salespeople ignorant, incompetent, or uninterested. Salespeople's attitudes must reflect their understanding of the dependence of customers on salespeople and of the customer's need for help and advice. Their attitude should reflect an awareness of the fact that customers are guests—their guests as well as the store's guests, and invited guests at that.

As for activities, they are whatever is needed to achieve self-improvement. They include such obvious practices as the analysis of selling attempts in order to identify elements of strength and elements of weakness. In particular, the well-managed salesperson searches for the causes of lost sales and lost customers. Another activity involves the collection of all information needed; information about merchandise, customers, and how to sell the merchandise to the customer. Still another activity is that of the improvement of memory. Otherwise, the information about merchandise, customers, and selling techniques will be of limited use because of its limited life. Then there is the matter of developing and even trying to perfect a pleasing personality. Finally, there is the never-ending practice of trying to be of greater help to the real boss: the customers.

SUMMARY

In retail selling, potential buyers come to the salesperson. These buyers are physically, financially, and emotionally close to buying. Retail salespeople are responsible for selling many more products than are organizational salespeople, and the number of buyers encountered is greater.

Retail salespeople have three principal types of duty or responsibility: selling merchandise, nonselling duties, and responsibilities to employers. Salespeople are expected to exercise good manners and show genuine interest toward customers. They should be helpful and give reliable information.

A retail salesperson must be informed about store, merchandise, and customer matters. Store policies and procedures must be familiar to the salesperson. The salesperson must understand how buyers can use the products the store carries. The retail salesperson does not know who the next customer will be, so a personalized preapproach is almost impossible, but the salesperson must assume that every customer is in a buying mood.

The first step in retail selling is greeting the customer. Next, the customer's wants are determined. They can be ascertained through observation, listening, headlining, and questioning. When serving decided customers, a short sales interview is desirable. More work and time are necessary when helping undecided customers make their choices. Casual lookers pose a difficult problem. It is the salesperson's duty to work toward achieving the goodwill of every looker. When goodwill is achieved, a serious attempt at a close can be made.

During rush hours, there may be several customers needing attention. Prompt service and serving shoppers in the order they arrive are very important.

After greeting the customer and determining what he or she wants, the salesperson must select merchandise to show and recommend. While standard presentations are usually inappropriate, key phrases are very effective. Demonstrations should almost always be done because the merchandise is easily accessible. Customer participation should be encouraged.

Most objections relate to product, price, and time. Avoidance of objections is effective here; objections should be explained away before the customer raises them. Closing should be handled in the same way it is for other types of sales.

The objective of suggestion selling is getting the customer to make unplanned purchases. Salespeople's suggestions may identify unrealized needs. Tact and moderate intensity are vital, or customers can be driven away.

After making the sale, assurance that the purchase was a wise one and a warm "thank you" should be offered. Retail stores need continued patronage, and salespeople should develop regular customers. Therefore, sound customer relationships must be built. Learning customers' names, remembering likes and dislikes of customers, and maintaining records are all effective.

Returned goods are expensive to the seller. Salespeople's mistakes, high pressure selling, mistakes in filling orders, and liberal return policies all lead to returns. Self-management is not complicated for retail salespeople. Their schedules and duties are established by management. Still, the salesperson does control his or her attitudes and personal activities.

1. What customer-related differences are there between retail selling and other kinds of selling?
2. List three types of duty or responsibility of retail salespeople.
3. What store information is needed by retail salespeople?
4. What is the first step in retail selling?
5. How can a salesperson determine what the customer wants?
6. What should a salesperson do when confronted with a number of customers?
7. How should the salesperson handle groups of customers?
8. What is trading up?
9. Why is substitute selling done?
10. What is the objective of suggestion selling?
11. If no sale takes place, what should the salesperson do?
12. List three methods for building sound customer relationships.
13. List five reasons why retail sales are lost.
14. What are some reasons for returned goods?
15. What aspects of self-management can a retail salesperson control?

DISCUSSION QUESTIONS

1. Much retail selling is done by very young, inexperienced people doing part-time work. How can such individuals be trained and convinced of the importance of maintaining the same standards of performance that professional salespeople maintain?
2. Discuss the compensation systems most widely used in retail selling. Are they similar to those used by wholesalers and organizational selling firms?
3. Discuss the following statement: "Most retail salespeople are not rewarded for truly outstanding efforts."
4. What closing techniques are especially effective in retail selling?

CASE STUDY 18

Read the following situations in which no sale was made when a particular product was unavailable.

SITUATION 1: The Men's Department at a Major Department Store in a Shopping Mall

Salesperson: Good afternoon. May I help you?

Customer: Yes, please. I'm looking for a Gant shirt for my husband, the shirt with the new collar style that uses a gold pin to hold the collar together.

Salesperson: I'm sorry, but we don't carry Gant. There are two other stores in the mall, though, that do. They're ____ and ____.

Customer: Thanks for your help.
Salesperson: Come back to see us.

SITUATION 2: A Hardware Store

Customer (an older man) to salesperson: I've been looking everywhere for old-fashioned brace and bit sets. My brace has finally broken after 22 years and I need to replace it. Do you have any in stock?

Salesperson (also older): I can see why you'd want to get a replacement. I still use my brace and bits. But we don't have any braces in stock right now. There's not much demand for them anymore except from us older folks. Can I sell you anything else today?

Customer: No thanks. That brace is all that I wanted. I'm sorry you don't have it.

Salesperson: Well, better luck next time.

What could the salesperson have done to increase the chances of making a sale?

SALES MANAGEMENT
part VII

Building the Sales Force

Building the Sales Force

After studying this chapter you should be able to:

- Break the management process down into four functions
- Describe a firm's promotion budget
- Contrast line organization with line and staff organization
- Distinguish among job analysis, job description, and job specification
- Explain the tools widely used in selecting salespeople
- Discuss training programs for salespeople

For many companies that sell over a wide geographical area, the key employee is the salesperson in the field. The climax of promotional efforts for those sellers occurs when a salesperson presents the product line to a buyer. That salesperson *is* the company to many buyers; consequently, the salesperson's influence on company-buyer relationships is great.

THE NATURE OF MANAGEMENT

Before considering sales management, we need to look very briefly at management in general. This text breaks the management process down into four functions: planning, organizing, directing, and evaluating.

Planning

To plan, the manager thinks ahead. Forecasting is part of planning, and forecasts become goals and objectives. Managers are decision makers. In reaching a decision, managers first identify and study a problem or an opportunity. Then they develop a number of possible courses of action to take. After evaluating each, they select the one that seems best. Budgets, quotas, and standards are established in the planning stage.

Organizing

In organizing, the manager establishes the jobs that will be necessary. The manager then defines the authority, responsibilities, and relationships of each job. Resources (people, machines, money, materials, etc.) are committed and their uses coordinated.

Directing

Directing consists of administering the planned program. In leading subordinates, the manager guides and supervises, inspires and motivates. Effective directing demands effective two-way communication between the manager and subordinates and between the manager and other managers.

Evaluating

In evaluating, the manager checks actual performance against planned performance and notes what progress is being made (often by month) toward objectives. If the differences between what was planned and what was actually done are too great, the manager tries to determine why and then takes the appropriate corrective action.

THE PROMOTION BUDGET

The biggest constraint on the sales manager is the sales budget, an element of the overall promotion budget. A few comments about the promotion budget are in order.

Budgeted promotion makes each promotion activity *dollar-* specific, and the scheduling which budgeting includes makes each *time-* specific. Proper promotion budgets permit the seller to avoid the extremes of wanton extravagance and pathetic inadequacy. The sales forecast is the basic influence in the setting of promotion budgets. Budgeting for promotion is one of management's most difficult tasks.

Annually, each firm's management must determine the make-up of the next year's promotion mix—how much personal selling, how much advertising, and how much sales promotion to buy and use in the effort to reach that year's goals. This is a critical decision because the promotion program is seldom changed to any great extent during a year. For many firms the building and managing of the sales force is the largest operating expense.

Once these three budgets have been set, then each is broken down according to: (1) *product* (how much effort will salespeople put behind Product A vs. Product B); (2) *time* (should the manufacturer drop TV advertising in the summer as some do); (3) *buyer* (what point-of-purchase items should be designed for large-volume retailers and what for small-volume retailers); (4) *sales territory* (New England vs. Pacific Coast); and (5) *expense classification* (should an ad in a school annual be charged to advertising or to public relations). These breakdowns are essential because of variations in type of product, market potential, share of market now held, competition, stage of business cycle, and so on.

INTRODUCTION TO THE SALES MANAGER'S JOB

The sales manager's main concern and responsibility relate to the firm's sales revenue or income budget, the first budget in point of time and importance. A business's most basic figure as it starts each fiscal year is the sales forecast, and the attainment of that figure is the sales manager's main objective. All cost and profit forecasts and all planning for purchasing and production are based on the sales revenue forecast.

The sales manager establishes goals and requests budgets; plans the nature and the direction of the firm's personal selling efforts; organizes the personal selling function; and staffs the sales department and the sales force. The sales manager directs this sales force in productive activities and effective operations, and exercises control to keep the staff on course.

The sales manager's job includes providing support for salespeople and equipping them with *selling tools and aids.* Examples include samples of the product, catalogs, manuals, visual aids such as photographs and motion pictures, the company advertising schedule, and samples of point-of-purchase items available to retailers. Salespeople may need *assistance from nonselling employees* in the firm. Specialists (engineers, chemists, accountants) can help salespeople analyze buyers' technical problems and select (even help present and demonstrate) the solution to recommend. For certain products, specialists install and then provide maintenance service. The sales manager must see that salespeople get the *information* they need about their customers and prospects and the geographical markets for which they are responsible. With it, they can work their territories most profitably and increase their performance.

ORGANIZATION OF SELLING ACTIVITIES

The two principal types of organization for any firm or selling division are line organization, and line and staff organization. Line organization is usually found in very small firms; line and staff organization is adopted as a firm grows in size.

Line Organization

In line organization, authority flows in a direct line from a top executive to the first-ranking subordinate, from this first subordinate to a second-ranking subordinate, and so on. This is comparable to the military system of organization in which the line of authority may go from major to captain, from captain to lieutenant, and so on. Each subordinate is responsible to only one person on the next higher level. There are no specialists or advisors. The sales manager of a field sales force in a small company is often the head of a sales department organized on the line pattern. All the planning for the department and administration of the department are done by the sales manager.

This type of organization is relatively inexpensive to implement, results in speedy action and decision making, is fairly simple and clear to operate, and permits good control because authority and responsibility are centralized. Disadvantages of line organization are that it suffers from the absence of specialization and tends to reflect the weaknesses of any one-person situation. Expansion tends to result in too many levels of authority.

Line and Staff Organization

As a firm grows, line organization often becomes unwieldy, and the need for a line and staff organization develops. With this type of organization, the top marketing executive may no longer be the sales manager but rather a vice-president of marketing. This individual represents the top of the "line" of marketing authority, and may have a staff consisting of a sales manager, an advertising manager, a sales promotion manager, and a marketing research director. The line of authority thus goes from vice-president of marketing to sales manager to regional sales manager (if there is such a position in the firm), to field salespeople. The vice-president's staff gives advice and makes suggestions on how best to conduct marketing activities. People holding staff positions have no authority over such line individuals as field salespeople, but they do have line authority over their own assistants.

Line and staff organization allows the utilization of experts in a specific area and results in the effective division of effort toward a common goal. Staff members plan and make suggestions; the top executive administers, controls, and coordinates. Responsibility and authority can be clear in a line and staff organization, but maintenance of such an organization can be expensive. Troubles can arise if a staff member usurps authority and issues orders to subordinates improperly.

Fragmentation

As a company continues to expand, fragmentation often results. This fragmentation is a subdividing of some already existing phase of an organization. For example, a manufacturer may subdivide the market area geographically so as to have a number of manageable units instead of one large, unwieldy area. In their various territories, the field salespeople report to a district or branch sales manager who may be responsible for three or four states. The district sales manager may report to a regional or divisional sales manager who may be responsible for fifteen states and may report to the sales manager in the home office. Just as the district sales manager has line authority over the district's salespeople, the regional sales manager has line authority over the district sales managers.

Products are a second base on which to divide line authority. A manufacturer of food items and drug items, a manufacturer of a line of consumer

A LINE AND STAFF SALES FORCE ORGANIZATION CHART

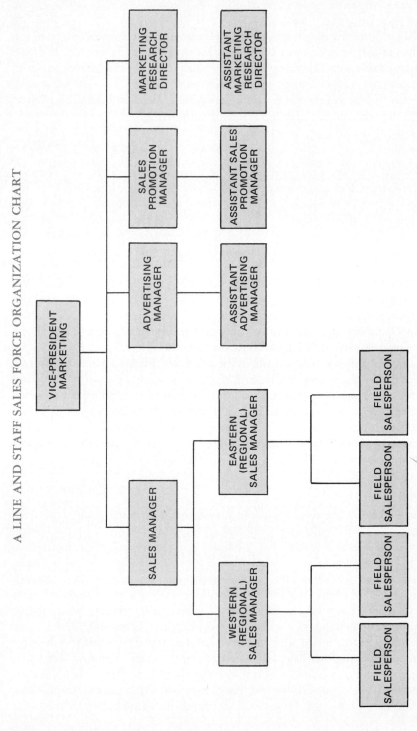

ILLUSTRATION 19-1. Line and staff organization allows the utilization of experts in a specific area and results in the effective division of effort toward a common goal.

products and a line of industrial products, or a manufacturer of a line of men's clothing and a line of women's clothing may decide to set up each product classification separate from the other. For example, the food line could have its own sales force and sales manager, as could the drug line. These two sales managers could logically report to a field sales manager.

Type of customer is a third basis for subdivision. Understandably, some marketers think of this as a division on the basis of distribution channel. A typical two-way split has one sales manager and sales force selling to domestic customers, with another sales manager and sales force selling to foreign customers. A three-way split might be made by a manufacturer who sells to the industrial market, to the government, and to wholesalers and retailers. A four-way split might find one sales force selling to mass retailers, another selling to foreign customers, a third selling to institutional buyers, and a fourth selling to wholesalers.

RECRUITING THE SALES FORCE

No job in sales management is more crucial than that of hiring salespeople. Hiring starts with recruiting. Unsound recruiting leads to unsound hiring, and hiring the wrong person for a selling job can be both expensive and harmful. The more recruiting, selecting, and training a company does to replace unsatisfactory salespeople, the greater the expense to the company. Inept salespeople can make unfortunate, costly decisions and can do damage to their brand's and their firm's image. They usually fail to develop the most desirable relationships with customers and to maximize sales to those customers; therefore, their shares of the market are lower than they should be. When personal selling does not function as it should, other executives, such as the advertising and production managers, are apt to feel that their efforts are handicapped. If many of a firm's salespeople are weak, high supervisory and selling costs can result in undesirably high selling prices of the firm's products.

How can the sales manager handle recruiting activities so as to reduce the number of problems involving inept salespeople? First, adequate amounts of attention and time must be earmarked so that a thorough job of recruiting can be done. Similarly, an adequate amount of money must be budgeted for this purpose. The sales manager must keep abreast of the better techniques of recruiting and must make sure that recruiting efforts are planned and systematic.

Job Analysis

Job analysis is the determination of the responsibilities and assignments that a particular salesperson is expected to have. The sales manager's first step in job analysis is to determine whether there is just one type of selling job or more than one. If there is more than one, the sales manager then classifies the types of selling job, making as many individual classifications as selling operations demand. The sales manager may, for example, separate missionary salespeople from regular salespeople, salespeople selling to retailers from those selling to purchasing agents, or salespeople selling standard products from those selling products bought on specification. The sales manager may even establish one classification for senior salespeople and another for junior salespeople.

In job analysis, the sales manager may consider several of the following questions. What do my best salespeople do, and how do they go about doing it? What are their problems and difficulties, and how do they handle them? What do the district and regional sales managers think their salespeople should do? Just what do my salespeople think their jobs should consist of?

Job analysis should precede recruiting and selection. In addition, the nature of the training program obviously cannot be decided until you know what duties the new employee should be taught to perform. How much and in what manner a salesperson should be paid should reflect the work performed. Finally, the salesperson's performance must be measured against some standard, and job analysis makes the establishment of these standards less difficult.

Job Description

Job description formalizes the findings of job analysis. A job description is a written statement of what the salesperson is to do, a statement reflecting management's conclusions after executing a job analysis. Typical items found on many job descriptions follow: (1) the official title of the job, (2) the amount of authority the salesperson will have, (3) the salesperson's accountability to others, (4) the relationship of the salesperson's job to other jobs, (5) the salesperson's daily assignments and activities (what products will be sold, the types of buyer to be contacted, the nature of the selling to be done, a breakdown of working time by duty to be performed, routine duties, and self-management and administrative responsibilities), (6) the method of compensation, and (7) the opportunity for advancement.

Job Specification

Job specification is a logical extension of job description. A job specification names the personal qualities needed by the individual who is to function successfully in a described job. Items that are often included in job specifications are physical factors, mental factors, environmental factors (such as social class), experience factors (in sales, other business situations, and the military), and personality factors (temperament, maturity, persuasiveness, and empathy).

There is, however, disagreement on how various subjective factors should be weighted. How important is age or education? How attractive in appearance should a salesperson be? Is it possible or even desirable to measure motivation or maturity? How much value should be attached to intelligence? Can a sales manager develop a person into a superior salesperson if that individual ranks low in self-confidence or mental agility? Do high ratings in enthusiasm and health compensate for low ratings in experience and maturity?

Sources of New Salespeople

A sales manager should experiment to find out what sources of recruits are the most fruitful. The wise sales manager identifies a number of sources and then sets up continuing relationships with them, even when not immediately in the market for trainees.

In many circumstances, the sales manager's company can be a productive source of recruits. Nonselling personnel in the sales department, clerical personnel, and engineering and production personnel may have capabilities and knowledge applicable to selling jobs. One approach is to request salespeople and top executives to be on the alert for nonselling personnel to fill selling positions. Seldom, however, does this internal source supply all the recruits that are needed.

Advertisements, employment agencies, and unsolicited applications are also sources of a considerable number of recruits. Placing "help wanted" ads in the classified section of newspapers and in certain business publications often brings much response, although sometimes of questionable quality. The screening of large numbers of applicants who respond to these ads can be costly. Stipulations in the copy of the ad may aid in screening out undesirable applicants. Some sales managers glance regularly at the "situations wanted" ads placed in newspapers and business magazines by individuals who are unemployed or who want to change jobs.

Some selling firms conduct a recruiting program in which they visit college campuses and interview persons interested in selling jobs. Most recruits from colleges, universities, business schools, or high schools will have had little selling experience, but they can be trained specifically for the selling job in question.

Some salespeople may also come from other firms—competitors, allied firms, suppliers, or customers. However, raiding another business for salespeople is certainly unethical and can be illegal.

THE SELECTION PROCESS

When stripped to its essentials, the selection step consists of (1) determining whether applicants measure up to the firm's specifications, and (2) hiring , if possible, the best who do. Who selects a firm's salespeople? In a small company, the president often does. In a medium-size company, the sales manager usually does. In large companies, a group of sales department executives may do the selecting, aided perhaps by individuals from the personnel department. Even though the sales manager should have the final responsibility and authority for the selection of salespeople, the personnel department may be asked to help in the recruiting, initial screening, and designing of the selection tools. Five basic selection tools will now be discussed: the application blank, personal interviews, references, psychological testing, and physical examinations.

Application Blanks

The application blank and the personal interview are the two most widely used selection tools. The application blank supplies background information on the applicant's qualifications and is a record of employment history. Once submitted, it can serve the personnel department as a permanent record. Some firms use a brief preliminary application blank and a brief screening interview. If the applicant is still under consideration after these have been evaluated, he or she is then asked to fill out the firm's detailed application blank.

Because of their major role in the selection process, application blanks demand careful design. Listed below are the headings found most often on application blanks and the subheadings that might also be included:

1. *Personal* (home address, citizenship).
2. *Education* (years of schooling, degree, major, grade average).
3. *Military* (branch, duties, rank, length of service).
4. *Activities* (clubs, organizations, athletics, hobbies).
5. *Employment* (former employers, selling experience, salary, reasons for leaving former jobs).
6. *References* (business, educational, character).
7. *General* (expected starting salary, relatives currently with the company).

Personal Interviews

The interview can be used to verify and to add to the information contained in the application blank. Also, there is no substitute for face-to-face presence and two-way oral communication when evaluating an applicant on such observable matters as quality of voice, vocabulary and conversational ability, manners, physical characteristics and appearance, ability to impress and persuade, and tact.

One type of interview may be described as a structured interview. Its basis is a standard, written questionnaire which is followed by all people in the firm who interview job applicants. The interviewer may read each question directly and record the applicant's answer as it is given, or may memorize the questions and their sequence and record answers only after the applicant has left. Answers recorded after the interview tend to be less accurate than those recorded during the interview.

Another type of interview is described as an unstructured interview. Here the interviewer does little talking, asks few direct questions, appears to exercise little or no control, and encourages the applicant to talk freely.

Most companies probably conduct interviews which are somewhere between these two types. In every instance, interviews need to be planned carefully. Rating scales, charts, or forms are often used to organize and summarize the results of and reactions to an interview.

APPLICATION BLANK

APPLICATION BLANK

PERSONAL INFORMATION

Name _____
Last   First   Middle Initial

Address _____
Apartment No. (if applicable), Street No., and Street

_____
City   State   Zip Code

Are you a United States citizen?   YES_____   NO_____

EDUCATION

High school attended   _____
                              Name of School

                              _____   _____
                              City   State

                              _____   _____
                              Years Attended   Did you graduate?

College(s) or univer-
sity(ies) attended   _____
                              Name of School

                              _____   _____
                              City   State

                              _____   _____
                              Years Attended   Degree(s) or Hours Earned

                              _____
                              Name of School

                              _____   _____
                              City   State

                              _____   _____
                              Years Attended   Degree(s) or Hours Earned

MILITARY EXPERIENCE

Did you serve in the United States Armed Forces?   YES_____   NO_____

Branch of service _____

Rank attained _____

PROFESSIONAL ORGANIZATIONS

Please list the professional organizations of which you are a member and any
offices held or committee assignments in those organizations.

_____

_____

_____

Continued on next page

EMPLOYMENT EXPERIENCE

Employers

Name of Company

Street Address

City   State   Zip Code

Supervisor's Name and Phone No.

Employment dates: From_____ , 19____ to_____ , 19___

Last Position Held

Final Salary   Reason for Leaving

Name of Company

Street Address

City   State   Zip Code

Supervisor's Name and Phone No.

Employment Dates: From_____ , 19____ to_____ , 19___

Last Position Held

Final Salary   Reason for Leaving

REFERENCES

References may be business, educational, or character references. Please supply at least two references.

Name of Reference and Phone No.

Street Address

City   State   Zip Code

Name of Reference and Phone No.

Street Address

City   State   Zip Code

OTHER INFORMATION

Position desired_____

Expected starting salary_____

ILLUSTRATION 19-2. The application blank supplies background information on the applicant's qualifications and is a record of employment history.

When should the personal interview or interviews be scheduled? A short, preliminary interview can be the first screening step, and it can precede the preparation of the detailed application blank. Much college recruiting follows this pattern. Often when the more lengthy interviewing starts, a number of interviews may be scheduled. Sometimes the first long interview is at a branch office, with subsequent ones being held at the home office. Generally, there should be more than one interview, and they should be conducted by more than one interviewer.

References

It is not uncommon for an applicant to be asked to supply a number of references. The sales manager knows, of course, that no one will list people who might be inclined to speak ill of the applicant. Even though not very reliable, the comments of some references may be helpful. References frequently report more freely face-to-face or over the telephone than they would when writing a letter.

Personal references are usually friends of the applicant. They are reluctant to report unfavorably; some may not know as much about the applicant as the sales manager would prefer. Business references are usually former employers; occasionally they are present or former customers of the applicant. Once in a while, a sales manager is justified in trying to contact neighbors, retailers, teachers, or bankers not mentioned by the applicant.

Psychological Testing

The premise behind the use of psychological testing as a selection tool is that tests can be designed which will determine the presence or absence of personal traits essential in successful selling, and the presence or absence of other personal traits found in weak salespeople. There are four general types of tests in use: intelligence tests, personality tests, interest tests, and sales aptitude tests.

Intelligence tests, or mental ability tests, are used to measure how well the applicant can learn, reason, and solve problems. A bothersome question, however, is whether or not a high score on an intelligence test guarantees that the person being tested will be an outstanding salesperson. *Personality tests* are intended to measure purely subjective traits such as confidence and poise. *Interest tests* are intended to identify the vocational areas which appeal to the applicant. *Sales aptitude tests* are designed to measure such selling-related traits as tact, memory, verbal facility, extroversion, persistence, and persuasiveness.

Psychological testing can often make a valuable contribution to the selection of salespeople. Sales managers act on subjective bases when they rely on their reactions to personal interviews and on the reports from references. Psychological tests—if they are soundly designed, administered, and interpreted—can help supply some objective bases. There is some feeling that this tool may be of greater value in screening and rejecting the weak applicant who should not be hired than in identifying the applicant who should be hired. Psychological tests should never be the sole selection tool used. The personal interview and the applicant's experience as recorded on the application blank are more significant than are test scores. Psychological testing can be a worthwhile aid to, but not a substitute for, the sales manager's judgment.

Physical Examinations

Selling is hard work; any physical handicap can be quite a burden, and any health problem can be troublesome to both the salesperson and the sales manager. If an applicant cannot qualify physically for the job, this should be determined as soon as possible.

ESTABLISHING THE TRAINING PROGRAM

The need for sales training is common to all sellers. New, inexperienced employees obviously must be taught certain principles and procedures to help them become successful salespeople. But the experienced salesperson also can benefit from training. New types of products appear each year, and the proliferation of brands continues. The increased competition which results calls for salespeople who are more competent. Because the boundaries of the typical selling job are continually expanding, the need for more effective training is also growing.

A sound training program can justify its cost on several bases. The more expert the sales force is, the larger the sales volume and the greater the gross margin on that volume. Salespeople become productive and profitable more quickly if they are well trained, and their performance approaches their potential sooner than it otherwise would. The better trained salespeople are, the better able they are to control and even reduce direct selling expenses. Good training leads to fewer resignations and fewer dismissals, and the drop in turnover permits reductions in recruiting, selection, and supervisory expenses. The drop also encourages higher morale, makes for more satisfactory relationships with customers, and has a favorable effect on the firm's image.

Organizing the Training Program

Each training program must be tailored to the circumstances of the company in question. We have noted various bases of difference among companies. Products can be paper clips, or they can be turbines. Buyers can be homemakers, or they can be purchasing agents. Salespeople can merely take orders, or they can serve as engineering consultants. Some firms hire only experienced salespeople; others hire graduates with no selling experience. These are just a few of the differences which demand that the training program be tailored to the needs and resources of each company.

Who should be responsible for training a firm's salespeople? Certainly, just one person should be given the authority and the responsibility. If the company can afford it, this person should be a staff executive who does nothing but plan, organize, train, and supervise. There are, of course, many firms which cannot see their way clear to house training in the office of some staff executive. Usually these firms assign training to a line person—sales manager, district sales manager, or sales supervisor. Outside training organizations are used in certain cases for certain purposes. A firm's personnel department sometimes does some of the training of salespeople (in company history and organization, for example), but the sales manager is usually responsible for what the salespeople are taught about buyers, products or services, product applications and uses, and how to sell.

Training can be done in the home office; it can be done in the field where the salesperson is working or will be working; or it can be a combination of home office and field training. A strong case can be made for training a salesperson in the field. And a strong case can be made for certain training at the home office in a somewhat formalized school—training on company history, policies, products, manufacturing processes, and the like.

Initial Versus Refresher Training

In many firms, there are two types of training, one for inexperienced recruits (usually young), and another for salespeople who have been with the firm for some time, often for years. Initial training is for new salespeople. It is dominated by on-the-job training; the recruits learn by doing. The recruits are under the supervision of a senior salesperson, a sales supervisor, or a sales manager. They participate in actual selling situations and get critiques, coaching, and counsel on their performances. Mistakes and weaknesses are spotted and corrected; improvement is noted promptly; the recruit gains experience and confidence before taking over the responsibility for a territory. Trainees with exceptional ability need less of this on-the-job training than typical trainees, but they are scarce and expensive to hire.

Some initial training is done in classrooms. Newly hired salespeople may be given a comprehensive training course before they report to their territories and begin selling. Or new salespeople may be given a short, fundamental course, receive on-the-job training, and then return to the office for advanced training.

Refresher training deals with such problems as experienced salespeople's drifting into bad habits, and it provides up-to-date information. Any changes the firm makes in the marketing areas of product, distribution, price, or promotion can be announced and explained.

Refresher training encourages all salespeople to subscribe to an ever-continuing program of self-improvement. In a sense, training should never end because in addition to any changes in the firm's marketing, frequent changes are taking place in competition, regulations, availability of raw materials, buyers, problems, personnel, and opportunities.

If retraining and review occur often, they virtually amount to continuous training. A brief training session every Saturday morning for all salespeople could be considered continuous training. Much refresher training is done at sales meetings, and some is done through special courses.

Techniques of Sales Training

Certain training techniques are appropriate for classroom use, whereas other techniques are more suitable to the field. Lectures have a place in the classroom. Panel discussions and group discussions can be effective classroom techniques. Demonstrations of "how-to-do-it" and role playing can also be valuable in the classroom. Analysis and discussion usually follow demonstration and role playing.

Most sales managers consider on-the-job training essential. Although the classroom is acceptable for informational training, mastery of good work habits and the elimination of bad work habits demand some on-the-job training.

Among the more common training aids are manuals, textbooks, teaching machines, movies, sound-slide presentations, records, charts, graphs, products, and models.

Content of Training Programs

The training program should teach salespeople how best to spend their time. The content of the training program should reflect what salespeople need to know, what they should do, and how they should do it. The program should also show salespeople how to handle common and troublesome problems—buyers' problems as well as their own. It should teach them about their buyers, their products, and how to sell those products to buyers.

The following topics and subtopics are found in most training programs: (1) *company*—history, organization, and policies, (2) *company procedures*—credit, shipping, expenses, and complaints, (3) *products*—manufacturing, features, prices, and uses, (4) *buyers*—buying motives, buying habits, problems, and attitudes, (5) *market*—territory, routing, business conditions, and competition, (6) *selling*—presentation, demonstration, objections, and closing, and (7) *non-selling duties*—planning, prospecting, customer service, and paperwork.

SUMMARY

Managers perform four functions: (1) planning, (2) organizing, (3) directing, and (4) evaluating. The biggest constraint on the sales manager is the sales budget. Each promotion activity is dollar-specific and time-specific. Budgets are broken down on the bases of product, time, buyer, sales territory, and expense classification.

The sales manager's main concern is the firm's sales revenue budget. The sales manager provides selling tools and aids to salespeople, gives them assistance, and supplies information.

The two principal types of organization are line organization and line and staff organization. In line organization, authority flows in a direct line downward. Each subordinate is responsible to one individual. People holding staff positions have no authority over line employees other than their own assistants. As a company expands, it may become fragmented, or subdivided. Fragmentation can be done geographically, by product, or by type of customer.

Recruiting salespeople is a crucial sales management function. Unsound recruiting leads to unsound hiring, and unsound hiring leads to increased expenses and lower sales.

Job analysis is the determination of the responsibilities and assignments that a particular salesperson is expected to have. It must be done before recruiting begins. A job description is a written statement of what the salesperson is to do. A job specification names the personal qualities needed by the individual to do a good job.

Sources of new salespeople include the sales manager's company, advertisements, employment agencies, unsolicited applications, recruiting programs at colleges, and other firms. The sales manager should experiment to find out which sources are the most fruitful. The selection process has two steps: (1) determining whether applicants measure up to the firm's specifications, and (2) hiring, if possible, the best who do.

The application blank and the personal interview are the two most widely used selection tools. Personal interviews are used to verify and add to the information contained in the application blank. Interviews can be either structured or unstructured. Multiple interviews are often conducted before an individual is hired. References may offer useful personal information about the applicant. Psychological tests are designed to determine the presence or absence of personal traits necessary to successful selling. The four general types of psychological test are intelligence tests, personality tests, interest tests, and sales aptitude tests. A physical examination may be used to determine whether the applicant can qualify physically.

Training programs are needed for inexperienced employees and can also be helpful to experienced salespeople. One person should be responsible for the training program. Training can be done in the home office or in the field. Initial training is for new salespeople. Refresher training deals with problems such as experienced salespeople's drifting into bad habits, and it provides up-to-date information.

Lectures, panel discussions, demonstrations, role playing, and on-the-job training are training techniques. Topics such as company, company procedures, products, buyers, the market, selling, and nonselling duties may be included in training programs.

REVIEW QUESTIONS

1. What are the four primary functions of managers?
2. How are promotion budgets broken down?
3. Describe a line organization structure.
4. Why does fragmentation occur?
5. List four possible outcomes of unsound recruiting.
6. What must the manager consider when doing a job analysis?
7. What is the difference between a job description and a job specification?
8. List five sources of new salespeople.
9. What is a structured interview?
10. What are the advantages of psychological testing?
11. Why are physical examinations necessary?
12. How can the expense of training programs be justified?
13. What training techniques are best used in the classroom?
14. List five topics usually covered in training programs.

DISCUSSION QUESTIONS

1. React to the following statement: "Psychological tests are used by managers who cannot conduct effective hiring interviews."
2. How would you respond to a complaint by a senior salesperson that a required refresher training program is just a waste of valuable time that could better be spent on selling?
3. How can on-the-job training be used to improve customer goodwill and even increase sales while individuals are being trained on sales calls?
4. Where is there greater room for ingenuity by the interviewee—in a structured or unstructured interview?

CASE STUDY 19

The Electro-Dynamics Corporation is a western firm that sells circuit boards, electronic cables, and electronic hardware to computer manufacturers. The firm has been growing and a new sales representative is needed. The sales manager has advertised in the newspapers for a salesperson to fill this position. After screening applications and reviewing information obtained in interviewing the applicants, the field has been narrowed down to two candidates. Their qualifications are listed below.

	Dorothy Dromboski	*Joseph Van Weele*
Appearance:	Neat, well-groomed, attractive appearance.	Well dressed but hair a little long.
Personality:	Quiet, reserved, but talked easily. Seemed familiar with uses for products.	Outgoing, friendly, hearty manner. Likeable.

Education:	Business Administration degree. Major in marketing, minor in computer science technology.	Has completed two years of degree work in marketing. Plans to complete Business Administration degree at night school.
Experience:	No experience but very interested in a selling career.	Three years experience selling automotive parts.
Reason for application for this position:	Wants to get started on a selling career.	Wants to get into a field with more opportunity for growth.
References:	College professor said she was very intelligent, ranked high in class, used creative approach in preparing projects. Got along well with others.	Former employer said he was a very dependable, steady worker. Well liked by fellow employees. Performed work capably.

As advisor to the sales manager, answer the following questions:

1. Which one of these candidates do you recommend that the sales manager hire? Why?
2. Give your reasons for rejecting the other candidate.

Managing the Sales Force

Chapter 20

After studying this chapter you should be able to:

- Understand the problem of establishing sales territories
- Describe three approaches to sales forecasting
- Comment on the establishing of sales quotas
- Name and explain the methods of compensating salespeople
- Identify the ways of handling salespeople's expenses
- Recognize the techniques of directing salespeople

The first topics in this chapter deal with establishing sales territories, making sales forecasts, and setting sales quotas. Certain terms are common to each of these topics; before beginning our discussion, it would be well to define these terms.

Market potential is the estimate of the dollar or unit amount of a certain product that an entire market could be persuaded to buy from all sellers of that product during the coming year. *Market forecast* is the realistic estimate of what that entire market will actually buy during the coming year. The *sales forecast* is the estimate of how much of the market forecast a specific firm will sell if it follows a certain marketing program. A company may consider two or three marketing programs, each having its own sales forecast, before adopting a single one.

When *market share* is a projected figure, it is the ratio of a firm's sales forecast to the market forecast; when it is an actual figure, it is the ratio of the firm's sales for a previous time period to market sales for that period. *Sales quotas* are the portions of the total sales forecast after it has been broken down by buyer; by day, week, and/or month; by sales territory and basic unit; by product and/or product line; or by salesperson. Each salesperson and sales territory will have a quota. A *sales territory* is the specific portion of a firm's total physical market that is assigned to a certain salesperson.

With these concepts in mind, let us now look at the sales management activities of establishing sales territories, making sales forecasts, and setting sales quotas.

ESTABLISHING SALES TERRITORIES

A sales territory may be viewed as the geographical area in which a salesperson works—an area ranging from part of a city up to a number of states—or it may be viewed as a group of buyers assigned to a salesperson. For a number of reasons, sales efforts and sales management are much more effective when each salesperson has his or her own territory. The salesperson can budget the appropriate amount of time and selling effort for each buyer in the territory. No buyer is neglected, and no buyer is visited too often. Responsibility is clear when each salesperson has a certain territory, and this works to reduce the friction among salespeople and between each salesperson and the company. Duplication of selling effort is avoided, and no profitable market is overlooked. Planning and control are more efficient. Each salesperson can be assigned a reasonable quota, and budgeting becomes more precise. Profitable and unprofitable markets can be readily identified. Selling costs can be cut because of reductions in travel time and travel expenses.

Deciding on the Basic Territorial Unit

The first step in establishing sales territories is to determine the basic unit of which territories will be composed. Ideally, the basic unit will be small, somewhat homogeneous, and have a stable geographic size. Five possibilities for this basic unit are (1) the city, (2) the county, (3) the Standard Metropolitan Statistical Area, (4) the wholesale trading area for the product in question, and (5) the state.

The City. Using the single city as the basic territorial unit is not usually satisfactory, partially because of the continuing growth of the suburbs. It is common for a city to expand its corporate limits frequently, and this change in geographical area complicates sales management efforts. A city too large to be one salesperson's territory must be subdivided by blocks, precincts, or perhaps census tracts; but few data of help to sales managers can be obtained for such subdivisions.

The County. A second possibility for the basic territorial unit is the county, and this is the most widely used basic unit. The boundaries of the county are firm; it is generally a small unit; and a wealth of marketing information is broken down by counties. There are over 3,000 counties in the United States; a few of these, instead of being basic units comprising a salesperson's territory, are too large to be covered by one salesperson. Los Angeles County, Cook County (Chicago), and Wayne County (Detroit) are examples. For most manufacturers, however, most counties are considerably smaller than their sales territories.

The Standard Metropolitan Statistical Area. This basic unit avoids some of the weaknesses of the city unit. Established by the Bureau of the Budget, the Standard Metropolitan Statistical Area consists of one county or a group of contiguous counties. The area must contain a city with a minimum population of 50,000, or two contiguous cities with a combined population of at least 50,000. Total population for the area must be not less than 100,000. The counties must be metropolitan in character; and the contiguous counties must be closely tied, both socially and economically, to the central city. Large cities within twenty miles of each other can comprise such an area; Tampa-St. Petersburg is an example.

The Standard Metropolitan Statistical Area is, thus, a homogeneous economic unit. It observes county lines but ignores state lines; for example, the Kansas City area consists of four counties in Missouri and two in Kansas. Much statistical information is available on or can be compiled for this unit because it consists of whole counties. Standard Metropolitan Statistical Areas account for the majority of retail and wholesale sales.

Wholesale Trading Area for a Product. A fourth possibility for the basic unit is the wholesale trading area for the commodity involved, a natural marketing unit determined by buying and selling patterns. A trading area consists of two elements: the central market or wholesale trading center (usually a medium- or large-size city), and the commercial area dominated by the central market. The boundary of this territory marks how far from home market-based firms sell or how far from the market are located buyers who concentrate their purchases with market-based sellers.

Delineating wholesale trading areas is not always easy, and market researchers use various techniques to determine the breaking points between competing central markets. Because breaking points sometimes ignore county lines and because the majority of marketing data are compiled for units no smaller than counties, it is sometimes difficult to locate comprehensive marketing data on a particular trading area. For this reason, many manufacturers delineate trading areas as precisely as possible but make sure they consist only of whole counties.

The State. Finally, the state can be selected as the basic unit of which sales territories are constructed. The small manufacturer who sells throughout the national market can justify the use of this basic unit perhaps better than anyone else. For other manufacturers, using the state as a basic territorial unit poses problems. States obviously differ widely in geographical area, population, transportation facilities, buying power, nature of their economies, and size and number of cities. Also, trade ignores state lines. Thus, for many manufacturers, the state is too large and too diverse to serve satisfactorily as a basic territorial unit.

Delineating Sales Territories

Each territory consists of one or more basic units and usually consists of many basic units. In delineating specific sales territories, the seller must recognize various influences:

1. The basic nature of the product and its price.
2. The buyers on whom salespeople will call, including the number of buyers who are prospects and the number who are customers, who they are (purchasing agents, retailers, or homemakers, for example), where they are located, an estimate of the annual purchases per customer, and the number of buyers a salesperson can satisfactorily handle.
3. The sales volume necessary to support a salesperson.
4. The salesperson's call pattern, including the number of calls made each day or week and the frequency of calls scheduled for each group of buyers.
5. Identity of competitors.
6. Transportation facilities.
7. The salesperson's ability.
8. Sales trends.

Two approaches, the buildup approach and the breakdown approach, may be used to delineate sales territories after these influences have been considered. The *buildup approach* is particularly appropriate for the manufacturer of consumer products. A manufacturer using the county as its basic unit might select those counties containing large cities and then add to each a county or counties geographically and economically related to that particular county.

When using the *breakdown approach,* the manufacturer has two choices. First, the sales forecast can be broken down into quotas for each basic unit and basic units can be combined into what the manufacturer feels are territories of the proper size for profitable coverage by one salesperson. Second, the manufacturer can determine the average sales volume that the salespeople are expected to achieve for the period, divide that figure into the total sales forecast, and thus determine the number of sales territories needed. Basic units are then combined to produce that number of territories.

Revising Sales Territories

Sometimes a firm reduces the sizes of some of its sales territories. Perhaps they were not correct from the start. Or, more often, a territory's potential becomes too big for one salesperson to cover thoroughly, and the work load becomes too heavy. The company reduces the *space* the salesperson will be covering (and travel costs, too) so as to increase the *time* spent with individual buyers.

Reducing their territory usually upsets salespeople. They may fear a drop in earnings. Occasionally, a good salesperson resigns. So, there should be adequate preparation of salespeople if their loyalty, enthusiasm, and morale are not to suffer—even to the extent of the firm's guaranteeing no drop in earnings for a period of time.

If certain territories are too small, if their sales potentials are inadequate for the salespeople to make satisfactory incomes, increases in territory sizes may be necessary. Increasing his or her territory usually pleases a salesperson who foresees greater sales and earnings.

A firm has been known to withdraw voluntarily and completely from some distant, unprofitable markets. Wholesalers or agent middlemen may be substituted for salespeople in these markets, or the markets may be ignored completely.

APPROACHES TO SALES FORECASTING

The sales forecast is basic to all company planning. Sales managers who make short-run forecasts are concerned with seasonal matters and developments; those who make long-run forecasts, perhaps of two to ten years' duration, are interested in trends. Our principal concern in the following discussion will be with the short-run forecast made for the next calendar year. This forecast should be reviewed after at least six months and preferably at the end of each quarter. Some firms choose to check actual sales against budgeted sales every month or even every week. As a general rule, the shorter the forecast period, the more accurate the forecast.

Because sales forecasts are estimates of sales revenue, forecasters try to identify and evaluate the determinants of *demand.* They start by determining the number of buyers (customers and prospects) who can use the product to advantage and finance its purchase. They compare their products with competing products to learn competitive advantages and disadvantages. They review their firms' marketing policies, particularly those involving pricing and promotion. They investigate the strategies and tactics of competitors. They take a look at the economic state of the industry and at the current stage of the business cycle.

There are various approaches to the establishment of sales forecasts. Three approaches will receive most of our attention: the executives' judgment approach, the salespeople's judgment approach, and the projection of past sales approach. Typically, the method used to arrive at a given sales forecast reflects aspects of all three approaches.

Executives' Judgment Approach

In this approach, a group of executives develops a group prediction or forecast. The individuals may include executives from marketing, production, statistics, research, and finance. Some of the group may attempt a buildup route to the forecasts; some may prefer a breakdown technique; still others may start with predicting Gross National Product, refine this down into an industry forecast, then try to forecast share of market.

The executives' judgment or opinion approach can be quick, easy, and inexpensive. Data, experience, and judgment are from several sources instead of from a single source. But, on the other hand, the forecast can be nothing but an average of guesses. Nonmarketing executives may be poorly qualified to engage in sales forecasting. Facts and data relating to the market may be grossly inadequate. Breaking this type of forecast down into quotas can be difficult.

Salespeople's Judgment Approach

Here the sales forecast is made by the sales force rather than by the company executives. This is a buildup approach, starting with each salesperson's estimate of what he or she will sell next year. If thought desirable, the salesperson and the district sales manager can develop the forecast together. Or all the field salespeople can come up with an overall sales forecast; all the district or branch sales managers can come up with their total estimate; and all the regional or divisional sales managers can submit their total forecast. If the executives still want to make their forecast, they can; then the four can be compared.

Salespeople in the field know their market and their customers' plans and thinking better than anyone else in the firm. The people forecasting are the ones to whom quotas will be assigned; they know they will be expected to sell the volume forecast. The dangers and risks of one-person forecasts are avoided. Finally, operating breakdowns of the forecast by product, customer, territory, and by salesperson should be relatively easy.

But some salespeople are too optimistic; some are too pessimistic; some will underestimate in the hope of getting a smaller quota. Because the method is time-consuming, some salespeople may resent having to participate. And while most salespeople are conscious of local, current conditions, they may not be well informed about broad economic developments and changes.

Projection of Past Sales Approach

This approach recognizes that today's sales activities flow into tomorrow's sales activities, that last year's sales extend into this year's sales. The influence of the past on the present and the influence of the present on the future are so strong that, in all probability, all forecasting methods include some version of the projection of past sales. Here is one way to think of the projecting procedure. Let this year's sales volume be 100 percent. It may be believed that next year will contain favorable changes which will work for a 10 percent greater volume in sales. But unfavorable changes may be expected which will result in a 5 percent smaller volume. The net is a plus 5 percent; the forecast for next year is 105 percent of this year's sales volume. This line of reasoning should be applied to each of the firm's sales territories and to each basic unit.

This projection of past sales is relatively simple and easy to do. No one can deny that each year's sales are related to the sales of the previous year. But the approach often puts entirely too much weight on past sales and not enough on other influences, such as competitors' activities. New companies and new products are obviously denied this approach.

Other Approaches

Some forecasters try to base their forecasts on the future behavior of the factors which determine demand. The number of births per month might well be the most influential factor for a manufacturer of baby foods. The number of four- and five-year olds could be a major factor for manufacturers of products used in the first grade. If the seller puts a number of such factors into a composite guide, the resulting statistical maneuvers are far beyond the scope of this text.

Some forecasters include buyer surveys in their overall approaches; these are also called "surveys of buying intentions." Basically, a sample of a buyer group is asked what it plans to buy during some short period of time. Perhaps these surveys are of greater value in arriving at market forecasts than in setting sales forecasts.

ESTABLISHING SALES QUOTAS

Sales quotas are sales assignments or goals; they are management's expectations in dollars or units for a specific future period. Sales quotas are assigned to various marketing units. The salesperson and the sales territory form what is by far the most basic of these marketing units. The district sales manager and the district, and the regional sales manager and the region are somewhat similar units. Sales quotas must be set up for each item in the product line. The buyer is a marketing unit which calls for a quota. If salespeople are to meet their quotas, they can do so only by selling certain quantities of merchandise to each of their customers. Larger quotas can be applied to groups of homogeneous buyers; there can be a quota for sales to the government, for sales to purchasing agents, for sales to wholesalers and retailers, for sales to foreign buyers. Finally, there is the time variable. The year, the quarter, and the month may each be assigned its own quota.

Purposes

Why assign sales quotas? First of all, quotas are established to aid in planning and control. When the sales manager edited and approved the final versions of the job descriptions, what the salespeople were supposed to do was spelled out in a qualitative way. Quotas quantify those responsibilities. The sales manager who assigns an annual quota of $400,000, and breaks it down by month and quarter, can compare the salesperson's actual sales against the monthly and quarterly quotas to see how sales are going.

Second, the quota can serve as a specific objective or target for salespeople. Some sales managers take the realistic sales forecast for a sales territory, increase it a bit, and assign the salesperson's quota for that territory. This may function as an incentive quota, but if the increase is too great, it does more harm than good.

Third, sound compensation and promotion of salespeople demand sound assignments and sound quotas. The quota is usually one of the more important elements in compensation plans and promotion decisions.

Quotas can be used to check on the suitability of the sales territories previously delineated by the sales manager. Analysis of salespeople's quotas and salespeople's sales can suggest strongly that some territories are too large and others too small.

Types of Quota

There are five commonly used types of quota: (1) dollar volume quotas, (2) unit volume quotas, (3) gross margin quotas, (4) net profit quotas, and (5) activity quotas. By far the most often used quota is that based on dollar volume. For example, a salesperson may be told that during the coming year, sales must total at least $400,000; this is a clear and specific goal. However, sales volume in dollars means little unless it contributes to net profit. A salesperson can reach the dollar quota with an unbalanced and thus undesirable sales assortment and an unacceptable profit showing. Margin and profit quotas urge the salesperson to sell a healthy portion of higher-profit items which are usually higher in price and often harder to sell. These quotas, however, may not be readily understood or accepted by salespeople and can also be expensive to administer.

Mention of gross margin quotas and net profit quotas is incomplete until one thinks of expenses. Gross margin less expenses equals net profit. Typically, a salesperson is told what his or her expense allowance will be, or is offered some sort of reward if expenses do not exceed a budgeted amount.

Activity quotas are based on points rather than on dollar volume or unit volume; points are awarded for sales and for other accomplishments. Salespeople may earn points for calls made, new customers, product demonstrations, point-of-purchase items installed, missionary sales work, or collections.

Setting Dollar Volume Quotas

In thinking about how to set sales volume quotas in dollars, the sales manager visualizes sales territories, each consisting of its own basic units. The basic unit, you recall, is the fundamental geographic unit (county, state) in setting up sales territories and forecasting. So what is needed first is the sales forecast by basic unit and by sales territory. If we use the salespeople's judgment or opinion approach, we automatically have forecasts by sales territory. If we use the projection of past sales approach, this was done or should have been done by basic unit and the figures totaled to get sales territory forecasts. But we may have followed the executives' judgment or opinion approach and have only a total sales forecast. What should be done in this case? The total figure must be apportioned over the sales territories (and probably even over basic units) according to some market index. One of the better-known and widely used indexes of this sort is *Sales and Marketing Management's* annual "Survey of

Buying Power." Regardless of the index used, the odds are great that it will reflect past sales and market potential.

At this point we have sales forecast by sales territory, and the sum of these territorial forecasts equals the overall company forecast. What we need are sales quotas for the sales territories. Our initial recognition is that in many instances, perhaps even in the vast majority of instances, the forecast becomes the quota. This makes sense. We commit ourselves to make 100 percent dollar sales next year. But some sales managers might add something to the forecast. We referred to these as incentive quotas because the real sales forecast remains 100 percent. There are downward adjustments, too. The quota may be tied to the compensation plan in the following manner: a quota of 90 percent of forecast, a bonus for a sales volume of 100 percent, and an additional bonus to salespeople who reach 110 percent.

Quotas do harm if they are too high or too low; this argues for a realistic, accurate quota which the salespeople can make if they work reasonably hard. To be of maximum effectiveness, the quota must be understood and accepted —hopefully, even approved—by the salesperson. The simpler the computations, the less the risk of friction, suspicion, and resentment. Salespeople's participation in quota setting may contribute to the achievement of this objective. Quotas must be fair and accurate; they must reflect territorial potential rather than the sales manager's guess or hunch, prejudice, or whim. Administration should not be complicated. Adequate flexibility is desirable. Perhaps the annual figure should be reviewed each month. Many sales managers have benefitted from posting their salespeople frequently on how they are doing.

COMPENSATION OF SALESPEOPLE

One of the sales manager's heaviest responsibilities is that of getting the desired amount of production from each salesperson. Some of the tools used in this endeavor are financial in character. The most direct financial motivation is, of course, money. Fringe benefits are considered to be indirect financial motivators; these include insurance, hospitalization, sick leave, paid vacations, and retirement income.

What Sales Managers Want

Sales managers want a compensation plan that will attract, hold, and develop good salespeople. Such salespeople are able to acquire, hold, and expand desirable customers. Such salespeople do not overload their customers, nor do they skimp on service to customers.

The compensation plan must keep costs within reason. Minimum cost to the company is not compatible with maximum pay, which salespeople desire, and a compromise must be reached. The plan must not be too costly to administer. It dare not force the company to raise its prices to a noncompetitive level.

Sales managers hope the compensation plan provides them adequate control over salespeople's efforts and activities. Managers want hard work, done in accordance with approved methods and company policies and procedures. But the plan should motivate and stimulate; it should encourage more sales and more profitable sales. When making quota depends largely on the salesperson's hard work and the salesperson has few nonselling duties, this incentive element should be prominent.

Finally, sales managers recognize that there are real differences between salespeople, sales territories, products, and buyers. So they want compensation plans flexible enough to be tailored to company circumstances, objectives, and problems. They know that the plan for paying salespeople must be in harmony with the plans for paying the firm's other employees.

What Salespeople Want

The salesperson's first interest is, of course, in amount of income. The salesperson wants an acceptable standard of living, and the opportunity to raise it over time. Most salespeople prefer two types of income. First, they want a certain part, perhaps enough to cover basic living expenses, to be regular and steady. This is to provide some security regardless of sales volume, and to prevent wide fluctuations in income. Second, they want an incentive element which rewards them for certain specific accomplishments.

The compensation plan should be simple to understand and compute. Salespeople want to be able to figure correctly how much they earned last week or last month, or their acceptance of the plan will be less than complete.

Finally, salespeople must feel that their compensation was determined fairly. They want it arrived at objectively. And they feel unfairly treated if made to wait three or four months for pay they earned.

Levels of Compensation

The term *level of compensation* is applied to what the sales manager must pay in order to hire and hold the type and quality of salesperson wanted. Type and quality can involve such matters as education, training, ability, and experience. Compensation level consists of income plus fringe benefits.

Level of compensation is greatly affected by the job description. From the job description, one can infer the difficulties and other unattractive features of the job. From it one can picture the type of salesperson needed and his or her current standard of living.

Another influence is the pay received by competing salespeople or the income range for comparable selling jobs. The gross margin potential of the product involved, which limits how much the sales manager can afford to pay, is an influence. Closely related is the worth of the salesperson to the firm. Still another influence is what the firm pays other types of employee. Finally, there is the relative bargaining strength of firm and salesperson.

The following discussion will examine the compensation methods of straight salary, straight commission, and salary plus incentive. In all three methods, earnings or income are separate from expense allowances or reimbursement.

Straight Salary. This method of compensation is fixed. A salesperson may be paid a specified amount regardless of sales volume or performance. Several advantages are credited to the straight salary method. It is simple, specific, and economical to administer. Stability of income gives the salesperson security. Straight salary is particularly appropriate when the sales manager wants the salesperson to do a well-balanced sales job. The salesperson's income does not suffer when the sales manager assigns educational, public relations, service, or missionary tasks. When the trainee is new, when the product is new and its initial potential is low, or when the firm is entering a new market, straight salaries are logical.

Straight salary ranks low as to incentive. Consequently, the sales manager must be responsible for stimulating and motivating the salespeople. The sales manager must also pay close attention to them, give close supervision to their activities, and do much checking up.

There are also other disadvantages to straight salary. Unit selling costs cannot be predicted with confidence because future sales volume is unknown. The ratio of selling costs to sales volume, as a percentage, goes up and down as sales volume goes down and up. There is a problem of fitting salaries to salespeople; old salespeople may be overpaid, and new salespeople may be underpaid. Unless reviewed and revised frequently, the salary structure can become out of date.

Straight Commission. Under straight salary, sales managers buy salespeople's time. Now we see them buying salespeople's accomplishment, paying according to productivity, which is usually measured in sales volume. This is variable compensation.

The great asset of the straight commission plan is its powerful incentive; the more a salesperson sells, the greater his or her income. Under this method, the salesperson enjoys considerable freedom of operation. Straight commission may attract the better salesperson. It can be as simple as 5 percent on net sales, or it can be flexible and tailored. Different rates can be assigned to different products, for different types of buyers, for in-season and out-of-season sales, and to different salespeople and sales territories.

There are, however, several disadvantages to straight commission. The job of setting commission rates which are fair is not easy; sales territories often vary in potential, as do assignments of nonselling tasks. Dollar income can fluctuate, sometimes wildly, causing some feeling of insecurity or even some temptation to resort to high-pressure selling. High-pressure selling is bad in itself, but it can also result in the salesperson's neglecting nonselling duties and the firm's interests. House accounts (sold by a company official and, therefore, ineligible for commissions) can be a cause of friction. If two or more salespeople contribute to making a sale, dividing the commission between them can be a problem.

Salary Plus Incentive. Salary plus incentive is by far the most popular of the compensation methods because it combines the advantages of the two plans just discussed and avoids many of the disadvantages. There are four principal types of salary-plus-incentive plan: salary plus commission, drawing account plus commission, salary plus bonus, and the point system.

Salary Plus Commission. This is perhaps the most common of the salary-plus-incentive plans and may be appropriate for the salesperson responsible for both selling and servicing. The salary portion can range from 30 percent to 90 percent of the salesperson's total income; the commission may apply on all sales or may apply only to sales over a certain amount per month.

Drawing Account Plus Commission. A drawing account is a fixed advance of money to the salesperson which is to be repaid from commissions earned. *Guaranteed draws* do not have to be repaid if the salesperson's commissions for the drawing period are less than the draw; thus, the guaranteed draw is really the same as a salary. The *nonguaranteed draw* works as a short-term loan against future commissions; the salesperson must repay the amount advanced.

Salary Plus Bonus. A bonus is a lump sum given to the salesperson for superior performance in some area of selling. A bonus is unlike a commission in that it is not related in any quantitative way to specific achievement. A bonus may represent appropriate recognition of the salesperson who has had few cancellations of orders, who submits reports promptly over a period of time, or whose relationships with customers are characterized by much goodwill. Two questions that sales managers must answer are how large the bonus should be, and the basis on which it should be distributed.

Point System. This combination plan is usually a variation of salary-plus-commission or salary-plus-bonus plans. Because it can be extremely complicated to implement, it is not widely used. With this plan, the salesperson earns points for various types of accomplishment. A certain number of points may be earned for every $100 of sales volume and other points may be earned for such things as the number of calls made, point-of-purchase displays installed, and product demonstrations made. There can be penalty points as well as credit points.

Fringe Benefits

Fringe benefits have been defined as "supplementary wage benefits provided salespeople regardless of their performance as long as they remain on the payroll." Most sales managers are pleased with their fringe benefit programs for salespeople and the results of those programs. These benefits boost morale and

PERCENT OF COMPANIES USING ALTERNATIVE SALES COMPENSATION AND INCENTIVE PLANS

Method	All Industrial 1974	All Industrial 1975	Consumer Products 1975	Industrial Products 1975	Other Commerce/ Industry 1975
Straight salary...................	23.4%	25.5%	14.1%	25.3%	52.4%
Straight commission.............	1.4	0.9	2.1	0.7	—
Draw against commission.........	4.6	5.3	9.9	3.9	4.8
Salary plus commission...........	23.6	25.6	23.3	27.7	15.8
Salary plus individual bonus.......	25.3	28.4	34.5	28.5	14.3
Salary plus group bonus..........	6.7	3.8	6.3	3.3	1.6
Salary plus commission plus individual or group bonus.......	6.9	7.2	4.9	7.8	7.9
More than one method of payment	8.1	3.3	4.9	2.8	3.2
	100%	100%	100%	100%	100%

Source: *Sales and Marketing Management* (February 9, 1976), p. 61.

ILLUSTRATION 20-1. Methods of compensation vary.

reduce turnover. They are often essential to attract, hold, and increase the loyalty of desired salespeople.

Federal old-age and survivors insurance (social security), workers' compensation, and unemployment insurance are required by law. Other benefits offered by some companies include: hospitalization, medical, and life insurance; paid holidays and vacations; moving costs; sick leave; loans; stock purchase plans; and educational aid.

METHODS OF HANDLING SALESPEOPLE'S EXPENSES

A salesperson's business expenses are often sizable, and it is understandably easy for them to get out of proportion. Thus, it is important that sales managers carefully watch the expenses of their sales personnel. For an expense plan to be effective, the salesperson's earnings must be handled separately from expense reimbursements or allowances; a salesperson should neither make money nor lose money on an expense account. The company should pay all the legitimate expenses that the salesperson incurs. Most sales managers consider the following to be legitimate business expenses: transportation, out-of-town lodging, out-of-town meals, telephone and telegraph charges, and business entertainment.

Expense plans should be simple and economical to administer, and their design and operation should minimize friction between the sales force and management. Every expense plan must be flexible. It should harmonize with the firm's compensation method, should recognize the nature of each sales territory, and should reflect awareness of the type of buyer the salesperson contacts.

Expense Plan #1—Salesperson Pays

A few salespeople working on straight commission pay all their expenses. The commission rate is set high enough to allow for expenses that the salesperson will incur. Thus, an 8 percent commission may represent 5 percent for income and 3 percent to cover the salesperson's expenses. Although this method of handling expenses is extremely simple, it is not widely used because management has little control and because salespeople may skimp unnecessarily on what they spend, even when the expenditure would enhance sales productivity.

Expense Plan #2—Unlimited Reimbursement

The most widely used method of handling expenses requires the salesperson to submit an itemized expense report. The salesperson receives an advance and then, when the itemized expense report is approved, he or she is reimbursed if expenses exceed the advance. Any money not spent is turned in. Because each salesperson knows that his or her reports will be examined, the likelihood of padding is reduced.

Expense Plan #3—Limited Reimbursement

There are also two versions of the limited reimbursement plan. In the first version, itemized expense reports are required, and there is a maximum budget figure which cannot be exceeded. The salesperson typically has some freedom within such a budget because there is a ceiling on total expenses but not on any specific item.

The other version includes an additional restraint: it places a ceiling on expenditures for specific items, such as transportation, meals, and lodging. This can be an effective plan if the ceilings imposed are realistic.

Expense Plan #4—Flat Expense Allowance

In this plan, the salesperson receives a certain amount of money each week to cover that week's expenses. There is little administration, and there are no expense reports and no disputes about the legitimacy of a certain expenditure. The sales manager must constantly review the flat allowance to see that it is set at the proper level. With this plan, it is easy for the sales manager to determine selling costs; however, there is always the possibility that salespeople may try to make money on their allowances, or they may curtail their activities as soon as they have run up expenses equal to the allowance figure.

TECHNIQUES OF DIRECTING SALESPEOPLE

Every sales manager must direct salespeople in such a way that they effectively carry out their assignments, work according to plan, observe company policies, develop their territories as expected, and maximize their own potential. Direction consists of such activities as training, control, encouragement, and guidance.

In smaller firms, the sales manager directs salespeople, mostly from the home office. In larger firms, district sales managers are responsible for direction in the field. Very large companies may have groups of field supervisors or sales supervisors who may do some selling as well as directing. Finally, in some firms senior salespeople may do some directing of junior salespeople. Regardless of title, those who direct salespeople must know how to sell and how to supervise. Many individuals who excel in selling do not have the ability to supervise others.

Objectives in Directing Salespeople

One of the goals of those who direct the work of salespeople is to continue the training of these salespeople. Usually there is an initial training program in the home office or branch office. This may be followed by on-the-job training in the field. A second objective is that of follow-up. Someone must see that salespeople understand and follow instructions, that they conform and comply.

A third objective involves communication. Salespeople must be kept current and posted on matters which bear on their work. And management needs to stay informed about what is going on in the various sales territories. Two-way communication, thus, is a goal. Fourth, direction tries to achieve better morale; it seeks to encourage the most desirable attitudes toward products, company, buyers, and selling in general. Finally, better planned selling is an objective. Better planning leads to more skillful selling, to more productive work. Better routing and better budgeting of time lead to a maximum of face-to-face selling time and a minimum of travel and waiting time.

Methods for Directing Salespeople

First, because there is no substitute for *personal contact,* we find sales managers and supervisors logging time with salespeople. The sales manager may travel with a salesperson as the latter works in his or her sales territory. As the salesperson sells, the manager observes and identifies points of strength and points of weakness. Later the manager may fill out a rating form on the salesperson. After a day's work, the two may analyze and discuss the salesperson's efforts. Personal contact makes for understanding and two-way communication. Directing in person is, of course, costly.

Sales managers use various types of *communications* in the direction of their salespeople. Letters are good in some respects for communicating, but unfortunate in others. Telephone conversations are another type of communication. Periodic mailings, such as house organs and weekly or monthly sales reports, are still another type of communication.

Sales meetings are a third technique useful in directing salespeople. Some retail firms start each day with a brief sales meeting. Saturday morning is meeting time for some sales forces. Quarterly, semiannual, and annual sales meetings are not uncommon. Most meetings are devoted to the salespeople's daily problems and what can be done about them. Salespeople can exchange experiences and solutions.

A fourth managerial technique in the direction of salespeople is the *conference.* Most are annual, two to five days long, and either regional or national. Conferences can be inspiring and stimulating when they permit salespeople to chat with top management. Training sessions might take up promotion plans, new policies, new products, or better solutions to current problems; these training sessions are often explaining sessions. Plant tours may be scheduled. Salesperson-to-salesperson exchanges of ideas, tactics, and experiences are facilitated. Because big conferences are expensive, because they pull salespeople off their jobs, and because some salespeople attending conventions act as if they are on vacation, conventions by closed-circuit television are being investigated by more and more companies.

Reports are a fifth tool employed by sales managers in directing their salespeople. Reports are designed to provide information from and about sales territories, information sales managers need to direct, to control, and to supervise. Often reports place information in the sales manager's hands from which a salesperson's performance can be rated or graded. Management's great hope is that a system of reports will encourage salespeople to plan their work and then to analyze their productivity and profitability. There is considerable variety from company to company as to the reports salespeople are expected to submit. Commonly reported matters include daily sales, daily calls made, routing, and expenses.

Contests are a sixth managerial tool. A competitive spirit is almost a prerequisite to even average success in selling. Because so many salespeople are competitive and because salespeople are engaged in competitive situations every week, contests can stimulate and motivate with powerful force. Competition can be based just on the amount of performance during the contest period or on the amount by which contest period performance exceeds performance for some earlier period of time.

Every contest needs a purpose or an objective. In most instances, the general, overall purpose is to increase sales volume. The contest must have a theme and a scoring pattern or basis. Boat racing, gold mining, baseball teams, stamps (such as trading stamps), points, wild game hunting, poker hands, and military campaigns are well-known formats. Contest length must be set. Prizes must be determined; cash, merchandise, and travel are the popular types of prizes. The contest must be promoted, executed, judged, and then the winners rewarded.

Sales contests have both advantages and disadvantages, and managers favor contests more strongly than do salespeople. Those who are enthusiastic about contests stress the stimulating effects of competition and the use of contests to encourage performance along desired lines. Contests can be designed to emphasize certain products or to concentrate sales power on certain types of buyers. Most contests *do* increase sales volume during the contest period. Special awards to leading salespeople and mention of them in house organs or sales bulletins increase the prestige and feed the ego of salespeople who make an extra effort and achieve greater performance. Contests can show certain salespeople just how much they can sell, bolstering their confidence. Contests can make hard work more attractive and acceptable.

Opponents of contests think them childish and undignified. Customers may be overstocked, service to them may be neglected, and future sales may slump. Some contests divert and distract salespeople. Because of technicalities, some people who deserve prizes may fail to get them. Salespeople who don't do well can easily develop a defeatist attitude. Intense rivalry can damage morale and even generate hostility. Some salespeople resent the pressure-to-win that some sales managers expect from the salespeople's families.

A final managerial technique is that of giving appropriate *recognition* to salespeople. Recognizing superior efforts builds good morale in an organization.

The capable sales manager tries in various ways to build each salesperson's pride in achievement, self-respect, and sense of belonging to the sales force and the company. Whether this recognition takes a tangible form—such as a promotion or award announced at a sales convention—or an intangible form—such as private congratulations on a job well done from an executive other than the sales manager—recognition can be an important incentive for a salesperson to work toward better sales efforts.

A promising *opportunity to advance* within the sales organization spurs many of the better salespeople to achieve greater performance. Such salespeople want to be told what they must do in order to be considered for promotion. Among any group of young, inexperienced sales trainees, at least a few of the superior ones are eager for advancement. Some may even be striving toward the sales manager's job.

Evaluating Salespeople's Performance

Sales managers must evaluate salespeople's performances if total productivity is to be improved. A sound compensation plan demands that each salesperson be paid in direct relation to productivity, and this demands some measurement of that productivity. Promotions and transfers should be based on performance, and this also demands measurement of that performance. Evaluation of salespeople's performances can lead to the identification of company policies needing revision and can help indicate how well the sales manager is succeeding in supervisory efforts.

The first step in evaluation obviously is to set up a standard which represents satisfactory performance. Next, actual performance is determined, and actual performance is then compared with the standard. The following measures of accomplishment represent one type of standard for evaluating performance: sales volume by product and customer, the relationship of sales volume to quota, gross margin, the relationship of expenses to sales volume, orders classified as to size, and the ratio of sales to calls made. The following measures of activities represent another type of standard: calls per day or week, days worked, product demonstrations made, point-of-purchase displays distributed or installed, or sales meetings held or attended. Qualitiative features are a third way of evaluating performance. Customer goodwill, planning ability, imagination and creativity, ambition, product and company information, and appearance are examples of qualitative features.

Evaluation is a prerequisite to the personal growth and development of each member of the sales force. Evaluation is not easy because territories vary, factors other than the salesperson's efforts can have a bearing on sales volume, and some criteria are subjective. But sales managers cannot supervise their salespeople properly unless they know who needs assistance and where this assistance is needed.

A survey of 405 sales managers provides the following listing of causes of friction between a salesperson and the firm with the percentage of sales managers mentioning each cause.

Cause	Percent
Poor communication	41
Unfair compensation	21
Weak leadership	19
Disagreement with company policies	18
Reports	17
Inadequate recognition of performance	17
Personality clashes	16
Management's ignorance of salespeople's problems	15
Poor cooperation	13
Salespeople not company-oriented	11
Lack of proper training	11
Lack of initiative	11
Poor performance	9
Failure to follow instructions	9
Unsatisfactory job specifications	9
Unrealistic sales quotas	8
Lack of mutual confidence	7
No advancement program	6
Product inferiority	5
Inequitable territorial potentials	5
Disagreement over performance	5
Poor human relations	5
Salespeople not customer-oriented	3
Salespeople's resistance to change	3
Lack of confidence in product	3
Rumors	2
Bad hiring techniques	2
Unpleasant job features	2
Disloyalty	2
Lack of mutual respect	1
Salespeople's feeling of not contributing	1
Public criticism by management	1

ILLUSTRATION 20-2. One of the responsibilities of sales managers is to provide as pleasant an atmosphere as possible in which their salespeople can work. One feature of a pleasant atmosphere is a minimum of friction, and the first step in reducing friction is to identify its causes.

A sales territory is the geographical area in which a salesperson works. Territories are composed of small, homogeneous areas called basic units. Basic units can be cities, counties, Standard Metropolitan Statistical Areas, wholesale trading areas, and states. The build-up approach and the breakdown approach are used to delineate territories. Sometimes territories must be revised.

Sales forecasts are estimates of sales revenues over a period of time. The executives' judgment approach calls for executives from different departments to make estimates. Sometimes the sales staff is asked to make estimates. The projection of past sales approach uses past sales as a basis for predicting future sales.

Sales quotas are sales assignments or goals. Quotas are established to aid in planning and control, to serve as specific objectives, and as a basis for compensation and promotions. There are five types of quota: (1) dollar volume, (2) unit volume, (3) gross margin, (4) net profit, and (5) activity. Quotas must be understood and accepted by salespeople. Participation in quota setting often helps to improve sales performance.

Money is the most direct financial motivation. Fringe benefits are indirect financial motivators. Sales managers want a compensation plan that will attract, hold, and develop good salespeople at a reasonable cost. The plan should be simple to understand and compute, as well as fair. Factors influencing the level of compensation include the salesperson's qualifications, the job description, the pay received by competing salespeople, the gross margin potential of the product involved, and the employee's worth to the firm. Straight salary, straight commission, and salary plus incentive are the three basic types of compensation plan. Expenses can be handled in the following ways: (1) the salesperson pays, (2) unlimited reimbursement, (3) limited reimbursement, and (4) flat expense allowance.

Sales managers must direct salespeople in such a way that they effectively carry out their assignments, work according to plan, observe company policies, develop their territories, and maximize their own potentials. Continued training, follow-up, good communications, improving morale, and better sales planning are the objectives in directing salespeople. Personal contacts, various types of communications, sales meetings, conferences, reports, contests, and recognition are tools used to direct salespeople. Managers must evaluate salespeople's performances if total productivity is to be improved. Standards must first be established. Then actual performance is determined and compared with the standard.

REVIEW QUESTIONS

1. What is the difference between market potential and the market forecast?
2. List four factors that influence the size of sales territories.

3. What are the advantages and disadvantages of the salespeople's judgment approach to sales forecasting?
4. Why are sales quotas necessary?
5. List five types of sales quota. Which is the most often used?
6. What do salespeople want from a compensation system?
7. What are the advantages of a straight commission?
8. What are the principal types of salary-plus-incentive plan?
9. List three examples of fringe benefits.
10. What are the disadvantages of a system where the salesperson pays all expenses.
11. List five ways that managers can direct salespeople.
12. Why is the evaluation of salespeople difficult?

DISCUSSION QUESTIONS

1. Assume that you are the sales manager of a sporting goods company and you supervise ten salespeople. You have set up an excellent training program and otherwise closely manage your subordinates. Your most senior salesperson, who also happens to have the greatest sales volume, has just complained to you that you are supervising him too closely and he feels as if someone is constantly peering over his shoulder. How would you answer this complaint?
2. Generally speaking, employees want the most money possible for doing their jobs while employers or managers try to keep expenses down. What goals do both salespeople and managers share in regard to the compensation system used?
3. Which compensation plan would you prefer to work with—salary, commission, or salary plus incentive? Why?

CASE STUDY 20A

When salespeople are reimbursed for their expenses, the job of budgeting for field selling expenses is primarily that of the sales manager. When sales representatives must cover their own selling expenses, the budgeting problem is primarily the responsibility of the individual sales representative.

1. If you were in charge of making up a selling expense budget, what categories of expense would you include?
2. Assume that your territory includes customers in major metropolitan areas along the West Coast (Seattle, Portland, San Francisco, Los Angeles, and San Diego), that you are on the road 80% of the time, and that you spend the same amount of time in each city. Make whatever additional assumptions you need, and then develop a budget for a month. (Your professor may prefer to assign you a territory nearer you. For help in figuring out various sales costs, you may wish to consult *Sales and Marketing Management*'s annual "Survey of Selling Costs.")

The Midwest Manufacturing Company makes a line of appliances, including automatic washers and dryers for the home. The line is marketed through distributors and retail dealers. Distribution is national, and the products are well-advertised. The size and quality of the sales force are in line with those of Midwest's leading competitors.

It has been the sales manager's practice to spend as much time as she can in the field. During such trips, she has conferences with members of the sales force and accompanies individual salespeople on their calls. In every instance, the sales manager and the salesperson discuss and plan strategy in advance for each call. The sales manager feels that buyers' and salespeople's reactions to this type of call are decidedly favorable, but she realizes that these three-person interviews are more restricted than are two-person interviews.

The sales manager recently received word from one of the company's good customers that he was dissatisfied with the salesperson managing his account. The buyer expressed a desire for a confidential conference with the sales manager. As she returned to her office from this interview, the sales manager did some thinking about a potential course of action. She debated whether she should begin calling on various buyers alone and without notifying in advance the salesperson concerned.

The unaccompanied, unannounced calls the sales manager has in mind are not to be selling calls. She feels strongly that she should engage in no selling activities unless she is accompanying one of her salespeople. If she were to make a sale, there would be the problem of taking credit away from the salesperson. Also, each sale calls for follow-up and service by the individual who made the sale. The sales manager's calls, then, would not be to sell but to cultivate buyer goodwill. The sales manager knows that she would learn what impressions the salespeople are making and feels that the calls would keep salespeople on their toes.

The sales manager sees some disadvantages in the plan, but she believes she can avoid any serious problems. She thinks her calls can be made without detracting from a salesperson's standing and without harming the salesperson's status in handling the account. She is positive that personnel problems exist in every sales force; she wants to identify just what these problems are before attempting to correct them. The sales manager does not see these calls as a breach of business etiquette, and she does not think her leadership or her relationship with her salespeople will suffer.

1. What would the sales manager of the Midwest Manufacturing Company gain specifically from solo calls?
2. If you were one of her salespeople, how would you be affected by them?

index

creative listening, 218, 219
creative selling, 34–37, 354
credibility, 77, 78
credit, 98, 99, 307–309
credit information, 307, 308; sources of, 308
credit management, 308, 309
culture, 52–54
current circumstances, 307, 308
custom(s), 54
customer(s), and demonstrations, 238, 239; classifying, 291, 292; in retail selling, 375–377; lost, 306; records on, 327; sound relationships with, 383–385
customer complaints, dealing with, 304, 305
customer information, in retail selling, 373, 374
customer relationships, 290–311
customer service, 104
customer support, securing, 296–299
customer wants, determining, 375

daily call record, 327, 328
deal(s), 130; consumer, 133
dealer-selling salespeople, 34–36
dealer services, and sales promotion, 129, 130
dealing, exclusive, 337, 340; with customer complaints, 304, 305
deceptive practices, 337
decided customers, 375, 376
decline, 89
decoding (a message), 83–85
demand, 121, 122
demonstration(s), 212, 232–243, 254, 260; of merchandise in retail stores, 379
denotative meaning, 84
department stores, 106
dependability, of salespeople, 22, 23; of supply, 359
desire, 161
determination, 22, 23
development, a systematic program of, 295
difficult prospects, 221, 224
diplomacy, 251, 253
direct-action advertising, 122
direct appeal close, 277, 278
direct channels, of distribution, 104
directing, 392, 393
direct-mail, as a source of prospects, 146
direct mail promotion, 82, 128
direct promotional forces, 119–136
direct sales manager, 395
direct selling, 353
discount(s), 98, 340
discount stores, 106, 107
discrimination, price, 337–340
discriminatory pricing, 338–340
disparagement, 341
display, influencing, 301
disposing of a single obstacle, 275

distortion, fog, 87; mirage, 87
distribution, 6; and salespeople, 109–111; decision areas, 110, 111; direct channels of, 104; exclusive, 112; fairly selective, 112; indirect channels of, 104; intensive, 112; physical, 109
distribution system(s), 93, 94, 104–113
distributors, truck, 105
diversification, advantages of, 262
diversion, and agreement, 259
divisional sales manager, 395
dollar volume quotas, setting, 417, 418
double question method, 273
draws, guaranteed, 421; nonguaranteed, 421
drawing account plus commission, 421
drop shippers, 105
Dun & Bradstreet, Inc., 308
duties, creative selling, 34, 35, 37; nonselling, 35, 37, 42, 317, 318, 370; of missionary salespeople, 36, 37; of salespeople, 33–44; service selling, 35, 37

early adopters, 88
early majority adopters, 88
earnings, of salespeople, 10
economic growth 6, 7
80–20 principle, 292
employment, 6
emotional close, 277
encoding (a message), 79–82
endless chain technique, 142, 143
enthusiasm, 22, 23
environment, 62
equipment, 194–196
ethical behavior, 341
ethical responsibilities, 336, 341–345
ethics, codes of, 343–345
evaluating, the performance of salespeople, 392, 393, 427
evaluation, of advertising, 122, 124; of sales promotions, 134
examinations, physical, 400, 404
exclusive dealing, 337, 340
exclusive distribution, 112
excuses, versus objections, 249–251
executive gifts, 130
executives' judgment approach, to forecasting, 414, 415
executives' opinion approach, to forecasting, 414
expense(s), 329; of salespeople, 423, 424; records on, 328
expense allowance, 424; flat, 424
experimental attitude, of salespeople, 332
experimentation, in routing, 320
external house organs, 130
external interruptions, 221, 222
external stimulus, 62

face to face (selling) time, 320
facility (storage), 110, 111
fairly selective distribution, 112
family(ies), 52, 53, 60, 61; and attitudes, 68
federal legislation, 336, 337
federal old-age and survivors insurance, 423
Federal Trade Commission, 337
Federal Trade Commission Act, 336, 337, 340, 341
feedback, 86
field sales manager, 397
figure, 63, 64
first call difficulties, 202
fishyback service, 111
flat expense allowance, 424
flexibility, in routing and scheduling, 322, 323
FOB price, 97, 98
fog distortion, 87
folkways, 54
forecast, market, 410; sales, 394, 410; sales revenue, 394
forecasting, 392; sales, 414–416
fragmentation, 395, 397
franchise systems, 108
free checking, 342
free on board price, 97, 98
frequency, 124
friendly nature, of salespeople, 25
fringe benefits, 418, 421, 423
functional discounts, 98

geographic considerations in routing, 319
gifts, executive, 130
goal(s), 67; definition of, 69, 70
goal conflicts, 67
goal-objects, 67; selection of, 70
goods, returned, 306, 385, 386
goodwill, building, 310, 311; using the telephone to cultivate, 324
Green River Ordinances, 338
greeting the customer, 374
grooming, of salespeople, 27
gross margin, 329
gross margin quotas, 417
ground, 63
group(s), buying, 362–364; identification with, 57; involved in advertising, 120, 121; play, 56; reference, 52, 53, 56–60; selling to, 362–365; of customers in retail selling, 377; prospect information in terms of, 153, 154; work, 56
group selling, 362–364
growth, 89; economic, 6, 7
guarantee(s), 93, 102, 254, 261, 338
guaranteed draws, 421
guaranteed price, 98

habit-based behavior, 65
harassment, 340
headlining, 210, 375
health, 331, 332; of salespeople, 27, 28
hearing, sense of, 28
hearing the prospect out, 255
high-pressure selling, 31, 342
horizontal cooperative campaign, 121
hostile communication, 86, 87
hostility, of prospects, 224, 247
household, 60
house-to-house selling, 43, 145

identification, with a group, 57
illegal practices, 338–341
imagination, 22, 24, 25
immediate refutation, 262
inactive accounts, 296
inattentiveness, of prospects, 223
incentive(s), for manufacturers' salespeople, 135; salary plus, 420, 421
incentive quotas, 416, 418
income budget, 394
indecision, of prospects, 223, 224
independence, of salespeople, 12
independent research findings, 211, 212
indifference, of prospects, 223
indirect-action advertising, 122
indirect answer, 255, 257, 258, 260
indirect channels, of distribution, 104
indirect promotional force, 119
indirect selling, 353
industrial wholesalers, 353
industry information, 93–95
influence, centers of, 144
information, about competitors, 227; about customers in retail selling, 373, 374; about organizational buyers, 355, 356; about prospects in terms of groups, 153, 154; about prospects in terms of territories, 154; company, 93–96; confidential, 342, 343; credit, 307, 308; industry, 93–95; merchandise, 372, 373; needed about prospects, 147–150; needed by retailers, 147–150; needed by salespeople, 162, 163; product, 93, 96–104; provided by salespeople, 8, 9; sources of about prospects, 152, 153; store, 371, 372; types of about prospects, 150–152
initial training, 405
initiative, 22–24
innovators, 88
installment terms, 263
institutional advertising, 122
institutional campaigns, 123
insurance, federal old-age and survivors, 423; unemployment, 423
intelligence tests, 403
intensive distribution, 112

National Association of Credit Management, 308
need, 69, 163–167, 177; and organizational buying, 352, 353; establishing, 252; objection to, 258, 259
net cost, 97
net price, 97
net profit, 329
net profit quotas, 417
noise, 84
nonguaranteed draws, 421
nonphysiological motives, 65, 66
nonselling duties, 35; handling, 317, 318; of missionary salespeople, 37; of retail salespeople, 42, 370
nonselling personal tasks, of salespeople, 29
nonverbal communication, 81
nonvisual physical factors, of salespeople, 28
norms, 54

objections, answering, 246–266; handling in retail selling, 379, 380
obligations, of salespeople, 28–33
observation, to determine customer wants, 375
old-age and survivors insurance, 423
one-cent sales, 133
on-the-job training, 405, 406
opening remarks, examples of, 199–202
opening the sales conversation, 198, 199
opinion followers, 59
opinion leaders, 56, 60, 88, 89
optimism, 22
optimum coverage, 320
oral communication, 76
order, request for, 279
order cycle, 109, 110
order placement, 109
order processing, 109, 110
order shipment, 110
organization, of advertising management, 122, 123; of selling activities, 394–397
organizational buyers, 352–365
organizational market, 353, 354
organizational sales interviews, 361, 362
organizational salespeople, 359, 360; the nature of their job, 354, 355
organizational selling, marketing channels in, 353
outside ideas, 359, 360
overall cost, 264

packages, cents-off, 133
packaging, 99, 101, 102
parallel track answer, 250, 251
percent-of-sales approach, of advertising budgeting, 124
perception, 52, 53, 61–64; and meaning, 83, 84
perceptual field, 63, 64

personality, and selling, 22, 23
personality tests, 403
personal rating chart, 330, 331
personal references, 403
personal satisfaction, in selling, 10, 11
personal selling, 1–49, 119; and advertising, 124–126; and sales promotion, 134, 135; influencing, 301, 302; laws affecting, 337, 338
persuasion, 8
physical appearance, 194
physical characteristics, of salespeople, 26–28
physical distribution, 109
physical examinations, 400, 404
physical product, 93
physiological motives, 65
pie-in-the-sky, 342
piggyback service, 111
planning, 392; of demonstrations, 234, 235
play groups, 56
plus points, a review of, 265
plus versus minus goal conflicts, 67
plus versus plus goal conflicts, 67
PM's, 130
point-of-purchase advertising, 128, 129
point-of-purchase displays, and salespeople, 129
point-of-purchase promotion, 82, 128, 129
point system, 421
poise, 26
policy(ies), advertising, 125; store, 372
position, in reference groups, 57, 58
positive attitude, of salespeople, 332
positive reinforcement, 64, 65
postponing, of objection to price, 263
post-purchase dissonance, 71
postsale activities, 279–284
postsale behavior, 382, 383
posttest evaluation, of advertising, 124
posture, of salespeople, 27
preapproach(es), 162, 163; using the telephone for, 324, 325
predatory pricing, 338, 339
premiums, 131
preparation, advance, 234, 235; for meetings, 303, 304
prepared prospect lists, 146
preselling, 141–183; the role of advertising in, 120
presentations, canned, 180; sales, 26, 160–183, 207–227, 363, 364, 378, 379
pretest evaluation, of advertising, 124
price(s), 104, 164, 173–177, 222, 261, 358, 359; anticipating an increase in, 264; FOB (free on board), 97, 98; guaranteed, 98; list, 97; net, 97; objection to, 262–264; opposition to, 252; of products, 97, 98; zone, 97
price discrimination, 337–340
price-fixing, 337–339
price increase, anticipating, 264

pricing, discriminatory, 338–340; predatory, 338, 339
pricing actions, 338–340
primacy, principle of, 81
primary advertising, 121
primary demand, 121
private warehouses, 111
problem-solving behavior, 65
procedures, store, 372
product(s), 164, 167–170, 177; company support for, 102; competitive, 103, 104; demonstrating the features of, 235, 236; introduction of, 89; making them look their best, 236, 237; new, 34, 35; objection to, 259–261; opposition to, 252; physical, 93; prices of, 97, 98; related, 103
product attributes, 99–102
product comparison, 254
product guarantees, 102
product information, 93, 96–104
production, 6; Age of, 6; mass, 6
production-oriented warehouses, 111
product knowledge, 359
product life cycle, 89
product line, composition of, 103
product-promoting advertising, 122
product research, 93, 96, 97
product service, 102
professionals, selling to, 40, 41
profit, net, 329; selling at a, 29, 30
projection of past sales approach, to forecasting, 414, 415
promotion, 7; direct-mail, 128; point-of-purchase, 82, 128, 129; sales, 119, 120, 126–136; store, 372
promotional forces, 119–136
promotion budget, 393, 394
promotion programs, 119–136
promotional communication, and the adoption process, 88, 89
proof, company-supplied, 211; obtained by survey, 265; principles of presenting, 210–212
prospect(s), achieving agreement of, 238; and demonstrations, 233, 237, 238; attitudes toward closings, 269, 270; capturing the attention of, 198; consideration for, 215; difficult, 221, 224; encouraging participation of, 238; fitting answers to, 251, 253; hostile, 224, 247; inattentiveness of, 178, 179; indecision of, 178, 179; indifference of, 223; interruptions by, 221, 222; point of view of, 178, 179; publications as a source of, 146; qualifying of, 148; records on, 327; resistance to buying by, 247; sellers as a source of, 144; sources of, 147; respecting the wishes of, 150; silence of, 153, 154; skepticism of, 224
prospect information, 153, 154; need for and

prospect information (*cont.*)
use of, 147–150; sources of, 152, 153; types of, 150–152
prospecting, 142–154; using the telephone for, 324, 325
prospect lists, 146
prospect record cards, 153
psychological characteristics, of salespeople, 21–25
psychological moment, 273
psychological motives, 66
psychological testing, 400, 403, 404
psychology, 52
publications, as a source of prospects, 146
publicity, 119, 120, 136
public warehouses, 111
purchase, 70, 162
purchasing agents, 354–361; selling to, 38–40; what they buy, 358, 359
purchase order, 353
push money, 130

qualifying prospects, 148
qualitative standards, 330
quality, 358
quantitative standards, 329, 330
quantity discounts, 98, 340
question(s), 261; additional, 250, 251; asking, 254; handling, 222; using, 220; why, 250, 254
questioning, tactful, 250, 251; to determine customer wants, 375
quotas, 316; sales, 410, 416–418

rate of delivery (of the sales presentation), 218
rationalization, 67, 68
reach, 123
readership studies, 124
reasoning, logical, 211
receivers, of communication, 78, 79
receiving (a message), 82–84
recency, rule of, 81
recession, 7, 8
reciprocity, 340
recognition, of salespeople by their managers, 426, 427
reconstruction (of a message), 84
record(s), as a source of prospects, 147; on customers, 327; on daily calls, 327, 328; on expenses, 328; on prospects, 153, 327; on sales, 328; on time, 328; tickler file, 328, 329
recordkeeping, 326–329
recruiting, of salespeople, 397–399
reference(s), 299, 400, 403
reference groups, 52, 53, 56–60
referents, 80
referrals, 143, 144
refresher training, 405, 406

refund, cash, 133
refutation, immediate, 262
regional sales manager, 395
regular dealer-selling salespeople, 34–36
rehearsal, of the sales presentation, 26, 220, 221
reimbursement, limited, 424; unlimited, 423
reinforcement, 64, 65
related products, 103
relating new items to current stock, 296
repeat business, 8; building, 293, 294
reports, 425, 426; lost order, 281, 282
representatives, manufacturer's, 105, 106
reputation, company, 95, 96
request for an order, 279
research, independent findings, 211, 212; manufacturing, 96; market, 96, 97; product, 93, 96, 97
resistance, to buying by prospects, 247
respect, for salespeople, 12
response, 63; to a message, 85–87;
responsibilities, basic selling, 289–336; ethical, 336, 341–345; legal, 336–341; social, 336, 345, 346
restraint of trade, 337
restrictions, channel/market, 340
retailer(s), 104, 106–108; contests for, 130; selling to, 33; selling to for wholesalers, 35, 36
retailer cooperative chains, 108
retail salespeople, 42, 369–371; information needed by, 371–374
retail selling, 42, 43, 301, 302, 369–386
retail stores, selling in, 42, 43
returned goods, 306, 385, 386
reviewing the five buying decisions, 275
Robinson-Patman Act, 336, 339, 340
role(s), 58; of salespeople, 112, 113, 345, 346
routing, and the telephone, 325, 326; experimentation in 320; flexibility in, 322, 323; geographic considerations in, 319; principles of, 319, 320; skip-stop, 325; techniques for, 318–320
rule of recency, 81

safety-risk standard, 307, 308
salary, 10; straight, 420
salary plus bonus, 421
salary plus commission, 421
salary plus incentive, 420, 421
sales, by telephone, 323, 324; closing, 269–284; one-cent, 133; records on, 328; terms of, 93, 97–99
sales agents, 353
sales aptitude tests, 403
sales branches, manufacturers', 106
sales budget, 393
sales effectiveness, increasing, 148–150

sales force, building the, 392–406; management of the, 410–428
sales forecast, 394, 410
sales forecasting, approaches to, 414–416
sales income budget, 12
sales interviews, securing and opening, 188–202, 361, 362; organizational, 361, 362; when to call for, 189
sales managers, as buying influences, 356; branch, 395; district, 395; divisional, 395; field, 397; regional, 395; the job of, 394
sales management, 391–428
sales meetings, 425
sales offices, manufacturers', 106
salespeople, 392; and demonstrations, 233, 234; and point of purchase displays, 129; and the distribution system, 109–111; as a source of prospects, 147; attitude of, 194, 195, 197; boundary role of, 8, 94, 112; characteristics of successful, 21–28; compensation of, 418–423; competitive, 225, 226; dealer-selling, 34–36; duties of, 33–44; earnings of, 10; evaluating the performance of, 427; expenses of, 423, 424; experimental attitude of, 332; importance of a positive attitude, 332; incentives for, 135; independence of, 12; information needed by, 162, 163; information provided by, 8, 9; introduction of, 197, 198; junior, 144; laws affecting, 336–338; manufacturers', 135; missionary, 36–38; obligations of, 28–33; organizational, 354, 355, 359, 360; professional, 20, 21; recruiting of, 397–399; respect for, 12; retail, 42, 369–374; roles of, 112, 113; security for, 11, 12; selection of, 399–404; sources of, 399; techniques of directing, 424–427; training of, 134, 135, 424
salespeople's judgment approach, to forecasting, 414, 415
sales performance, 329–332
sales presentations, 207–227; delivering, 378, 379; planning, 160–183; rehearsing, 26, 220, 221; to groups, 363, 364; see also sales talks
sales promotion, 119, 120, 126–133; and advertising, 134–136; and personal selling, 134, 135; evaluation of, 134; management of, 134
sales quotas, 410; establishing, 416–418
sales revenue budget, 394
sales revenue forecast, 394
sales talks, 180; making them interpret the demonstration, 236; see also sales presentations
sales territories, 410; establishing, 411–414; revising, 413, 414
sales training, 404–406; techniques of, 406
sales volume, 316, 328, 329
sampling, 131
saturation, 89